WOMEN IN INTELLIGENCE

HELEN FRY

WOMEN IN INTELLIGENCE

The Hidden History of Two World Wars

YALE UNIVERSITY PRESS
NEW HAVEN AND LONDON

For information about this and other Yale University Press publications, please contact:
U.S. Office: sales.press@yale.edu yalebooks.com
Europe Office: sales@yaleup.co.uk yalebooks.co.uk

Set in Adobe Garamond Pro by IDSUK (DataConnection) Ltd
Printed in Great Britain by TJ Books Limited, Padstow, Cornwall

Library of Congress Control Number: 2023943513

ISBN 978-0-300-26077-9

A catalogue record for this book is available from the British Library.

10 9 8 7 6 5 4 3 2

For the women in intelligence, past and present,
those who are known and those who cannot be named

and

for Jonathan, David and Edward,
whose resilience, hard work and spirit of dignity
towards others is an inspiration

I wanted to do more for the war effort than bake sausage rolls.

Charlotte Betty Webb, codebreaker, Bletchley Park

CONTENTS

ILLUSTRATIONS

TERMS AND ABBREVIATIONS

Abwehr	German military intelligence
ACIU	Allied Central Interpretation Unit
AOC	aircraft operating company
ATS	Auxiliary Territorial Service
AWCS	Association of Women Clerks and Secretaries
BUF	British Union of Fascists
Comintern	Communist International organisation
CPGB	Communist Party of Great Britain
CSDIC	Combined Services Detailed Interrogation Centre
EMFFI	État-major des Forces Françaises de l'Interieur (French Forces of the Interior)
FANY	First Aid Nursing Yeomanry
GC&CS	Government Code and Cypher School
GCHQ	Government Communications Headquarters
GHQ	General Headquarters
GPO	General Post Office
I/O	Intelligence Officer
IRD	Information Research Department
ISOS	deciphered messages of the German secret service
ISTD	Inter-Services Topographical Department
JBC	Joint Broadcasting Committee
MEW	Ministry of Economic Warfare
MI5	Military Intelligence for national security within Britain
MI6	Military Intelligence for Britain's security abroad
MI(R)	Military Intelligence (Research)
NID	Naval Intelligence Division

NKVD	Soviet intelligence agency
NSDAP	National Socialist German Workers' Party
OIC	Operational Intellig ence Centre of the Admiralty
OSS	(US) Office of Strategic Services
PI	photographic interpreter
PID	Political Intelligence Department
P/O	Petty Officer
POW	prisoner of war
RAF	Royal Air Force
RNVR	Royal Naval Volunteer Reserve
RSS	Radio Security Service
SAARF	Special Allied Airborne Reconnaissance Force
SHAEF	Supreme Headquarters Allied Expeditionary Force
SIS	Secret Intelligence Service
S/O	Second Officer
SOE	Special Operations Executive
STS	Special Training Schools
VI	voluntary interceptor
WAAC	Women's Auxiliary Army Corps
WAAF	Women's Auxiliary Air Force
WRNS	Women's Royal Naval Service

ACKNOWLEDGEMENTS

My first thanks are to Heather McCallum, the Managing Director at Yale University Press and my commissioning editor, for her enthusiastic support for this book and my career. She is an inspiration and, with her staff, an incredible support to authors during both the writing and publication process. My sincere thanks to Katie Urquhart for her meticulous edits, patience and care over this book. I am grateful to my agent Andrew Lownie for his continued support throughout.

During the course of my research over two decades, I have enjoyed a close relationship and friendship with a number of veterans whom I interviewed: Evelyn Barron, Elisabeth Bruegger, Susan Lustig and Fritz Lustig, Eric Sanders, Cynthia Turner and Lesley Wyle.

A book on this scale could not have been written without the generosity of other historians, researchers, family of the personnel and archivists. I am indebted to historians Lee Richards and John Howes, who have given support from their respective decades of research. My thanks to Dr David Abrutat, Richard Aldwinckle, Dr Jim Beach, Dr Nick van der Bijl, Michael Bottenheim, Professor Hugo de Burgh, Anna Somers Cocks, Melissa Davis, Linda Eberst, Neil Fearn, Col. (Rtd) Nick Fox, Rebecca Halliwell, Barbara Hennessy, Prudence Hopkinson, Joyce Hutton, the late Professor Keith Jeffery, Caroline Jestin, Jennifer Jestin, Loftus Jestin, Dr Stephen Jolly, Bobbie Jones, Fred Judge, Dr David Kenyon, Hilary Knight, Frances Knight, William Knight, Carinthia Knight Gibbins, Katherine Laing, Karl Lehman, Robin Libert, Barbara Lloyd, Robin Lustig, Stephen Lustig, Stella MacKinnon, Michael Maslinski, Robert Maslinski, Nigel Morgan, Louise Morris, Ingram Murray, Sebastian Neave, Stephen Newman, Derek Nudd, Marion O'Hara, Jamie O'Shaughnessy, Kate Osborne, Brigitte d'Oultremont,

Brigadier Brian Parritt, Sarah Paterson, François de Radiguès, Florence de Radiguès, Rodolphe de Radiguès, Giles Sandeman-Allen, Major Mike Shearer, Steven Schwitzer, Mark Scoble, Dr Michael Smith, Iain Standen, Major Bill Steadman, Wolf Suschitzky, Phil Tomaselli, Peter Verstraeten, Dr Kate Vigurs and the family of Margot Morse.

I am indebted to staff at the following museums and archives for their support in research, photographic material and sound archival material: Bletchley Park Trust, the Imperial War Museum, the Military Intelligence Museum, the Medmenham Collection, the National Army Museum and, in Belgium, the Cegesoma Studies and Documentation Institute and the National Archives. In addition, I have received much support from the trustees of the Military Intelligence Museum (MIM), trustees of the Friends of the Intelligence Corps Museum (FICM) and trustees of the Medmenham Collection.

My appreciation to those who helped with the book who have asked not to be named. To my family, for their loyal support and encouragement over all the years – thank you.

PROLOGUE
I NEVER KNEW HIS NAME

Leicester Square, London, October 1942

The ground floor café of the Quality Inn in Leicester Square was bustling with men and women, some in uniform, grabbing what little relaxation and pleasure they could. London had been heavily bombed and the fears that Hitler planned to invade England persisted. Standing in the doorway, Lesley Wyle strained to see if any of the tables were free. A waitress approached and showed her to the only vacant table, and she ordered a cup of coffee.

Lesley Wyle was not her original name. Born Ilse Eisinger in Vienna in 1921, she had fled Nazi-occupied Austria after Kristallnacht on 9/10 November 1938, when Jewish businesses and shops had been smashed leaving shattered glass across the pavements of the once cultured city. Within weeks of the Anschluss, as Nazi Germany's annexation of Austria was called, thousands of male Jews had been rounded up and taken to concentration camps. Nazi command had singled out Europe's Jews as enemies of the regime – and that included Lesley. She had been lucky to escape to the safety of England.

As she sipped her coffee that day in autumn 1942, she reflected on Britain's ignorance of the military might of the German war machine – which she herself had witnessed on the streets of Vienna. The country's naivety shocked her. With little understanding of how the odds were stacked against them, however, Britain's fighting spirit and resolve endured – and the previous December the Americans had joined the fight.

Her thoughts were interrupted by a slight clearing of the throat and a male voice: 'Excuse me, madam. May I join you?' She glanced up to see a man in RAF uniform.

'There are no spare tables,' he added. 'May I join you? I won't disturb you.'

'Yes, of course.'

They sat in silence for a few minutes, before he said, 'I couldn't help noticing your accent. Do you speak many languages?'

'Yes, German. I am originally from Vienna. I have been working as a nanny in Banbury.'

He leant slightly across the table, his voice urgent. 'You are wasting your time. With your fluency in English and German, you should be working for the Ministry of Information or the BBC. I am going on a dangerous mission tonight and I might not come back. I want you to promise me something.' He handed her two postage stamps. 'Please, take these stamps and stick them on the envelopes of the two letters you are going to write.'

He scribbled two addresses on a scrap of paper and slid it across the table. 'Promise me . . .' he said.

'I promise', she replied.

He stood up and tilted his head in respectful goodbye. She watched him weave his way across the room and suddenly he was gone.[1]

That evening, she posted two letters to the addresses on the scrap of paper, offering her services. And four months later, in February 1943, she joined a secret section of the BBC Monitoring Service, first at Evesham in Worcestershire and then at Caversham in Berkshire. Wearing a set of headphones, she listened in to German broadcasts: 'we had a very primitive recording equipment device behind us and a radio in front of us', she explained. 'There were cylinders and we touched a button to turn it on and cut grooves into the cylinder. We recorded everything, then transcribed and translated.' The listeners worked in three shifts, including throughout the night, because foreign broadcasts transmitted at different times. They monitored for Bletchley Park, the codebreaking site in Buckinghamshire and the War Office. Lesley went on to carry out intelligence duties, attached to the civil censorship division of the US army in post-war Germany, where she monitored German correspondence and translated letters.

When I interviewed Lesley over Zoom during the pandemic in 2020, she was approaching the age of 100.[2] She sat in her room in

Canada, still so bright and mentally alert, her memory sharp, as she regaled me with events from her wartime career. She recounted the story of the RAF officer, then added something which has remained with me.

She said, 'I never saw him again. I never knew his name, or whether he ever came back from his dangerous mission, but that chance encounter changed my life.'

It sent goosebumps down my spine.

Over eighty years later, she still had no idea whether the man who had recruited her for intelligence work had survived the war. He was prepared to sacrifice his life to defeat Nazi Germany, for freedom, and it touched something deep within her. She trusted him that day in October 1942 and was prepared to do what she could for the country that had saved her from certain death in the Holocaust.

Lesley's story is one of many inspirational accounts that I have discovered during the course of writing this book. Many of those involved kept their experiences working for British intelligence secret, even from their own families. For instance, it was not until two decades after Margot Morse died in 1994 that her family went through her jewellery box that had been in storage and discovered an assassin's pen. It left them with a number of unanswered questions – had she ever used it? What covert life had she hidden from them? Margot was one of the 'Baker Street irregulars' who worked in utmost secrecy for the Special Operations Executive (SOE). Her file has been declassified, but its slim contents raise more questions about the work she really did for SOE than it answers.

Lesley and Margot are typical of the thousands of women whose stories have been obscured behind official secrecy. Charting the contribution of women in intelligence from the First World War through the 1920s and 1930s and into the Second World War is a monumental task. The challenge is underlined by the fact that some aspects will never be known as they are still classified under the Official Secrets Act.

This is the hidden history and legacy of women's involvement at the heart of British intelligence operations, espionage, deception and unorthodox methods of warfare across two world wars.

INTRODUCTION
RECLAIMING A LOST PAST

In a striking Tudor portrait that survives at Hatfield House, Hertfordshire, Elizabeth I proudly gazes at the viewer. She is swathed in a resplendent cloak decorated with a curious pattern – of human eyes and ears. The representation of such peculiar embroidery was intended to make a grand statement about Elizabeth's prowess in surveillance and espionage. Here, the painting is saying, is the ultimate spymistress.

After all, Elizabeth I was the first monarch to establish and head a secret service. With Sir Francis Walsingham, her private secretary, she had the foresight and vision to create a network of spies that operated in England and abroad. Walsingham devised secure codes and ciphers to protect diplomatic and military messages. Meanwhile, while travelling on Crown business, Elizabeth's ambassadors acted as agents, and English students studying abroad spied for her. When Elizabeth's cousin Mary Queen of Scots supported a conspiracy to overthrow her and place herself on the throne of England, the plot was unmasked by Walsingham's early censorship service, which monitored the correspondence of Elizabeth's subjects. The consequences were fatal: Mary was found guilty of treason and executed in 1587.[1]

However, it was not until 1909 that a formalised British intelligence service, named the Secret Service Bureau, came to be established. This was a period of heightened fear: Major James Edmonds, the new head of MO5, a section of the Directorate of Military Intelligence, was not alone in being convinced that German spies were overrunning British streets and undermining the nation from the shadows.[2] Edmonds's idea of a secret organisation to deal with counter-espionage in Britain and oversee Britain's agents abroad was endorsed by a sub-committee chaired by Richard Haldane, the Secretary of State for War. They believed that a new organised approach to counter-espionage was required – hence the formation of the Secret Service Bureau. Its existence was to be kept totally secret, and only a few officials in Whitehall knew about it. Commander Mansfield Cumming of the Royal Navy and Captain Vernon Kell of the Army were chosen as joint heads of the new bureau.

Fifty-year-old Mansfield Cumming was an extrovert, jovial character who was prone to exaggeration – qualities considered ideal for the world of espionage. Kell was fourteen years younger, an optimist whose experience in military intelligence began in 1902. He had travelled widely and had a knowledge of languages. Cumming was responsible for espionage abroad; Kell was given charge of intelligence at home. On 3 January 1916, the bureau split into two separate organisations to become MI5 and MI1(c), the latter a forerunner of the Secret Intelligence Service (SIS/MI6).[3]

How women came to be involved in these institutions and the vast array of organisations and theatres that intersected with them from the First World War, through Second World War to Cold War, is the theme of this book.

In 1715, the 1st Duke of Marlborough, one of England's greatest military generals, had intoned, 'No war can be conducted successfully without early and good intelligence.' Yet, before 1914, there was a positive distaste for regular officers and soldiers to be permanently employed in intelligence gathering. Espionage was deemed to be ungentlemanly, but occasionally necessary. Employing women in intelligence in this period was 'absolutely unthinkable'.[4]

Two hundred years later, Major-General David Henderson, then director of Military Intelligence, declared, 'Women are frequently very successful at eliciting information; they require no disguise; if attractive they are likely to be welcome everywhere, and may be able to seduce from their loyalty men whose assistance or indiscretion may be of use. On the other hand, they are variable, easily offended, seldom sufficiently reticent and apt to be reckless.'[5]

Such views are markers against which to measure, first, the trailblazing presence and groundbreaking progress, and, second, the real roles and achievements of women in intelligence, often pushing against a backdrop of sexism and inequality.

There is a comparative lack of evidence for women working in intelligence – a result of the continuing classification of files, as much as ingrained biases of operational histories which gloss over the kinds of roles that many women performed, as well as the prejudice that existed against them at the time. But this book will reveal the wealth of intelligence roles that women took up across the twentieth century, making a profound contribution to operational intelligence, as well as in strategic and support roles. The former engaged women behind enemy lines in such work as intelligence gathering, deception and sabotage. The latter involved women in providing intelligence elicited from the analysis of photographic interpretation, radio communication, codebreaking and interrogation. Women, whether as civilians or in uniform, served at the very heart of some of the most significant intelligence activities.

The somewhat egregious comment quoted above, and from the Military Intelligence chief no less – that is, assessing and valuing women intelligence operatives based primarily on their presumed seductive qualities – is also emblematic of a very real and persistent problem with popular portrayals, and therefore general understanding, of female spies. Such an issue has plagued women in intelligence quite literally for millennia.[6] No one embodied the contradictions of this position better than the emblematic spy-seductress Mata Hari.

Her real name was Margaretha Geertruida Zelle. Born in 1876 in Leeuwarden in Holland, she was a dancer and courtesan spy who 'represented the decadence of Salome with her erotic dancing, the hidden female threat with her sexual exploits, and the enemy within through her espionage'.[7] After a failed marriage, she moved to Paris where her risqué performances extended to dancing naked. She embarked on affairs with high profile men and military officers, and was cast as the archetypal *femme fatale*. In London, MI5 opened a file on her.[8]

During the early part of the First World War, Mata Hari undertook missions to Spain and Belgium on behalf of France, but by the autumn of 1915 the Germans had 'turned' her and she agreed to spy for Germany. She travelled to Spain in autumn 1916 to meet a German military attaché, then to England, where she was arrested at the port of Falmouth in Cornwall. She was taken to London and interrogated by the assistant commissioner of New Scotland Yard, but vehemently denied being a German spy. French officers could not establish her allegiance either and placed her under suspicion. She was allowed to leave England.

The following year, on 13 February 1917, Mata Hari was arrested in Paris by the French authorities, who had intercepted a German message and decoded an agent's codename, 'H-21', which pointed to her being that double agent. Her trial by a French court took place in closed sessions. The British petitioned French military intelligence to transfer her to London, so she might be 'turned' again to work for the Allies, but the French executed her by firing squad.

It is now clear from declassified files that MI5 did not find concrete evidence that Mata Hari had worked against the Allies, and today her case retains an element of unsolved mystery.

Whatever the truth, her fame and notoriety exploded into the public arena through a slew of books, films and sensationalist articles in the international press. For over a century, her glamour and glamorisation has served to reinforce unhelpful stereotypes of female spies as dangerous, duplicitous sexual predators. Coming to define the image of the female spy, she obscured the real history and legacy of women working in intelligence across two world wars. As we shall see, these women acted with great courage in carrying out resistance activities, gathering intelligence on enemy troop movements and positions, organising sophisticated spy networks and acting as couriers carrying secret messages and documents. They used invisible ink in letters, ran observation posts and distributed propaganda for the Allies. The history of women in intelligence is not, in fact, the world of honeytraps, alluring agents, fast cars and Bond-girl glamour – that is fictional entertainment. The true story is one that evokes awe and respect.

It is now well over a century since the formation of the British Secret Service in 1909, yet our picture of women's crucial work in intelligence has heretofore been murky. Women have been the missing dimension in intelligence history, but that is changing, especially through the work of contemporary female historians. In the words of a senior Army figure, in 'both operational and support intelligence there has been a remarkable, albeit painfully slow, recognition of the capability of women to successfully gain intelligence'.[9] This book contributes to that broader consciousness.

It does much more than just acknowledge that women 'were there'. It reveals many untold stories of women as practitioners in the field of intelligence – civilian and uniformed – as well as female spies, both well known and unknown, and assesses their contribution. The time is right to reveal and reclaim their stories and provide a measured assessment of the legacy of women in intelligence across two world wars. In doing so, I hope that, even if only partially, I can help give them the public recognition they deserve.

It will probably never be possible to provide a complete picture of women in intelligence. Due to the nature of their work, many of the women's identities will remain protected by British intelligence forever. Neither is it possible in this book to do justice to women's contributions to intelligence operations from the Cold War until today – that would require several volumes and, again, much remains classified. There are challenges in bringing to life the history of women in intelligence, often relating to the material available – or lack of it. MI5 occasionally releases files, but MI6 never declassifies its files. This means that we can have only a limited view of the contribution of women as professional intelligencers. SOE was shrouded in mystery for over seventy years, but its operational and personal files are gradually being released and provide a deeper insight into the achievements of its agents.

Progress can be made by working through (literally) tons of declassified files of air, military and naval intelligence. The level of detail for women is variable, and it is a matter of picking out relevant information to reconstruct exactly what they did. During my research into other aspects of military intelligence, the discovery of women's unusual intelligence roles was purely accidental – as in the case of the female interrogators. We will see how the 'secretaries' – so often overlooked by other histories – were, in fact, coordinating and organising some of the most important agent-running in networks across Europe and elsewhere. All this has been hidden for so long, but it is clear that, behind 'ordinary' roles as clerks, secretaries, translators and typists, women emerged as experts in their field or department. This understanding, running through this book, serves to remind us that all our previous assumptions about women in intelligence are about to be changed . . .

From the shadows of secrecy emerges an understanding and admiration of the roles of thousands of often nameless women who became intelligencers and made a material difference to the outcome of both world wars. This is a tribute to those women who can now be named, as well as those who cannot – from the dedicated intelligencers to the courageous spies. All were heroines who played their part in securing democracy and freedom for their generations and ours.

It is an inspirational history, and one full of surprises.

1
INVISIBLE SPIES

In the decade leading up to the First World War in 1914, Britain was in a heightened state of alert over German spies operating both within and outside of the country. By 1909 the fear of German spies had risen to fever pitch, bordering on a national paranoia. Although this apprehension was exaggerated, Germany's wider threat to the stability of Western Europe was not. In the early 1900s spying was extended to colonial territories; and South Africa (part of the vast British Empire) became fertile territory for Britain to recruit intelligence officers and agents to conduct espionage against German-occupied regions, like south-east Africa. Between the end of the Boer War in 1902 and the outbreak of the First World War, British agents gathered intelligence on new weapons that the Germans were rumoured to be developing, in particular a new gun. The diamond mining regions of South Africa, with their international connections, created an ideal cover under which British spies could travel and observe the state of Germany's military forces in the region, including any mobilisation or increase in those forces.[1]

Concerns about Germany's expansionist ambitions, especially in Europe, were ultimately proven to be correct. On 4 August 1914, German forces crossed the border into Belgium and occupied the country for the next four years. Britain declared war on Germany. Neighbouring Holland and France remained neutral and unoccupied, and they would become important bases from which to conduct espionage and intelligence missions for both Britain and Germany.

On 13 August 1914, the War Office in London despatched a number of special army personnel to France under the direction of Major (later General Sir) Walter Kirke.[2] They were the embryonic Intelligence Corps and consisted of one major, four captains, seven lieutenants and over forty 'scouts'; the latter would be sent out to gain intelligence from reconnaissance missions. There were no women among them, but that would change three years later. War was very much a male domain, and women were not permitted to serve in fighting forces or on the front line. However, it would not be long into the conflict before civilian women began to play a crucial role as intelligencers and spies.

Before 1914, women had already been working as nurses and governesses across Europe. After the outbreak of war, some of these women were prepared to operate behind enemy lines, though they did not see themselves as spies. Often their common link was a knowledge of languages, and none had had any prior intelligence training. Female spies behind enemy lines were valuable because they were inconspicuous. Their male counterparts stood out in a population where most younger men were fighting with their regiment; young men not in uniform immediately fell under suspicion of espionage and were arrested. Women could move much more freely in occupied countries, using their 'invisibility' to gather and deliver sensitive and valuable information for the Allies.[3] Given this relative freedom, some male spies occasionally disguised themselves as women.

Edith Cavell

The woman who is most synonymous with heroism in the First World War is the British nurse Edith Cavell, who aided French and British soldiers to escape from Belgium into neutral Holland.

At the outbreak of war in 1914, Edith Cavell was forty-eight years old and, since 1902, had worked as a nurse at 149 Rue de la Culture in Brussels. From August 1914, it is well known that she headed an escape organisation, smuggling British and French soldiers from Brussels into neutral Holland, and Belgians who wished to join their king in exile. It was perilous work and involved many secret meetings in her home.[4] With Belgian architect Philippe Baucq, she founded a clandestine organisation which came to be known as the Cavell–Baucq Organisation. She recruited women and men who were prepared to risk their lives to save wounded soldiers and escort them out of enemy-occupied Belgium. She used guides to escort soldiers over the border and engaged forgers to provide fake identity papers. Further precise details of how she operated are scant as she left no paper trail and there are no operational files for her organisation in a national archive. More insight can be gleaned about the individuals who worked for her than about Cavell's own clandestine life. Among them were Abbé Vallez, whose home was used as a safe house on the French side of the Belgium border. In her network were Belgian aristocratic women like Princess Marie de Croy.

Marie de Croy was born in London in 1875 to a British mother, Elizabeth Mary Parnell, and a Belgian father, Prince Alfred Emmanuel de Croy. When war broke out, de Croy was staying with a friend in England, Violet Cavendish-Bentinck, whose mother, Louisa Scott, was well connected as the maternal grandmother of Queen Elizabeth the Queen Mother and great-grandmother of Elizabeth II. De Croy left England for Château de Bellignies, her ancestral home in Belgium, which was being used as a hospital by Cavell. She went on to shelter Henri Giraud, then a junior French officer (and future general and leader of the Free French Forces), whose escape had been assisted by Cavell.

Other women aiding Cavell were Countess Jeanne de Belleville, whose stately home was a safe house at Montignies-sur-Roc, and Louise Thuliez, a French school teacher who operated as a guide for the organisation.[5] It is believed that around 15,000 French soldiers were secretly escorted into Holland by Cavell's organisation. The exact number of British escapers is harder to ascertain, but thought to be in the hundreds.[6]

On 20 July 1915, Cavell received a visit from Count de Borchgrave, whose daughter was working as a nurse for Cavell. Borchgrave's wife was living in England at the time.[7] The purpose of his visit is unclear, but when he arrived at Rue de la Culture he found three plainclothes Germans searching Cavell's house for papers. Nothing was said to him by Cavell or the men. As Borchgrave left, one of the men signalled to another man to follow him. The following morning a young English girl, whom the Count did not know, arrived at his home with a message from Cavell. It was to be delivered urgently to the Belgian consul in Rotterdam and to Cavell's mother in England to warn them both about German spies operating in the UK and urging them not to give any information about Cavell's whereabouts in Belgium. Undercover

German spies in Britain were trying to obtain details about her by penetrating her circle of family and friends. Although MI5 was already tracking most of the German spies, there was a need to safeguard Cavell's security and operations in Belgium.

Cavell warned them about one man whom she described as having 'a reddish face, fair, short military moustache and a very cockney accent', and who had admitted to her that he visited England whenever he wanted.[8] Count de Borchgrave wrote to his wife in England the same day. When she received the letter eight days later, she immediately sent it to the local authorities to forward on to Cavell's mother, whose address she did not have. They local authorities passed it to MI5, who posted it to Cavell's mother.[9] By the time Mrs Cavell received the warning, her daughter was already dead.

With informers everywhere, the risk of betrayal was high and Cavell had known it. She was betrayed, arrested on 5 August 1915 and taken to St Gilles prison in Brussels.[10] At her two-day trial that October, Cavell was accused of hiding officers in her house and at a convent, then escorting them by night via trams to Brussels station to board a train for the Dutch border.[11] Crucially, what sealed her fate were allegations that she, along with Prince Reginald de Croy and Countess de Belleville, was running an espionage organisation.

Cavell and thirty-five members of her organisation, thirteen of whom were women, faced charges. Twenty-six were found guilty and five received the death sentence.[12] Cavell and Philippe Baucq, who had forged identity papers for her and planned escape routes, were sentenced to death by firing squad. Miss Louise Thuliez, Countess de Belleville of Montignies-sur-Roc, and Princess de Croy all stood trial during October 1915 on charges of espionage. The trial initially condemned them to death, but their sentences were commuted to life imprisonment in the case of Thuliez and Belleville, and ten years in jail for Princess de Croy.[13] Thuliez was held in a cell with Cavell and was the last person to say goodbye to her before her execution.

In the weeks before her death, Cavell reflected on the meaning of her life. She was visited in prison by a British chaplain, Revd H. Stirling Gahan. He found her brave in the face of her imminent fate. She said to him: 'I have seen death so often that it is not strange or fearful to me.

I thank God for these ten weeks quiet before the end. I must have no hatred or bitterness towards anyone.'[14]

At 2 a.m. on 12 October 1915 Cavell and Baucq were taken to the execution ground of Tir National in Brussels and shot.[15] Afterwards, the German chaplain who was present at the execution reported to Revd Gahan that Cavell was 'brave and bright to the last. She professed her Christian faith and that she was glad to die for her country.'[16] Cavell's execution was widely covered in the newspapers and provoked condemnation and shock in wartime Britain. Vernon Kell, the head of MI5, received photographs in the post from the French authorities of the execution ground and Cavell's grave with its simple wooden cross.[17] He wrote a compassionate letter to her mother and enclosed the photographs in the hope that it would be helpful to her in her grief. MI5 did not officially exist then, and Mrs Cavell had no idea that Kell was the head of the Security Service. She replied to him via the War Office, using black-edged notepaper, as was customary at the time of bereavement in a household. She expressed her appreciation at receiving the photographs during her 'time of great loss'.[18] The letter and photographs, in declassified files, still have the power to move the reader over a hundred years later.

British intelligence mounted an investigation into Cavell's death, conducted jointly by MI5 and MI1(c). They passed her case to British officers of the Intelligence Corps, based in France, working on military intelligence and running agents behind enemy lines.[19] They succeeded in identifying Cavell's betrayer as a man called Georges Gaston Quien.[20] Quien was interrogated three times by Captain Sigismund Payne Best (Intelligence Corps), who later joined SIS (the Secret Intelligence Service) and was betrayed in the famous Venlo incident of November 1939, when two MI6 officers were arrested on the Dutch–German border in a sting operation by the Germans. Quien claimed to have been drafted into Cavell's organisation for a few days and ferried messages from Cavell and Princess de Croy to Prince de Ligna and Lieutenant Colonel Desprey in Holland. Quien told Payne Best that he was arrested by the Germans on 19 November 1915, having arrived at the organisation's headquarters from a mission in Holland to find Cavell and much of her network had been arrested. He was kept in solitary confinement at St Gilles prison from November 1915 to 23 July 1916, then transferred to a civilian prison at Sennelager and finally an internment camp in Switzerland.

Suspicions in Cavell's organisation about Quien possibly being a German agent started to materialise after he told different stories to people about his background and identity as a doctor, a flying officer and a Frenchman.[21] Payne Best struggled to obtain a true picture from his interrogations and concluded that Quien's account lacked both detail and documentary evidence to support his version of events.

Quien was sentenced to death for his betrayal of Cavell. Princess de Croy was among the women who gave evidence at his trial.

A Spy?

Opinion has been divided for decades on whether Edith Cavell was a spy behind enemy lines for the British Secret Service in the First World War. With the benefit of declassified files in Britain and Belgium it is now possible to answer this question conclusively and reveal that Cavell performed espionage and ran a spy network for British intelligence. This was conducted alongside her work in the escape and evasion of Allied soldiers. Of relevance is the fact that the Germans believed she was guilty of espionage and executed her for that reason.

After Cavell's death, and on the instructions of British intelligence, Payne Best interviewed a number of Belgian women who had been part of her clandestine organisation.[22] Their testimonies provide a much clearer idea of their activities and confirm that the Cavell–Baucq organisation was engaged in intelligence gathering. (It is not possible to verify whether Cavell set up this intelligence operation under the formal direction of the British Secret Service because SIS/MI6 does not release its files.) Whether formally or informally working for the British, Cavell was recognised as the organisation's leader. Miss Louise Thuliez, Countess de Belleville, Elise Grandprez and Princess de Croy were among the prominent women engaged in intelligence gathering for Cavell. Also included was Princess de Croy's cook, Charlotte Matha.

Scant details survive about these women's backgrounds and how they were recruited but it was primarily via family members and trusted friends. They had no formal training and used their judgement on what information would be useful to British intelligence. They worked with Hermann Capiau, an engineer by profession, who guided soldiers to Cavell. He was witness to their intelligence work and wrote a report which reveals as much.[23]

Madame L'Hotelier was another member of Cavell's network who was questioned by Payne Best. She relayed how she had been imprisoned in eight jails for sheltering a French agent who was subsequently arrested and taken prisoner by the Germans on the Dutch border.

Louise Thuliez and Mrs Cavenaile had direct contact with British and French intelligence agents.[24] Thuliez travelled to Cambrai to obtain plans of German ammunition depots and took the diagrams to an architect, Mr Bauk, in Brussels, to be passed on to his British contact. It was while she was with Bauk that she was arrested by the Germans on 31 January 1915.[25] Her sister, Mrs Aubertine Houet, who was married to a telegraphist, also worked for Cavell. Thuliez and Houet corresponded in invisible ink.[26] Their letters were carried by soldiers from Siburg to Brussels, where they were copied and forwarded to MI1(c) officers in Saint-Waast, northern France. Through Houet, British intelligence received details of the whereabouts of men who were suspected of working for the Germans as agents and spies. This is espionage and counter-espionage work, not escape and evasion.

With the constant threat of discovery, there were precarious moments for Cavell's agents – as in the case of Mrs Bodard who, fearing imminent arrest, bundled up and hid incriminating papers and special maps to be used in crossing the frontier.

Further insights into this clandestine world can be found in the National Archives of Belgium, including interviews with others who worked with Cavell. One testimony is provided by Octave Malice, who confirmed that he and the network sheltered English soldiers at the home of Baucq.[27] Baucq handed letters to the soldiers to post once they were back in England. Malice first met Cavell at a house on Rue de la Culture, and in subsequent days was introduced to some of Cavell's senior agents, Prince Reginald de Croy, Mr Capiau and Miss Thuliez. Malice was given folders of material by Capiau to deliver to a duke at Roosendaal in Holland. It is clear that Malice was recruited by Cavell as an important courier, for the purpose of espionage, and he operated via her agents who acted as handlers and gave him his instructions.

Malice undertook intelligence work alongside escape and evasion; frequently, the lines between them were blurred. On 30 September 1914 Malice escorted nine evaders to the military hospital at Mons, and a further twelve English soldiers on 5 October. A week later, on 11 October, he was asked by a Miss Manners and Miss Hozier, who were involved with the Cavell network, to undertake a secret mission to the Admiralty in London. No further details have emerged about these two women, but it is known that Malice escorted a seriously injured English soldier to Villerot and on to Dunkirk. Three days later, they left by boat for Dover. Malice recalled how he stayed with Winston Churchill (then First Lord of the Admiralty); after three days of rest, Malice left the Admiralty and returned to Belgium via Folkestone. MI1(c) had one of its principal offices in Folkestone, although Malice does not mention whether he met any intelligence officers there. He returned to the English Ambulance Service in Mons and handed over the precious mail from London.[28]

Malice's secret mission to the Admiralty provides a rare glimpse into the high levels at which at least one of Cavell's agents was operating, and a concrete link between her organisation and British intelligence in Whitehall.

A wide network of Belgian aristocrats worked for Cavell, among them Baron and Baroness Crombrugge, who escorted soldiers to the Dutch border. They also worked with the English Ambulance Service in Mons. Intelligence was written on handkerchiefs and cloths which were then sewn into escapers' clothes and hidden in the soles of their shoes.

Marie Charlet had been rescuing soldiers for Cavell since September 1914, including sheltering in her own home two aristocrats who were attached to the French secret service.[29] On 6 September 1914 she escorted eleven Belgian prisoners of war to the frontier to rejoin their battalion. She hid Belgian spies in her home, including Joseph Goris, who undertook the clandestine mail service for British intelligence behind the lines in Belgium; he was given a room in Charlet's house for sorting that mail. The correspondence was then taken to whoever it was intended for within the network, carried by a woman called Marie Pinnoc. Charlet also hid weapons and pigeons for Cavell's network. Pigeons were important carriers of secret messages, which were placed in tiny capsules tagged to their legs; the birds would then fly back to their loft in France, which was being run by British intelligence officers of MI1(c).

Charlet was arrested by the Germans on 22 June 1916. In prison, she was placed in solitary confinement for twenty-one months, but never gave anything away. She was transferred to a harsh labour camp, which she survived until the Armistice brought her release. In her testimony she said that she suffered torture by the guards during her long internment, but she never regretted what she had done for her country.

It is clear that Cavell ran both male and female agents in her intelligence network. This discovery is significant because, historically, her spy status has been ambiguous or contested. Until recent times, a combination of official secrecy and lack of evidence has obscured her true legacy not only as a spy, but as a spymistress – a woman who founded, established and ran the beginnings of an amateur intelligence network behind enemy lines for SIS. That Cavell was an exceptionally important spymistress for the British Secret Service may explain why an experienced SIS officer, Payne Best, conducted the investigation into the betrayal that led to her execution.

The Alice Service

The fact that Edith Cavell, as a woman, headed an espionage organisation in wartime was not unique. Women were very capable of setting up and running intelligence networks for the British Secret Service. Louise de Bettignies, for instance, founded the Alice Service in January 1915, a spy network for the British that covered the region of Lille and had deep connections to agents in Brussels.

Born in 1880, Bettignies was the daughter of a Lille porcelain manufacturer, a devout Catholic, educated at Girton College, Cambridge, and spoke several languages.[30] Prior to 1914, she was employed as a governess to nobility in Austria and Italy. At the outbreak of war, she joined the Red Cross and was stationed in Lille when the Germans occupied the region. When she escaped to England the following year, she brought valuable information about the German military positions and offered herself to British intelligence. She received no formal training (which was no different for male recruits at this time), except a briefing from intelligence officers on invisible inks, safe houses, dead letter boxes and codes. She operated under the pseudonym Alice Dubois and received a salary from British intelligence. In January 1915 she left England for Lille to set up a clandestine headquarters from her family home. She recruited friends and family into the nascent network.

Bettignies represented 'the beginning of a new phase in espionage, when women were trained to fight and spy for their countries in resistance movements'.[31] The women were trained in personal security and how to hide in plain sight, and were instructed on the kind of information that was needed about the enemy. They also learnt how to identify German battalions and regiments, uniforms and insignia – such details offered vital eye-witness evidence to enable British intelligence to assess the types of enemy forces and troops being moved towards the front line. They were thus in essence operating as intelligencers. Bettignies herself operated under different guises, as a teacher, peasant and lace seller. Messages were hidden inside rosaries and the headdress of Catholic nuns. The Alice Service helped Allied POWs to the borders, but also gathered intelligence on German troop movements, camouflaged installations and military positions that was of great value to the British. Bettignies sent secret messages about the precise time and date that the imperial train was carrying the Kaiser of Germany to the front line at Lille. The British attempted to bomb the train, but missed it.

Bettignies was so successful in her intelligence work that she was dubbed 'the Queen of spies' by officers in Military Intelligence.[32] General Sir Walter Kirke, British director of Military Intelligence at headquarters in France, described her as a 'regular, modern Joan of Arc'.[33] She travelled between France and England more than a dozen times for British intelligence and commanded men and women of all ages. One of the women known to have operated as an agent for the Alice Service was Marie Leonie Vanhoutte (aka 'Charlotte'). Twenty-seven-year-old Vanhoutte came from Roubaix, France, and worked on the French–Belgian border. She and Bettignies expanded the Alice Service around Cambrai, Valenciennes and Saint-Quentin. Reports of what they witnessed of German troop activities were secretly ferried through Belgium and Holland. Vanhoutte was arrested on 24 September 1915, survived the rest of the war in prison, but gave away Bettignies during brutal interrogation by the German secret police.

On 20 October 1915, Bettignies was arrested near Tournai and was found to be carrying forged passes. Just prior to her arrest, she had managed to alert French intelligence to the fact that the Germans planned an offensive at Verdun in early 1916, but her information was mistrusted and ignored. She was taken to St Gilles prison in Brussels and later sentenced to death, which was commuted to hard labour. The Alice Service did not survive her arrest and disintegrated without its visionary leader.

Bettignies was held in a punishment cell in solitary confinement and, in midwinter, issued only with thin cotton blankets – treatment intended to break her spirit. She contracted pneumonia and was close to death. She recovered, only to develop a small tumour on the breast. She was operated on in the prison, but it was unsuccessful. She died in prison on 27 September 1918, aged thirty-eight, just six weeks before the end of the war. After the Armistice, she received a full military funeral, her coffin draped in the French flag, placed on a gun-carriage and escorted through the streets of Cologne to the railway station. The French General Deboutte and General Simon of the British Army marched behind her coffin. Her body was laid to rest in Lille.

General Sir Walter Kirke wrote: 'I cannot speak too highly of the bravery, devotion, and patriotism of this young lady. Her services to British intelligence . . . were simply invaluable.'[34]

The Woman Who Saved London

When Marthe Cnockaert (later McKenna) was first approached by her friend Lucelle Deldonck to spy for the British she was horrified. Unbeknownst to her, following the occupation of Belgium by German forces in August 1914 Lucelle had begun operating as a courier behind enemy lines. Marthe started work as a nurse at the hospital in Roulers, West Flanders, in January 1915, helping German soldiers wounded on the front line. Born in Westroosebeke in 1892, Marthe hated the occupation and secretly wanted to support the Allies but, as she admitted, she was afraid of a German firing-party in the cold dawn.[35] And things became more complicated for her after the Germans asked her to betray fellow Belgians. For a short time, she became a spy for both the Germans and the British. She offered information to the Germans which she believed would not harm Belgians or the British, but which her handler 'Otto' would believe to be important.

She was honest about the dilemmas she faced and admitted to feeling guilty if the intelligence she passed to the British led to the fatality of German soldiers. Her situation changed after the sudden death of her German handler, bringing an end to her double life, and she made a decision to work solely for the British. One of her first actions was to undertake, alongside another secret Belgian agent, the dangerous task of dynamiting a German ammunition depot. Overcoming her fear of death by firing squad, she went on to provide British intelligence with information that would ultimately save London.

By day, Marthe gathered intelligence from wounded German soldiers in the hospital. In the evenings she worked as a waitress at her parents' café and this gave her another opportunity to pick up information from the conversations of German officers and soldiers. The intelligence was passed to an intermediary. Marthe worked with two other female agents, one of whom she only knew as 'Canteen Ma', a vegetable seller, and the other an agent called 'No. 63'. Canteen Ma was an older woman whose activities did not arouse suspicion as she travelled the countryside selling her vegetables. She was able to deliver coded messages and instructions to Marthe. Canteen Ma disappeared and her fate remains unknown. Marthe never met No. 63, who dropped weekly reports for the Allies through the window of a small shop in Westroosebeke. As a result of her intelligence work, the Allies were able to bomb military targets – ordnance, train and ammunition depots.

In May 1916, Marthe was in the shop when German Commander Fashugel entered with one of his lieutenants. He spoke about a church parade for a whole battalion of German soldiers the following day. He turned to Marthe and asked if she would bring some of the wounded soldiers to the service. She knew that if she passed this information to the chemist on the square, it would cross the frontier by dawn; a coded message would be sent to Allied commanders such that Westroosebeke would receive a visit from their bombers. The fact that she was going to be at the parade with wounded German soldiers did not deter her from acting.

The following day, just as the bishop was finishing the morning service, there came the roar of Allied aircraft overhead, dropping their bombs. The battalion, including Commander Fashugel, was virtually wiped out, with just a handful of survivors and deserters. Marthe survived. The German NCOs and officers brought their heavily wounded casualties to one area and awaited the ambulances. One of the officers despatched Marthe with a lorry to attend to the men at the German hospital. The irony for Marthe was not lost – she had been responsible for the intelligence that had led to all this suffering. It was a traumatic experience for her: she coped by refusing to let herself think.[36]

In the autumn, the German authorities asked her to requisition medical supplies which she was to collect from Rumbelle aerodrome.[37] It was the perfect excuse for her to observe the aerodrome to provide intelligence for the Allies without arousing suspicion. For weeks, she had received messages asking for intelligence on the airfield and now was her chance.

The hospital porter who delivered the requisition form commented to her that all gossip in the canteen pointed to a massive raid on England soon that would cripple the country and evoke fear in the British population. This was supported by comments from Sergeant Schweitzer, who had been posted to the aerodrome and already knew Marthe from the hospital. She charmed Schweitzer, and he boasted that a colossal raid on London was planned for 1 October; Heinrich Mathy, commander of Zeppelin air raids on London, was to lead eleven Zeppelins, two from Bruges and the rest from Germany. Schweitzer then started to made advances, grabbing and kissing Marthe. She struggled and screamed. It alerted one of the pilots on duty nearby who rushed to her aid. The pilot recognised her as the nurse who had tended him when he was wounded. Schweitzer was dealt with harshly for his behaviour. The pilot invited her to come back that same evening to dine with him at the aerodrome.

At dusk, as she crossed the complex, she took a mental snapshot of the scene around her. She spied five single-seater biplanes of a type that she had not seen before. She made an innocent comment to the lieutenant about the planes. He had already consumed a fair amount of alcohol, and he trusted her. He told her the planes were little Albatrosses and were designed for speed. 'They climb like rockets,' he said, 'answer to the slightest touch, and what is better, go a good twenty miles faster than anything the Allies can put in the air.'[38]

After supper, while the lieutenant left the room to shout to his batman for more brandy, Marthe saw two sets of papers: one was authorisation for the lieutenant's leave for Germany, and the other was a half-written report on the new biplanes. She swapped the papers inside each envelope, knowing that the report on the biplanes would mistakenly be sent to the brigade major (who was supposed to authorise the form for the lieutenant's leave). Marthe knew the brigade major's clerk, Stephan, and, although he was not working for the Allies, he liked her and occasionally passed her useful information. She knew that he would copy the report for her.

The lieutenant drank more brandy and his tongue became looser. He regaled her with tales of his bravery and how that coming Friday he was due to escort some heavy bombers on a night raid against the British line at Poperinghe in the region of West Flanders. Leaving the aerodrome, Marthe went straight to the chemist's shop to send a coded message about the Zeppelin raid on London and the bombing of Poperinghe. This was not without danger: there was a curfew in place, and she only had a permit to travel in and out of the hospital, not to private houses or shops. There was a tense moment as police detained her outside the chemist, but she made an excuse about needing urgent medicine for her father and the police allowed her to enter.

The following morning, she used a trusted contact called Alphonse to contact the clerk at the aerodrome for a copy of the report on the biplanes. Within hours, Stephan arrived at the shop with the report. But it was too big to pass over the counter without arousing suspicion. Marthe cut the paper sheets into strips and numbered them, then sewed them into the hem of an old skirt. When Canteen Ma arrived the following day with her usual haul of vegetables, the old skirt was handed over to her and onwards to British intelligence. British bombers were duly scrambled and headed for Rumbelle aerodrome to attack the biplanes before they could take off. But they arrived too late, and instead met the German bombers already en route for Poperinghe. A furious dogfight took place overhead, with losses on both sides. The German planes continued to Poperinghe, but the town was prepared with its defensive barrage. One German aircraft fell and the others left without inflicting any serious damage. Poperinghe survived.

At 5 p.m. on 1 October Marthe heard the drone of Zeppelin engines overhead. As she stared up into the darkening sky, she prayed that Commander Mathy and his Zeppelins would fail. She did not hear about the result of the raid until years later. Mathy died that night. The defences of London were well prepared and the Zeppelin L31 was shot down over Potters Bar, to the north of London. Through the intelligence she had passed to the British via her channels, Marthe saved London, and Germany lost its foremost air commanders.

The Risks

The extent of Marthe's work behind the lines was not limited to providing intelligence on German raids. She and her friend Alphonse discovered a series of underground medieval sewers that ran under a German ammunition dump.[39] Taking the initiative, she persuaded him to help in a pre-planned operation, descending into the sewers in the middle of the night and surfacing, unnoticed, through a cover near to the ammunition dump. They placed two sticks of dynamite at strategic points and returned to the hospital where they worked. That night the ammunition dump was destroyed. The Germans never worked out who had done it or how.

Marthe could not evade the Germans forever, and in 1916 she was suspected of espionage, arrested and questioned by the police, and detained behind bars. In prison she was threatened with the one fear that had initially prevented her from working as a spy for the British – the firing squad at dawn. She was scared and intimidated, but denied everything and held her nerve. With little food and drink, and desperately cold, she became ill and suffered periods of semi-consciousness. Her mother was permitted to visit her once and brought extra food. She raised Marthe's spirits by informing her that the German surgeons and staff at the Roulers hospital were going to give her a good character reference at the court martial. She was transferred to the military hospital in Ghent.

At her trial in November 1916 she was sentenced to be executed at dawn on a day of the court's choosing. Defiant, she told the court that she did not recognise the German court or its verdict, and 'If you think the might of Germany can keep down the spirit of the oppressed Belgian nation, you are mistaken. You will have to arrest, imprison and murder every man, woman and child born with the spirit of freedom in Belgium . . . Vive la Belgique! Vive les Allies!'

The months passed in prison and Marthe grew frail, but she was not shot. Because of her dedication to German soldiers in the hospital and her consequent award of an Iron Cross, her sentence was commuted to life imprisonment. She spent the remainder of the war in Ghent prison and was liberated by Allied soldiers.

She returned to her former home in Westroosebeke, of which not a single brick was still standing. A kind young British officer came over to her and asked if the rubble had been her home. He was the man she married a short time later and they settled in Belgium.

Defiance and Heroism

Nurses like Marthe Cnockaert and Edith Cavell worked tirelessly to provide medical care and pastoral support to wounded soldiers. They were the maternal figures who comforted the men after the horrors of the battlefields, but these women, already well established and living in German-occupied Belgium, were also in a unique position to help British intelligence behind the lines. Alongside their daily work, they risked their lives to smuggle Allied soldiers and enable their escape back to England or France. Aiding soldiers to escape was dangerous enough, and carried the risk of arrest and imprisonment, even a death sentence, but they were prepared to go yet further and engage in intelligence activities for the British.

Today, Marthe's legacy is largely unknown by the public in narratives of women's history, even less so in the wider telling of the First World War. On the other hand, Edith Cavell has become a household name, and it has been possible to say, with certainty, that she was a spy for the British. There is an important, oft unacknowledged, dimension to her legacy – that her defiance and heroism in 1915 inspired women to take up resistance and intelligence activities for the remainder of the First World War. But her legacy goes further. Cavell could not have anticipated during her lifetime that her spirit of resistance would go on to inspire a new generation of women behind enemy lines two decades later when the world went to war again.

2
ESPIONAGE BEHIND ENEMY LINES

France was never successfully fully occupied by the Germans during the First World War; consequently, the country became an ideal staging post from which British intelligence could run espionage operations into the German-occupied countries of Belgium and Luxembourg. MI1(c) stationed its senior British officers in Paris and other locations in northern France. The uniformed male intelligencers were often attached to the Intelligence Corps, nominally working for the War Office, but really working for MI1(c), the British Secret Service. MI1(c) ran its clandestine networks behind the lines from a number of offices, two of which were in England. These were located at 7 Lincoln House, Basil Street, London, under the command of Major Ernest Wallinger, and in Folkestone under the auspices of Captain Cecil Cameron. A train-watching network behind enemy lines in Belgium was set up by the Folkestone office, with some overlap between the work of Folkestone and London. Unfortunately, there was competition, rivalry and friction between the two offices and that hampered intelligence work.[1]

After the German forces entered Brussels on 20 August 1914, Belgians were prepared to resist and work with the British. The most critical early intelligence network behind enemy lines in the country was instituted in late 1914 by a Belgian, Dieudonné Lambrecht. Initially it had forty-one agents, including women, who worked from six observation posts around Liège, Jemelle and Stavelot. Its primary task was to watch the movement of trains across Belgium in order to track the transfer of German troops and equipment towards the front line, and these observations were sent back to British intelligence in Folkestone and London. Following the arrest and execution of Lambrecht in April

1916, which sent shockwaves through the organisation, the network continued under the leadership of Walthère Dewé, Herman Chauvin and Father Jean Desonay. It was given a new name, Service Michelin, and continued to recruit and engage women in its activities.

One of the other independently run networks to work closely with Service Michelin was the Service de Monge, which was named after its chief, Countess Gabrielle de Monge.[2] She had initiated an escape line organisation and recruited its early members, such as her friend Thérèse de Radiguès, who lived in the château in Conneux, from where many of the clandestine activities for Service de Monge were organised and coordinated. A team of women were appointed to recruit other members. In operation since November 1914, the escape line sheltered Allied soldiers in abbeys and aristocrats' homes and escorted escapers and evaders to the Belgian–Dutch border, where they could be smuggled out of the country. The organisation had a section for forgery, printing photographs and producing fake identity cards. Further, it collected intelligence for the British. This underground network was compromised at the same time as Lambrecht was arrested. Gabrielle de Monge as its leader, along with some members, were imprisoned, with the countess sentenced to three years' hard labour – but not before the Service de Monge had saved more than 400 soldiers.

The women who were not discovered remained steadfast in their loyalty to the Allied cause and bravely continued their intelligence work for the British by working for another Belgian intelligence network, La Dame Blanche (p. 30).

The Petit Network

Twenty-two-year-old Gabrielle Petit was formally recruited by an officer of the British Secret Service in the summer of 1915 while crossing the Channel by boat to England.[3] The Belgian had told the British officer that she aspired to help the war effort and wanted to volunteer for medical work. Her bold, fearless character made an impression on him and he asked her to become an agent for the British in Belgium. She was excited by the prospect and accepted.

After training with British intelligence in England, she returned to the Tournai region under the alias 'Mademoiselle Legrand' and formed a new intelligence organisation called 'Petit' that was distinct from other such networks in the country. Petit was delighted to be back in Tournai, the place of her birth in 1893. She came from a middle-class background, but had had a troubled childhood. Rejected by her father after the death of her mother, she was sent to an orphanage and made a failed suicide attempt at the age of fifteen.[4] Drifting between jobs and accommodation, she was taken in by a kind Belgian couple, Mr and Mrs Collet-Sauvage. In July 1915, having enlisted into the intelligence services in Belgium, she was sent to England for a period of training by the British Secret Service as a professional spy. She returned to her country and was given a letter box for dropping off intelligence at the home of none other than the now widowed Mrs Collet-Sauvage.

From the autumn of 1915, under the codename Mrs Legrand, Petit travelled to the Ypres sector in Maubeuge to live and move among enemy troops and take note of the units, their movements, the position of troops, morale, uniforms and weapons. Her mission was complex and dangerous. She adopted a multitude of false identities, including a bakery delivery woman, a nanny, a barmaid, a fisherman and a beggar in order to slip between the German lines, appearing and disappearing under these different disguises. Her observations were written on minuscule, thin sheets of paper using invisible ink and taken to Collet-Sauvage. From there, couriers collected the messages and passed them on to British intelligence. Three other young girls are known to have worked in the Petit network; all were conscious of the perils and the possibility of betrayal.[5] They proved very successful in recording the movement of trains and German troops and passing their observations back to British intelligence.

Petit sent a total of fifty intelligence reports during her relatively short time working for the British. She was ultimately betrayed by a German mole called Wepiar d'Ougrée and, as a result, the Germans placed her under surveillance, recording her visits to the dead letter box.[6] She went to the Logemont café on 26 August 1915, 24 January 1916 and 2 February 1916, and on that final visit she was arrested. As she was driven away by her German captors, she shouted, 'I am Belgian and I am captive of the Boches.' They threatened her, but she calmly retorted, 'Just try it . . . I will pierce your hand with the hairpin of my hat!'[7] Why did she risk her life? In her own words, it was 'to do my duty, come what may'.[8]

Petit was imprisoned in the infamous St Gilles prison in Brussels. An eyewitness account of her treatment at the hands of the Germans and her defiance towards them was provided by a prisoner in the next cell. Petit faced trial and, although there was insufficient evidence of her espionage activities, the Germans sentenced her to death. The prison priest tried to persuade her to send a plea to the German Kaiser for a pardon. She flatly refused, telling him, 'I will not abase myself before a German, even less for the Kaiser. I want to show them a Belgian woman knows how to die.'

On 1 April 1916, at the age of only twenty-three, Petit was shot by the Germans for espionage. She was heroic and defiant even moments before her death, refusing to be blindfolded before the firing squad in Schaerbeek and, as they raised their guns, shouting out, 'Vive la Belgique! Vive la Belgique!'[9]

La Dame Blanche

The Germans knew there was a leakage of intelligence to the British, as well as spies, smugglers and fighters passing in and out of occupied Belgium and into neutral Holland, where the British Secret Service had a station in Rotterdam, run by SIS man Richard Tinsley. In an effort to prevent these clandestine activities, the Germans constructed an electrified wire fence in May–June 1915, known as 'the wire of death', along the border from Knokke on the Belgian coast to the German city of Aachen. It was almost 450 km in length. Belgians could only leave for short visits via a gate, with the entire length of the border guarded every 50 to 100 metres. During the war, over 3,000 people lost their lives trying to cross the fence. Leonie Rammeloo and Emilie Schatteman, two teenagers of peasant background, lived in the border village of Bouchaute.[10] They helped *passeurs* (smugglers) to get information and people through the wire into Holland. To prevent electrocution, some of those going through the wire wore rubber suits and gloves, or used specially made collapsible wooden frames to wedge open a gap.[11] It was ingenious. When the Germans became wise to these activities and the situation became trickier, members of the network threw messages over the wire to be collected by agents on the other side.

The electrified fence posed enormous challenges for MI1(c) in trying to obtain intelligence from behind the wire. There were some successes with Service Michelin, but this was compromised again in 1917 when Father Onays was arrested. The British Secret Service decided to instigate changes and, for the first time, members of the network were militarised, becoming soldiers as the Corps d'Observation Anglais au Front (English Observation Corps of the Western Front). The organisation also changed its name to La Dame Blanche – the White Lady.

The network took its name from a legend of the ghost of a white lady who, when she appeared, would herald the demise of the Hohenzollern royal dynasty, the ruling family of Brandenburg-Prussia and later imperial Germany.[12] The implication was clear: by its work, La Dame Blanche would facilitate the end of German rule in Belgium. Three men from Liège – Walthère Dewé, Herman Chauvin and Joseph Falloise – led La Dame Blanche, and South-African born Captain Henry Landau oversaw military espionage activities in Germany, Belgium and France for MI1(c). The number of agents in Belgium and France connected to La Dame Blanche was estimated to be over 2,000, a least a third of whom were women.[13]

Recruits took an oath of loyalty upon joining the network:

> I declare and enlist in the capacity of soldier in the Allied military observation service until the end of the war. I swear before God to respect this engagement, to accomplish conscientiously the offices entrusted to me . . . not to reveal (without formal authorisation) anything concerning the organisation of the service, even if this stance should entail for me the penalty of death.[14]

Despite such explicit wording, there was reluctance from MI1(c) in London to grant women soldier status. It took the lobbying of a number of British intelligence officers and La Dame Blanche chiefs for women to be recognised in a military capacity and given a military rank; in some cases they even outranked their male colleagues. This was a crucial development, giving women the opportunity to serve in roles traditionally fulfilled by men and placing both sexes on an equal footing in this work.[15] La Dame Blanche was forward-thinking in permitting its female recruits to 'function in so-called masculine roles, such as spy, courier and saboteur'.[16] Women played a central and sophisticated role in La Dame Blanche. With occupations tending to be as educators, domestics or of no official occupation, they attracted less attention than their male counterparts, yet could ensure they were in the right place at the right time.

The network quickly increased its surveillance of German troop movements to fifty-one railway observation posts across occupied Belgium and parts of the Grand Duchy of Luxembourg. These posts operated twenty-four hours a day, every day of the year. The houses and cottages nearest the railway lines served as the best locations and in a sense were the new 'front line'. Families involved in the network divided up the day and night into shifts to cover all hours. Women from the ages of eighteen to eighty sat outside their cottages and houses appearing simply to be knitting; in reality they were observing the troop movements as the trains passed by their doors. They knitted coded messages into their jumpers and scarves, with certain types and numbers of stitches representing particular German troops and regiments and their strength. The knitted items were sent over the lines to MI1(c)'s headquarters in France to be decoded by an intelligence officer.

Nuns acted as informants and passed to the network information that they overheard from the conversations between German soldiers in hospitals. Reports from observation posts, like the Hirson–Mézières line, were brought by courier to Sister Marie-Mélanie in the French convent at Chimay. Sister Marie-Mélanie and Sister Marie-Caroline, both active members of La Dame Blanche, ran a small shop which was frequented by German soldiers from the front line.[17] The soldiers chattered away, giving snippets of information that seemed innocent to them but which were valuable to the Allies. The sisters' reports covered German military activity and information about new German concrete gun-platforms and ammunition pits along with their precise locations. The intelligence was passed on to Landau, who sent the reports to the British military attaché, Colonel Oppenheim, at The Hague in Holland. Oppenheim sent the daily intelligence summary by telegraph to British

GHQ. The intelligence which they gave not only aided the military picture of German forces and supply lines in Belgium, but also saved the lives of British agents who could be killed going near the front line to gather intelligence.

Sister Marie-Mélanie gave gentle support to one particular (unnamed) German soldier who had a spell of convalescence in the convent. He spoke to her about his war and she listened; he did not suspect that she was spying for the other side and passing information to MI1(c) officer Henry Landau. Just before the German gunner left the convent to return to the front line, he spoke proudly about the big gun, the Kaiser Wilhelm Geschütz. It could fire 120 km and would reach as far as Paris, and, he said, it was the weapon that would win the war for Germany. Sister Marie-Mélanie doubted it, but he boasted that he had seen the installation himself in Laon. She remembered how a French refugee had been given shelter in the convent a few weeks earlier and spoken about Crépy-en-Laon being deserted by civilians because the Germans had moved them out and placed artillery there. The German military had constructed concrete gun-platforms and ammunition pits at one of the farms. This intelligence was passed to Landau and on to London and corroborated other intelligence coming from Allied agents in Germany of a high-trajectory gun with a barrel 30 metres long.

Sister Marie Angèle, mother superior of the convent at Les Hauts Buttes in the Ardennes, was recommended for an honour for her 'patriotic collaboration . . . and precious services rendered' in the war, which was personally signed by Henri Philippe Petain, Field Marshal of France.[18] She sheltered Allied airmen in the convent, working for a network headed by Paulin Jacquemin. The principal agents of the Paulin Jacquemin platoon were killed by the Germans. Mrs Hélène Levy of Charleville was one of the prominent women of this network. She managed the intelligence reports and aided escape and evasion and the Pigeon Service.[19] She was ultimately arrested, faced trial and sentenced to death but this was reduced to life imprisonment.[20]

Women distinguished themselves in positions of responsibility in the daily running of the network. In a secret service section, Lieutenants Julienne and Anne Demarteau, who were sisters, worked as secretaries. Julienne undertook the same liaison duties as two male liaison officers, and was of equal status. Her position was extremely important – and dangerous – as she oversaw the centralised intelligence documents coming in from the various units and then organised their delivery to Holland. She founded several observation posts in Luxembourg and recruited for the platoons.

Families ran letter boxes, safe houses and courier networks. The Weimerskirch sisters Emma, Alice and Jeanne ran a bookshop in Liège that became a letter box and functioned until the end of the war without being betrayed. Sergeant Emma Weimerskirch was personal assistant to the commander of an observation post and was keeper of its reports.[21] The three sisters were in the Service of the Guard and responsible for security.[22] An elite security section was headed by François Rodelet, with Juliette de Brualle, Julie Brever and Germaine van den Berg conducting liaison with prisons. An auxiliary section was responsible for counter-espionage; eight of its members were men, with one woman, Sergeant Isabelle Wauthier.

After Anna Kesseler lost her only son fighting on the front line in 1914, she and her four daughters all decided to help British intelligence by working for La Dame Blanche. Two of the daughters, Germaine (aged twenty-three) and Maria (aged twenty-one) worked as couriers between Brussels and Liège. They represented a growing number of women who have previously not been written about or named in the history of espionage, and who were part of whole families who worked for the network. It was at great risk to themselves, but also other members of their family if they were caught.

Expansion and Leadership

Four specialist extension squads for La Dame Blanche which were responsible for expanding the network across Belgium consisted entirely of women.[23] In addition to the recruitment squads, women directed battalions and established new observation posts. Miss Laure Tandel was one of them. In her forties, she was the headmistress of a school and carried out her duties for La Dame Blanche in her spare time. She operated with her sister Louise in establishing new observation posts at Malines, Gard and Mons.[24] Their section observed trains passing through Malines, Mons, Louvain and Charleroi, and the movement of German military equipment and troops via these routes. In 1918, with the rank of captain, she commanded Battalion III from Brussels and directed the observation posts and networks of Mons, Tournai, Gard, Louvain and Brussels. The battalion had 190 agents, 59 of whom were women. The women acted as couriers, passing documents and reports between agents and locations. Some maintained correspondence with the main leaders in Liège. Of these women, 60 per cent were married, 7 per cent widowed and 34 per cent unmarried.[25]

In November 1917 Laure's sister, Adjutant Louise Tandel, accepted the role of manager at the head office of La Dame Blanche in Brussels.[26] From there she set up a network of observation posts west of Brussels. In September 1918 she became deputy commander of Battalion III – her sister Laure being commander – which had under its direction four observation companies in the west region. The sisters were awarded an OBE by the British.[27]

Marie Delcourt was twenty-seven years old, unmarried and living in Liège without a profession when she joined La Dame Blanche. She established the Luxembourg observation post in January 1918, recruited members and carried out secretarial duties from its creation until it was dissolved in September 1918.[28]

By autumn 1918, as the final stages of the war approached, there were legitimate concerns about how La Dame Blanche could continue if its male leaders were arrested. A decision was taken by the leaders Dewé and Chauvin that a trusted group, made up solely of women, would take over the command if that happened.[29] From September 1918, all battalions and companies of the network were asked to put women in place as reserve personnel. The main board of La Dame Blanche would be taken over by Juliette Durieu (commander), Thérèse de Radiguès (deputy commander), Laure Tandel (deputy commander, if de Radiguès was compromised), Julienne and Anne Demarteau, Emma Weimerskirch and Marie Delcourt.[30]

Platoon 49

In April 1918, Thérèse de Radiguès created, organised and directed a new observation post at Conneux known as Platoon 49. It was run from the castle in Conneux and consisted primarily of the local nobility, who gathered intelligence from locations in eastern Belgium.[31] De

Radiguès's three daughters, Marguerite (aged twenty-six), Marie Antoinette (aged twenty) and Agnes (aged fifteen), worked for the platoon, as did many of the old members of the Service de Monge. Her sixteen-year-old son Gérard, the only one of her four sons not sent to fight in a regiment, also worked for La Dame Blanche.[32] He was arrested with his friend Jean d'Huart in the vicinity of Eupen, near the Belgium–Germany–Netherlands border, on 30 October 1917. They were betrayed by their guide, who handed them over to German border guards. They were released from prison on 25 November 1918, fifteen days after the armistice. Here was a woman, Thérèse de Radiguès, whose children were all involved in some way in fighting for the Allies or as enlisted agents of La Dame Blanche – not to mention her own contribution. What a sacrifice she and her family were prepared to make.

Every week, aristocratic women took the risk of carrying a considerable number of reports to the meetings attended by the chiefs. The women did not shy away from leadership roles. They volunteered to activate and command new observation posts for British intelligence. Twenty-three-year-old Baroness (Corporal) Clémie de L'Epine established a new intelligence post at Charleville. Clémie readily accepted a dangerous reconnaissance expedition towards Monterme to prepare for a new surveillance post at Charleville.[33] Twenty-two-year-old Countess Françoise de Villermont and her sister, twenty-four-year-old Countess Anne de Villermont, set up a new observation position at Givet. Both women had been working for Platoon 49.

Another courageous woman was Elise Grandprez, an unmarried woman in her forties, who operated in the Ardennes region. She undertook train-watching duties and supplied a significant amount of information to the Allies on the movement of German troops. She ran a letter box and worked as a courier with other members of her family, including her sister Marie. Using invisible ink, Elise and Marie wrote secret reports onto ordinary objects, such as packing paper, box covers and bookplates. These reports were taken to the chief, Walthère Dewé, in Liège. These women had originally worked for the founder, Dieudonné Lambrecht. All members of the Grandprez family were arrested in 1917 on charges of espionage. In the moments before she was shot, Elise Grandprez raised her hand toward the sky and shouted, 'Courage! Vive la Belgique!' Her spirit of defiance followed her role model, Edith Cavell.

Miss Eglantine Lefebvre, a Belgian agent, was employed on the *Post Française* newspaper and acted as a courier for La Dame Blanche from April to October 1918. She conducted surveillance of enemy troops moving through the countryside and passed this information to the British.[34] She was incredibly courageous. Although suffering from ill health, Lefebvre wanted to accomplish her duty as a soldier despite everything, and succeeded in accomplishing one final perilous mission. She did not survive the unnamed mission and died for her country on 23 October 1918 at the age of twenty-eight.

Villa des Hirondelles

Villa des Hirondelles in Wandre, a suburb of Liège, was the home of the Collard family and the headquarters for La Dame Blanche and SIS operations in that area. In March 1918 it was raided by the German secret police and a number of arrests made, including the two Collard brothers, Louis and Antony. They were caught with coded messages and reports scattered across the floor of an upstairs room. The arrest of the brothers, who were aged twenty-one and twenty, was swiftly followed by the apprehension of their father and six others. La Dame Blanche stepped in to financially support those families who were left with small children after the breadwinner had been arrested. Eighteen-year-old Marie-Thérèse Collard was not arrested. She and Irène Bastin (whose parents had been arrested) enrolled as members of La Dame Blanche to restart the network. They ran contacts between couriers and agents, operating under false names as 'sisters' Martha and Madeleine Vailly. The secret police became suspicious of them for travelling regularly to Namur and Liège and arrested them. They gave nothing away and were released. On 18 July 1918, Louis and Antony Collard were shot at Fort de la Chartreuse in Liège.

The women of La Dame Blanche remained defiant and determined to continue their work, even when members of their own family were arrested and shot by the Germans. As Thérèse de Radiguès commented,

'The feeling of danger hanging over our heads night and day did not dishearten us, far from it, it seemed that the greater danger became, the more enchanting was our work.'[35]

The Sacrifice

At least 300 women were imprisoned by the Germans at Siegburg prison, near Köln in Germany, for their intelligence work for the Allies across all networks, although the true figure may be higher.[36] They endured harsh treatment with only a wooden plank for beds, unheated cells and an insufficient subsistence of watery potato soup and stale bread. During their incarceration and hard labour punishment, the women resisted the Germans by refusing to give away any information that might be used as ammunition against the Allies. They were punished with a period of solitary confinement, and yet demonstrated their extraordinary bravery, lack of fear and refusal to be intimidated by a brutal regime.

In 1917, Jeanne Delwaide was arrested and sent to Siegburg prison. She was among the first twenty agents recruited for La Dame Blanche and one of the few people privy to the names of the three main leaders. If she had given them away under interrogation, the fall of La Dame Blanche and its vital intelligence networks would have delivered a severe blow for the British. Walthère Dewé, the supreme chief, sent her a coded message while she was in prison, imploring her to keep silent, and told her: 'Remember you are a soldier. Remember your oath. Deny everything.'[37] Delwaide never gave the network away.[38] She concluded, 'We have done our duty – as good British soldiers – our patient labour was not in vain.'[39]

Another young woman who kept silent amidst the hardships in prison and intense interrogation was Jeanne Goeseels. She, like so many other women, was a loyal, patriotic, effective and courageous soldier and intelligence agent. In spite of all their suffering, 'not one of these brave women, from Princess de Croy down to the humblest peasant, regretted having served her country'.[40]

At the end of the war, Landau petitioned the British Secret Service to accept these women as soldiers for military awards because 'they ran exactly the same risks as the men'.[41] In 1919, British intelligence honoured this request and over 3,000 awards were given to male and female agents, often a military division of an order, because they had been part of a militarised unit. A thousand of these awards were for members of La Dame Blanche. More than a hundred members lost their lives and were shot by the Germans.

The women of La Dame Blanche were irrefutably engaged in espionage, gathering military intelligence and doing courier and resistance work. They were, as Henry Landau stated, 'as brave and efficient as the men'.[42] Official MI6 historian Keith Jeffery wrote that La Dame Blanche was 'the most successful single British human intelligence operation of the First World War'.[43]

From Censorship to Intelligence in the Field

While La Dame Blanche functioned from within Belgium, British military intelligence was operating from a number of secret locations in France. Military intelligence was no different from any other section of warfare at this time in being traditionally the province of men. However, Field Marshal Douglas Haig, commander-in-chief of the British Expeditionary Force in France, recognised 'the principle of employing women in this country [France] is accepted and they will be made use of wherever conditions permit'.[44]

The first female intelligencers began to arrive in France in 1916. That same year, Charlotte Bosworth was posted to the Ministère de la Guerre (Ministry of War) in Paris from London, where she had been deputy assistant censor at the Censorship Office. Her role there had involved scrutinising the mail taken off neutral ships and gathering intelligence that could be useful for the war.[45] This gave her important experience that was soon needed abroad. She was selected for a new post in Paris precisely for her skill in ascertaining useful intelligence from documents and being fluent in French and German. Her new role was to extract information from the pay books of German prisoners of war.

Charlotte spotted an advertisement for the recruitment of linguists for intelligence work and was able to recommend her sister Sylvia. A job like this could only be secured by knowing someone already in the clandestine world. Sylvia arrived in Paris in 1917 and was drafted alongside Miss L. Brooking, who was already stationed at GHQ there.[46] They operated from Rue d'Alésia in Montparnasse, looking over documents taken from German POWs by personnel of the Intelligence Corps, extracting and collating intelligence from them. These two women were particularly valuable because they could read difficult German script; they also supported a nascent signals intelligence service in France. Useful information derived from the analysis of captured documents was passed back to Intelligence GHQ, which helped the British to understand enemy tactics. James Marshall-Cornwall, a major at Intelligence GHQ during the war and, after it, head of the MI3 section of the military intelligence directorate, concluded of the women's contribution: 'This success delivered into our hands a welcome mass of intelligence material, including von Below's Army Orders and documents showing the complete organisation of their rear services.'[47] The women continued this work until nearing the end of the war, when the information from soldiers' pay books became sporadic and no longer useful.[48]

Military intelligence in France was able to use a small number of talented women on translation and cipher duties. Among them was Miss Gwendoline Edith Watkins who, under the auspices of MI1(b), the forerunner to GC&CS, worked in Paris on administrative duties and German field codes. From GHQ in France, Miss Hannam and June Spurling worked on German field codes. Like Watkins, they spoke fluent French and German.[49] On 7 January 1914 MI5 posted Miss D. Bourie to Paris until 5 December 1918 on undisclosed intelligence work.

A small number of women were attached to the clandestine Pigeon Service that sent pigeons with messages over enemy lines into Belgium and Luxembourg from various mobile pigeon lofts in France. Staff Officer Ellemont worked for the service, as did Junior Commander Biard. The latter represented the British Organisation of Pigeon Soldiers.

As both sides in this war developed more sophisticated weapons, the need for knowledge of the enemy's new equipment and military plans become more urgent. By 1917 the intelligence work had increased to such an extent that the Intelligence Corps needed to expand. That same year, the Women's Auxiliary Army Corps (WAAC) was created to carry out non-combat roles that had traditionally been the duty of men. They were not permitted to wear military ranks or badges, but freed up the men to fight on the front line. Many of the WAACs went on to become codebreakers and interceptors. At the end of September 1917, twelve British women (all WAACs) arrived in France to provide support in intelligence roles on the Western Front. They were known as the 'Hush-WAACs' and made history as the first women ever to be employed in uniform on intelligence work abroad.

The 'Hush-WAACs'

The Hush-WAACs were given the nickname because of the secrecy of their job, which involved deciphering German codes alongside their male colleagues. Among them was Mavis Peel, whose war diary provides a unique glimpse into daily life for these women. Although she does not betray precise details of their work, she writes that it required 'the greatest concentration and was of the highest responsibility'. As officers, they had their own orderlies. She described the first day at the headquarters at Saint-Omer: 'We sat there, with sheets of paper in front of us on which were arranged in the form of sentences, meaningless groups of letters. We were told that they were codes, wireless messages (coming from the Germans and tapped by our operators).'[50] Their job was to decode the messages, a job for which they had no prior experience or training.

Peel began her wartime service as a censor in the War Office. University educated and with a knowledge of German, she was already acquainted with an officer in Military Intelligence whose name she does not disclose. He was establishing a new section and needed twelve women fluent in German. He recruited Peel and she underwent a series of selection interviews in London, and was enlisted into the WAACs. A fortnight later, on 28 September 1917, she was despatched to France with five other women. Crossing the English Channel, they were the only women on the boat, which attracted attention from the male passengers. She commented: 'We were going out to do some mysterious work, the nature of which we knew no more than anyone else.'[51]

After an overnight stay at Boulogne, the initial group of six Hush-WAACs arrived at headquarters at Saint-Omer, then located 28 miles behind the front line. Even at this distance from the front, they were not spared the German bombing raids, with the enemy often shelling the place night after night. They were billeted in a small, hutted camp, their sparse rooms containing a bed, four army blankets and a straw pillow. They were soon joined by a further six Hush-WAACs.

In the first few weeks, the women struggled with the coding and required help from their more experienced male colleagues, but within three months they could decode the daily messages without any help. Their decrypts were signed off direct by the head of the room. The work was interesting, but the hours were long. They worked up to seven hours a day, every day, including weekends, with only a half-day off a week. They were entitled to only a fortnight's leave a year, in contrast to the male officers doing exactly the same work who had a fortnight's leave every six months. The Hush-WAACs became extremely fatigued after half a year without a proper break. Peel recalled, 'For six months we had done work requiring the greatest concentration and of the highest responsibility,'[52] and the women persisted in their request for the same period of leave as their male colleagues. Finally, the commanding officer secured for the Hush-WAACs a fortnight's leave every six months. The proper leave prevented the risk of breakdowns and enabled them to continue their intelligence duties with energy and efficiency.

Despite the grim situation of the war, there were moments of relief and joyous spirits. Christmas 1917 was celebrated with a dinner and dance in the Officers Mess, its walls decorated with holly and mistletoe, attended by women from the Hush-WAAC, the FANY (First Aid Nursing Yeomanry) and nurses. Parcels were opened, sent from generous relatives and friends back home.

In spring 1918, Peel was able to take leave back in England. She returned to France a fortnight later to find that, due to heavy German bombing raids, the intelligence HQ had moved from Saint-Omer to a villa called Joyeuse at Étaples. GHQ was located nearby at Montreuil-sur-Mer and various British Army units had been moving up and down the front line. The Hush-WAACs stayed there for the next seven months. Peel had her last period of leave in October 1918, before returning to Étaples for the final three weeks of the war. After the Armistice of 11 November 1918, the work of the Hush-WAACs ceased and they either took up administrative work in France or England, or put in a request for demobilisation. Tasked with closing it down, Peel was the last of the Hush-WAACs to leave the office in France. She was awarded the Victory Medal and the War Medal, and from 1925 she worked for the British Legion in Rouen, aiding unemployed ex-servicemen.[53]

Rue Saint-Roch – Secret HQ of SIS

In the icy winter of January of 1917, thirty-four-year-old Captain George Bruce (later 7th Lord Balfour of Burleigh) arrived in civilian clothes at 41 Rue Saint-Roch, a street just north of the Louvre and the River Seine in Paris. A descendant of Robert the Bruce, he had been wounded in action in 1915 while serving in the Argyll and Sutherland Highlanders. Fluent in French and German, he was despatched to Paris to run a clandestine headquarters for MI1(c), the forerunner of SIS.[54]

On his first day, Bruce entered the building and stepped in the cat's saucer of milk. He looked up and saw Miss Dorothy Done, a secretary at 41 Rue Saint-Roch, who was carrying out 'mysterious duties'. In 1914, when the war began, the twenty-nine-year-old Dorothy had volunteered to work for the Red Cross in London. Having heard nothing, she applied to and was accepted by the French equivalent, the Croix Rouge Française, working first in the French Ministry of War, where there was an exchange of information on German spies. General Walter Kirke, British director of Military Intelligence at headquarters in France, was seeking potential spies to operate for him. As an Englishwoman in a French organisation, Dorothy Done was conspicuous and came to his notice. Kirke recruited her to work for him and moved her to MI1(c)'s headquarters at 41 Rue Saint-Roch. From there she ran a Parcel Fund, sending 'ordinary' parcels to British POWs in German camps that concealed secret escape gadgets. She would later marry Bruce, and was awarded an MBE in 1920 for her work for British intelligence.

The five-storey building at 41 Rue Saint-Roch had opened as a permit office, issuing permits for French civilians and refugees to travel to England in the days before the formal establishment of passport control offices. Bruce could monitor the movement of civilians and refugees flooding into the country from Belgium. Among them might be foreign agents, especially German spies masquerading as refugees. Five such permit offices were established and information and intelligence emanating from them was sent to British GHQ at Montreuil. The premises at 41 Rue Saint-Roch provided a cover for British clandestine operations, where MI1(c)/SIS could run its spy networks behind enemy lines. It was too risky to train agents at this headquarters, so instruction took place in a house in Rue Soufflot, not far from the Sorbonne. A network of military intelligence officers and local trusted civilians coordinated the intelligence coming from behind the lines, especially from La Dame Blanche in Belgium.

The Reluctant Spy

Bruce was concerned that German-occupied Luxembourg had no cover at all. The Grand Duchy of Luxembourg was at the centre of the railway network and, as such, was an important hub between Germany and fighting in the Western Front. Bruce needed a trustworthy, suitable agent to operate in Luxembourg.

At 137 Rue d'Alésia, a middle-aged bourgeois woman, Madame Camille (Lise) Rischard, was staying with her cousin Madame Vanvers. Camille had received a desperate letter from her son by her first marriage that he was about to be sent to the front line and he wanted to see her before he left France. When Rischard arrived in Paris, she discovered that her son was not going to fight but needed money. She longed to return to Luxembourg, but was trapped in France, having handed over her passport to Swiss authorities when borders were lax at the beginning of the war.

During her stay, the permit regulations had changed and she now needed a visa to return home to Luxembourg via Switzerland. The French authorities refused her a visa because she was travelling onwards to German-occupied Luxembourg and that would entail travelling through Germany. She appealed to former French minister to Luxembourg, Armand Molland, whom she knew, repeatedly calling on him at the Quay d'Orsay, the street below the famous basilica the Sacré Coeur, in the Montmartre district of Paris. Each time she visited, he told her that he could not help her: she was trapped in France. In January 1917, her father died and she was desperate to return to Luxembourg. Still, she could not leave. In mid-March 1917, she decided to try Molland again. Unexpectedly, in a theatrical gesture, he pulled aside a curtain in the sitting room to reveal a door, which he opened. Standing behind it were two men. She recognised only one of them – Captain Bruce, in disguise.

They asked, 'Will you spy for us? And if so, your training must start immediately.'

Rischard was shocked by the suggestion. As a respectable bourgeois woman, she did not engage in espionage. She left again. Bruce and his military intelligence colleagues visited her four times at her temporary lodgings, explaining that all they wanted her to do was to conceal a rolled-up piece of paper in her ear and take it into Luxembourg. Each time she stubbornly refused.

Rischard became restless. After a number of sleepless nights, she went out to wander the streets of Paris. Passing the imposing Madeleine church, like an enormous cathedral, with steps the length of the building leading up to the entrance, she felt drawn to enter. In the stillness of the vast ornate church her eyes adjusted to the darkness, and she made out a confessional. She found a priest was there, explained her dilemma to him and asked him what she should do. He told her that it was her duty to help France and the Allies. She left the church and walked for a further twenty minutes to the Quai d'Orsay, behind which she saw the golden dome of St Louis-des-Invalides rising majestically into the sky. This was the soldiers' church, where Napoleon was buried. In that moment, having reflected on what the priest had said to her, she knew what her duty was. She would spy for the Allies.

Rischard called on Bruce at SIS headquarters in Rue Saint-Roch and told him she would work for him. Bruce was relieved that he had secured the only route he had for gaining intelligence from behind enemy lines in Luxembourg; Rischard's would be an SIS intelligence network running in parallel to La Dame Blanche in Belgium. Bruce instructed her to recruit her own husband, Dr Carville Rischard (a doctor to the railway workers), and to then get him to recruit a network of train-watchers at the marshalling yard. The railwaymen trusted the couple. Bruce then explained to Rischard that she was to head the whole network and expand it beyond her husband's immediate workers to provide intelligence for the British. Her training began immediately at secret locations in Paris. She was taught how to recognise German uniforms, insignia, transport, weapons, types of train, letters and symbols. She studied German military handbooks and was asked to identify uniforms from dead German POWs displayed on tailors' dummies. Her codename was 'Madame Léonard' and she became a code expert. She was to send back to Bruce reports and coded messages detailing German troop movements by train heading towards the Western Front. Coded messages sent to her from Paris would confirm whether her messages had been received. What Bruce had not told her was that a similar SIS operation in Switzerland, albeit unoccupied by the enemy, had been beset by failures. Had Rischard known this, she might well have pulled out of her mission.

With the training complete, Bruce issued a visa for Rischard's return to Luxembourg. The war was taking a new turn. After a wet winter, the Germans recommenced their offensive on the Western Front in March 1917, and Bruce desperately needed intelligence from the marshalling yard in Luxembourg on the movement of trains carrying German forces and equipment there. Meanwhile, on the Eastern Front, the Russian army was plagued by poor morale and deserters; if the Russian front collapsed, Germany could move its units from the east to reinforce the west.

Having completed her training, on 17 June Rischard finally arrived at the border into Switzerland – the first hurdle to cross in order to re-enter Luxembourg. The police stamped her new French passport. As she glanced around, she saw Bruce watching her from afar; his presence gave her the assurance she needed to continue her mission. Its gravity was not lost on her. She was about to cross the frontier as an agent of a foreign power and, if things went wrong, she would pay the price with her life. But, in the interim, the rules had changed again. Rischard now required a visa from the Foreign Ministry in Berlin as well, which could take up to six weeks. She was trapped inside Switzerland. Bruce was concerned that the delay would undermine her confidence in the whole operation and she would return to Paris. She held her nerve, but in August 1917 wrote to Bruce from Lausanne with troubling news: Berlin had refused her request to leave Switzerland. The German military command was planning a renewed offensive that autumn, with talk of a large offensive in spring 1918 – Bruce *had* to get Rischard into Luxembourg before that time. Her husband appealed for help from the Grand Duchess of Luxembourg, whose sister he had been treating. Luckily, she intervened, and a visa was on its way to Rischard by January 1918.

On 7 February, Madame Rischard took the early morning train from Zurich to Luxembourg. As the other passengers settled down to their newspapers, she smoked a cigarette and gazed casually out of the window. As the train sped through Germany, she observed everything – the condition of the fields, the appearance of towns, activity at railway stations and sidings. Her espionage for the British had already begun. The train pulled into Offenburg and she disembarked for an overnight stay in a hotel. From there she wrote her first postcard to Bruce, informing him how different Germany was since she was last there two years ago. She told him how the people were starving and demonstrating on the streets. There were riots and strikes, and curfews had been introduced. The German people were thin, their faces gaunt and they lacked the energy for war. This was important information for Bruce on the morale of the German population and its ability to tolerate or support the war.[55]

Rischard finally arrived back at her home at 20 Boulevard Royal. Her husband noticed the change in her and she filled him in on all that had happened. He agreed to work for Bruce behind the lines with the railway workers. She set up a safe house in her home to shelter Allied agents. The property was ideal as it had five different doors leading directly onto three different streets – her agents could come and go undetected. Through coded reports and newspaper articles, she passed vital intelligence about the enemy back to Bruce at 41 Rue Saint-Roch. A week after her return home, she sent him a coded message to tell him that no German troops had passed through Luxembourg that week. For Bruce, this was a vital indicator that new German troops were not moving to reinforce the front line.

During the final year of the war, at such a crucial time, this courageous, once reluctant spy, built a successful – and currently the only known – intelligence organisation behind the lines in Luxembourg for the British Secret Service. Her legacy would remain secret for decades until the discovery of a locked chest at the Bruce ancestral home in Scotland.[56]

The Spies Who Should Be Remembered

The intelligence successes by the British Secret Service, then known as MI1(c), could not have been achieved without the actions and heroism of over 3,000 women and men in occupied Belgium and Luxembourg who were prepared to risk their lives smuggling out intelligence. These were the women and men of the Service Michelin, the Service de Monge and La Dame Blanche. They included nurses like Edith Cavell and her organisation, and formidable and courageous women like Thérèse de Radiguès and Madame Rischard. Alongside them, the British women in uniform for the first time in intelligence roles abroad made their mark.

It is clear that women of all ages were prepared to play their part in enemy-occupied countries for the ultimate goal of freedom from tyranny and occupation. They left a history and legacy within their own circles that would make them incredibly valuable and experienced in intelligence gathering in any future conflict. Theirs had been a war that gave them roles previously never imagined in their restricted civilian lives, a war fraught with real personal danger, but providing them with the satisfaction that they had made a difference.

It was exceptionally hard for these women in the years immediately following the First World War as they were expected simply to return to their traditional roles as mothers and wives. This did not mean that women had no role in intelligence in the 1920s and 1930s, though. MI1(c), soon to become the Secret Intelligence Service (SIS) in 1919, continued to engage women in intelligence work, but at much reduced numbers compared to men.

How many women realised in their lifetime the huge significance of their intelligence work is not clear. The leaders of La Dame Blanche were, however, told quite clearly by Mansfield Cumming, the first head of SIS, that the intelligence obtained by them 'was worth thousands of lives to the allied armies'.[57] Their work accounted for 70 per cent of the intelligence obtained by the Allied armies, not only via the Netherlands but through other neutral countries. The Allies came to depend on the intelligence provided by La Dame Blanche on enemy movements in areas near the front line. It was one of the great successes in the early history of the British Secret Service and one in which women had played a central and indispensable role.

3

INTELLIGENCE ON THE HOME FRONT

Intelligence roles on the home front in the First World War mined every available source and employed a huge variety of strategies to provide information on the enemy. This included combating enemy spies in counter-espionage operations by MI5, postal censorship through the War Office and the Home Office, secret work for Special Branch, cracking and deciphering German naval codes by Naval Intelligence Division (NID) at the Admiralty, and interception and cryptanalysis by MI1(b). With tens of thousands of men leaving for the various theatres of war overseas after the introduction of conscription in 1916, across these intelligence organisations and agencies as elsewhere, women began to take on duties that in peacetime had been carried out by men.

On 8 August 1914 the British Parliament passed the Defence of the Realm Act, which gave the government powers of interception to open and study all mail and letters passing through the country, including the post of foreign nationals. It enabled British intelligence to discover if enemy spies already residing in Britain were communicating with the German intelligence services in Germany. At the outbreak of war, the postal censorship department in the UK consisted of just one man. By December 1914 the department's personnel had risen to 170 men and women. By the end of the war in November 1918 there were 1,343 men and 3,318 women engaged in censorship. Of these, 1,247 women were based in special premises in Liverpool, with the remainder in London.[1] The majority of the war's censorship work was, therefore, undertaken by women. And what work it was: in total, around 2 billion letters and 14 million parcels passed through the hands of the censors. Women thus played an important part in uncovering a number of German spies operating in the UK who had used mail and cable to transmit information to the continent. From the censorship department, some women transferred to MI5 or Special Branch, the latter the organisation responsible for security and policing.

Room 40

Room 40 at the Admiralty in London was the centre of naval intelligence operations during the war. It was located inside the citadel, overlooking Horse Guards Parade in Whitehall. From the outbreak of war in 1914 Naval Intelligence Division and the War Office worked together as part of MI1(b), the branch of military intelligence for codebreaking. It comprised of a small team of male officers and cryptographers from the Admiralty and the War Office who worked closely together on enemy codes.[2] Women joined their ranks, and Sir Reginald 'Blinker' Hall, the new director of Naval Intelligence, had basic criteria for who should be recruited: they had to be the daughters or sisters of naval officers, be fluent in at least two languages and have the ability to use a typewriter. These women became known as 'Blinker's Beauty Chorus'.

By 1916, twenty women were operating in Room 40. The secretaries and typists were supervised by Lady Hambro, wife of the banker Sir Everard Hambro. She was said to shock her male contemporaries 'when she smoked a cigar at a social function'.[3] Among the high-class female staff working for Lady Hambro were Miss Joan Harvey, daughter of the Secretary of the Bank of England; Miss Violet Hudson, daughter of a soap magnate; and Catherine Henderson, daughter of Admiral Henderson. Mrs Margaret Bayley, the wife of a doctor, joined Room 40 in November 1917. There were wealthy men in Room 40, too.[4]

Other women whose names are known include June Spurling, one of the elite cryptographers, who had worked in GHQ France on German field codes. For decades, British naval attachés posted abroad had been sending back intelligence to the UK from their postings in embassies abroad.[5] Now in wartime one of the main central intelligence roles for NID was breaking enemy codes and ciphers. Miss Watkins, Miss Spurling, Miss Marreco and Miss Anderson all decoded, and Miss Haylar worked on Italian codes. Alastair Denniston, joint deputy head of Bletchley Park in the next war, commented that 'the services of these ladies are invaluable. They are experienced in the working out of all kinds of codes.'[6] They were so valuable that they retained their jobs in the Admiralty after the war.[7]

Unfortunately, so little mention is made of the women in code-breaking at the Admiralty in the First World War that it is impossible to properly assess their achievements. In contrast, more information is available in declassified files about the roles of civilian women on the home front in MI5.

MI5

The Security Service was formed in 1909, initially as part of the Secret Service Bureau, and for the first two years of its existence had no female employees at its headquarters at 64 Victoria Street, SW1.[8] Vernon Kell, its first chief, had just one male assistant who acted as his second in command: William Melville, the former superintendent of Special Branch, who had gained respect there for successfully tracking down anarchists and subversives. His experience proved invaluable to Kell as he built up counter-intelligence operations within the UK. The first woman was hired in January 1911 for the post of typist. In October that same year, the first woman was appointed as the private secretary to Vernon Kell. Her tasks included opening his letters, the custody of all secret and confidential documents and the formation of a card index of the bureau's records. In February 1913 a second female secretary was engaged and a third in January 1914.

The responsibility of MI5 was, and remains, counter-espionage and security within the UK, including the monitoring of civilians entering the UK. The nature of its work occasionally takes its personnel abroad if there is a specific threat or case to be solved. In the years leading up to the First World War, the primary security concern for Kell's new organisation was to track down enemy spies operating in Britain. It was believed that a German espionage system as successful as the one in France was being established in the UK. A list was drawn up of possible suspect characters thought to be operating as German spies, and this was passed to the chief constables around the country. With the declaration of war on 4 August 1914, these suspects were arrested and interned in camps at places like the Isle of Man to ensure that German intelligence could not operate on British soil. The frenzy around possible

German agents would not diminish during the war and would be the main focus of the service's work.

In August 1914, the MI5 staff consisted of nine officers, five civilians, three male clerks and just four women, three of whom were secretaries and one a typist.[9] This number would soon change as MI5's administrative workload dramatically increased and with it the number of personnel. It would see the employment of over 650 women between 1914 and 1918.[10] The women became a fundamental and integral part of the smooth, efficient administration and running of both MI5 and Special Branch of the Metropolitan Police, and in some cases they made valuable changes to working organisational practices that benefited the service.

Kell acknowledged that the Germans used female spies and wrote: 'The employment of women as German spies in this country [Britain] is on the increase and one must consider the fact that the class of information they can acquire is very often of more value than what the ordinary male spy can obtain, and just as effective.'[11] But, although he recognised the potential danger of the enemy using women as spies, he was slow to employ British women for duties within MI5 beyond those of secretaries, clerks or typists. In the early stages of MI5's history, women were selected from a middle-class or upper-class background, and usually with another source of income to supplement their earnings as their wages alone could not support independent living.

Intelligence is a long, slow game, and no more so than for secretaries or the patient and methodical female workforce, who worked eight-hour shifts on very precise and detailed material in the Registry (the repository for all MI5's card indexes and files). Much of their time was spent processing papers and compiling card indexes on suspect persons operating as potential enemy spies in the UK. The office never closed, operating twenty-four hours a day, seven days a week. This generated such a volume of paperwork that the shifts proved insufficient for the women to complete the work that was so vital to national security. They frequently undertook unpaid overtime, which they did from a sense of patriotic duty and service to their country.

By 1915 the rates of pay for MI5's women were in no way commensurate with their value and ability and, as the cost of living rose, their salaries became even more inadequate. Male officers were conscious of this and the issue of a rise in salary for the women and their right to a living wage was discussed. Increases in the salaries of female personnel were given according to their value as a clerk or secretary as shown by the quality of their work, rather than by seniority or prominence of position. This was measured and decided by their male superiors.

MI5 was reorganised in November 1915 to include control officers at Britain's ports, and women became part of the work surrounding port security. In April 1920 an internal report was written on the significant roles played by its female personnel since MI5's beginnings.[12] It noted that 'in many cases they were women of particular ability'. Now declassified, the report provides an important insight into the developing roles of women within MI5. It was almost certainly written by a woman, although she is unnamed.

MI5 in War

In August 1914, the War Office was flooded with letters from British citizens reporting people whom they suspected of being German spies, or who were possibly signalling to the enemy and using wireless messages and codes. The information was passed to MI5 for investigation. In the first two months of the war, MI5 staff worked up to twelve hours or more a day, including Sundays, with only two half-day holidays during that period, and for the next eighteen months they continued to work at least ten hours a day. During 1915, they dealt with up to 3,000 papers monthly, which necessitated the opening of over 1,000 new personal files on individual suspects. The name of a suspect was registered in full on a card index, with aliases if any, permanent address, occupation and nationality all recorded for the purpose of identification. This mass of information proved useful to other departments, and so the women found themselves processing numerous requests by them.

When MI5 was established, there were comparatively few files and these were known individually to the staff. But the sheer volume of work, with thousands of new files opened every month, made it impossible to keep track of individual subjects and suspects. The explosion in the overall workload in turn escalated MI5's administrative work too, and women were hired to cope with the huge demand.

By February 1915, the female staff had grown from the pre-war strength of just four to thirty-two, two-thirds of whom were employed in the Registry. As the war progressed, the amount of information became overwhelming and necessitated dividing some of MI5's branches into sub-sections dealing with intelligence from different parts of the world. Each sub-section had its female secretaries and clerks who processed the paperwork and became experts in their field, including on aspects of intelligence. The first sub-section, the Indian section, was formed in July 1915 with one female secretary to the officer-in-charge, and another woman responsible for records, looking up information when required by various departments, filing and indexing. The foreign sections had a heavy workload.

A subsidiary section located abroad or elsewhere in the UK was staffed and organised by women from MI5's central headquarters in London. These women obtained excellent results in their identification of suspects through their own intuition and intelligence. This was something which the male officers, and even Kell himself, had not anticipated because of preconceived ideas as to women's suitability for only particular, restricted roles in society. A number of university-trained women were soon part of MI5's workforce; they were engaged in compiling monthly reports and summaries of the contemporary work of MI5 as a record for the organisation, drafting précis of the files and compiling lists when needed. This began to build a reference library as a database if information was required by any MI5 officer or other departments during future intelligence work.

The MI5 switchboard was operated by two female telephonists who transferred from the General Post Office. Although this work might be seen as relatively straightforward, these women had to sign the Official Secrets Act and exercise discretion when answering telephone calls so as to not give away classified information inadvertently.

In January 1916, there was a major change in the way MI5 conducted its accounts. Rather than them being the responsibility of each branch within the service, the work was undertaken in a new accounts office. The male officer accountant called in his secretary to aid him with the accounts. Three months later, in April 1916, he handed over the entire finance section to her charge. Although her name is not yet known, she became the first and only female employee in this period to be in charge of the finances of a government organisation or department. Her position was unique and underlined a principle that began to emerge within military intelligence of using the right person for a job, irrespective of gender. She was placed in charge of all accountancy and statistics, and the preparation of estimates and balance sheets.

In the summer of 1916, it was decided that historical records should be compiled from the papers generated within MI5, for future reference. At first this work was undertaken by one or two junior male officers and one university-educated woman who had been engaged for the purpose, but eventually it came to be done entirely by women who were trained in historical methods. They worked initially under the direction of a senior officer who had been selected because of his literary experience. At this time, the sheer number of documents in MI5's archives and the increase in staff to cope with the workload meant that the service had to extend from Watergate House to include the adjacent Adelphi Court, which afforded less cramped space.

By the end of 1916, the female staff had increased to 161. They could be categorised into three main areas of work – the Registry, the Secretariat and the Historical Section.

The Registry

The Registry was the hub of operations and one of the key places where women made their mark in the early days of MI5. Also known as Section H, it held the most significant organisational role within MI5 and was run entirely by women. The Registry had charge of MI5's records, the filing and preparing of the papers and the compilation of an adequate index for these records. It oversaw the engagement and control of the staff, the keeping of office accounts and the purchasing of stationery and furniture, and it acted as the liaison between the service and the War Office. By 1917 it had become so large that it had to be sub-divided into several sections.[13]

All letters and material arriving at MI5 from the public or other departments was opened by an officer, then taken to the Registry where the women placed each letter or piece of paper in a suitable cover and marked it with its own number. The indexes were consulted to see if the same subject had been filed before and, if so, those papers were found and the new material added. The file was then passed to the relevant branch within MI5 for processing. The Registry had a trace of all material and subjects being dealt with by MI5 currently or in the past. When a section had finished with papers, they were filed away by women in the Registry and correctly indexed. This highly organised system meant that a paper could be traceable from the moment it entered the office. The job of indexing, which was solely the work of the women, was described as 'the lifeblood of MI5'. The women who searched in the indexes for relevant material for other departments were known as the 'lookers up'.

The first woman superintendent was appointed head of Registry on 2 November 1914. She was Lily Steuart and was in the role until she resigned the following year on 7 February 1915. She was replaced by Edith Annie Lomax, who proved to be 'one of the ablest administrators in Service history'.[14] With the help of two assistants, she succeeded in 'gradually extricating it [the Registry] from the tidal wave of documents by which it had been almost overwhelmed'.[15] She ensured that the number of staff increased to cope with the escalating workload, eventually being responsible for forty-nine female clerks. Even the secretaries of various sections were unable to keep up with the workload, and assistant secretaries were employed. New branches, and sections within those branches, were opened and old branches reorganised. The volume of work was staggering. At one point, between 10,000 and 12,000 papers were received and dealt with every month, not including letters and telegrams addressed to officers in MI5. The average number of new personal files opened every month was about 2,000, and some 16,000 to 20,000 letters were written and posted monthly. H branch eventually had to divide into eleven sections. Suggestions were sought from the women in the Registry on how certain methods could be made more efficient or speeded up. Taking up some of their practical ideas, a detailed reorganisation of methods was undertaken and working practices changed.

Female personnel who were engaged in the Historical Section on the compilation of historical reports needed particular skills and special qualifications. Knowledge of historical methods was essential for the job, preferably a degree in history, because the work involved scrutinising vast quantities of material and then being able to present a complicated subject in a readable form. These women displayed exceptional attention to detail, precision and accuracy. They studied newspapers for relevant information and cut out extracts that were likely to be of interest. This material was sent to the relevant branch officer within MI5.

A reference library was formed, with relevant books that could be consulted by officers and other staff. Any documents taken from suspects which were too heavy for filing were stored here. A female clerk from the Registry was put in charge of the museum, where any objects of interest to espionage, such as specimens of secret ink, were stored and catalogued.

By the autumn of 1916, the sheer volume of circulars, lists and memoranda that needed to be duplicated and sent out to various ports necessitated the installation of a printing machine. By the end of the year, two sisters, who were members of the Women's Printers Association, began work in a small room on the top floor of the building, using a hand press to print labels and lists of statistics. The work was labour-intensive but the women managed to print 2,000 copies of a list of British-born people of alien parentage (known as the grey list), even though the machine could only print two pages at a time. They had no proper paper cutter either, and had to improvise with a tool usually used for cutting photographs that only took five sheets at a time. In June 1917 a large monotype machine was installed in the annex building of MI5 and three rooms were allocated on the ground floor for the printing department. This was known as section H.9. The sisters took it in turns to attend a training course on how to use the new printing machine, and while one did so, the other ran the printing press. The staff increased and soon numbered fourteen women, plus two men who carried out the heavier physical work. The eldest of the two sisters remained in full technical control of the printing department and oversaw the staff, including the men. When they were busiest, the printers worked from 8.30 a.m. to 8.30 p.m. and printed all the lists, circulars and memoranda as well as special reports, the historical summaries prepared by Section H.1, index cards and all stationery used by MI5.

A similar taking on of roles which had previously only been carried out by men occurred in the Photographic Section. Originally the department was responsible for taking photographs of censored letters of suspect persons and making copies of the images of suspects for distribution to the port authorities in case the suspect entered or left Britain. This section also developed invisible inks. Until April 1916 the Photographic Section was run solely by a male manager. When he required an assistant, a female worker was attached to his section. He showed her how to operate the equipment and, from 1 January 1917, she took charge when he temporarily left MI5 on confidential business. Before she left MI5 in September 1918 she taught another woman, who in turn took charge with a female assistant.

Across the war, the volume of information obtained from all sources grew to such a point that the Registry became a powerful resource. The need for specialisation grew, such that the female secretaries and filing clerks who had a good command of their areas of expertise became experts. Their specialist knowledge contributed to the success of MI5.

Clerks and Other Roles

MI5 recruited its female clerks from the ranks of educated women who as 'gentlewomen' would naturally be supposed to have a code of honour and appropriate behaviour. They were from good schools and, in some cases, university educated. Recruitment to MI5 could not be advertised publicly. Candidates were recommended by existing members of MI5 and known personally to them or officers in other government departments tasked with the recruiting of women workers, or they were headhunted from leading ladies' colleges such as Cheltenham, Holloway, St Hugh's and Somerville, the principals of which were asked to recommend suitable pupils or ex-pupils.[16] MI5 required female clerks and secretaries who had qualities of discretion, intelligence, conscientiousness and physical fitness.[17] Knowledge of languages was deemed useful in any capacity. Comparatively little stress was placed on their technical abilities, although a typing speed of more than thirty words per minute was desirable.

In this era there was an important difference in the enrolment of the sexes into the security service. From the First World War on, MI5 recruited its women mainly from the universities of Oxford and London. The men, however, were not recruited from universities until after the

Second World War. This meant that MI5's female personnel came from higher up the social scale than its male employees, and it had more upper-class female recruits than any other British government department or agency in wartime.[18]

After an application was completed, interviews were arranged by MI5's controller of women clerks. She decided whether an applicant was trustworthy, discreet and mentally and physically suitable for a job that required constant energy. There were age parameters. Candidates had to be between the ages of twenty and thirty and not of alien background (i.e. they could not have a non-British parent). If successful, a woman was hired for a three-month probation period, at the end of which a confidential report was submitted on whether or not she should be appointed on a permanent basis. By the time of the Armistice in November 1918, the number of female clerks had steadily increased across the war from 4 to a total of 291. As the organisation developed, the entire female staff came to be placed under the charge of a Lady Controller. Her duties were defined as the 'control, selection and discipline of female staff, and the compilation and custody of their records of service'.[19] She supervised their work, was in charge of their welfare and even petitioned for an improved salary for her workers.

Women came to take up a vast array of roles in MI5. The organisation's chauffeurs, for instance, were recalled to the army in January 1917 and replaced by women, a succession of whom came from the WAACs. It was relatively rare for women to drive cars before the First World War; prior to 1914, cars were the domain of the rich, and usually drivers were male. These female chauffeurs were drawn from the same societal class as MI5's secretaries and clerks. They worked long hours and, because much of MI5's work was of an urgent security nature, they could be working late into night. Their male superiors noted that the women behaved with the same level of professionalism as had the men. Such a view reflects the patriarchal world at that time – the surprise that women could match the competence of their male colleagues in carrying out a traditionally male role.

Initially, MI5 employed Boy Scouts to run messages and carry papers to and from the different branches and its headquarters. Change came in September 1915 when they were replaced by eleven Girl Guides.

Their numbers gradually increased until, by August 1916, they numbered thirty-four girls. They took on the same duties as had been undertaken by the Scouts. Their work hours were between 9 a.m. and 7 p.m. daily, with a half-day off every week and every second Sunday of the month. A week's holiday was given in the summer and some short leave at Christmas and Easter. They were selected as messengers on the recommendation of their Guide Leader, with work references provided by their schoolteachers or a local clergyman.[20] The girls had to sign a basic contract which was countersigned by a parent or guardian and the captain of her company. They had to be between the ages of fourteen and sixteen and were engaged first on three months' probation.

Girl Guides were allocated as messengers to particular floors at MI5 headquarters, with each floor having a patrol leader who was responsible for discipline and good behaviour. A parade was held every Monday at 2 p.m. for half an hour on the roof of Waterloo House. The initial rate of pay was 10/- a week, plus lunch and dinner. Guides who had special responsibilities received a higher rate of pay. Part of their duties between 9 a.m. and 10 a.m. included dusting all the rooms on their floor, cleaning and filling the ink pots on the desks and disinfecting the telephones. After 10 a.m. they carried out collections for Registry from the despatch room, ran messages to various offices, collected files and emptied the wastepaper baskets and rolled up the paper ready for burning. In the printing room and the stationery office, the elder guides were taught how to clean the typewriter and carry out minor repairs. Although the Girl Guides were not on intelligence duties per se, they were an essential part of the support staff for MI5. Their duties were vital in the daily efficient running of this highly secret intelligence organisation.

Many of the MI5 secretaries were gifted linguists and were assigned to the translation of documents; others compiled monthly reports which were circulated to other government offices. They were reliable and totally trustworthy in the handling of the boxes of secret papers. They oversaw, too, the personal records of serving MI5 officers. Bearing in mind that MI5 did not officially exist, their ability to keep secret the names and identities of serving MI5 staff was paramount. Notably, this was especially true for the women working in the Directorate of Intelligence. Miss Bidwell became departmental secretary for the directorate. Miss Hope Symons was assistant to the Foreign Section of the Directorate of Intelligence and handled and registered all highly secret material. Miss E. Symons worked there as a temporary clerk. Miss McCulloch, who had previous experience in postal censorship, was appointed assistant in the Labour Department of the Directorate of Intelligence. Towards the end of the war, MI5 promoted a few of its women to fulfil the post of officers (though frustratingly, further details are not forthcoming from the files).

The most important sources of information about German espionage and agents travelling through Holland to arrive in Britain came to MI5 from SIS. By mid-1915, as German intelligence realised that the cover of its agents had been blown, it began to change its methods. This led to MI5 shifting its work from simple espionage to using double agents to impersonate German agents and pass misinformation to the enemy. The double agents were used for deception purposes, and this formed a basic model that would be developed further and scaled up in the Second World War. By 1918, as a result of a number of successful double agents, the reputation of MI5 stood very high. Although MI5 had no female double agents in this period (according to currently declassified files) that would change in the Second World War.

It was believed at the time that the work of the Registry could not have been carried out to the same degree of success if the roles had been reversed and men had replaced women. The work required slow, meticulous analysis and research to identify suspects from records and indexes, for which it was found, as a rule, that men lacked the patience, instincts or interest to do well. Women, however, were said to have particular 'feminine characteristics' of intuition and a love of detail. MI5 came to realise that it increased its value by 'employing a staff of women who carried out faithfully and conscientiously the work entrusted to them, and that no branch of war work had a more earnest band of workers than the women of the War Office department of MI5'.[21] As with much of society and government departments in this era, there was a culture of inherent sexism in MI5, as reflected in these comments, as appreciative as they are.

The British government formally acknowledged the work of MI5's women with a number of awards. On 1 January 1918, Miss E.A.

Lomax, the controller of women staff, was awarded an MBE. In September that same year, two senior women in the Registry and three of the original secretaries were mentioned in the *London Gazette* for valuable war services.[22] In August 1919, ten female staff were similarly recognised.[23] Immediately afterwards, Vernon Kell wrote to Lomax, expressing his pleasure on seeing ten of MI5's ladies mentioned and sending his congratulations. In the New Year's Honours List of January 1920, Lomax was raised from MBE to Officer of the British Empire (OBE), and Miss Elsie Lydia Harrison (later Mrs Akehurst), the superintendent of Registry, received an MBE.

MI5's internal report on women in the organisation, dated April 1920, concluded: 'The value of work done by the women did not exceed the value of the work done by the men employed in MI5. It was the union of men and women in the work to which the department owed its success, each bringing into the common stock their own peculiar qualities and thus complementing the work of the other.'[24] As a result of women's increased presence in MI5, the organisation developed better working relationships and an esprit de corps between its male and female staff which would stand it in good stead during the challenges ahead.

Special Branch

One area that is often overlooked in regard to women in intelligence roles is the Metropolitan Police's Special Branch. It liaised closely with MI5 and, similarly, its early history is marked by very few female personnel. There could be very practical operational reasons for this. For example, in 1903, Special Branch's superintendent William Melville was attached to the War Office overseeing the investigation of suspected German spies within the UK. The suspects were tracked by 'watchers' – an onerous and labour-intensive task for which men tended to be recruited because, on the rare occasions that a female assistant was present, she was subject to unwelcome attention from the male watchers, which hindered intelligence gathering.[25] Into the 1920s and 1930s, female watchers on counter-intelligence operations were still scarce. The first real success came with the Percy Glading case and the Woolwich Arsenal spies (see Chapter 4).

At Special Branch headquarters in London, however, women undertook roles in intelligence successfully. MI5 and Special Branch were so closely connected in their type of work that women from Special Branch often transferred to MI5 because of their expertise in handling secret material. Women were most prominent in running the Special Branch Registry, handling secret documents and files, indexing papers and creating a card index. One of the women singled out in the early history was Miss Eggett, confidential clerk to Sir Trevor Bingham, deputy acting commissioner since 1919. She had already been in the organisation for twelve years and was knowledgeable 'on the whole confidential work of MI5 and Special Branch since the inception of the Directorate of Intelligence'.[26] She also had practical experience in dealing with informants outside the office. Other women mentioned in connection with the Registry were Misses Appleton and Bracey, both of whom had fourteen years' service, seven as permanent staff.[27] Alongside Miss Eggett, they received an extra allowance for special duties – the handling of top secret information and files – beyond their roles as, respectively, clerical officer and typist. For several years the Registry at Special Branch was headed by Miss Symons, but, with ill health, she required extra help.

As Special Branch moved into the 1920s and 1930s, discussions were undertaken with the Home Office about pay conditions for women being recruited into the organisation. The commissioner was realistic in stating that new female staff could not come in on the low salaries being offered, and that the Home Office did not appreciate 'the necessity of being able to pay a wage commensurate with secrecy and responsibility'.[28] There were senior officers, including the commissioner, who were conscious of the need to pay a fairer wage to female employees – although that did not extend as far as suggesting salaries equal to those of their male colleagues.

Up to 1 December 1928 women received different amounts of the 'special allowance', depending on their responsibilities. The decision about whether an extra allowance could be paid to secretaries, clerks and typists carrying out special duties depended on three criteria: whether the woman was working long and irregular hours; whether she was entrusted with secret and highly confidential work; and whether she had been given more responsibility than the usual duties of the post.

In 1929, in a new development, salaries were increased for those women in Special Branch who took on jobs that had previously been carried out by middle-aged ex-servicemen in the Registry. The men had been receiving 63/- a week, but younger women now received over 70/-. This appears to be a groundbreaking example of women receiving a higher salary than men for doing the same work. It was justified, stated Bingham, 'by the fact that, not only is the work very confidential, but it demands educational qualifications of a high order'. He went on: 'We should aim at getting a class of clerks in the Secret Service Registry who are acquainted with foreign languages [and] have a knowledge of home and foreign affairs'; the 'ex-servicemen now available', he explained, 'falls short of the mental calibre required to work in an Intelligence Registry'. He concluded that 'the post is worthy of a salary commensurate with the considerable responsibility attached to it'.[29]

In a further development, Bingham wrote to the Home Office on 6 February 1931 requesting a change to the salary structure for female clerks. Currently they had no provision for annual increments in their salary unless approved ad hoc by the undersecretary of state. He said that the value of female staff doing confidential duties increased considerably with experience, and requested a structure be put in place for regular salary rises. Miss Eggett, he said, was already receiving an additional allowance of £50 per annum. Bingham wrote, 'My safe is full of documents about which nobody but she [Miss Eggett] and Colonel Carter know anything, and from time to time I must ask her assistance examining these . . . Her knowledge of secret affairs is extensive.'[30] Bingham's request was approved and marked an important step forward for women working in a professional capacity.

This correspondence provides a rare glimpse into the background fight for the betterment of women in the intelligence workplace, albeit a far cry from total equality of pay. These early attempts to champion more pay for women on equal terms with men and for the same work were happening in a climate where it was still a universal principle that female employees in government service were paid less than the men. And any progress in equality at work for women could only come if sanctioned by the (inevitably) male hierarchy. Nevertheless, the intelligence community seems to have been at the forefront of recognising women's capabilities.

The New Threat

When the guns fell silent on 11 November 1918, relief swept across Europe that the long bloody war was over. It had squandered millions of young lives on the bloody battlefields, and those who did survive were scarred for life, physically and mentally. The work of MI5 at home and the SIS networks of La Dame Blanche and Edith Cavell's organisation in Belgium, and Madame Rischard's agents in Luxembourg, had laid the foundations for methods of military intelligence going forward.

For MI5, there was a realisation of just how much the organisation needed its female workforce. There would be no turning back to restricting their roles to secretaries and clerks. From the 1920s, women were to be an indispensable part of MI5 and would gradually take on responsibilities traditionally assigned to the male officers. This was forward thinking, especially given the other civilian employment options then open to women, not to mention the general public perception of a woman's place to be running a home and raising children.

The Europe which emerged from the destruction and death of war was very different from the Europe of 1914. Not only had the continent been physically and psychologically scarred by the conflict, but Russia experienced a cataclysmic political and ideological upheaval with the Revolution of 1917. It ended with the Bolsheviks and Communists seizing power, overthrowing the Russian monarchy and the brutal murder by firing squad of Tsar Nicholas II and his family. Communism, the new ideology, came to dominate in Russia. Advocating full societal equality and public ownership of the means of production, the reality that emerged was far from the utopian world it claimed to usher in. Communism was felt to be the new threat to Western democracy and capitalism. In March 1919, Soviet leader Vladimir Lenin established the Comintern to promote world revolution, potentially inciting a wave of civil wars and infiltrating other countries' armed forces.[31]

From 1909 to 1918, British intelligence had devoted almost all its attention to counter-measures against German intelligence and therefore no serious efforts were made to detect espionage activity by any other power. After the Russian Revolution, MI5 created Section 6, which was tasked with addressing Russian espionage against the West and Britain specifically. Problems with the Comintern and Russia's secret agents remained under the jurisdiction of Special Branch until 1931, when the specialism was transferred to MI5. British intelligence had to adapt swiftly to the changing threat which had emerged at the end of the First World War, but it did so against a scaled-down intelligence workforce in peacetime and a wholly inadequate budget. It sought to deliver results, in spite of the severe strain placed on its personnel and lack of resources.

By the late 1920s, the serious deliberations about women's salaries in Special Branch, as we saw above, reflected the changing perception and increasing appreciation of women in intelligence at whatever level they were engaged. Even so, progress for women across all areas of intelligence work was slow and it would be decades before the first female head of MI5 was appointed. Nevertheless, stories are emerging about the clandestine work of female intelligencers in the 1920s and 1930s that are thrilling and revelatory. They were very much at the heart of operations against the new Soviet threat.

4
SPIES AND INFILTRATORS

In times of conflict, Britain needed good and reliable intelligence, but in peacetime also the same level of accurate intelligence was crucial to counter threats to national security. The inter-war years of the 1920s and 1930s were defined by two primary threats to mainland Britain: communism and the Comintern spies who sought to enter the UK and conduct espionage under cover of the Communist Party of Great Britain (CPGB); and right-wing fascist groups like the British Union of Fascists (BUF). The BUF was anti-Semitic and nationalistic, headed by Sir Oswald Mosley, who led its members in Nazi-style rallies and demonstrations across the UK. The most famous was the Battle of Cable Street in the East End of London on 4 October 1936, which saw barricades erected in the streets and violent clashes between the BUF and the Jewish communities, dock workers and labourers.

In their own ways, communism and fascism both posed a real and credible threat to democracy and the stability of the nation. MI5 spied on their adherents to find out what coups or revolutions were planned and to identify direct links and communications with foreign powers, particularly Moscow. It was of paramount importance to avoid a socialist revolution in Britain as in Russia in 1917. MI5 instigated a long-term programme to monitor individuals, including fascists like Mosley and communists like Edith Suschitzky, a Viennese Soviet agent who had been under watch since 1929. Throughout the early 1930s, MI5 tracked her movements while she was in the UK, and SIS when she returned to Vienna. In 1934 she married an English professor, Ethan Tudor-Hart, in Vienna and settled in England. The marriage did not last, but she remained in the UK and her involvement with the CPGB continued to be watched.[1]

The Comintern was successful in attracting members of the Communist Party of Great Britain. Arguably its biggest coup was the recruitment of Kim Philby via his Viennese wife, Litzi Friedman, and her friend Edith Tudor-Hart (née Suschitzky). In 1934 Tudor-Hart introduced Philby to a Russian recruiter, 'Otto' (Arnold Deutsch), on a bench in Regent's Park, and Philby was recruited as a Soviet penetration agent. After covering the Spanish Civil War and the Battle of France as a journalist, he began working for MI6 in 1940 and steadily rose within its ranks, at one point even being touted as a future head of the organisation. Philby recommended Guy Burgess, Donald Maclean and Anthony Blunt, his friends from Cambridge, for recruitment, and, from the 1930s, they passed British secrets to the Russians from their roles within the establishment. It was not until the defection to Moscow of Burgess and Maclean in 1951 that suspicion fell on their associates.

The failure to uncover the Cambridge Five spy ring continues to cause embarrassment in intelligence circles today, but there were successes against communism. During the 1930s, MI5 officer Maxwell Knight (aka 'M' when behind his desk or 'Captain King' in the field) recruited agents to 'M Section' in MI5 to penetrate communist and fascist organisations and groups within Britain, and this included the deployment of women undercover. He was the first intelligence officer in MI5 to use female agents.

He later said, 'It is frequently alleged that women are less discreet than men; that they are ruled by their emotions and not by their brains: that they rely on intuition rather than on reason: and that Sex will play an unsettling and dangerous role in their work . . . yet it is curious that in the history of espionage and counter-espionage a very high percentage of the greatest coups have been brought off by women.'[2] Kell, the head of MI5, had once declared that women do not make good secret service agents. He was proved wrong, and his view changed after a number of female agents brought in outstanding results in terms of intelligence.

Olga Gray

Historically, MI5 operations had been hampered by a lack of funds and its officers had worked from a sense of patriotism, almost as a hobby, rather than understanding their roles to be vital to the security of Britain. That changed with Knight's operations. One of his female agents was twenty-five-year-old Olga Gray, an educated young woman from a middle-class background who grew up in Birmingham. In 1931 she attended a local event of the Conservative Party and it was here that she met another young woman about her own age, Dolly Pyle. She asked Gray a strange question: 'Have you ever thought of working for the Secret Service?'

An avid reader of spy fiction, Gray was fascinated with the world of spies, but she knew nothing of the reality of espionage. Dolly was serious, and, although Gray believed she would damage her reputation and prospects of marriage if she were to become a 'Mata Hari figure', she was curious enough to say 'yes'. Pyle introduced her to Captain King (aka Maxwell Knight), who was keen to recruit her to spy on members of the CPGB and expose spy rings. Knight interviewed her, asking about her background, hobbies and opinions. She seemed to have a good sense of humour, even though she had had a difficult childhood, having had an abusive father who had then been lost in action in the First World War. Knight was struck by her patriotism and anti-communist stance. As a secretary with more than five years' experience, she could be ideally placed undercover as a typist in one of the communist organisations. Having passed the interview, Gray was sent to London for training at M Section headquarters, which happened to be Knight's flat at 38 Sloane Street in Knightsbridge; he preferred to run his agents from there initially, away from the eyes of those working in the main MI5 office. Later he despatched his agents from Dolphin Square, Pimlico. Gray found him a charming and charismatic spymaster who was unconventional, attractive, with a certain presence. He had a fascination with animals and could be seen at home with various exotic creatures, including a parrot on his shoulder.

Knight gave Gray a crash course in espionage and advised on the kind of information he needed about the CPGB, including underground networks and closed groups of party members who met separately. She was tasked with finding concrete proof of a link between Moscow and the CPGB, and to infiltrate the Woolwich Arsenal spy ring, something which he had had little success in doing thus far. It was to be a case 'full of plots and plans, illicit photographs of naval guns, shifty foreigners, fateful attaché cases deposited in left-luggage compartments, conspicuous brown paper parcels passing from one impassive conspirator to another at Charing Cross Station', wrote another of Knight's female agents later.[3] Gray's codename for her reports was 'M/12' and she was paid on a weekly basis. She and Knight both knew that she would have to play the long, slow game of patience to reap results.

Woolwich Arsenal Spy Ring

Surrounded by high brick walls and electric fences, the Royal Arsenal, situated on the banks of the River Thames at Woolwich, was known as the Secret City. Military and naval armaments were being developed there, including a new big naval gun. On 14 December 1928, almost four years prior to Gray's recruitment, an unnamed 'reliable source of information' had reported to MI5 that certain of its workers were active and dangerous communists. They all had access to top-secret drawings and blueprints of new quick-firing guns being tested by the Admiralty. The leader of the spy ring, Percy Glading, was already under surveillance for his prominent communist activities in the UK.

Glading was co-founder of the CPGB and was active in promoting the communist cause, visiting India on a mission on behalf of the Communist Party as well as attending a conference in Amsterdam and other communist meetings around the UK. In the 1920s, he was known to be closely connected with inner circles of the Communist Party and made numerous journeys abroad on behalf of the Comintern.[4] He worked in the Naval Department at Royal Arsenal but was dismissed from his job as a gun examiner on 14 October 1928 on security grounds, due to his communist activities. He took a job with Russian Oil Products Ltd, a company that was set up to trade in oil directly with the West, but which was a cover for Western industrial secrets to be sent back to Russia. He travelled to Moscow under the pseudonym James Brownlie and attended the Lenin School, a Comintern spycraft training school. The Russians sent him back to the UK as one of their spies to secure information on the British big naval gun. Although he no longer worked at Royal Arsenal, he still had contact with workers there.

Blueprints were smuggled out overnight and he photographed them and other sensitive plans for the Russians. The men who did this were assistant foreman of the works George Whomack, examiner in the Inspectorate of Armaments Department Albert Williams and assistant chemist Charles Munday (though the latter was not prosecuted later for lack of evidence).

In September 1929, Glading was appointed a member of the Political Bureau of the CPGB, a position in which he controlled the communist 'cells' operating in all Soviet institutions in the UK. An MI5 report commented, 'All the military espionage reports compiled in this country and intended for Moscow are sent to Glading.'[5] He was interested in acquiring plans of new aircraft to pass on to Russian intelligence in Moscow.[6] He set himself up in a nicely furnished office on the top floor at 23 Great Ormond Street in London, where all secret reports were sent, ready for despatch to British colonies or the Soviet Union. It was there that he received agents. MI5, aided by Special Branch, tracked his movements – who he was meeting and where. All his mail was opened and his telephone calls monitored, but MI5 lacked proof of his treacherous photographing of top-secret documents that would hold up in court. MI5 needed somebody to get close to him and obtain such evidence. This was to be Gray's mission.

In 1931, Olga Gray was placed undercover in the CPGB and given the codename 'Miss X'. It was relatively easy for Knight to plant her inside an organisation that was administratively chaotic and needed a competent secretary. In August 1932 she came to the attention of Isabel Brown, an influential member, who offered her a part-time position in two organisations, both of which were communist fronts that had direct links to Moscow. It was an ideal scenario – Gray had not pushed herself forward, which might have aroused suspicion, but was engaged at the target's own invitation. Knight's belief that female agents would be incredibly valuable when disguised as secretaries was about to pay off.

Gray swiftly became secretary to Harry Pollitt, leader of the CPGB. She came into contact with Glading and other CPGB members, gaining their full confidence and trust. Glading began to confide in her and recruited her to aid his espionage work. It was a game of patience on the part of Gray and Knight, but by May 1937, at Glading's insistence,

Gray gave up her day job to work for him full-time as a photographer. She photographed documents at their safe house at 82 Holland Road, West London. As the films were being developed in the basement dark room and the photographs hung out to dry, she noted the serial numbers of the blueprints for MI5, so they knew exactly what was being passed to the Russians. As an eyewitness to the documents being copied, developed and distributed, Gray was now a highly valuable agent.

MI5's surveillance team was closing in. On 21 January 1938, they tailed Glading to a meeting at Charing Cross station and caught him exiting the station with Albert Williams, a worker at the Royal Arsenal, who had smuggled out special documents to be copied overnight. Glading was observed receiving from Williams an envelope concealed in a newspaper. Officers of Special Branch swooped in to arrest them. Glading dropped the parcel in the hope it would not be seen, but it was too late. George Whomack was apprehended a week later.

In a search of Glading's various premises, MI5 and Special Branch found military and naval design documents, copies of blueprints and designs for new aircraft. Because Glading had travelled abroad for the Comintern, MI6 had been monitoring his movements too and shared their intelligence with MI5.[7] As part of evidence for the trial, MI6 acquired photographs of pages of Glading's diary.[8] Major Valentine Vivian at MI6 believed the diary to contain coded entries and asked for MI5's opinion in deciphering them. For example, mention of '1.B.W.' was thought to be Albert Williams, employee of the Royal Arsenal. Another accomplice, 'Lawson', was indicated by a cross within a circle, but his exact identity was as yet unidentified by MI6.[9]

But it would be Olga Gray's evidence and her testimony in court that would clinch the case. Glading, Williams and Whomack were tried at the Old Bailey in March 1938, charged under the Official Secrets Act, and they each received a prison sentence. Gray's evidence given in the courtroom secured the conviction but necessarily blew her cover – and provoked a violent outburst from the accused. The stress took a toll on Gray's mental health: she was terrified of reprisals and feared for her life. Like so many women working in intelligence, Gray bore the responsibility of secrecy on her young shoulders, relying on Knight as her strength through six long years of hard work and a double life within the heart of the CPGB. Without Gray's long, patient work deep undercover in the CPGB, these convictions would not have been obtained.

In October 1939, Glading received a visit in prison from MI5's expert on Soviet espionage and most competent interrogator, Jane Sissmore (Mrs Archer).[10] She explained to him that the war situation had changed and the Soviet Union was now an ally and asked him to give up the names of those who had been placed undercover in the UK by Soviet intelligence. Glading's only response was that the figures he had known were mercenaries and not activated by ideological motives. Archer concluded that he was unshaken in his communist views.[11] Glading served his sentence until 1942.

The triumph of the Woolwich Arsenal case enabled Knight to justify increasing his staff to twelve, but it also meant that he had lost one of his most cherished agents. Olga Gray received £500 from MI5 and emigrated to Canada.

Joan Miller

Another of Knight's successful agents was nineteen-year-old Joan Miller, who came from an upper-class background, having been raised by nannies and then attended a boarding school. Her gilded life had not been easy: she spent most of her school holidays with relatives rather than her socialite parents, her father gambled away the family fortune and her parents divorced. After leaving school, she worked as a typist for Elizabeth Arden and was gradually promoted within the company to work in the advertising department. She was recruited to MI5 by a woman – an old school friend, Janet Withers, who worked in MI5's Registry.[12]

At the outbreak of war in September 1939, Miller was working for MI5's transport section when instructions came for her to board an unmarked bus outside the Natural History Museum in London. She and the other young women on the bus were taken to MI5's new headquarters at Wormwood Scrubs prison, relocated there from Thames House because of security concerns about a German invasion and to give MI5's rapidly expanding staff more space. The majority of the prison inmates had been evacuated elsewhere and MI5 staff moved into the cells, where working conditions were horrendous. The cells were unventilated and had a terrible odour, especially those which still had unemptied chamber pots in them. The staff had to ensure that they did not close the cell door because it had no internal handle and they could be locked in. In an attempt to boost morale among the women, it was arranged for a ladies' hairdresser to come to the prison and a more flexible female dress code was permitted: women were allowed to wear trousers for the first time in the workplace because of the open staircases inside the prison. In October 1940, after the prison was hit during the Blitz, MI5 moved out to Blenheim Palace in rural Oxfordshire, a complete contrast from Wormwood Scrubs. Blenheim became known as 'the country office'.

Knight occasionally visited the canteen during MI5's time at the prison, and it was here that he looked out for potential recruits to his section. He had been watching Miller for some time. Knight explained that he required a personal secretary, until such time that she was ready for other 'real tasks' (he meant as agent). She agreed. He soon appointed her in place of Olga Gray as an agent provocateur, working out of an MI5 flat at 10 Collingwood House in Dolphin Square. By this time, Knight himself was operating out of a flat at 308 Hood House, also in Dolphin Square, and ran his special agents from the flat that belonged to his brother-in-law. Miller lived with Knight as his mistress until 1943, although it was said that their relationship was never consummated.

Miller was tasked by Knight to infiltrate political and social organisations like the Right Club, which was a right-wing, deeply anti-Semitic, anti-communist organisation with around 230 members. Members of the Right Club included MPs, aristocrats and public figures whom MI5 needed to monitor for their political views and likely security risk to Britain. Knight asked Miller to join the club and pass herself off as an ardent fascist who was opposed to war with Nazi Germany. She was to get close to its members and gather intelligence on their activities, their associates, contacts and plans. This she did.

The Russian Tea Rooms

By the time Knight infiltrated Joan Miller into the Right Club, he already had another female agent there. She was forty-one-year-old Mrs Amor (codename 'M/Y'), who worked undercover using her maiden name.[13] Knight was concerned about Captain Archibald Ramsay, a Scottish Unionist MP, who was known to boast to members of the

Right Club about his own connections to people in the Foreign Office, the War Office and the Admiralty. He was heard commenting that he really needed a contact in the Postal Censorship office, and, upon learning this from Amor, Knight immediately placed her there. One day at the Right Club, Amor duly let slip to Ramsay that she was working in postal censorship. Ramsay and his wife began to press her for confidential information. Having gained their trust, Amor was introduced to the Wolkoffs, a privileged White Russian family living in Britain who had fled the Russian Revolution in 1917. The family had once enjoyed prominence in Russia as Admiral Wolkoff had served as the Russian naval attaché in London under the Tsarist regime.[14] MI5 was already tracking Admiral Wolkoff's thirty-five-year-old daughter, Anna, who was a member of the Right Club.[15]

Anna Wolkoff ran the Russian Tea Rooms, a family business at 50 Harrington Road in South Kensington. She frequently held meetings of an inner circle of the Right Club in the flat above. One of her clients was Wallis Simpson, mistress and later wife of the Duke of Windsor, Edward VIII. Amor gained Wolkoff's trust and joined this intimate circle, reporting back to Knight about their activities and views. By early spring 1940, the group was engaged in anti-war propaganda and extending their activities to political and diplomatic circles. Knight suspected them, too, of espionage. Amor reported back that the group aimed to gain contacts inside the War Office, so Knight posted Joan Miller there. This meant that Amor could introduce Miller to Wolkoff.

Anna Wolkoff invited Miller to meet her at the Russian Tea Rooms, something which Miller made a habit of doing regularly thereafter. Wolkoff distrusted most people, and being forced to flee her homeland after the Revolution had made her tough, but once her trust was gained she could be generous and kind. Miller made a point of expressing strong anti-war sentiments against the British government, which endeared her to Wolkoff. She was invited to become a member of the Right Club. In the tearooms Miller often sat with Admiral Wolkoff, listening to his reminiscences of life in Russia. Knight had engineered two of his prized female infiltrators to be right at the heart of the action.

In late February 1940, Amor discovered that Admiral Wolkoff had made the acquaintance of an official at the United States embassy in

London. Meanwhile, Anna had successfully established contact with Jean Nieumanhuys, who was second secretary in the Belgian embassy in London. Nieumanhuys allowed her to use the diplomatic bag to communicate with William Joyce (aka Lord Haw Haw), one of Britain's leading traitors, who was broadcasting anti-British propaganda in Germany. Anna gave letters to Nieumanhuys which she had received from Joyce to pass on to her friend Count or Countess de Laubespin, who worked at the Belgian Foreign Office in Brussels. With this news, Knight decided to infiltrate another woman into the network to get close to the Wolkoffs.

She was Hélène de Munck, a twenty-five-year-old Belgian woman, who had been educated in a convent and, fortuitously for Knight, had known Admiral Wolkoff since 1936. Knight gave her the codename 'M/1' (aka 'Miss Z'). What Hélène really desired was British nationality, and this Knight promised her if she would work for him.[16] She agreed, and Knight tasked her with convincing the Admiral that she had a great many diplomatic contacts that could be useful to him. Over tea in the Russian Tea Rooms, she lied to him about knowing someone in the Romanian Legation. He reported this to his daughter, and, when Anna discovered that Munck had high-level contacts, she asked her to help her smuggle letters into Germany. Munck agreed to pass letters to 'her friend' at the Romanian Legation who would place them in the diplomatic bag and send them on to William Joyce.

Munck immediately passed the letter to Knight, who had it copied. It was resealed, but, before it was sent, Anna Wolkoff asked to add a postscript to the letter. She visited Munck's flat and opened it in front of Munck, completely unaware that it had already been opened once. Wolkoff added an Eagle and Snake (the emblem of the Right Club) to the bottom of the letter and signed off 'P J', which stood for the anti-Semitic slogan 'Perish Judah'. She resealed it and was none the wiser that Knight had copied an earlier version. Once she had left the flat, Munck secretly gave the letter back to Knight to copy again. As the contents were coded, Knight took it to Bletchley Park for decoding.

In April 1940, just a month before the German invasion of the Low Countries, Munck informed Wolkoff that she planned to visit her family in Belgium. Wolkoff asked her to make contact with the Right

Club's principal agent in Belgium and obtain translations of certain Russian documents. She was asked to visit Count and Countess de Laubespin to establish whether Nieumanhuys could really be trusted. Munck was given a list of questions to memorise and left for a four-day visit to Belgium on 16 April. On her return, she reassured Wolkoff that Nieumanhuys was loyal and trustworthy. Thus, she efficaciously 'double-crossed' Wolkoff and held on to her own MI5 cover.

Anna Wolkoff

Around the same time as Munck visited Belgium, Knight asked Joan Miller to stop collecting intelligence on the Right Club and focus solely on Anna Wolkoff, who was suspected by MI5 of far more serious activities.[17] A leak had occurred of top-secret communications between Winston Churchill (then First Lord of the Admiralty) and US President Franklin Roosevelt – communications that had to have been decrypted first – and wireless traffic between Rome and Berlin had been intercepted to suggest that the source of the leak was the Italian embassy in London, at which Wolkoff had a contact. In February 1940 she had also met Tyler Kent, a code and cipher clerk who worked in the US embassy for Ambassador Joe (Joseph) Kennedy and who was a regular visitor to the Russian Tea Rooms. Kent was deeply concerned that Roosevelt wanted the United States to join the war against Germany and had begun collecting evidence of this, making copies of correspondence between Churchill and Kennedy. In May 1940 he showed this to Wolkoff, who made copies, and Miller later testified that the documents were then passed to the Italian embassy. With Kennedy's agreement to waive Kent's diplomatic immunity, Special Branch raided his flat and arrested him. Inside they found over 1,500 documents which he had stolen from the US embassy. That same day, Anna Wolkoff was arrested and interned under section 18B of the Defence Regulations, allowing for the detention and confinement of persons who were deemed to be a threat to national security. Other members of the Right Club were arrested a few days later.

Wolkoff and Kent were tried at the Old Bailey behind closed doors. They were charged under the Official Secrets Act and Defence Regulations and found guilty. Joan Miller gave evidence at the trial, and there was a dramatic scene when Wolkoff realised she had been betrayed by her supposed friend and screamed at her from the dock. Wolkoff received ten years in jail and Kent seven years. Knight's agent Mrs Amor was 'imprisoned' with other female members of the Right Club who had been interned under section 18B, acting as a stool pigeon for MI5 and writing reports about the women's conversations and political views. It is not certain whether MI5 hid microphones in the cells, but it was already tapping the telephones of the Communist Party's headquarters in King Street.

The trial of Wolkoff and Kent blew Miller's cover and thereafter she took a desk job at MI5. Knight took her to weekend parties at Worplesdon, a large estate near Guildford and home of Ian Menzies, brother of the head of MI6. She described the parties as 'full of Greek shipping magnates, middle aged, lecherous and wearing pure silk shirts, and gambling for high stakes that would go on after dinner'. Back at 'the Office', as MI5 headquarters was known, she was trained how to open letters and reseal them, break into a trunk of documents and crack open safes. Her new target was an Indian lawyer, Rajanu Palme Dutt, a supporter of Stalin and General Secretary of the Communist Party of Great Britain. Miller broke into Dutt's flat in order to examine documents in a box under his bed which Knight was interested in, but these revealed nothing pertaining to national security. Miller did not enjoy the work and told Knight that she did not wish to do break-in assignments again. Knight gave the task to Munck, whose priorities were the far left and their activities.

Resilient Spies

Knight had a number of female agents who infiltrated communist and fascist groups in Britain. As well as Joan Miller and Hélène de Munck, there were Mona Maund, Marjorie Mackie, Kathleen Tesch and Friedl Gärtner. These women undertook vital intelligence gathering while operating as undercover agents, at a time when the country faced a potential military coup from right-wing activists and MI5 was receiving disturbing intelligence regarding a communist revolution in Britain. The importance of these female spies cannot be overestimated.

Mrs Marjorie Mackie (aka 'M/Y') was infiltrated into the Right Club in late September 1939 because Knight believed that the club was building its own network of agents, 'fifth columnists' who would work with Hitler if Germany invaded Britain. Mackie, who was a single mother, had carried out public cookery demonstrations outside various shops. She was excellent at explaining and embellishing if needed. This was precisely what Knight needed in her – to be able to convince members of the Right Club that she was ardently anti-Semitic. She achieved this after being invited to tea with the wife of Captain Archibald Ramsay and, having gained Mrs Ramsay's confidence, she met Ramsay himself. He boasted to Mackie that he had a network of agents who had infiltrated every right-wing group in the country and even operated inside Whitehall. Mackie convinced him that she was very well connected in military circles and could introduce these figures to him.

Mona Maund (aka 'M/2') was run as a typist and attended meetings of various left-wing organisations in the hope of picking up intelligence for Knight. Like Olga Gray, she had had a sad childhood – her mother died when she was four years old; but her father, a staunch Conservative, was devoted to her. Knight saw one particular quality in her – resilience – and believed that she could be extremely useful to him. Some communist organisations had become suspicious that they might have been infiltrated; in particular, the CPGB distrusted those members who refused to canvass on its behalf. They were deemed suspect and this led to a series of spy hunts to unmask moles in the organisation. The mistrust increased after the Glading trial, when the role of Miss X (aka Olga Gray) became publicly known.

Knight therefore planted Maund as a secretary at the headquarters of the Communist Party in King Street, Covent Garden; ironically, the same office as Gray had been in during her time as an agent. Knight succeeded in infiltrating the organisation for a second time. Maund provided him with regular, precise intelligence about the spy hunts and soon became one of his most valuable agents. To deepen her cover, she joined a trade union called the Association of Women Clerks and Secretaries (AWCS) and eventually sat as a member of its executive committee. This opened further contacts for her and placed her above suspicion because of 'her extraordinary perseverance, as well as her ability to persuade so many Communist party members to see past her right-wing background, even if this had taken several years to achieve'.[18]

In her position with the AWCS, she had crossed paths with Melita Norwood, who was an honorary secretary of the Cricklewood branch. Maund had a hunch that Norwood was a Soviet spy; there was an air of mystery about her, and she alluded to not being able to take on further work for the party because she was too busy. She had alerted Knight in April 1938, and had even made an accurate sketch of Norwood, all of which was passed by Knight to Jasper Harker, head of a counter-espionage section at MI5.[19] Harker took the decision not to follow this up – which proved to be one of the most disastrous decisions in the history of MI5. In 1999, Norwood confessed to having been an agent of the Russian intelligence agency, the NKVD, who passed atomic secrets to Moscow. She turned out to be the longest-serving Soviet spy in Britain.

An Unsuspecting Agent

MI5 recruited agents who unwittingly believed they were working for German intelligence. One example was Merita Perigoe, a woman of mixed Swedish and German origin living in the UK, who wanted to be a spy, not for Britain but for Germany.[20] She joined the BUF, where she crossed paths with a bank clerk whom she knew as Jack King. Unbeknownst to her, Eric Roberts was an MI5 agent and 'Jack King' (aka 'Agent Jack') was his codename. Maxwell Knight had recruited a network of 'German agents' in the UK who believed they were passing him intelligence for Nazi Germany. It was a perfect way for MI5 to see what intelligence was being sought and passed to Nazi Germany, intercept it and prevent it from reaching the German intelligence services. Roberts lied to Perigoe and told her that he was the Gestapo's man in London. She believed him and began passing intelligence to him for the Abwehr in Berlin. Ironically, she enthusiastically started recruiting agents for 'Agent Jack' and thereby formed a network that she believed was aiding Nazi Germany, but in reality was fictitious. The intelligence from these agents went no further than MI5's office. It was such a clever ruse.

There were a number of German organisations within the UK that were seeking to change British public opinion on Britain's aggressive anti-Nazi policy and its hostility towards Hitler. MI5 had to insert agents undercover within right-wing groups, like the British Union of Fascists, to ascertain what precise links they had to Nazi Germany. One of those British pro-Nazi groups was called 'The Link'. Kathleen Tesch (aka 'M/T'), the daughter of a Yorkshire engineer, was recruited as an agent in July 1939 to get close to members of The Link. Her surname came from her husband, Leonard Robert Tesch, whose father was Danish-born and a British citizen. The Link planned a trip to Nazi Germany in the summer of 1939 to meet with Nazi figures in the country. It was essential that Knight had coverage of the trip. Tesch was tasked with joining them.

On 2 August 1939 the group visited the Eagle's Nest at Berchtesgaden, Hitler's mountain retreat. Tesch's German surname brought her to the attention of Hitler, who was in residence there at the time and had looked through the names of the visitors. She was called off the coach, escorted into the house and entered a room where Hitler was sitting. Hitler believed her to be a German and did not suspect that she might be a British agent. He presented her with an autographed copy of *Mein Kampf*, embossed with a silver eagle. It was only a month before the outbreak of war, and the extraordinary nature of this experience left her quite shaken.

Another prominent Nazi organisation of great interest to MI5 in the UK was the Arbeits Front which operated from a house in Cleveland Terrace, London. The woman chosen to infiltrate it was Friedl Gärtner.

Spies and Fascists

Friedl Gärtner was strikingly beautiful, exotic and alluring to men – qualities which had come to define the public image of the female spy after the execution of Mati Hari. Born Friedl Stottinger in Austria, Gärtner had worked as a stenographer in Vienna in the 1930s. She married a German Orthodox Jew, whose name is blanked out in the MI5 files, and they emigrated to Palestine. The marriage did not last, and they divorced. With no remaining ties in Austria, except a mother who was said to be slowly dying, she came to Britain in April 1938, a month after Hitler annexed Austria.[21]

It appears that Gärtner was already working for SIS in the 1930s and was part of the inner circle of the Menzies family. In March 1937, her sister Lisel married Ian Menzies, the brother of Stewart Menzies, the latter then a senior counter-intelligence officer who would become the new head of MI6 in 1939. It is not known how or where Lisel met Ian and whether she too was engaged in intelligence. On the instructions of SIS, Friedl Gärtner was asked to get in close contact with the German secret service prior to coming to Britain in 1938. It is highly likely, therefore, that, while living in Vienna, she was working for SIS spymaster Thomas Kendrick.[22] Kendrick was part of Stewart Menzies' circle; their intelligence relationship stretched back twenty years to the First World War, when Kendrick worked with Menzies in France. Declassified files do not reveal further precise information on Gärtner's work for SIS in the 1930s.

As soon as Friedl Gärtner was living in London, Stewart Menzies wrote to Guy Liddell, the head of counter-espionage at MI5, asking him to find work for her. He suggested that she could mix at parties hosted by the German colony in Britain and report back to British intelligence on their views and activities.[23] Her MI5 file describes her as 'extremely level-headed and intelligent, well versed in the political situation in Europe', but adds a comment that she would need training on the National Socialist German Workers' Party (NSDAP) in Britain.[24] She was left-wing, but 'not so much so as to cause embarrassment to British intelligence'.[25]

In late September 1938, Gärtner arrived at the Arbeits Front headquarters. She had been advised by a clerk at the German embassy in London that as a 'good German' she could build up friendships at the Arbeits Front and feel less isolated in England, so he provided an introduction for her. In spite of still holding a German passport and having a personal introduction from the German embassy, Gärtner faced intense questioning at Cleveland Terrace which she had not anticipated. The interrogation began immediately.

'What will you do if there is a war?' an unnamed official asked.

'I am on my way to getting a work permit as a mannequin,' she replied.

'I don't think the English pigs will want to employ you or any other good German,' he said.

She was quick to respond. 'Wherever possible I refrain from committing myself politically with my English friends and I'd like to make use of them. They probably won't think of me in political terms at all.'

He grunted and seemed convinced. 'The English are such swine and liars that you cannot depend upon anything they say.'

With a war likely, Gärtner was asked why she had not returned to Germany.[26] She explained that she had no home to return to and was relying on the generosity of her younger sister, who was married to an Englishman. The official wished to know her sister's name, address and occupation, which she duly gave. Fortunately, the German official did not recognise the Menzies name, nor did he suspect that Gärtner and her sister were, through marriage, part of the intimate circle of high-ranking members of the British Secret Intelligence Service. He agreed to contact others in the organisation and said he would be in touch with her soon. She left the headquarters that day, having successfully begun her penetration of the most prominent Nazi organisation in Britain.

Knight gave her the codename 'M/G' – the set of initials which she used to sign off intelligence reports for MI5, which were periodically also passed to Menzies if of direct interest to MI6.[27]

Agent M/G

As agent M/G, Gärtner went on to infiltrate the British Union of Fascists and the British People's Party. She passed detailed reports to Maxwell Knight on Nazi front organisations, as well as pro-Nazi individuals in Britain and the Right Club.[28]

In October 1938, just three weeks after Prime Minister Neville Chamberlain signed the Munich Agreement to appease Adolf Hitler, Gärtner attended a dinner of the Anglo-German Fellowship at Claridge's. Three hundred guests were present, half of whom were British from the middle and upper classes. Opinion was intensely divided in Britain over going to war with Germany just twenty-one years after the last conflict. Gärtner observed several inappropriate after-dinner speeches by figures such as Lord Brocket and Lord Rennell, who expressed pleasure that the Anglo-German Fellowship was providing a means of rapprochement between Britain and Germany. In his view, 70 per cent of Britons felt friendship towards Germany; he stated that Britain should 'trust Germany and that Britain and Germany should arm or disarm together'. The keynote speech was given by General Tholens, a distinguished ex-officer of the German navy, and lasted over an hour. Gärtner reported to MI5 that it was 'so dry and boring that even the most enthusiastic member ceased to listen'.[29]

A fortnight later she attended a cocktail party thrown by the Anglo-German Fellowship for over a hundred guests at the Hans Crescent Hotel. She described the guests as being more intelligent than those at the dinner. She was introduced to the journalist Dr Karl Silex, the main speaker that evening, who proceeded to tell this social circle that it was dangerous for Britain to feel humiliated by the signing of the Munich Agreement, and he endorsed Chamberlain's actions.[30] By December, the dinners had shifted in tone to focus less on propaganda for Germany and more on social issues relevant to Britain, so as not to appear too pro-German. But even this change of emphasis could not mask the fact that the Anglo-German Fellowship sought appeasement with Nazi Germany.

With her Austrian background, Gärtner was able to mix with complete ease in Austrian aristocratic circles in London, observing their social connections and movements and compiling reports about them. She followed the movements of a number of personalities of interest to MI5, including the Hungarian Manci Gertler. Gertler had married Lord Howard of Effingham, which, Gärtner ascertained, gave her a title and British nationality – all of which would be useful to Gertler's Abwehr handler, Edward Stanislas Weissblatt. Weissblatt was believed to be running Gertler as a spy for Germany, for which he paid her between £250 and £300 a month. On occasion he paid her in precious stones, and in one instance in the form of a million-franc diamond collar which he had purchased in Paris.[31] Gärtner was tasked with gathering intelligence for MI5 on Weissblatt's mistresses and financial affairs, and that included information about Gertler. Gärtner established that Weissblatt was secretly using Gertler as an intermediary for his business dealings when she travelled with her husband to the United States and Egypt, the latter of which included clandestine work linked to Weissblatt's negotiations with an arms dealer.[32]

Gärtner's work in counter-espionage enabled MI5 to keep abreast of Weissblatt, whose activities she was still tracking in March 1939. He was just one of the figures of interest to MI5 who she was following in this period. For instance, on a number of occasions she met with an unnamed pro-Nazi friend of Unity Mitford. Unity was one of the famous Mitford sisters, known for her closeness to Hitler and support of National Socialism and whose sister Diana was married to Sir Oswald Mosley, leader of the BUF. Unity, her friends and family were all being tracked by both MI5 and SIS. From casual conversations, Gärtner learnt that German Prince Loewenstein had recently visited Britain to acquire special gramophone records for use in illegal broadcasts to Germany.[33] From her continuing observation of members of the Arbeit Front in Cleveland Terrace, she learnt that Berlin was disappointed with the weakness of the Anglo-German Fellowship, such that some of its extreme right-wing members transferred to The Link. Like Kathleen Tesch before her, Gärtner infiltrated The Link for MI5.

In the months leading up to the war, Gärtner was very effective at providing intimate personal details of people under surveillance by MI5. By 18 July 1939 she was tracking a female German spy called Ilsa von Griesheim, who was operating under the instruction of the German embassy in London. Gärtner reported her movements to MI5 and the people whom she met. During the early years of the war, Gärtner continued to investigate the activities of suspect pro-Nazis by feigning to be on the side of Nazi Germany. She gathered valuable intelligence on the Anglo-German Fellowship, carried out first-class work in the Wolkoff case and was the linchpin in a sting operation against Ben Greene, a former Labour Party politician. Greene had joined the far-right British People's Party, which had brought him to the attention of MI5. Gärtner's story was that she needed Greene's help to contact her fiancé in Austria. She discovered Greene had strong defeatist views and was an ardent believer in National Socialism. He said he could help her because he had recently met with a member of the German Sturmabteilung in London, whom he knew from Germany. This meeting he had failed to report to the British authorities, and MI5 used this as the basis for arresting him on charges of treason.[34] This was just the start of Gärtner's career in British intelligence.

The Legacy

What had Maxwell Knight's female agents achieved?

The women of M Section were the first major operational female agents in the field in the history of MI5. Hitherto, MI5's male officers had not commissioned female agents in the field or seriously conceived of the possibility of doing so; this was due largely to false prejudices about the reliability or stamina of women. Knight thought differently. His foresight in engaging women at all turned them into 'successful government spies'. They gathered intelligence deep undercover and contributed to, and were instrumental in, the success of Knight's operations. Their intuition often proved to be accurate and helpful, and, Knight said, 'this ability can at times save an intelligence officer an enormous amount of trouble'.[35]

The female agents proved essential to security operations in the UK and gained intelligence that protected Britain at a time when the country was most vulnerable. Agents like Olga Gray brought conclusive evidence against the Woolwich Arsenal spies who, if not unmasked and prosecuted, would have continued to pass British military and naval secrets to their Russian handlers in Moscow. This could have had potentially devastating consequences for the balance of power in the early part of the war, when Russia was on the side of Nazi Germany. Indeed, Knight believed that the long-term threat was Russia, and in this respect he was correct, especially in light of the successful and long-lasting penetration of the Cambridge Five and other atomic spies revealed later. The impact of the intelligence gathered by Knight's female agents would be felt especially in 1940, when Britain faced the reality of a German invasion. These agents had spent the 1930s tracking prominent fascists in Britain and 'without their intelligence, gathered during the thousands of hours of painstaking and often boring undercover work, it would have been extremely hard, perhaps impossible, to execute the order in May 1940 to detain all senior British fascists'.[36] Their greatest legacy in this crucial period was to help neutralise the fascist threat in Britain ahead of the Second World War, such that it never gained a major foothold in Britain again.

5
SECRET SECRETARIES

The ideological clash between East and West and the communist threat to democracy came to define SIS operations abroad in the 1920s, just as it was the focus of MI5 within Britain. The Treaty of Versailles, signed in Paris on 28 June 1919, had imposed huge reparations on Germany for waging war. It limited Germany's ability to rearm and permitted no more than 100,000 troops and no air force. The once vast Austro-Hungarian Empire was divided up to form the new countries of Austria, Czechoslovakia and Hungary, and parts of Poland were conceded to Germany. In reality, instead of providing security, this caused instability in the region as communism sought to overthrow democratic rule in the newly created countries of Eastern Europe.

The most urgent priority for SIS was to monitor Soviet spies and agents across Europe. To do so, SIS embedded a number of its senior intelligence officers in British passport control offices across Europe to carry out counter-espionage activities. The most important SIS station at this time was Vienna. The Austrian capital had become the centre of espionage and one through which the spies of all nations passed between east and west.[1] The SIS chief in Vienna from December 1919 to October 1922 was Captain Ernan Forbes Dennis, followed by an unnamed officer, with the post then being taken up in 1925 by Captain Thomas Joseph Kendrick.[2] Berlin was another significant posting and this was held by SIS man Frank Foley until 1939.[3] Kendrick and Foley had served together in France in the First World War, in MI1(c), attached to the Intelligence Corps.

The SIS heads of station formed their own networks of agents, spies and informers and sent intelligence back to Hugh 'Quex' Sinclair, 'C', the new head of SIS. Undercover with them were a number of women working as 'secretaries'.

The SIS 'Secretaries'

The secretaries of SIS are especially interesting as they provide a rare snapshot of the work of SIS women in this period. It is impossible to tell the stories of the vast majority of SIS personnel, men and women, because their identities and operations largely remain classified. The stories of the SIS secretaries who worked in Vienna or Berlin do provide a view, albeit limited; a proper assessment of their contribution to the intelligence world cannot yet be undertaken.[4]

The most acute insight into the work of the women of SIS in this period can be reconstructed from the secretaries who worked with Kendrick in Vienna between 1925 and 1938: Clara Marguerite Holmes, Evelyn Stamper and Betty Hodgson. Well educated, highly efficient and feisty characters, these women had already served in intelligence in the First World War. During the course of their work for SIS/MI6 in the 1920s and 1930s they became experts on Austria and Eastern Europe – something that would prove essential to British intelligence in the next war.

For these secretaries there was often a fine line between their regular clerical duties and extra assignments in running spy networks – work that has hitherto been hidden and unacknowledged. The SIS chiefs of station and their secretaries received no formal intelligence training. Instead, they had to learn on the job and develop their own ways to recruit and run agents. As we shall see, they played a key role in developing SIS's methodology of intelligence gathering and operating spy networks.

Working from a back room of the British passport control office in Vienna, Holmes, Hodgson and Stamper aided Kendrick in running spy networks into Czechoslovakia, Hungary and Italy. They gathered intelligence, decrypted messages and compiled reports for London. After Kenneth Benton was posted to Vienna in March 1938, he discovered that his real work would not be concerned with visas and passports, but aiding Holmes, Hodgson and Stamper in their handling of, and correspondence with, agents for Thomas Kendrick. On his first morning, Benton was taken to a room at the rear of the building where on a desk there was a letter in Czech, a small open bottle of colourless liquid and a brush. Holmes dipped the brush in the liquid, passed it over the front of the letter and red writing in German appeared at right angles to the Czech text. She turned the letter over and repeated the process to reveal a German report from one of their operatives. Benton was able to translate the German. He commented, 'it was obviously from somebody in Czechoslovakia reporting about events in the Sudetenland where the Germans were already planning to take over. After that, almost all my work was of this kind.'[5] Benton learnt that Holmes and Hodgson were using invisible ink in their letters to secretly correspond with agents in Czechoslovakia, Hungary, Italy and Sicily. They decrypted messages and compiled intelligence reports for London.

There are scant details on the backgrounds of Hodgson and Stamper. The latter was born Evelyn Bruce Graham Stamper on 9 June 1884 to a surgeon. In 1940 she married Guy Maingy (who also went by the surname of Le Feuvre) in the registration district of Kensington.[6] Hodgson never married and was living in Vienna with her father, a retired officer of the Indian army. She had served in MI5 during the First World War in a section commanded by Claude Dansey, then a British intelligence officer who had already served in military intelligence in South Africa prior to 1914. After working for a short time in MI5, both Hodgson and Dansey began their lifelong careers in SIS/MI6, the latter rising to become assistant head. Hodgson, like Holmes, was an expert skier who enjoyed travelling the region and ski resorts, sometimes as part of the gathering of geographical intelligence for MI6. The women were also part of the social whirl of cocktail parties and musical soirées, mixing with high society guests, intellectuals and spies – always building their circle of trusted friends and agents for their friend and ultimate spymaster, Kendrick.

We know more about Holmes, who was affectionately known by her friends and SIS colleagues as 'Bill' and by her family as 'Midge'. Prior to the First World War, at the age of nineteen and under her maiden name Clara Bates, she had travelled to Kiel to teach English to the daughters of a respectable German family.[7] When war broke out with Germany in 1914, she returned to England as a fluent German-speaker, which would soon become a valuable skill for the intelligence services, and she went on to work for SIS in the First World War. In 1917, she was posted to Berne in Switzerland on secret intelligence work for SIS, the nature of which she never disclosed in her lifetime. Her daughter Prudence Hopkinson recalled: 'The only mention she made was that it was all unofficial and not based in an embassy. My mother stayed in Berne for two years.'[8] The story of her recruitment which has been passed down to the family goes as follows. While working for the Ministry of Munitions in the basement of the Metropole Hotel in London, Clara and her sister Freda went out one evening to a girls' club in Trenora Road, near Earl's Court Road. There they met a woman called Mimi Munro, who told the two sisters that she could find them interesting war work. Clara volunteered her services. Mimi was posted to Malta to take up an undisclosed intelligence role with the Admiralty, so it was from a Miss Parry that Holmes, while staying with a relative in Ireland, received word she had been offered a job in Switzerland. Clara left the Ministry of Munitions, attended three days of training in ciphers and codes, then left for Le Havre.

She recalled:

> On a Sunday in the Autumn of 1917, I set sail for Le Havre which was still being shelled. I arrived at the Gare du Nord at about midnight in a blackout on only my second trip to the continent. A certain Captain Bellier was supposed to meet me, but there was no sight or sound of him. I wandered in to a bar opposite the station where an English captain took pity on me. He knew the manager of the Ritz and so I spent my first night there. I was twenty-two by then but still very young. The following morning Captain Bellier appeared. How he managed to find me I never did discover. We spent the day in Paris together and then he put me on the night train at Gare du Lyons, bound for Geneva and then Berne. Through the night we rumbled across war torn Europe and all of the next day until we arrived in Berne in the early evening – I shall never forget that journey.[9]

At Berne she was met by Mrs Godfrey, believed to be Bertha Margaret Godfrey Hope, who in the next war worked at Bletchley Park, and whose husband John Godfrey became director of Naval Intelligence. Holmes worked in Berne for Swiss-born Hanns Vischer of British intelligence.[10] Before he left Berne for the British passport control office in Prague, Vischer extended an invitation to Holmes's sister Freda to come to work in Berne with her. Holmes later commented, 'We decoded and encoded, and worked out of a lovely villa which looked up to the mountainside to the Jungfrau and Eiger.' By 1918, the sisters had moved into accommodation with Daisy Ashford, famous author of a novella *The Young Visiters*. With war coming to an end, Freda returned to England, while her sister Midge stayed behind to close down the Berne office.

In May 1919, Hanns Vischer had travelled to Vienna to set up the SIS station there under the cover of the British passport control office. He then went on to Prague and Warsaw to do the same. He asked Holmes to accompany him to Vienna and she was billeted at the Hotel Bristol. She worked with Captain McEwan to get the passport control office open and the undercover operations established. In the autumn of 1919, Vischer wired for her to come to Prague and she operated from there until June 1920. She returned to England, transferring back to Vienna in August 1921, where she worked in the passport control office for Carlile Aylmer Macartney, a British specialist on Austria and Hungary.[11] In 1926, when attending her sister Freda's wedding in England, she met Reginald (Rex) Trayton Holmes, the brother of Freda's husband. Midge married Rex the same year and they started a new life in Kenya. After he died three years later from malaria, she returned to England with their one-year-old daughter, Prudence.

It was precisely because of her knowledge of running SIS spy networks that in the summer of 1930 Holmes was invited back to the passport control office in Vienna to work for Kendrick, head of the SIS station there since 1925. Holmes was one of the cases, albeit rare, when women with children could and did work for SIS. Doing so was not easy as a single mother, but the other secretaries and friends provided support and childcare when necessary.

Communists versus Fascists

By the 1930s, the work of SIS increased substantially across Europe to monitor the twofold threat, from communism and Russia on the one hand, and Adolf Hitler and the Nazi regime on the other. To do so, one of the British intelligence networks abroad in the 1930s, closely tied to SIS, was the Z Organisation, which was run out of Switzerland by Claude Dansey. Very little is known today about the organisation, except that it comprised male officers and collected industrial intelligence for the British while working undercover within industry in places like Berne and Geneva. Whether women were part of the Z Organisation is currently not known. Did Dansey engage women? It is true that he was reluctant to send female agents into the field during the next war because of the dangers it posed to them; however, he may not have had the same qualms about engaging women undercover in industrial intelligence work, possibly as secretaries, in peacetime. To not have used women would stand as a missed opportunity by Dansey because they provided great cover and opportunities for intelligence gathering as they were least suspected of it.

While the Z Organisation gained industrial secrets for British intelligence, SIS continued to monitor other threats in Europe, with one of its most important stations being in Vienna. During 1933 and 1934, the right-wing regime in Austria clamped down on communists, labelling them enemies of the state, so the communist activists and spies went into hiding, often in the city's sewers. Kendrick, his agents and secretaries were tracking their movements through journalists like Eric Gedye and a young graduate, Kim Philby.[12] In addition to the immediate situation in Vienna, Kendrick, Holmes, Hodgson and Stamper had a vast geographical area of Europe to cover and gather intelligence for 'C' in London, including from Czechoslovakia, Hungary, Germany, Italy and Romania. Kendrick despatched Holmes to Italy and instructed her 'to get close' to an unnamed Italian naval officer. Enticing him with the offer of English lessons, she gleaned useful pillow talk for Kendrick. The honeytrap is one of the oldest tricks in espionage tradecraft, but one not frequently used historically by British intelligence.

Agents were recruited in Italy and tasked with sending back reports on military and naval activity by the Italians. The reports were mostly written in German, sometimes Italian. Benton recalled that some of the reports were from Augusta in Sicily and gave details of Italian battleships and other vessels in the naval base. A number of reports were received about the Tenth MAS Flotilla (Decima Flottiglia MAS), the special naval unit headed by Prince Borghese, which employed E-boats. The Admiralty in London needed intelligence on this, in particular on 'very fast boats, each with two torpedo tubes, and the idea was that they would penetrate our naval ports like Alexandria and Gibraltar, loose off their torpedoes under cover of night, and escape by sheer speed from the immediate response of our guns and aircraft'.[13]

Holmes was responsible for intelligence about the ports of Venice, Trieste and Gorizia, and the movements of the Italian navy. She was particularly interested in small quick motor torpedo boats and it was her job to keep track of their movements. She maintained a close friendship with Ernan Forbes Dennis, former passport control officer in Vienna, and his wife, Phyllis Bottome. They travelled on expeditions together, driving through the mountains of Slovakia and visiting towns like Dubrovnik on the Adriatic coast, as well as other parts of Europe, such as Poland and Yugoslavia.

The Legation in Vienna was run by Kendrick's close friend Vice Consul John Taylor, who had been posted to the capital in 1933. His wife, Margot (née Simpson), whom he married in 1926, had worked for the military attaché in the British embassy in Prague. She was accustomed to life in diplomatic circles and the frequent parties. In a sense, the wives were part of the job and provided important support as hostesses of these social events that garnered friendships and contacts that could be drawn on in a future crisis. Her daughter Grizel recalls, 'a lot of people came to our house in Vienna, like Sigmund Freud. I remember dinner parties and coming downstairs in our nightclothes to say hello before going back upstairs again.'[14] Margot and friends took weekend holidays around Europe in the 1930s, including to Budapest. It is possible that they were involved in some kind of casual intelligence gathering.

Annexation of Austria

On 12 March 1938, the anticipated German occupation of Austria took place. Acquiring intelligence on Germany's threat to other neighbouring countries, like Czechoslovakia, was never more urgent for SIS. Czechoslovakia – the country saved temporarily by the Munich Agreement in September 1938 – was believed by SIS to be next in Hitler's expansion plans. It would be occupied by Nazi Germany in

March 1939. SIS's Vienna station struggled to run its agents and informers because of the immediate humanitarian crisis that engulfed the British passport control office. Hundreds of Jews sought to flee the country every day, and understandably this placed the intelligence work under extreme pressure. The SIS staff now combined their intelligence duties with rescue efforts and spent up to twelve hours a day working to issue visas and fake documents to get Jewish people out of the country.

From new research, it is evident that Kendrick headed an 'Austrian circle' of rescuers, including his 'secretaries', who worked tirelessly to save up to 200 Jews a day. Among this circle were Ernan Forbes-Dennis and his wife Phyllis, who were living in Kitzbühel in the Austrian mountains, where they were running an international school: one of their most famous pupils was Ian Fleming. Just a week after the Anschluss, Phyllis wrote to her friend, the American journalist Frank Adams, and his wife Esther, describing the horrors in Austria, the threat to Sigmund Freud, who was rumoured to have been arrested, and how she and Ernan were trying to save the daughter of a Jewish psychiatrist, as well as two doctors and a dentist. 'The state of things in Vienna is past belief,' she wrote. 'The German soldiers have burst out of their prison, half-starved and desperate for the sake of loot. All Jews are visited night and day for foreign money, weapons and subversive literature . . . There is no escape and no hope . . . We both do what we can, from morning to night, to try to get a few little broken winged birds out of this snare.'[15]

The Austrian scene was not exclusive in the rescue efforts. Across Europe a number of British spies and diplomats, including the SIS secretaries, placed their intelligence work under strain to rescue Europe's Jews. In so doing, they saved tens of thousands of Jewish people from being murdered in the Nazi concentration camps.[16]

Due to the overwhelming workload and immense strain on the staff in Vienna, Marjorie 'Peggy' Weller was transferred from the British Legation in Sofia, Bulgaria, to aid them. She is another of the secret 'secretaries' in MI6's history.

Marjorie Weller

Educated at Cheltenham Ladies' College, and fluent in French, Weller was recruited to MI6 through the old-school channels by the principal of St James's Secretarial College, where she was studying.[17] She was interviewed in London by a man in civilian clothes who was of a military bearing. He asked if she would like a job abroad, to which she replied 'yes'. She left on a second-class ticket on the Orient Express bound for Sofia, and became attached to the Legation. Of her duties, she recalled, 'We had these queues outside and I used to say, I had this pile of passports here and a pile of secret ink letters there and I was doing both.'[18]

Weller never spied on the country she was living in, but Kendrick sent her on espionage missions during the Abyssinian crisis of 1935. She attended many parties and mixed in social circles as part of the espionage scene. Like the other SIS secretaries, she became highly experienced in running agents, communicating with them using invisible ink and helping to run spy networks across Eastern Europe and Italy.

These were dangerous times for all personnel in the passport control office, but none more so than the SIS officers and secretaries. Kendrick was betrayed by a double agent and arrested on 17 August 1938. This was a profound shock and a disaster for British intelligence operations in Europe; his arrest was deemed the most serious incident to befall SIS in its thirty-year history. During the eight-hour 'Soviet-style' interrogations at the Hotel Metropole in Vienna, apparently one of the first questions Kendrick was asked was, 'Where are the secretaries?'[19] They too were being firmly implicated in espionage. These were incredibly perilous times for the women because, like their boss, they had no diplomatic immunity. Kendrick said nothing.

Unknown to him then, the secretaries had fled; the Gestapo had arrested Kendrick's office manager (also a spy) two days earlier and they knew the net was closing in. Just hours before fleeing the office, they had destroyed all evidence of their intelligence activities. Every secret paper and file had to be burnt in case they fell into the hands of the raiding Gestapo. Holmes and her daughter Prudence left Vienna, travelling with Stamper via Innsbruck and then to the border. Although the Austrian frontiers were on alert for the women, the guards were looking for two lone secretaries rather than two women with a ten-year-old girl. They attached themselves to two other British families and crossed the border into Switzerland, arriving in Amiens two days later. They lived in Paris until the outbreak of war in September 1939, in a flat near the Étoile. Did they carry out any work for SIS from Paris? Midge never spoke about it. Her only comment in her unpublished memoir was, 'Things were getting worse and worse, so we both got involved again by word of mouth. It was so interesting and we met such nice people even with the moments of worry.'[20]

The spy's life was hard to give up for strong, intelligent women like these, and they were clearly highly valued and respected within SIS for their expertise. They already had over a decade of valuable experience as intelligencers, in handling agents and secret communications and in espionage activities. That they got out of Nazi-occupied Europe in August 1938 was hugely significant because, with the next world war on the horizon, they were about to make an astonishing contribution to the secret intelligence world that has thus far not been recognised in histories of the secret service or SOE.

Joan Osborne

Kendrick's arrest was the greatest disaster to befall MI6 in its thirty-year history. The MI6 network across Europe was recalled because it was believed that the Germans had the names of all its personnel and agents. Once the panic was over, a few weeks later, the SIS network returned; Kenneth Benton was back in Vienna for a short period with his wife Peggie, for instance. But in May 1939 a new secretary arrived in Vienna. She was twenty-three-year-old Beatrice Joan Osborne (having changed her surname by deed poll from Oppenheim). Whether she was working for SIS in Vienna is not known, but by the war's outbreak she was working for MI6.

Like the MI6 secretaries before her, Osborne never disclosed the exact nature of her work, but it is known that she developed an expertise on Austria and Hungary as well as other parts of Eastern Europe. She had been born in India on 25 January 1916; her father worked in the Indian Civil Service and she was sent to boarding school in the UK. In 1937, she graduated in history from Newnham College, Cambridge, from where it is possible that she might have been recruited by MI6. She studied in Germany, Italy and France during her university vacations and, during 1937 and 1938, in Dresden and Munich, then

Innsbruck. In October 1938 she took a job as research assistant in the Press Cutting Service of the Royal Institute of International Affairs. From here she was sent to Vienna as a 'secretary'.

In a letter home, she made no mention of the nature of her work, but informed her mother Elaine that any letters could be sent to her via the diplomatic bag, c/o 54 Broadway, London SW1: this was headquarters for MI6 and the passport control department. One can imagine the glint in her eye when she mentioned how 'the papers have been making an awful howl about us using the consulate and particularly the passport office as an espionage centre'.[21] She said she was having 'quite a pleasant life' in Vienna, and had been invited with her colleague Stella to dinner with the British Consul-General Donald Gainer and Vice Consul King. Osborne and her colleagues, including Nancy Brown, took day trips and spent weekends out of the city to explore castles and the Austrian mountains. In early August 1939, she travelled by train to stay for the weekend at the home of Baroness Johanna Freiin von Pirquet in Ebensee, near Salzburg, after an introduction from Irene McIlwraith, head secretary at the Legation. The purpose of the visit is not known; it might have been for intelligence, although Osborne could have been a paying guest.

Osborne's work in Vienna did not last as war was imminent. At the end of August 1939, she was tasked with destroying records at the Legation and then returned to the UK.[22] Her expertise on Austria and the surrounding region saw her take up further intelligence duties, first as a civilian secretary at MI6, then from November 1939 as a research assistant in the German section of Foreign Research and Press Service (FRPS). The following November, she was attached to the Political Intelligence Department (PID) in Whitehall, working on Czech and Polish intelligence, among others. She helped to research and write political and economic papers on the state of these countries and compiled weekly political intelligence summaries. From 1943, she specialised in Germany and Austria, in particular assessing problems facing the economy in Austria. She gathered relevant information from newspapers and other sources to aid these intelligence summaries. At the end of the war, Osborne's work took her back to Austria. By now she had met her future husband, Arthur William Knight, as both were working in intelligence for the Allied Commission.[23]

Joan Osborne is another prime example of how women could be drawn on to good effect by the secret service because of their existing knowledge, in her case derived from her intelligence work on Austria in the 1930s and 1940s.

Countess Marianne

Due to the ongoing secrecy surrounding MI6, it is impossible to map the full networks of its intelligence officers and agents. However, occasionally some light is shed on operatives. During the writing of *Spymaster: The Man Who Saved MI6*, new information emerged about one of Kendrick's female officers. She was Countess Marianne Szápáry – the mother of Her Royal Highness Marie-Christine, Princess Michael of Kent – who worked for Kendrick and SIS in the 1930s and probably also for Claude Dansey. Although the precise nature of her work for SIS is still unknown, there are reasonable conclusions that can be drawn from the material and these are explored in detail in *Spymaster*.[24]

Over the decades Princess Michael and her brother have weathered intense scandal and rumours about their father, Baron Günther von Reibnitz, on the basis that he was a member of the SS, a paramilitary organisation under the Nazi Party.[25] The media focus on him has meant that no attention was given to their mother. But this new information about her reveals the possibility that the Countess was actively on the side of the Allies, even if in ways that cannot be totally understood currently.

Countess Marianne Szápáry was the daughter of Count Frederick Szápáry, the last Austro-Hungarian ambassador to the Court of the Tsar in St Petersburg before the outbreak of war in 1914. The family estates fell within Austria, Czechoslovakia and Hungary, countries that were covered by Kendrick and the SIS station in Vienna. Whether the Countess ever met Kendrick's secretaries is not known, but she had been educated in Hungary and read history at the University of Vienna in the 1930s – this at the crucial moment when Austria was struggling with its political extremes of communism versus fascism.

Countess Marianne shared a number of inherited properties with her siblings in Austria, Czechoslovakia and Hungary. After their father's death in 1935 she lived in Heiligen (now Svetce, formerly in Bohemia), from where she managed the nearby family estate centred on Tachau (now Tachov), on the Bavarian frontier. As part of managing the family estate, she was a director of the family firm that dealt in timber. This meant that she often travelled on family business from Czechoslovakia to Austria and Hungary. Her observations of any movement of German troops would have been useful to Kendrick, especially in 1938 when Hitler threatened both Austria and the Sudetenland.

It has been claimed she participated in anti-Nazi demonstrations during the 1930s.[26] Although not illegal then in Czechoslovakia, as the country was not yet occupied, it pointed to her strength of character in being prepared to undertake such activities. It was not uncommon for discreet women like Countess Marianne to attend anti-Nazi rallies to observe what was going on and possibly report back to the British. A number of British women travelled in Germany and other parts of Europe in the late 1930s to give eyewitness reports of events and changes on the ground for British intelligence. Later, Countess Marianne's participation in anti-Nazi demonstrations was raised during her interrogations by the Gestapo. They had amassed a thick file of evidence against her.[27]

Shortly before the outbreak of war, she made a visit to England, during which she invited two Englishmen to stay at her home in Heiligen before their upcoming visit to Berlin. They were British Secret Service agents William Douglas Home and clergyman Peter de la Poer Beresford-Peirse. Home was already acquainted with her.[28]

Home and Beresford-Peirse stayed with Countess Marianne for about a week in Heiligen in August 1939. On 13 August she took them to see the Graf Zeppelin flight from Eger over the Sudetenland, which might have aroused some suspicions. They might have been observing whether the Zeppelin had any new features or aerial equipment, but with Countess Marianne they joined thousands of spectators of these propaganda flights. Some Zeppelin flights were espionage trips by the Germans to secretly collect information – in one case on the British radar system. The Zeppelin had flown along the coast of Britain as far as the Shetland Isles and photographed the new Supermarine Spitfire from a 'spy basket'.[29] Home and Beresford-Peirse travelled on to Berlin to try to persuade Unity Mitford to return to England, but they failed in their mission.

The Gestapo certainly believed that Home and Beresford-Peirse were SIS officers, and knew that they had stayed with Countess Marianne. This increased the German authorities' mistrust of her and she continued to fall under their suspicion until May 1945.[30] The Germans certainly believed that she had been a source of information to the British and claimed to have reliable evidence for it. They were, in fact, correct, as has been confirmed by a British source who wishes to remain unnamed.[31]

MI6 Station Berlin

Berlin represented another key SIS station. Headed by Frank Foley, its cover was again as the British passport control office. Foley operated much like Kendrick, running agents and spy networks to monitor the Soviet threat in the 1920s and 1930s, and, from 1933, the rise of Hitler and the extent of Germany's rearmament programme. Foley was considered by SIS to be one of their primary experts on the Comintern in the region.[32] His principal secretary was a woman called Sheila St Clair; little is known about her background. One of the cases that crossed her desk while working for Foley became one of SIS's most important 'walk-ins' (someone who offers themselves for espionage without previously being recruited). He was Johann Heinrich de Graaf, known as 'Johnny X', a Soviet military intelligence officer, who turned up at the passport control office in Berlin in June 1933 and offered his services to the British Secret Service. Johnny had spent some time working for the Comintern in the UK, but was returning to Moscow via Berlin when he decided to turn himself in to the British. Between 1933 and 1940, with the Soviets believing he still worked for them, this double agent provided SIS with current and extensive details of undercover operations by the Comintern and Russian military intelligence. His case provided 'an example of the outstanding success of penetration of Russian secret organisations' enjoyed by British intelligence.[33]

After Hitler's ascent to power on 30 January 1933, Foley and his staff were overwhelmed by the rescue efforts to save Germany's Jews, working twelve-hour days; the workload further increased after the passing of the Nuremberg Laws of 1935, which denied German Jews of all civil liberties. Against this backdrop, SIS staff struggled to send intelligence back to 'C' in London. The situation for Germany's Jews worsened further after Kristallnacht (the Night of Broken Glass) on 9/10 November 1938 that saw synagogues and Jewish businesses smashed and set on fire.

The following month, on 12 December 1938, twenty-six-year-old Margaret Reid was despatched to the SIS station in Berlin. Reid was the daughter of a doctor and a graduate of Girton College, Cambridge. Her employment in Berlin involved regular clerical duties as the Registry clerk during the day, and then, after hours, working for SIS, in which she helped Foley to run the spy networks and gather intelligence on German rearmament. They recruited intelligence sources, such as the German Jew Hubert Pollack, who worked closely and secretly with Foley to bribe German authorities into letting Jews out of the country, and Paul Rosbaud, an Austrian metallurgist who passed vital intelligence regarding the German weapon programme to the British because Foley managed to get his Jewish wife out of Germany to safety in England.

In August 1939, with war imminent, Reid destroyed all secret documents at the passport control office and prepared to leave Berlin. Foley left first and agreed to meet Reid in Copenhagen later that month. They travelled to Oslo where she continued to work as Foley's secretary and his main aid for intelligence operations in the region. Their presence in Oslo was initially awkward because the city already had a passport control officer and a vice consul – and the latter did not approve of secret operations being run from the British Legation. Foley found new premises from which to run the clandestine SIS missions; he and Reid revamped the rather chaotic and insecure SIS station and ran it on a professional, efficient basis. It was from Oslo that Reid aided Foley in running agents into Nazi Germany. These included German merchant seamen who still had access to Germany and to other workers, particularly railway workers, via their membership of the International Transport Workers' Federation.[34] Norwegian diplomats also proved helpful in acting as couriers. The network of agents being run from Oslo photographed German airfields, military installations and weapons, and observed German troop movements passing through Oslo.

On 9 April 1940, Germany invaded Norway. It was the first victim of Hitler's Blitzkrieg, 'lightning war', which had the aim of occupying the whole of Western Europe. Foley and Reid made a hurried and difficult escape as German troops advanced across the country. From her room in Åndalsnes, by a fjord and below the majestic mountains, Reid set up an ad hoc signals station to restore communication between Norway and London that had gone down during the German invasion. With her help in encoding a message using an MI6 codebook, Foley successfully made contact with MI6 headquarters again. Reid had received no formal training in codes – only a hurried explanation from Foley on the use of them while they were in Copenhagen. She demonstrated an ingenuity and strength of character that has come to exemplify so many of the SIS secretaries in this period.

Foley and Reid joined the British military attaché, Colonel King-Salter, and linked up with Norwegian General Headquarters in Helsinki. All would soon have to be exfiltrated from the country. To protect his staff, Foley requested they be given military ranks so that, in the event of capture by the Germans, they could not be shot as spies. Reid was given the rank of sergeant in the ATS. It had been a dramatic time, fraught with personal danger, but they were finally rescued by the Royal Navy on 1 May 1940 and returned to Britain.

For her 'extreme devotion to duty', Reid was awarded the MBE and the Norwegian Krigsmedaljen (War Medal), but Foley had to fight for such recognition for her. Foley went on to head SIS's coverage of intelligence on Norway and Germany, and was later involved with MI6 and MI5 joint Double Cross deceptions. Margaret Reid remained his secretary throughout the 1940s.

MI5 Secretaries

While not in immediate personal danger, the MI5 secretaries, like their SIS counterparts, would carve out extraordinary careers in this period. Two figures stand out in the history of MI5 at this time: Jane Archer and Milicent Bagot. Archer became MI5's first female officer and its main Soviet expert who, in 1940, interrogated the first Soviet defector,

Walter Krivitsky. Bagot was the first woman to reach senior rank in a career that spanned forty years as MI5's expert in international communism. The two women's careers will be examined below.

In the period immediately after the First World War, MI5 was still very much a formal organisation where the officers were only known by their surname and the women also addressed each other by surname. One officer commented that she did not know the first name of her colleagues for a number of years. Nevertheless, it did not prevent the ranks socialising and developing a close rapport. Catherine Morgan-Smith, who retired from MI5 in the 1960s having risen to superintendent, commented, 'we were a small closely knit group, friends among ourselves, keenly interested in our work and proud of it'; she called MI5 a 'happy place to work in'.[35] Occasionally she and her colleagues were invited to dine at the home of the chief, Vernon Kell, and his wife Constance, at Evelyn Gardens in Chelsea. Kell continued to be the primary recruiter of staff, a process which in the late 1930s he carried out with Miss Dicker. Changes to the criteria for recruitment saw an important departure from the traditional selection of staff from particular social backgrounds and education. Kell came to prioritise the knowledge of foreign languages as essential for MI5's work.

There were notable changes in working conditions for the staff, with a pay cut in 1931 due to the severe economic pressures caused by the Great Depression two years earlier. Prime Minister Ramsay MacDonald and his government were forced to make temporary reductions to salaries and this lasted three years, until 1934, when wages were increased to their former levels. MI5 staff were paid weekly in cash, with no deduction for income tax until after 1945. It was one of the perks of the job. Female staff queued up for their 'buff envelopes at the end of each month outside the office of a rather terrifying lady, Miss Dicker (lady superintendent), and her equally terrifying assistant, Miss Constant, who wore a monocle'.[36]

Jane Archer

From 1922, MI5 operated a much reduced Registry, but it had already in its ranks one of its most remarkable recruits, Kathleen Jane Sissmore (later Mrs Archer). She was recruited as a temporary clerk in 1916, aged eighteen, and rose rapidly through the organisation's ranks. The headteacher of Princess Helena College, Ealing, which she attended, described her as 'a strong character, very straight, well principled, industrious'.[37] Sissmore was destined to go far because of her sheer determination to succeed. This was no more evident than when she decided to train as a barrister in her spare time, alongside her full-time job with MI5; it clearly did not affect her ability to achieve results within MI5, as in 1923 she was awarded an MBE. She finished with first-class examination results and was called to the Bar in 1924. In 1928 she became controller of the Registry.

By 1929, Sissmore was in sole charge of MI5's department for covering Soviet espionage in the UK. Her promotion was a remarkable achievement, given that the department was almost totally dominated by men. In 1935 Kell wrote of her 'brilliant and devoted efforts'.[38] On 2 September 1939, the day before war was declared, she married Wing Commander John Archer during her lunch break. He died in action in September 1943. MI5 made no expansion of female officers in wartime and Jane Archer was its only female officer, but behind the scenes women continued to carry out the duties and responsibilities of a fully fledged intelligence officer, even though they were not promoted to that rank in this era.

One of Archer's greatest career achievements came in 1940 with her interrogations of Walter Krivitsky, the first major Soviet GRU officer to defect to the West. She interviewed him every day for three weeks in London's Langham Hotel. Her subsequent report was described as a model of its kind and 'the first really professional debriefing of a Soviet intelligence officer on either side of the Atlantic'. It gave MI5 'its first insight into the machinery of the Russian Secret Service'.[39]

Krivitsky revealed that the Soviet Union was 'growing agents from within a host country' – a veiled reference to the Cambridge spy ring and others – and how 'this method had a great disadvantage in that results might not be obtained for a number of years, but it was regularly used by Soviet Intelligence Services abroad'. The Soviets were prepared to play the long game and, if necessary, develop sleeper spies who might not be active for ten to fifteen years. Krivitsky claimed that an agent who had received an education at Eton and Oxford, and was based in the Foreign Office, was actually working for the Russians for ideological reasons. Krivitsky believed that the Russian agent handlers were Theodore Maly and Arnold Deutsch, who had subsequently returned to the Soviet Union. There were hints, too, about Kim Philby, although Philby was never overtly named.

The defector exposed to Archer how Moscow was prepared to pay for the university education of young men so they could secure top jobs within government, obtain diplomatic posts or work for British intelligence. These were shocking revelations to a Security Service that had ceased to believe Moscow was a threat, with Kell declaring the previous year (1939) that Soviet 'activity in England is non-existent in terms of both intelligence and political subversion'.[40] He was proved wrong in that evaluation; and it was an assessment that had left MI5 weakened in terms of resources and unable to monitor the Soviet threat. Moscow was incredibly successful in recruiting graduates from Oxford and Cambridge – as became embarrassingly evident as the case of the Cambridge spies unravelled in 1951 and 1963, rocking the core of the British intelligence services.

In spite of Archer's competent and professional interrogation of Krivitsky, and her expertise on the Soviet Union at a time when MI5 most needed it, she was sacked by Kell's successor, Jasper Harker, in November 1940, having denounced his predecessor's incompetence as director. Guy Liddell, head of counter-espionage at MI5, noted in his diary, 'I heard today that Jane Sissmore had been sacked for insubordination. This is a very serious blow to us all.'[41] He believed that, while she was wrong about the former director general, the incident should never have happened and was not entirely her fault. Two days later Liddell met her at the Bear Inn in Woodstock and asked her not to do anything further because he might be able to smooth things over.[42] The following day he met with Jasper Harker and told him that, while Sissmore had no right of appeal, 'in view of her long and devoted service she certainly had a moral right'. The response was that she had no right to have criticised the former director general, but if her comments were accurate, then Harker would have to resign. Harker was succeeded by David Petrie the following year.

Then, Archer's career in MI6 was disrupted when Philby moved her aside, fearing that her interrogations and research skills, especially after her direct involvement with the Krivitsky case, might unmask him as a Soviet mole. He could not allow that to happen.

Archer would have made a brilliant director general of MI5, but the world was not then ready for a female chief. It would be another fifty years before it appointed its first female head.

Leading Expert on Soviet Communism

Milicent Bagot entered the service of MI5 in 1931 as a twenty-four-year-old Oxford Classics graduate. Born in March 1907 and from an aristocratic background, she had been educated at Putney High School and then Lady Margaret Hall, Oxford. She had joined Special Branch of the Metropolitan Police in 1929, where she was engaged as a secretary. She transferred to MI5 with other colleagues who had all been tracking communist and foreign revolutionary movements for Special Branch. She developed such an expertise in international communism that she became MI5's most senior expert on the subject. It was a huge achievement for a woman in her day. She was known to be forthright and intimidating, a woman who did not suffer fools lightly.[43] She later became the model for the fictional character Connie Sachs, the Soviet expert in John le Carré's novels *Tinker, Tailor, Soldier, Spy*, *Smiley's People* and *The Honourable Schoolboy*.

During the Second World War, she worked as a clerk in the Registry and counter-subversion section at MI5, first at Wormwood Scrubs then Blenheim Palace. Her advanced knowledge of communism came to the attention of US FBI Director J. Edgar Hoover, who was said to be impressed by her. After the war she spent a short period in the Middle East, advising the British authorities there on how to counter Soviet subversion. In 1949, she was promoted from administrative assistant to officer rank in MI5, like her colleague Jane Archer one of the first women to achieve this position. She went on to serve in MI6 as well. As a Soviet expert, she became suspicious of KGB double agent Kim Philby and warned MI5 about him after discovering that he had been a member of the Communist Party of Great Britain. Philby denied this following the defection of Guy Burgess and Donald Maclean in 1951, but it was the reason for his resignation from MI6 that same year. (He was re-employed by MI6 later.)

In 1953, Bagot was promoted to assistant director of MI5, the first female intelligence officer to take on that role. She took charge of a whole section in the overseas branch of the Security Service. She was known to be a dedicated, tenacious intelligence officer who was completely at home in the world of counter-espionage and who served MI5 for over forty years.[44] In 1949 she was awarded an MBE, then received the CBE at Buckingham Palace in 1967. She was a trailblazer who paved the way for MI5's first female director, Dame Stella Rimington DCB, forty years later.

Other remarkable secretaries would emerge in MI5's history who would go on to become intelligence officers and counter-intelligence officers. Among them was Teresa 'Tess' Mayor, secretary to Victor Rothschild, 3rd Baron Rothschild, heir to the banking dynasty, and later his second wife.[45] Well educated, and a Newnham College graduate, Mayor was recruited by MI5 in 1939 and worked on anti-sabotage operations with Rothschild, who had founded MI5's first counter-sabotage department, known as B1c, in a cell at Wormwood Scrubs. In 1945, she was awarded the MBE for gallantry in dismantling booby traps at Rocquement.[46] Her recently declassified MI5 file reveals that she was questioned by MI5 in connection with the Cambridge spies; in particular, she was aware of MI5's suspicions that one of Philby's friends, Flora Solomon, was considered in intelligence circles to possibly be one of the Cambridge spy ring.

A Career in Intelligence

The attention paid to the MI6 and MI5 secretaries derives from a common thread: they had all developed an expertise that was indispensable to the British intelligence services, irrespective of gender. That did not mean there were no challenges for them in the workplace, but it does highlight how they were integral to not only the developing techniques and methodologies in intelligence but also the successes of intelligence operations, counter-espionage and deception. With the outbreak of another world war in September 1939, their experience was too valuable for MI6 or MI5 to ignore – and those services did not do so. A number of them, like Holmes, Hodgson and Stamper, were posted to SOE, and their expertise – in their case, in Austria – saw them run SOE missions behind enemy lines (more on that later).

As the history of the Second World War shows, and contrary to preconceived perceptions of women in intelligence, many went on to have long careers in MI5 and MI6 that were transformational for those services. However, the Nazi occupation of Western Europe from April/May 1940 meant that SIS heads of station and their staff made swift exits from the capitals where they were operating undercover. The only places they could operate from now were British passport control offices in neutral countries like Spain, Portugal, Switzerland and Sweden. From 1939 until 1942, MI6 struggled to gain adequate intelligence and coverage on Nazi Germany within Europe. That intelligence would have to be gathered primarily from clandestine sites on British soil, one of the most famous of which was Bletchley Park. This saw female intelligencers take centre stage again, and across all major intelligence operations.

6
THE CODEBREAKERS

The highest priority in wartime is to break the enemy's codes and ciphers; in the case of the Second World War, this meant the various German Enigma codes. A special site was required outside of London to crack the various encrypted messages between the different German services and the High Command, as well as between Hitler and his secret service (Abwehr). In the summer of 1938, Hugh Sinclair, the then head of MI6, purchased the estate of Bletchley Park in Buckinghamshire, once the country house of Sir Herbert Leon. Not wishing to wait for the government to release funds, Sinclair used £6,000 of his own private wealth to buy the estate, which became colloquialised as 'the park'. It provided the codebreakers and cryptanalysts with a discreet country location within easy travelling distance by train of London. In August 1938, 'Captain Ridley's shooting party' arrived there; in reality this was a cover for the men and women expecting to undertake the task of codebreaking. When war did not break out that summer, they were sent away again.

A year later, in September 1939, the men and women were back. Bletchley Park would go on to crack the 'unbreakable' German Enigma codes and thereby provide war-winning intelligence that saved millions of lives. One of the first women to arrive at Bletchley Park was Margaret Godfrey, the wife of Admiral Godfrey, head of Naval Intelligence. In the 1920s she had been educated at Girton College, Cambridge, but gave up her studies at the age of nineteen to marry.[1] Two days before the outbreak of war, she was posted to the codebreaking site; her daughters believed that she was in Oxford to collate data for the Admiralty. It was new ground for her because, for the first time in her life, she received a wage. During the four months she was at Bletchley Park she made no entries in her diary and never spoke about her work, but she was a firm believer in women having a much larger role to play in the modern world, and on a personal level she combined 'intelligence and experience with energy and common sense, firmness with warmth'.[2] In 1940 she transferred to Oxford University Press, working for Sam Bassett in the Inter-Services Topographical Department (ISTD), liaising over printed maps, illustrations and photographs. Admiral Cunningham wrote in 1942 that her work gave Operation Torch (the invasion of North Africa) 'a flying start'.[3] The sheer volume of work threatened to overwhelm the staff at the ISTD – but not Margaret. By the time she left in 1943 to accompany her husband John to India, she was in charge of the printing of all maps, illustrations and photographs for the ISTD. After her departure a new department had to be created to cope with the workload that she had been managing on her own.[4]

This kind of work stayed in the family, with Kathleen Godfrey, daughter of Margaret and John, joining Bletchley Park as a WAAF (Women's Auxiliary Air Force) officer, after a posting as a radio operator at Ventnor on the Isle of Wight. In the spring of 1941, having served for a year at the radar station, she was transferred to the codebreaking site in Buckinghamshire where she decoded messages.

Recruiting family members was true also for Edward Travis, who was deputy to Alastair Denniston until Travis became head of Bletchley Park in February 1942. Travis recruited his two daughters, Betty and Valérie, to work at the site. It is not certain what Betty did, except that later in life she spoke a lot about the naval section; it is likely she worked in some aspect of naval codes, before moving into central London on diplomatic traffic with Denniston. Valérie worked for Lieutenant Commander Tandy (RNVR) in Hut 4, Naval Section VI (Technical Intelligence). Apart from research, one of the main tasks of the section was to compile lists of technical terminology, based on captured documents, in order to help mine decrypted messages for any possible cryptanalytic or intelligence value. In 1944, she moved with the section to Block A and was working in Room 28.

Many of the earliest young female recruits were debutantes – high society, privileged and well-educated women who were the daughters of aristocrats and moved in closely trusted circles.[5] The 'debs' tended not to be codebreakers and instead were more involved in the clerical side. This probably explains why ladies like Lady Jean Graham (married name Fforde) found their work 'rather a dull chapter in an otherwise colourful life'.[6] She was the daughter of the 6th Duke of Montrose, whose family owned most of the Scottish island of Arran. She joined the Wrens (WRNS – Women's Royal Naval Service), considered to be the elite service for women, and was posted to Bletchley Park at the end of 1941. Her father had founded the Royal Naval Volunteer Reserve (RNVR). Her recruitment came at a time when operations on site were being drastically scaled up.

One of the key roles for the Wrens was running the Hollerith machines – among the earliest electronic computers in the world – in Block C, which supported the codebreaking. The work was extremely boring, but essential. It involved punching hundreds of holes into cards which stored information from earlier decrypts of encoded German messages. As operators the women often had no idea how their work directly impacted on the war. The job may have been of national significance, but living conditions were usually challenging, as recalled by Jean Tocher (Wrens): 'We were billeted in the servants' quarters [Woburn Abbey], eight double bunks to a room. The bats flew in and the condensation dripped off the ceilings.'[7]

From 1942 onwards, Wrens became the sole operators of the bombe machines, used by cryptologists on site to decipher the encrypted messages of German enigma machines. As we shall see, after 1943 women operated Colossus, the first programmable electronic computer, designed by British engineer Tommy Flowers, which helped to break the Lorenz SZ42 teleprinter cipher code (nicknamed 'Tunny'). Colossus was developed in the Newmanry, a section at Bletchley headed by mathematician Max Newman, which by the end of the war was staffed by 272 Wren cryptanalysts and 27 men.[8] This statistic is one example of just how central the women were to codebreaking and cryptanalysis at Bletchley.

The Debutantes

The young debutantes were recruited because the intelligence services believed that they were better able to keep a secret and were deemed to be more discreet than young women from humbler backgrounds. Of course, this was not necessarily true: there is ample evidence that women from less privileged beginnings could also keep quiet about their wartime work. Not all the women recruited to Bletchley Park in its early days were aristocratic, but they were all highly educated – from Oxford or Cambridge – or middle class.

Socialite Joan Stafford-King-Harman (later Lady Dunn) was already employed by MI6, having briefly taken 'a pioneering role as one of the first female desk officers'.[9] The eldest daughter of Sir Cecil Stafford-King-Harman, 2nd Baronet of Rockingham (Ireland), Joan had been tutored by a governess, then attended Abbot's Hill School in Hemel Hempstead, Hertfordshire. From there, she went to Munich for a year to study German and the piano. She commented, 'I came back [to England] madly pro-Hitler, thinking he had done a wonderful job for Germany, bringing them back from the horrors of the First World War. Of course, my family were all pretty furious when I got back and thought I was a silly young girl.'[10] Interestingly, she was recruited by John Godfrey in spite of these views, probably because her social status overrode her personal opinions, which were most likely dismissed as deriving from the naivety of youth. It was Joan's expertise in German that attracted Godfrey. On a trip to Scotland with friends he had asked them whether they knew any young women who could use a typewriter and keep a secret. Joan's name was put forward, and she accepted.

She received a letter for an interview at Broadway Buildings and was informed that she would be working in passport control – a cover for MI6 – in the countryside. MI6 had moved some of its sections to the mansion house at Bletchley Park because of the Blitz on London. Joan arrived there and was assigned as a secretary in the naval section of MI6, working for Captain Eddie Hastings and Lieutenant-Commander Christopher Arnold-Forster. The main liaison officer was Ian Fleming, with whom she had contact. The British intelligence establishment's obsession with recruiting young women from the right families continued after she joined MI6. Joan commented, 'People were always asking me if I knew of anybody else who would like to come and work for them and so one collected up friends and friends of friends.'[11]

At the end of 1939 she was transferred to St Albans to work for Section V of MI6, which dealt with counter-espionage. She worked alongside Nicholas Elliott, the intelligence officer in charge of German spies in Holland, and they became lifelong friends. When the Germans occupied Holland in May 1940, she and Elliott dealt with the influx of refugees, some of whom were German spies. The latter were either jailed or turned as double agents to feed false intelligence back to Germany. In counter-espionage, she found herself operating alongside Kim Philby, a close friend of Elliott, who worked in the next office. She said, 'We all knew him [Philby] quite well. Very charming, quite good looking. He behaved terribly badly. Talk about wine, women and song. Tremendous charm but terribly badly behaved.'[12] In a sign that Joan was respected and admired by her colleagues, when Elliott became seriously ill, Joan was asked to temporarily take his place at a time when 'there were no women officers [in MI6] then. They were all men.' In 1943 she married Captain George Dennehy of the Irish Guards and left MI6 after becoming pregnant with their first child.

English socialite Sarah Norton (later Baring) had been educated by a series of governesses before being sent to Munich to learn German and broaden her horizons. She commented on her time there that 'Hitler and his entourage used to take tea in the Carlton Tea Rooms in Munich, and my girlfriend and I would sit at a neighbouring table and pull faces at him . . . We weren't arrested, because at that stage the Germans were still being frightfully nice to us.'[13] After the outbreak of war, and back in England, Sarah joined an aircraft factory at Langley in Slough. With her linguistic skills, she was transferred to Bletchley Park, where she collated intelligence in Hut 4, using index cards. She recalled how the index cards were kept in long boxes like an elongated shoebox; 'each time a signal came in and was translated, you had to put down the salient points in that signal, such as the name of the U-boat commander on one card, the number of the U-boat on another, the coordinates or the person; anything related to that signal went on different cards'.[14] In October 1944, she transferred to the Operational Intelligence Centre (OIC) in the Citadel at the Admiralty in central London. She and three other girls from Bletchley Park were the liaison officers between OIC and Bletchley. They formed NID 12a, and all Ultra material – wartime signals intelligence obtained by breaking encrypted enemy teleprinter and radio communications – was passed through their small section and used as operational intelligence.

The story of the debutantes is only one aspect of the women's history in Sigint. Certainly not all the talented and intelligent young women employed in codebreaking and cryptanalysis were from an aristocratic background. By September 1941, 200 of the 1,000 young women in intelligence were graduates in economics, maths, law and languages from Oxford and Cambridge. Peter Calvocoressi, an intelligence officer who began the war at a CSDIC (Combined Services Detailed Interrogation Centre) eavesdropping site and himself attended Oxford University, transferred to Hut 3 at Bletchley Park. He commented, 'As a consequence of the recruitment, nearly all of us had had the same sort of education and shared a common social background. We made, unwittingly for the most part, the same assumptions about life and work and discipline and values.'[15]

But, despite such camaraderie and shared background, the female linguists at Bletchley were paid at least £50 less per year than their male counterparts.[16] Women were not promoted to the higher grades and were limited to being temporary clerks or paid as junior assistants. There was a level of injustice in terms of pay and promotion which mirrored women's experiences in wider society and their jobs in civilian life. This was before the modern movement that advocated and fought for equal rights, representation and pay for women in the workplace, a fight that is arguably still necessary in some places today. There were some male officers at Bletchley Park who sought increased salaries for their female employees, but it was a battle, and one that required a full written justification for the salary increase and why upgrading was necessary.

The Myth of 'the Debs'

The official history of GCHQ (Government Communications Headquarters) states that the image of glamorous debutantes breaking codes after a party or croquet on the lawn is a myth. Not all the first codebreakers were debutantes and 'the real history of women in British Sigint is unknown, and mostly forgotten once lived'.[17]

In the inter-war period, MI1(b) – the interception and cryptanalysis section – was based in the War Office in London. When it merged with other codebreaking organisations in 1919 to form the GC&CS (Government Code and Cypher School), it had just one female junior assistant. She was Emily Anderson, who was Irish, a music scholar and professor of German at the National University of Ireland, Galway. She had continued her academic career alongside her codebreaking work for a while, but in 1920 she left her university post to work full-time for GC&CS. In 1927 she became the head of the Italian diplomatic section. In 1939 she was posted first to Bletchley Park and then sent to GHQ in the Middle East on work for which she was awarded an OBE in 1943. She went on to have a long career in intelligence and codebreaking.[18]

Anderson persuaded her friend Patricia Bartley (later Brown) to join her at Bletchley Park, which could only come about via a personal recommendation. Bartley was born in India, the daughter of Sir Charles Bartley, an Irish barrister who was serving there as a judge. She was sent to boarding school in England at the age of ten and, unhappy, ran away from a succession of schools until she was finally educated with her siblings in an abbey in Brittany. Her father retired from the Indian courts in the 1930s and the family moved to Swanbourne. She studied philosophy, politics and economics at Lady Margaret Hall, Oxford. When she first arrived at Bletchley Park, it was all very low tech. She was handed a pencil and paper, and, because of her knowledge of languages, was given the task of working on the main German diplomatic code, a system that had been ignored because it was deemed too difficult to break.

Bartley was brilliant and meticulous in her attention to detail. Mistakenly believing that the doubly enciphered Floradora was unbreakable, German diplomats had become careless when using it, and their mistakes were seized upon by Bartley to help crack the code. She played a leading role in breaking Floradora.[19] And her cooperation with her US counterparts meant that it was achieved much more quickly than would have been possible otherwise.

In 1941, the diplomatic section of GS&CS, headed by Alastair Denniston, moved to Berkeley Street in Mayfair, and, at the age of only twenty-four, Bartley became head of the German diplomatic section. By May 1942, Bartley's team included American film star Dorothy Hyson and Ernst Fetterlein (once the Tsar's personal codebreaker). They began to successfully read a small number of messages between the German embassy in Dublin and Berlin, and by August 1942 were reading every message. One of Bartley's male staff attempted to take credit for this breakthrough, but Denniston intervened to ensure that it was she who received the recognition. He was always supportive, but as a woman in a position of authority Bartley encountered a number of challenges from some of the male colleagues. Frederic Freeborn, who controlled the Hollerith tabulating machines needed to break Floradora, frequently circumvented her and delayed her requests for time on the machines. Ultimately, the strain and stress led to a breakdown in Bartley's health and she left GC&CS. She returned after the war only to write two chapters of the internal GCHQ history of her section, then joined the Foreign Office, where she met her future husband Denys Downing Brown. She supported her husband's diplomatic career and postings to Egypt and European capitals, and, like many women of her generation, she spent the post-war period bringing up a family. Her civilian life hid a world of secrets in which she had been one of the top British female wartime codebreakers.

Hut 6 and Hut 8

There were numerous huts on site at Bletchley, each conducting their own specialisms in an operation that involved the tri-services cooperation of army, air and naval intelligence. Women and men working in one hut may not know what was going on in another hut – there were layers of secrecy within the site – but all contributed to the larger intelligence picture and codebreaking operations at Bletchley.

Hut 6, run by Gordon Welchman, dealt with German army and air force traffic.[20] Its first female recruit was Dorothy Chads, followed by Mary Wilson in early 1940, along with Sheila Dunlop and Jean d'E Mylne.[21] The role of Hut 6, the most top-secret section of Bletchley Park, was to understand the whole German wireless traffic organisation for the German army and air force, so that interception at Y stations (signals intelligence collection sites around the UK) could be maximised. June Canney was hired by Welchman as his secretary and played an important role in the administration of Hut 6. In its Registration Room, the women logged the enciphered Enigma messages, which were then deciphered, analysed and turned into intelligence for Allied commanders. Getting this intelligence – known as 'real-time intelligence' – out to Allied commanders in the field as quickly as possible was the primary aim. Hut 6 was constantly modified and streamlined to speed up the production of intelligence.

Jane Hughes (later Fawcett) played a key role in the sinking of the German battleship *Bismarck* in May 1941.[22] She had been recruited by a friend who was already working at Bletchley and who wrote to her one day: 'I'm at Bletchley and it's perfectly frightful. We're so overworked, so desperately busy. You must come and join us.'[23] Hughes was interviewed by Stuart Milner-Barry, who worked in Hut 6, whence she was assigned; her knowledge of German helped in decoding the enemy's messages.[24] Fawcett recalled, 'We had horrid little trestle tables, which were very wobbly, and collapsible chairs, which were also very wobbly, very hard. There was very poor lighting; single light bulbs hanging down from the ceiling. So we were really in semidarkness, which I expect is what the authorities wanted, better security.'[25] On 25 May 1941 the shift in Hut 6 received a briefing that the Royal Navy was hunting down the *Bismarck* in the North Atlantic. She typed out a message which she realised emanated from Luftwaffe headquarters in Berlin and indicated that the *Bismarck* was heading for the French port of Brest. The message was rushed immediately to the Admiralty. The following day, a Royal Navy flying boat was despatched and spotted the battleship. The navy gave chase and the *Bismarck* was sunk. It was an early example for the codebreakers of the tangible results of their meticulous operations.[26]

In February 1943, Hut 6 became Hut 16, still decrypting German army and air force Enigma messages. One of the women in Hut 16 was Valerie Glassborow (the paternal grandmother of Catherine, Princess of Wales), who helped decipher German codes along with her twin sister Mary. The sisters were not debutantes, but from a standard middle-class background. They worked in a section called Commercial and

Miscellaneous Y (or CMY for short). CMY assigned the interception of commercial and diplomatic traffic to the relevant Y Stations. Although commercial and diplomatic codebreaking had moved to Berkeley Street in early 1942, such was the complexity of interception that CMY was based at Bletchley Park as part of the WT Coordination section. This enabled CMY section to liaise more easily with those responsible at Bletchley for directing the Y section intercepts. For Valerie, the work included calculation of the productivity of different wireless networks and ensuring that they were allocated to particular Y Stations, according to interception priorities. Women like the Glassborow twins were part of the greatest wartime codebreaking operation, but neither spoke about their secret war to their families.

Joan Clarke (later Murray) was originally recruited for Hut 6 by Welchman, who had taught her geometry at Cambridge. When she arrived at Bletchley Park on 17 June 1940 she was met by Alan Turing and taken to Hut 8, which was tasked with solving German naval Enigma messages. She worked for the whole of the war as a cryptanalyst in Hut 8 and was promoted to its deputy head in 1944. Her role has been immortalised by Keira Knightley in the film *The Imitation Game*.[27]

Rozanne Medhurst (later Colchester) had been a codebreaker in Hut 8 since 1942. She was the daughter of Sir Charles Medhurst, then Vice-Chief of the Air Staff (Intelligence), who had been a First World War pilot and air attaché in Rome in 1937.[28] She was nineteen years old and back in England when he told her that an intelligence site in Buckinghamshire needed Italian-speakers. After she passed an interview at the Foreign Office, her father drove her to Bletchley Park, where she was assigned to Hut 8, working alongside Kathleen Godfrey. Rozanne recalled, 'it was so intense. There were such a lot of very clever and eccentric people shut away in the strange isolation. I remember Alan Turing. He was very shy and awfully sweet. We used to have coffee after lunch in the canteen.'[29] Their work was so completely confidential that no one was allowed to speak to anyone about it or even ask others in one's own hut what they were doing. Churchill described the codebreakers as golden geese who laid the golden eggs and never cackled. Medhurst added, 'we didn't cackle, because we were told not to, so we didn't'.[30]

They worked in shifts to cover the full twenty-four-hour period, usually in smoky and claustrophobic conditions. A convoy of buses brought the codebreakers into the site from nearby areas. Rozanne cycled daily from her billet in Fenny Stratford. She admitted, 'it was monotonous, sloggish work, but gradually I began to understand the codes'. To cope with the pressure, they went to the cinema, and at Christmas time the canteen was transformed into a theatre. During her years at 'the Park', Rozanne had little sense of how her seemingly humdrum work, or that of her colleagues, was impacting on the war. That changed late one night in 1943, when she decoded a high-grade Italian air cipher and was staring at intelligence which no one in the Air Ministry had yet seen.[31] Just over three hours later, at 4 a.m., the Italian air force was due to leave Tripoli and send its SM.79 Torpedo bombers to Sicily. The intelligence was sent to the appropriate commanders and the bombers were shot down, thus protecting Allied forces for the invasion of Sicily in the summer of 1943. Of the wartime years, Rozanne commented, 'everything was so intense, like a love affair'. At the end of the war Rozanne applied for a transfer to 'the Office' and was posted to MI6 in Cairo.

Codebreaker Dilly Knox, who was based in the cottage on site, required female mathematicians for his research section – women like thirty-six-year-old Margaret Rock, who had been educated at Bedford College, London, and Mavis Batey (née Lever), who was reading German at University College London when war broke out. Mavis left her studies to work in Broadway Buildings (MI6 headquarters) on commercial codes and checking the personal columns of *The Times* newspaper for coded spy messages. Her brilliant lateral thinking led to the uncovering of an illegal shipment of goods to Germany and so in 1940 she was transferred to Bletchley Park to work with Knox's team. On her arrival, aged just nineteen, Knox said to her, 'Oh, hello, we're breaking machines, have you got a pencil?'[32] Mavis received no training, but Knox relied on her ability to think for herself to solve problems. The team began on the Italian codes, and, even if they did not understand Enigma, Knox had 'devised a system of rods, strips of cardboard with rows of letters in the order they appeared in the wiring of each Enigma rotor, which were slid along under the encoded text to try to find a point at which the text of the crib began to appear'. Mavis compared it to a game of Scrabble or doing a crossword. In September 1940, working a shift on her own one night, she cracked the missing spaces and was able to read the whole of an Italian message. Dilly Knox obtained a salary increase for Mavis from Denniston, her pay going up from 35 shillings a week to 57 shillings, as per the rank of a linguist. He moved her from the back room to the front room to work alongside Margaret Rock, and took Mavis to a local pub for a celebratory meal.[33]

On another occasion, after an interception of an Italian encoded message at Chicksands in Bedfordshire, Mavis, with some help from her future husband Keith Batey, decoded a long message which confirmed that the Italian navy intended to attack and sink a convoy of British ships en route from Egypt to Greece. The intelligence was passed to Admiral Sir Andrew Cunningham, commander-in-chief of the Mediterranean fleet, and it led to the sinking of three Italian heavy cruisers and two destroyers, with the loss of 3,000 Italian sailors.[34]

Ahead of D-Day, Mavis Batey and Margaret Rock played a leading role in cracking the complex Enigma code of the Abwehr. Unlike other machines, Enigma had four rotors instead of the standard three, and they rotated randomly, with no predictable pattern. The settings were also changed every day at midnight. Hut 6 had been unable to break Enigma. But on 8 December 1941 Mavis Batey broke a message on the link between Belgrade and Berlin, allowing the reconstruction of one of the rotors. Within days Knox and his team had broken into the Abwehr Enigma, and shortly afterwards Mavis broke a second Abwehr machine.

The significance of their work cannot be overestimated. MI5 and MI6 were running double agents as part of the 'Double Cross System' and feeding deception and fake intelligence to the Germans. Being able to decode the messages between the Abwehr and their agents provided a way to ascertain that the double agents were really working for the Allies as well as to monitor whether the Germans had accepted the deception. It ensured the success of the D-Day landings because it evidenced the Germans' belief in the misinformation being fed to them by the Double Cross agents – that the invasion was to occur at Pas-de-Calais and not the real landing points in Normandy. Brigadier Bill Williams, Montgomery's chief intelligence officer, said that without cracking the Abwehr Enigma the deception operation could not have been mounted; the Germans would simply have moved their reinforcements from Calais to Normandy, and the events of D-Day, had it occurred at all, would have had a very different outcome.

Edward Travis and the Recruitment of Women

On 2 December 1941, due to shortages of women in the auxiliary units of the armed forces, the government announced conscription for women between the ages of twenty and twenty-five who were unmarried or childless widows. Soon the age range lowered to nineteen and extended to women aged thirty. This was a necessary step to increase recruitment into all services, and that included all branches of intelligence. However, six months earlier, in July 1941, the shortage of staff to cope with intelligence work was already a serious issue at Bletchley Park. Staffing levels in Hut 6 and Hut 8, in particular, proved insufficient to meet the increasing volume of intelligence work.[35] Bletchley Park was commanded jointly by Alexander 'Alastair' Denniston and Sir Edward Travis. Both men had worked in codes in the First World War.[36]

On 4 July 1941, Welchman wrote to Travis: 'As you know, the work of Hut 6 is getting more difficult. We need more staff and more space. The male staff will probably not need many additions, but I should like permission to engage up to 6 senior and 6 juniors in addition to our present staff.'[37] He sought authorisation to engage up to forty-eight more women, either as temporary assistants or as grade II clerks, and up to three more of the more senior rank of temporary junior assistant principals.

On 10 July, a letter was sent by Lieutenant Colonel Hatton Hall to Denniston that outlined grave concerns over the inadequate level of staff. In it, Hatton Hall wrote how he and Frederick Winterbotham, the RAF officer who distributed Ultra material, were not 'awfully happy that the codes section in Hut 3 is adequate for the strain that will be put on it in case of invasion and also in view of the two new outstations in Middle East':

> As far as I can gather, the present personnel detailed to do the encoding have also other duties to perform which may interfere with their work on coding when the strain arises . . . Winterbotham

> and I both think it is essential in the interests of efficiency and the quick passing of urgent operational messages that there should be no loophole for delay in the constitution of the codes section for this purpose.[38]

The question of increasing staff was a major issue in this period. A report at the end of the month stated that 'it appears that our work is still increasing and that we still need more staff . . . we should go on trying hard to get as many suitable girls of grade II and linguist standard as we can. It seems to me that before long we shall need about 100 of them spread between the four sections.'[39]

Delays in appointing sufficient staff were still a concern in October 1941. Ralph Curtis of MI6 in Hut 3 wrote to Denniston, 'I have mentioned this matter verbally on numerous occasions during the past six months, but I feel the time has come when I must put it on paper if I need to protect myself in the event of any serious delays occurring in reporting material of operational importance.'[40]

Failure by Denniston and senior management to deal with the requests for more staff led Welchman to take more drastic action. In late October 1941, a letter was written by Welchman, Alan Turing, Hugh Alexander and Stuart Milner-Barry – dubbed the 'Wicked Uncles' – and delivered by hand to Winston Churchill at 10 Downing Street by Milner-Barry. Churchill stamped it 'Action this Day!' and told General Ismay, his chief military assistant, 'Make sure they have all they want on extreme priority and report to me when it's done.'[41]

Authorisation had been received to increase staff but nothing happened in reality, thus placing further pressure on Denniston. A letter in late August 1941 from Hut 3(e)'s Ralph Curtis stated that the night watch in Hut 3, consisting of only two or three people, was 'completely inadequate to deal with the influx of material'.[42] He had discovered a large quantity of teleprinter material in the wrong pile that required action. This led him to say that, unless the situation was ameliorated soon, he would have no alternative but to 'draw the attention of my commanding officer to what is, in my opinion, a serious deficiency in the organisation. I would emphasise that in this organisation it is essential to cater for the maximum and not the minimum requirements.' The watches in Hut 3 were adhering to a fairly rigid eight-hour shift and, as he highlighted, in his section, their type of work frequently necessitated twelve- to fourteen-hour shifts.

In February 1942, with Churchill having sanctioned more personnel, and a personality clash going on between Denniston and Menzies, the head of MI6, Travis replaced Denniston as sole director of Bletchley Park. An undated report, thought to have been written by Travis, outlined how the site needed a substantial increase in personnel: 'We must endeavour to collect as many first-rate girls as possible. It is difficult to estimate the number required, but we need about 90 linguists and 20 to 25 in each of the four main parties. As regards space, it seems that we need additional accommodation equivalent to a quarter, possibly one third of our present space.'[43]

Travis dramatically scaled up the number of recruits, especially women, as well as instigating a major administrative overhaul that was quite visionary. In so doing, he prepared the codebreaking site for its greatest challenges ahead of D-Day. He had run out of contacts from the universities of Oxford and Cambridge and had to look further afield. Women from more diverse backgrounds were enlisted, a move that saw Wrens, as we have seen, becoming the sole operators of the bombe machines at Bletchley Park and its sister site at Eastcote, near Ruislip.[44] With Travis as director, productivity increased to such a level that Bletchley Park became an industrial-scale intelligence-gathering site.

Women of Expertise

At sites like Bletchley Park, and their counterparts in the United States and Canada, women became leaders in codebreaking and cryptanalysis. Their expertise was used by British intelligence, with little regard for their gender. This meant that it was possible for them to succeed in a traditionally male-dominated world. But it took the situation of wartime for these opportunities to present themselves for a larger number of women.

Caroline Chojecki (née Rowett) was a pioneering leading naval intelligence analyst at Bletchley Park. She was born in 1920, the daughter of a wine and spirits importer, and was educated at St Bride's School, Helensburgh. She lived in Paris with a French family to learn the language, then studied modern languages at Girton College, Cambridge. In June 1942 Frank Birch, head of the naval section in Hut 4 at Bletchley Park, recruited her from the university. Her work involved deciphering coded messages regarding the threat to Allied shipping during the Battle of the Atlantic. Britain could not survive without the supplies transported by the sea convoys which, with their Royal Navy escorts, received relentless attention from the Germans, who knew just how vulnerable the ships were; their U-boats could easily sink them and their precious cargoes. After Turing and his colleagues cracked the German navy's Enigma cipher, the Admiralty was able to reroute the convoys around the attacking groups of U-boats, known as 'wolf packs'. However, in December 1941, as we have seen, the Germans had added a fourth rotor to the Enigma machine, creating a new cipher which could not be broken, and the wolf packs had some success in attacking the convoys.

Chojecki was tasked with building up a database of information about the U-boats that could help provide 'cribs' – pieces of plain text to help the codebreakers crack the German naval Enigma again (codenamed 'Shark' by Turing) and decipher the messages. Chojecki was just twenty-three when she led a team of seven young women in Hut 4. She later recalled being plunged into a bleak world where the codebreakers were really struggling: 'I had arrived at an appalling time in the Battle of the Atlantic. Vast numbers of enemy submarines were prowling the convoy routes. Ships were under constant attack. The gloom in Hut 4 was indescribable.' Hut 4 'seemed rather decrepit and smelled of damp wood and was heated by an old iron stove which was prone to belching out smoke'.[45]

By the end of 1942, working conditions improved when the German naval section moved into a new concrete building. Chojecki amassed ostensibly inconsequential data in German messages to build up a wide-ranging picture of the threat, with information ranging from extensive detail of individual U-boats to details of their commanders. She and her colleagues recorded the intelligence on index cards and created a resource of known German text that might appear in the messages which the codebreakers needed in order to decode the Shark cipher. She recalled how initially the card index was 'the bane of my existence because it would be useless unless kept up to date. But it proved invaluable later on.'

On a grey day in December 1942, the codebreakers succeeded in breaking the German U-boat Enigma. It was an exciting moment, the culmination of months of painstaking labour that produced results. Chojecki said, 'The excitement built up to the moment when word went around that at last U-boat Enigma had been broken. There was no time for celebration, but I think there were many secret prayers of thanksgiving.'[46] Breaking the Shark cipher enabled the Admiralty once again to divert supply convoys away from the enemy, and they could instead concentrate on knocking out the U-boats. By the end of March 1943, the U-boat losses were so serious that Admiral Karl Dönitz, commander-in-chief of the German navy, withdrew them from the Atlantic. Over the next two years, Germany began to rebuild and replace its U-boats. Still intercepting and reading the Shark messages, Chojecki and her team knew that Dönitz was going to send them back into the Atlantic and continued to gather intelligence. Together they directly contributed to the Allied victory in the Battle of the Atlantic.

Chojecki gave her all to her work. On a bitterly cold day in January 1945, and carrying a volume of *Jane's Fighting Ships* and a copy of *Cassell's World Atlas* for research, she collapsed at the top of a staircase. The twenty-four-year-old was diagnosed with exhaustion and told to take two months' leave – a diagnosis which, she said later, was 'thoroughly unwelcome and I have never been so frustrated in my life.'[47]

After the war, she married Zygmunt Chojecki, a Polish exile. By the mid-1970s, having raised their children, she once again returned to intelligence work, making use once more of the expertise and skills gleaned from her time at Bletchley Park nearly thirty years earlier.[48] Her career is another example of how the legacy and expertise of women in intelligence have been hidden for so long, with her story only emerging publicly after her death in 1992.

Senior Codebreakers

Women continued to progress as experts in codebreaking at Bletchley Park, reaching high levels of proficiency. Helene Aldwinckle (née Taylor) became one of the most senior female codebreakers in Hut 6.[49] She was recruited in August 1942 directly from having graduated in

French and English at Aberdeen University. She was called to interview in London where a panel of twenty men sat around a table and asked the women interviewees 'about mathematics, crosswords and languages, with no mention of the work they would be doing at Bletchley Park'.[50] Helene was engaged in Hut 6 on sorting messages that could be linked together by the same callsigns or the length of the messages; those with the same number of groups might be a re-encipherment of the same German text, and this could help to break those codes.

Following the signing of BRUSA intelligence-sharing agreement between Britain and the United States in May 1943, US codebreakers arrived at Bletchley that summer. Helene was asked to take charge of their induction and training programmes and, in so doing, played a small yet important role in what became known as the 'special relationship'.[51] She recalled, 'They were full of banter and used to flirt at every opportunity, for example trying to accompany me to lunch, but it was always in good jest and they were enormous fun and a breath of fresh air in a rather stuffy environment.'[52] Helene was a good choice for the training because she was relaxed, quick-witted and vivacious, and able to get along easily with her American trainees. She was diplomatic in handling the sensitive situation when the British worried about the US codebreakers being less security-conscious with their work, quietly underlining to them the importance of keeping their work secret and not letting any of it come out.[53]

Afterwards, she returned to Hut 6 and worked in the Quiet Room on Enigma ciphers that could not immediately be dealt with by the Watch (the main codebreaking section). Codebreaking in Hut 6 was divided between two sections: the Watch and Research. The former operated in three shifts across twenty-four hours, working on keys that were breakable and operationally urgent. The Research Section focused on codes that the Watch could not break, and those codes that were breakable but operationally less urgent. Between the Watch and Research was a section known as the 'Quiet Watch' (nicknamed 'the Qwatch').[54] Helene worked in this section. Messages were handed to the Quiet Room if the Watch had been unable to break a code, often because a British intercept operator made a mistake or misheard a letter, or a number of letters, due to poor reception conditions.

Towards the end of the war, once intercept sites were linked to Bletchley Park by teleprinter, the teleprinter operator could make mistakes inputting the message. The job of those in the Quiet Watch was to find out where the mistake had occurred and to thereby decode the message. The Quiet Watch was an essential part of the codebreaking process, ensuring that as much as possible was done to break every message. It was also directly responsible for breaking a number of keys.[55] On 10 April 1944, Helene broke one of the keys called 'P'. This was almost certainly the Pink Luftwaffenführungsschlüssel (the Luftwaffe leaders' key), first broken on 1 January 1942, which was used for messages of the highest secrecy sent between the most senior German air force officers. It was rarely used and always difficult to identify.[56] Helene met her future husband, John Aldwinckle, an RAF navigator, while on a short course in Aberdeen.[57] He spent much of the war in Algiers, and then Italy, dropping SOE agents into occupied southern Europe. After the war Helene stayed on at Bletchley Park to co-write the official history of Hut 6,[58] before getting married and, as were then the terms of service, therefore being required to leave the Foreign Office.[59]

Aged just seventeen, Margaret Elizabeth Oliver (later O'Connell) volunteered for the Wrens. Her acute ability to solve crossword puzzles meant that she was selected to work in the Newmanry, the section headed by Max Newman to develop computational methods to automate codebreaking. Oliver was there when Colossus Mk 1, the prototype decoding machine, arrived and became operational in December 1943. By February 1944 the team was cracking Hitler's Lorenz messages, the cipher used to communicate with his generals. One of Oliver's roles was 'to load and unload the precious paper message data tapes, which had taken hours of meticulous work to create'.[60] At the time she had little knowledge of just how their work relating to the Lorenz messages impacted on the outcome of the war.

On arrival at Bletchley Park, Charlotte 'Betty' Webb (née Vine-Stevens) was initially tasked with cataloguing the intercepts of encrypted German radio messages. Born in 1923, she had acquired her knowledge of German from her German au pair, then became an exchange student in Germany in the 1930s. She commented, 'I wanted to do something more for the war effort than bake sausage rolls.'[61] She went on to make a huge contribution at the codebreaking site when she was transferred from work on Enigma to the Japanese section on site. She became one of the women to break intercepted Japanese codes – work absolutely crucial for fighting the war in the Far East. The work was long and strenuous: she recalled, 'We worked a shift pattern 8am–4pm, 4pm–midnight, midnight–8am. It sounds easy but it was tiring.'[62] With hostilities over in Europe in May 1945, she travelled to the United States where she assisted US codebreakers in the Pentagon with operations in the Pacific.

Elizabeth Balfour (née Ranken), a Wren cryptanalyst who worked alongside Webb in Japanese naval codes, commented, 'We learnt very quickly to ask nothing, do as you're told, do the job. It was boring in the extreme . . . But you couldn't say we got our teeth into our job. We didn't because we couldn't see what came out of it.'[63] It was not really possible for the intelligencers to know the material outcome of their intelligence work. They were told, and trusted, that what they were doing was impacting on the war in ways that they were not permitted to know.

During the Second World War, women were attached to the Intelligence Corps for the first time and were entitled to wear the cap badge. By war's end, at Bletchley Park, 270 women were entitled to wear the badge of the Intelligence Corps. Over 1,000 WAAFs worked as teleprinter and wireless operators. By January 1945, women made up 76 per cent of the workforce, in roles which in peacetime they would not have had the opportunity to undertake.[64] Much of their work involved long, tedious hours, and they rarely knew the direct outcomes of their job. And, like so many of the women involved in such top-secret work, they never talked about it, not even to the men they married after the war. They kept their vow of secrecy which they had made when signing the Official Secrets Act at the start of their war work.

There were examples in the United States, too, with cryptanalyst Elizabeth Smith Friedman who, in the First World War, had become interested in ciphers and codes.[65] She had taught the first cryptography classes to soldiers in the war and deciphered letters from a suspected spy. By the Second World War she led a team of codebreakers who were responsible for identifying Nazi spies and sympathisers in South America. They solved three different German Enigma codes; however, the credit was given to the FBI by J. Edgar Hoover (head of the FBI) and not to Friedman's team. Her story is an example of how history can be set right and her leadership and expertise as a senior female US codebreaker is now acknowledged properly.

In Britain, women made an equally important contribution to the Y Service, which fed into operations at Bletchley Park. These satellite listening stations represented a vital part of Britain's intelligence capability all around the country and abroad: at places like RAF Chicksands in Bedfordshire and Beaumanor near Loughborough.[66]

Radio Security Service (MI8)

MI6 had responsibility not only for the GC&CS at Bletchley Park, but also for the Radio Security Service (RSS).[67] It began as a branch of MI5, located in a prison cell at Wormwood Scrubs, then from March 1941 was taken over by MI6, Section VIII. It became known as MI8(c) or the Radio Security Service. Because of bombing raids on the capital, the RSS was relocated to the village of Arkley in Barnet, North London. Its postal address was simply 'Box 25'. Working in close partnership with Bletchley Park, it handled the interception of Axis wireless cable traffic, including diplomatic and military communications. It intercepted the post and telephone communications at foreign embassies and missions in British territories.

Across the country around 1,700 people worked as voluntary interceptors (VIs) during the war, only 3 of whom were women. The world of radio amateurs (or 'radio hams') in general was very much a male one; any women operating as such or engaging in the technological world at all were rare, and something of a curiosity. Nevertheless, the small number of female radio hams had the respect of their male colleagues. Each VI was issued with a specific frequency for listening in to German signals, as well as a specific band wave to record any sound they heard, whether it was a tone, Morse code or just a hum. These recordings, noted on special log sheets, were sent to Box 25 for identification, classification and deciphering, and if appropriate passed to Bletchley Park for deciphering by codebreakers. The personnel working at Arkley View sent messages back to the VIs, instructing them whether or not to continue with a particular lead.

The VIs were originally instructed to listen for enemy spies transmitting from within Britain. But they soon began to intercept radio signals from across the Channel, and it became apparent that these were issuing from German High Command on the continent. These short, rather odd amateur radio messages were originally dismissed by British Naval Intelligence, but they were actually communications between members of Hitler's innermost spy ring, the Abwehr, using the guise of amateur radio hams to avoid detection. The Germans never discovered that Britain was listening in to Hitler's closest network. The VIs gave the first warnings of a massive German offensive into Belgium and Holland in the spring of 1940. And, with the very real threat of a German invasion of England via the coast of Kent, their work assumed increasing importance.

One of those three female VIs in MI8 has come to light. She was Mrs Olive (Catharine) Milne Myler. She was remembered by locals in the North Devon village of Knowle where she lived as 'the mysterious Mrs Myler'. It has been possible to piece together aspects of her life and intelligence work.

The Mysterious Mrs Myler

Olive Myler lived in a bungalow high on a hill in Church Street in the tiny village of Knowle, near Braunton. She was married to Dr John William Glenton Myler, but the couple were separated and he was not seen in Knowle.

Olive Myler's intelligence career had begun in the 1930s when she had worked for the Foreign Office, possibly in the British embassy in Vienna, and travelled to and from an East European country. She spoke fluent German and had a knowledge of other languages. Former radio amateur Ted Verney, a Barnstaple man who worked in the radio branch of the GPO (General Post Office) as an investigation officer, serviced Myler's radio equipment. He recalled how on numerous occasions during the war he called on her to check her amateur transmitting equipment and to investigate when there was outside interference on the system.[68] She confided in him that she had been a violinist in the Vienna Symphony Orchestra and had been forced to flee Vienna when the Nazis annexed Austria in March 1938.[69] There is no evidence that she fled for being Jewish, but it appears that she was working for SIS as a spy, and most likely for Thomas Kendrick. On her return to England in spring 1938, unusually for a woman at that time, she registered as a radio ham. She was given the callsign G3GH.6, which affirmed her status as a highly trained radio operator. She passed the highest exams for admission to the Radio Society of Great Britain.

In September 1939, the government impounded all private radio equipment for security reasons. All transmitters owned by radio amateurs were to be put in sealed boxes until after the war when they would be returned their owners. Myler's equipment was duly confiscated. However, the GPO did not have suitable equipment for intelligence work to monitor German transmissions, so all the radio amateurs were given back their radio receivers and many were asked by the intelligence services to become VIs. They were tasked with listening for German signals and messages on a particular frequency band. Myler became a VI under the command of Captain Norton, whose regional office was at 27 Dix's Field, Exeter, and sent her radio intercepts to Box 25, where they were decoded.[70]

Myers was rarely seen by the villagers. She had her supplies delivered to her from the local shop and post office by eight-year-old Edmund David Fry, son of the local postmaster. He recalled once seeing a revolver on the kitchen table – enough in itself to arouse significant suspicion – and that she had a 50ft radio mast in her garden, screened by tall conifers.[71] She worked long hours in her bungalow, especially during the night, when neighbours might spot a chink of light through her blackout curtains.

A local became suspicious and reported her to the authorities as a possible enemy spy. A behind-the-scenes investigation by MI5 established that she was not, and in 1941, to avoid further suspicion, she was issued with the uniform of the Royal Observer Corps, which she wore on a very few occasions when she went into the village post office herself. When the neighbourhood boys became too interested in her work and peered through her windows, a large aviary was constructed across the French doors of the dining room to prevent them prying.

Uncovering Myler's story in official records was difficult because of her top-secret work, but the research yielded results. Rather than home-made, her radio transmitters and receivers (RME69) were commercially manufactured and supplied by Radio Manufacturers & Engineers Ltd. Shortly after her registration as a radio ham, an article appeared in print: 'The very fine rig illustrated here cannot strictly be called the other man's station, because actually it is owned and operated by Mrs CH Myler, Knowle, Braunton, North Devon, who has recently been licensed after a spell as 2CHY under the call G3GH . . . In welcoming Mrs Myler to the growing ranks of our feminine supporters in the game of amateur radio, dare we whisper that in correspondence with the local boys she has been known to sign herself Grandma.'[72] It is a great piece of reporting about her.

Myler made a particularly outstanding contribution to the work of the Radio Security Service, for which she was one of only six VIs and the only woman to receive a British Empire Medal in February 1946.[73] She probably never knew the precise reason why she received the BEM; she was simply informed that it was for 'exceptional service rendered during the war'. The real reason was that she was apparently the only VI in Britain to pick up signals one night regarding the location of particular U-boats.[74] This was at a time when U-boats were devastating in their attacks on Allied convoys and supply lines and, despite RAF bombings of the submarine pens around Brest, on the French coast, British supply ships were still being sunk. Myler intercepted signals from the German base control indicating that their U-boats were being loaded in special pens 25 miles inland. The base was subsequently bombed, hence protecting the British food and equipment convoys. An obituary described her as 'a first class operator in every way'.[75] She had a fund of good humour, was generous in nature and a good friend to all radio hams in the North Devon area; her passing was 'mourned by many amateur friends at home and abroad'. Her wartime career, however, seemed to be almost totally hidden in the shadows of MI6 secrecy.[76] Like so many of those who were stationed at top-secret sites like Bletchley Park and elsewhere, she took her secrets to the grave.

The history of women in codes and cryptanalysis is one of immense achievements and a source of national pride since the stories began to break in the 1970s, even though their contributions have been hidden for so long. Only today, with the benefit of declassified files, is it possible to begin to assess the impact of their codebreaking and analysis for the outcome of the war. Bletchley Park was one of the best kept wartime secrets. At its sister site at Eastcote, near Ruislip, hundreds of Wrens had operated the bombe machines.

After the war, Eastcote became the headquarters for the newly formed GCHQ. Women like Emily Anderson continued to be engaged at GCHQ. Others did not continue with a career in intelligence, often because of the restrictions on women's roles in society as wives and homemakers primarily responsible for raising children. They were demobbed and returned to civilian life.

7
WHEN THE WALLS HAD EARS

British intelligence believed that one of the most valuable sources of intelligence in any war was prisoners of war. The challenge was how to gain the information without contravening the Geneva Convention or using third-degree methods (physical violence or torture) – which in any case leads to unreliable results. A new branch of military intelligence, MI9, was established in December 1939 to handle intelligence from POWs, whether they were Allied personnel who had evaded capture or escaped from prisoner of war camps, or enemy POWs held in special sites in the UK. MI9 was as top secret as MI5 and MI6 and women were central to gathering intelligence from this vital source.

Under the umbrella of MI9, a new unit was created. It was the Combined Services Detailed Interrogation Centre (CSDIC); its rather obscure name was designed to mask its real identity as one of the foremost organisations for gathering intelligence about the enemy. It was commanded by MI6 spymaster Thomas Joseph Kendrick and secretly eavesdropped on German prisoners of war in their cells.[1] The covert operation functioned from September 1939 until December 1945 and was a tri-services unit of army, air and naval intelligence. Operating first at the Tower of London, then Trent Park at Cockfosters from the end of 1939, its importance in gleaning valuable information from POWs meant that two further country estates were requisitioned by Kendrick in 1941. These were Latimer House near Chesham and Wilton Park at Beaconsfield, both in Buckinghamshire.

Intelligence personnel first arriving at these sites came before Kendrick, who explained the nature of their work. They all had to sign the Official Secrets Act and were told that they could never divulge the location or nature of their work to anyone. Among the intelligence personnel were the male secret listeners – German émigrés fleeing Nazism, the majority of them Jewish. They worked in a special room known as the 'M Room' (M for miked), with equipment to covertly record the conversations of German POWs in their rooms. The POWs never found out about the existence of the M Rooms.

As Pauline Rubin, one of the many women who worked at these clandestine sites, recalled:

> What made this such a special unit was that it was the only one of its kind in that it employed what was at that time a very sophisticated and unique method of obtaining information from prisoners of war. Cells contained hidden microphones which were manned 24 hours a day and records were cut of any significant conversations that took place. These were the days long before tape recordings. The prisoners suspected that there might be microphones and on entering cells they searched for them but invariably failed to detect them.[2]

At the three secret sites, tiny microphones were hidden in the light fittings and fireplaces. At Trent Park they were even hidden behind the skirting boards and picture frames, as well as in plant pots, the billiards table and the trees in the grounds. The microphones were wired back to the M Room where the POWs' conversations were recorded onto 78 rpm acetate discs. The conversations were transcribed the same day, then the original German and English translation typed up. With three sites, this unit gathered intelligence on an industrial scale. By the end of the war CSDIC had amassed some 75,000 transcripts of conversations and intelligence reports.

After May 1942, a number of Hitler's generals and senior officers were taken to Trent Park after capture on the battlefields of North Africa.[3] Hitler's top commanders continued to arrive at the house after capture in Sicily and Italy and after D-Day. Given a life of relative comfort, they soon relaxed and began talking among themselves on a range of military subjects and German battle plans, little knowing that the hidden microphones were picking up everything they discussed. Thereby they inadvertently gave up secrets of the Nazi regime to British intelligence. Three 'M Rooms' in the basement at Trent Park gathered intelligence that would never have been obtained in an interrogation. It was such a clever ruse. The deception went even further, with the creation of a fake aristocrat to befriend Hitler's senior officers. He was 'Lord Aberfeldy', with estates and a castle in Scotland. In reality, he was senior Military Intelligence officer Ian Thomson Munro, who was 'briefed as to the imaginary land that he owned . . . His handkerchiefs had an embroidered coronet and he had a coat of arms on all of his belongings.'[4]

By 1942, a thousand intelligence personnel were working across the three sites, at least a third of whom were women. While it is true that women were assigned to clerical duties, translation work and the typing up of thousands of prisoners' conversations, they began to take on intelligence roles that traditionally had been assigned to men.

Female officers of the Air Intelligence Section (AD(I)K) were responsible for analysing and assessing the intelligence coming out of the 'M Rooms'. They sorted the material for its intelligence value and made decisions about which commanders or departments across the armed forces needed to receive a copy. It was a huge responsibility and the women were conscious of the trust being placed in them. The women in the small naval intelligence section became interrogators, and those serving in the army intelligence section were enlisted into the ATS and attached to the Intelligence Corps. For the first time, the latter were entitled to wear the badge of the Intelligence Corps.

The women attached to CSDIC from all three services contributed to one of the most far-reaching intelligence-gathering units of the war; the operation successfully bugged the conversations of over 10,000 German POWs of all ranks as well as Hitler's top generals. Pauline Rubin was just eighteen years old when she enlisted in the ATS and was sent for an interview to join an organisation that was recruiting German-speaking personnel. After being interviewed by five male army officers, she was sent for officer training and attached to the Intelligence Corps. She worked briefly at Trent Park, firstly in the rank of 2nd subaltern (equivalent to 2nd lieutenant), before moving to Latimer House. Promotion for the commissioned female officers was more or less automatic after a certain period of time.

Since the publication of the full history of the three sites of Trent Park, Latimer House and Wilton Park in my book *The Walls Have Ears:*

The Greatest Intelligence Operation of World War Two, further material has come to light on the roles of the female personnel employed there.

MI19

By 1942, MI9 had become such a large branch of military intelligence dealing with Allied and Axis prisoners of war that it split into MI9 and MI19. Both were headquartersed in the same administration block at Wilton Park. MI9 assumed sole responsibility for escape and evasion of Allied POWs, still under the command of Norman Crockatt, and MI19 dealt with intelligence from Axis prisoners of war (and included CSDIC under its wing). MI19 was commanded by Lieutenant-Colonel Arthur Rawlinson ('Rawli'), a man in his early fifties, skilled in delegating work to his staff so that he was free to make policy decisions. He kept nothing on his desk, except a blotter and two telephones, a black one and a red one. The red telephone was for scrambling and unscrambling messages of extreme secrecy.[5] His personal assistant was Dawn Rockingham-Gill (later Mrs Doble) and she liaised on his behalf between MI19 and other departments on all top-secret matters, as well as signing off and despatching classified intelligence reports.[6]

Working alongside her was ATS officer 'Tigger' Agar-Robartes whose job was to censor prisoners' letters and search for any small clues or information that could be useful for intelligence. Her colleague Junior Commander Elizabeth Angas worked in a key administrative and organisational role for CSDIC. Then, because of her fluency in French and German, she was transferred to CSDIC Mediterranean, where she gained knowledge of and expertise in the situation in Greece.[7] Working with CSDIC Mediterranean was Captain L. Landsberg. She had knowledge of German and Afrikaans and carried out the translation of X reports (the transcripts of the bugged conversations from the M Rooms). She was responsible for all the main Italian series of transcripts coming out of the CSDIC posts in the Mediterranean. Junior Commander K.H. Phillips had a good command of the French, German and Portuguese languages, and excellent secretarial qualifications, and therefore became personal assistant to the commander-in-chief of CSDIC Mediterranean. It was recorded that she 'knew the work of CSDIC thoroughly'.[8]

Back at Latimer House in Buckinghamshire, Cynthia Turner (née Crew) and Elisabeth Bruegger (née Rees-Mogg), both British-born, carried out important intelligence analysis for Denys Felkin, head of the air intelligence section attached to CSDIC.

Cynthia Turner had joined the WAAF in 1942 and trained at Morecambe in Lancashire, then worked as secretary to the camp commandant at RAF 61 Maintenance unit near Manchester. One day she had seen a poster on the noticeboard appealing for German-speakers and, aged just twenty-one years old, she submitted her name. She was transferred to Latimer House where she first began as a clerk, undertaking general clerical duties including maintaining a card index of the names of all the senior German air force officers being held as POWs across the CSDIC sites in the UK. She soon acquired more important responsibilities and was given secret reports (SR) in English and German from the M Room for assessment. She had to decide if the intelligence was urgent enough to flag up immediately, and to mark up the useful information that must be distributed forthwith to the various intelligence branches and commanders.[9] This was highly important analysis, relying on her acuity in understanding and assessing the vital information emanating from the eavesdropping on prisoners' conversations. Of interest to British intelligence was information on enemy positions, its aircraft and squadrons, new technology and, of highest priority, details connected to Hitler's secret weapons. Turner was to note information and anecdotal stories from the prisoners that could be used in the British radio propaganda broadcasts. There were rumours of gas chambers, concentration camps and discussions of atrocities – all to be flagged up for war crimes trials at the end of the war.

Elisabeth Bruegger's job was to receive unedited documents from the M Rooms, analyse the intelligence and extract useful information, then file it on card indexes. The system was frequently used by interrogators as a source of information. For example, if an intelligence report was being compiled about the movement of German fighter squadrons, the interrogator came to Bruegger and asked what relevant information she had on the subject from previous interrogations (which may have originally been carried out by a different interrogator). She worked directly for Squadron Leader Roffey of ADI(K) at Latimer House and recalled:

> We did not do any code-breaking, but some of us knew about Bletchley Park because the officers visited us from the code-breaking site. Our specialisation was important prisoners of war – the grumpy, middle-aged generals whose conversations were recorded and transcribed. There were other sources of information; for example, that came from brave Dutch sea-farers who crossed the North Sea to bring news of German activities in the Netherlands or the current situation at the Phillips company in Eindhoven.[10]

For Bruegger, their work represented the best of cooperation between army, navy and air intelligence, and, from the end of 1941, in conjunction with US intelligence. The working hours were long, but the women contributed to a unit that was gathering intelligence on an industrial scale. It became highly efficient.

M Room Tech

Twenty-one-year-old Catherine Townshend was another female intelligence officer who soon found herself undertaking work traditionally assigned to male officers. On 22 January 1942, she was asked to report to the War Office because she was a gifted linguist who was serving in the FANY. She had worked as a batwoman, orderly and staff car driver. Now she was about to undertake top-secret work for Kendrick's eavesdropping unit. She first reported to Major John Back of MI9 at the Metropole Building in Whitehall. He impressed on her the need for strict security in the work she was about to undertake. She received orders to proceed by underground from her home in South Kensington to Cockfosters station, with no idea of the final destination, except that it was a highly secret site. When she arrived at Cockfosters, an army car was waiting and transported her to Trent Park, which was also known as 'Cockfosters Camp'.[11] She wrote to her mother: 'I wish I could tell you about my work. I can only say that it sounds exciting and interesting.' Her first day at Trent Park was noted in her brief diary entry for 23 January 1942: 'First day at Cockfosters Camp, Barnet. Interview with Col. Kendrick. Signing papers. Seems most interesting work.'[12]

Townshend's work gave her an insight into just how valuable enemy POWs were for gaining intelligence: 'Each prisoner was questioned at length on German strategy, Hitler's domination of almost all of Europe, and the possible invasion of the British Isles. More important were subjects such as radar, scientific research, codes, spies, and troop movements. POWs were not maltreated, but were comfortably housed and fed according to rank.' She went on to praise the work of Mr J.F. Doust, a civilian and chief engineer at the Post Office Engineering Research Station, Dollis Hill, North London: 'J.F. Doust at the Post Office Research Department developed tiny and sensitive microphones; he was far ahead of the Germans in this field of engineering. Soldiers in every [Axis] army were warned that if captured they must beware of microphones in prison cells, but Doust's inventions were seldom, if ever, discovered by the enemy . . . [unguarded conversations were] recorded for subsequent typing and distribution to all branches of intelligence.'[13]

At Trent Park, Townshend's work began with typing duties, but she was too slow for interrogator Captain Marsh and he transferred her to the map room on site, where she was responsible for charting Axis army divisions on land and German ships at sea.[14] This included the daily plotting of key German battleships, the *Scharnhorst* and the *Gneisenau*. In March 1942, she plotted the famous British commando raid at Saint-Nazaire.

In early autumn 1942, Townshend was transferred from Trent Park to Wilton Park in Buckinghamshire to join MI19(e), the section within MI19 that was responsible for setting up new M Room sites, including the ordering of relevant equipment and maintaining oversight of the eavesdropping technology, acquisition of suitable personnel and gaining security clearance from MI5 for new staff members.[15] She was selected to join Back and a Miss Winifred Felce because 'none of the efficient German-speaking women officers at Trent Park could be spared from the daily pressure of typing reports'.[16]

On arrival at Wilton Park, she was greeted by Lieutenant-Colonel Rawlinson, who explained the nature of her work and that her immediate boss would be Major Back. Back kept no records of his time as head of MI19(e) because negotiations with the inventors and suppliers of microphones was highly classified. His only staff, Townshend and Felce, were expected to have an encyclopaedic memory and expertise in their specialist technological work.

Townshend wrote to her mother: 'The work is more important and varied than at Cockfosters. Felce and I can call upon three clerks – we ourselves never use a typewriter.'[17] That was as much as she was permitted to say.

On 5 October 1942 Townshend was called into Back's office. He explained that he and Felce were leaving that morning for (unspecified) secret work. He explained that as the only person who knew this highly classified job, Townshend was to be the new head of MI19(e). This young female intelligence officer became the expert on M Room technology, sending out listening equipment and recording machines to interrogation centres in England, the Middle East, India and Australia, as well as mobile listening vehicles.[18] It highlights an important point – that the intelligence services were often decades ahead of civilian life in appointing the right person for the job, irrespective of gender. Had they been held back by gender prejudice, it would have been easy to find a male officer to replace Back; instead, MI19(e) looked only for expertise and competence, and installed Townshend as its head.

The same morning that Back and Felce left Wilton Park, Townshend walked into her new office to find an alarming amount of material piled in the in tray. She was determined to succeed and immediately began to tackle the memos and correspondence. After drafting replies, she took them across the hall for Rawlinson, head of MI19, to approve. He also gave her the responsibility of keeping up the operations map in his office.

Townshend liaised with another top-secret site, Latchmere House – MI5's secret interrogation centre at Ham, near Richmond, known as Camp 020. Commanded by Lieutenant-Colonel Robin 'Tin Eye' Stephens, it played a crucial role in the Double Cross deception, whereby captured German spies and agents were interrogated and attempts made to 'turn' them to work for the Allies as double agents, which some did.[19] MI19(e) supplied microphones for Camp 020 to listen in to conversations of those being held there. Communication between Camp 020 and MI19(e) was conducted by scrambler telephone or correspondence.

Townshend recalled: 'For months, everything went smoothly until I received a request from the commandant [Stephens] for permission from the War Office to promote members of his staff. Rawli ordered me to refuse, with a polite explanation that the establishment of 020 did not permit higher ranks.' Exchanges became tense and Stephens threatened to turn up at Wilton Park, which he then did. Rawli was away in Whitehall, and Townshend faced the irate and formidable Stephens on her own: 'Tall, with a black patch over one eye, he strode along the corridors of Camp 20 [Wilton Park], flung open the door of my office, and stood for a moment in amazement before bursting into a loud laugh. "Are you Junior Commander Townshend?" he asked, "I thought you were going to be a fierce bureaucrat in her fifties!" '[20]

MI19(e) remained a small unit, consisting of Townshend and Junior Commander (Mrs) Enever, both of whom were engaged on duties relating to the administration and replacement of equipment for the M Rooms. Towards the end of the war, they were joined by Elizabeth Burton. These female officers were based at Wilton Park; their cover address on headed notepaper was Room 327, Hotel Victoria, Northumberland Avenue. They corresponded directly with chief engineer J.F. Doust at Dollis Hill and his secretary Miss Ward; the latter also became an expert on this top secret technical operation.

So, in an extraordinary turn of events, one of the most sensitive and secret roles in military intelligence was undertaken solely by young female intelligence officers. These stories of the women behind the sophisticated technology relied upon by British intelligence have hitherto been hidden by official secrecy.

The eavesdropping programme continued at the UK sites after war's end, until November 1945. CSDIC still had operations in India as the war was not yet over in the Far East.[21] The techniques were required too by new Allied intelligence teams in post-war Europe, and Townshend, Enever and Burton supplied the equipment necessary to set up M Rooms at CSDIC sites in post-war Germany and Austria. It was a huge financial investment. The cost of supplying eavesdropping equipment to Captain Copping of CSDIC in Germany to support military intelligence operations there amounted to a staggering £3,500 alone.[22] The US forces used M Room technology in post-war Austria for counter-intelligence operations. They were supplied by MI19(e) with five mobile units of recording equipment and bugging devices at a cost of £12,000.[23] On this occasion, it was Enever who coordinated what was required and despatched the equipment to the US army. At the end of 1945, Townshend received instructions from Doust on how to return all the listening equipment from the CSDIC sites in the UK to Dollis Hill. The women of MI19(e) – the sole workforce in this department of military intelligence – were responsible for decommissioning the three M Room sites in the UK.

Recruiting Secret Listeners

Running the M Room tech was not the only significant role that Townshend carried out while with MI19. With Colonel Kendrick, and two other officers (Major Corner and Major Le Bosquet), from 1943 she conducted interviews in London to expand the teams of secret listeners and recruit new personnel. The demand for native German-speakers as secret listeners had become pressing for Kendrick because the nature of the intelligence from the M Rooms often involved unfamiliar technological terms or dialects that were hard to understand for non-German linguists. Rawlinson asked Townshend to investigate a source that had not yet been tapped – the German and Austrian Jewish refugees in the army's Pioneer Corps. These young men had fled persecution and concentration camps in Nazi Germany and found sanctuary in England.[24]

Townshend recalled: 'I attended the interviews, sought security clearances through MI5 afterwards, and in the weeks that followed, sent successful candidates their instructions to report to Beaconsfield or Latimer. The long and careful questioning by Lt. Col. Kendrick prepared me for the role of interviewer, a task that I had to assume in the year ahead.'[25] In her scant personal diary, she noted in pencil 'interviews' on the days that she and Kendrick interviewed prospective secret listeners. She travelled from Wilton Park to London for these, often weekly, and in her absence, as the office work still needed to be done, Margaret Morley (ATS) became her assistant. They became firm friends.

Around a hundred male German-speaking refugees transferred to CSDIC as secret listeners, one of whom was Fritz Lustig. On 18 March 1943, he arrived at the Metropole Building to find about a dozen other candidates waiting for interview, all ex-refugees from Germany or

Austria. He was ushered into an interview room where a board of six officers, including one woman (now known to have been Townshend), awaited him. Lustig made a sufficiently good impression to be asked for a second interview after lunch, and he got the job. Later, at Latimer House, Townshend continued to help Lustig by correcting letters he wrote to her in English, improving his knowledge of the language.

Female Interrogators

Women like Townshend continued to be at the forefront of intelligence at this time, taking groundbreaking roles, including – for the first time in intelligence history – as interrogators. Interrogation was a role traditionally assigned solely to men, but, as an MI9 file boldly states, 'the right type of woman is as good an interrogator as a man'.[26]

The use of women as interrogators is borne out by declassified naval intelligence files and is supported by fascinating psychological analysis of what might provoke German prisoners into giving up information.[27] Placing two female interrogators in an interrogation room was a new move, designed to completely throw the German prisoners off guard. Not knowing what was to happen next, the prisoners instinctively became cooperative. Coupled with that, British intelligence understood that the men would feel humiliated to be interrogated by a woman – and these were emotions that could be exploited to break them. The employment of women in this role, as early as 1941, was a clever call and one that underlined a principle within British intelligence of using the right person, man or woman, to achieve results.

At the beginning of 1942, there was only one Wren officer in the naval intelligence section attached to CSDIC at Latimer House, but this was soon increased to four, all of whom were employed in interrogation. At its peak, the section consisted of five Wren petty officers and one chief Wren, the latter (in addition to her supervisor duties) being responsible for running the office. The female interrogators are named in naval intelligence files: Third Officer Esme Mackenzie (appointed July 1941), Second Officers Evelyn Barron and Jean Flower (appointed 1942), Miss Celia Thomas, Third Officer Claudia Furneaux (appointed 1943), Petty Officer Wren Hales (appointed

1943), Gwendoline Neel-Wall, Third Officer Betty Colls (appointed 1944), Petty Officer V. Lennard (appointed April 1944), Petty Officer writer M. Barton (appointed 7 June 1944), Petty Officer E. Duckers (also appointed 7 June 1944), K. Pearce (appointed 13 June 1944) and Petty Officer J. Day (appointed September 1944).[28] All were young women in their twenties, unmarried or widowed. It is not known whether their age was a conscious decision by Naval Intelligence, but possibly their youth and charm would be more effective on the German prisoners in encouraging those prisoners to be relaxed and open.

The first woman in the uniformed services to be appointed as an interrogator was Third Officer Esme Mackenzie. She was followed by Evelyn Barron on 25 May 1942. In a rare post-war interview, Barron revealed that the Wren officers in the naval intelligence section at Latimer House were recruited by Ian Fleming. She further commented: 'The German prisoners found it most unnerving to be interrogated by a woman and the interrogation was over before it started! They did not know how to respond to us and became cooperative.'[29]

Claudia Furneaux had an aristocratic background and was a cousin of the Earl of Birkenhead. She was reading modern languages at Somerville College, Oxford, when she appeared in a student revue in London to raise money for the friends of the French Forces Fund. She left the degree course to enlist in the Royal Navy because she wanted to serve her country. After a period of listening to German radio transmissions from various stations on the south coast of England, by 1943 she was commissioned and posted to Latimer House. While undertaking her regular duties, she was asked to escort two U-boat officers on a London pub crawl to soften up their attitude towards their British minders and reward them for providing good information.

Few personal details are known about the other female interrogators, except that Gwendoline Neel-Wall was widowed, and her only son lost with the submarine HMS *Tempest* in February 1942. Esme Jean Mackenzie was engaged to Captain Peter Watkinson of the Royal Regiment who accidentally and fatally shot himself with a German pistol in March 1941 half an hour before their wedding. She later married Brian Connell, whom she met during her time with CSDIC. It is also known that CSDIC stations that were established abroad occasionally used female interrogators, as in the case of CSDIC Cairo.

The work of the Wren interrogators, as with their male counterparts, involved familiarising themselves with all details that might come up during an interrogation. Each interrogator was a specialist in at least one area of the German navy. They kept the Admiralty fully informed on the new torpedoes which Germany was developing, often giving very detailed descriptions, which enabled the Admiralty to design countermeasures before the weapons became operational. One interrogator was able to provide a full description of the submarine bubble target, a device whereby U-boats were able to produce a false target and escape behind a screen. This kind of information was unique to CSDIC and did not come via other intelligence units, underlining the huge value of this work. By the middle of 1942, when the German navy began to develop new methods and technological services on a large scale, the results of interrogation became of the highest importance to the war. By then, the naval interrogators had built up a large background and the reliability of the intelligence was well known among the services.

As well as housing MI9 headquarters and one of the eavesdropping centres, Wilton Park was used to interrogate Allied escapers and evaders after their return to the UK.[30] Interrogation was always conducted by a specially trained officer as it was deemed better to have a few trained interrogators than a large number of untrained ones. Female interrogators Second Officer E.A. Hughes (WAAF) and Second Subaltern Jackson (ATS) carried out many of these interrogations. Hughes's signature clearly appears on reports of escapers and evaders. It was noted that 'besides being responsible for the whole of office routine [at Wilton Park], she carried out occasional interrogations very efficiently'.[31] The interrogations provided useful intelligence for MI9 in planning escape routes, updating escape and evasion training manuals and providing details of conditions in enemy-occupied countries. Information of interest to home security was passed to MI5.

Interrogation Reports

In the first half of the war, the writing and editing of reports of interrogation was largely undertaken by the interrogators themselves, until their workload became too heavy due to the influx of POWs. As the amount of work swelled, the Wren personnel were increased.[32] The Wren analysts who came to be attached to CSDIC vastly improved the quality and focus of the intelligence reports. They synthesised the different sources of data available to CSDIC, from interrogation reports to M Room transcripts, from which they produced a single view of the intelligence product and, importantly, of its reliability. The finest intelligence was useless unless it was believed and acted on.

Prior to 1942 the distribution of intelligence could be slow, but this changed with the increase in the number of shorthand typists. To ensure the swift supply and distribution of all intelligence available, a special staff of Wren officers in the Admiralty were trained to write and edit the summaries. They were assigned to writing the intelligence reports, while the Wren ratings dealt with the immediate distribution of interrogation reports. Based in the Admiralty, Miss M. Maggs was appointed in August 1942 as a civilian assistant officer to Colin McFadyean, head of the German sub-section. She was responsible for the circulation of German POW information in the Admiralty and assigned to the handling of documents and distribution of intelligence from prisoners of war. Later, she handled intelligence gained from captured documents from various departments once the Allied forces entered Germany.

By the middle of 1943, the amount of valuable information that needed to be shared with other departments and required quick promulgation became so great that a decision was taken to issue a weekly summary of the information obtained from German naval POWs. Depending on the amount of information available in any one week, the summary ranged from half a dozen pages to over fifty pages of A4. The female officers kept a daily record of the results of interrogation and, at the end of every week, compiled them into a summary of raw intelligence. Their hard work and efficiency meant that no information in the summaries was more than a week old. The summaries enabled recipients in relevant departments and branches of intelligence to have a constant overview of German naval activity, as well as developments in enemy torpedo technology and other new weapons. This work was duplicated by the officers working in the army and air intelligence sections of CSDIC.

Weapons Intelligence

CSDIC personnel were the first to hear accounts by prisoners of new German scientific and industrial developments, including information about the V-weapons being developed at Peenemünde on the north coast of Germany. Suspicions about Peenemünde had led to reconnaissance missions by the RAF in 1942, but nothing concrete had come of them. Intelligence on Hitler's secret weapons continued to come from a number of different clandestine sources, including agents behind enemy lines, but it needed to be corroborated by an indisputable source. That validation came in early 1943 from CSDIC's eavesdropping programme.

On 12 March, the secret listeners at Latimer House were the first to overhear a conversation between two German paratroopers concerning the V-weapons, but the ultimate corroborative evidence came around ten days later from Hitler's generals at Trent Park. The generals and senior German officers were thoroughly disillusioned by news that Stalingrad had finally fallen in early 1943. They worried that this meant they had lost the war. General von Thoma, captured in North Africa in November 1942, revealed to a fellow general (unnamed in the transcripts) that Hitler had a weapons programme that would win the war. This was when discussions turned to more detailed information on the V-1 vengeance weapon being developed at Peenemünde. As a direct result of these bugged conversations, Peenemünde was confirmed as the secret weapon site and was bombed on 17 August 1943, rendering it non-operational, and thus setting back Hitler's V-weapon programme by nine months. (For a fuller picture of the photographic intelligence operation behind the elimination of the V-1 programme, see p. 186.)

Cynthia Turner recalled how, on one occasion, Air Minister Sir Archibald Sinclair visited Latimer House to congratulate the teams on their fine work. Memories were vivid for her, too, of the early hours of 6 June 1944, with the non-stop drone of aircraft flying over Latimer House, heading for the D-Day operation.

On other intelligence gained, Pauline Rubin remembered how they first learnt for the Admiralty about the new secret German naval weapon, the one-man midget submarine. This type of diver propulsion vehicle enabled a single crewman to fix a limpet mine to the underside of Allied warships; the crewman was unlikely to return to base, hence they were referred to as suicide submarines.

In September 1944, the German generals were overheard talking among themselves about a much faster and more powerful vengeance weapon, the V-2. This 13-ton rocket carried a 1-ton warhead, and could travel 200 miles from its launch site, inflicting devastating damage where it landed. There was no warning of its approach and no deterrent. The hidden microphones picked up these conversations and alerted the Allies to search for the secret V-2 installations.

After the Allied landings in Normandy on 6 June 1944, intelligence began to take another form. There continued to be a stream of intelligence from German prisoners of war that had thus far been the primary source of detailed information on German naval weapons and technology. Now the Allies began to capture the equipment itself, along with various handbooks and documents. So, as well as continuing to collect ongoing intelligence from POWs at secret sites, it became important to extract intelligence from the captured evidence – a role undertaken by the female naval intelligence personnel, too. This gave the interrogators a new and continuous supply of the fullest possible information about the German navy. Previously, the greatest number of German naval prisoners had come from U-boats operating in the Atlantic, but now the Allies began to capture survivors from various types of small battle units, U-boats working close inshore and E-boats that were threatening Allied lines of communication to the continent. All prisoners continued to be interrogated, but efforts were particularly concentrated on the most vital intelligence, which was now chiefly operational rather than about new technology. This material was at the heart of the weekly intelligence summaries which continued to be issued until shortly after the surrender of Germany in May 1945. A total of 130 weekly intelligence summaries were compiled and edited by the women.

In the closing days of the war, there was a fear that Germany might yet have some weapon of mass destruction that would cause a new Armageddon. No evidence of such a weapon was found in post-war Germany; however, other interesting documents were discovered. Three aircraft a week, full of documents, began to arrive at Latimer House for analysis by the women and men of the air intelligence section. The sheer volume of material was overwhelming and the team – among them, intelligence officer Cynthia Turner – was moved to the Air Ministry building in Monck Street, central London.[33]

Émigré Women

From the summer of 1942, once Latimer House and Wilton Park were fully functioning alongside Trent Park, the volume of intelligence work from thousands of captured German POWs necessitated an increase in staff. Colonel Kendrick received authorisation to increase the quota of ATS women working across his sites, and this is when he began to draft in German Jewish émigré women who had been forced to flee Nazi Germany.[34] They were assigned to keeping Axis prisoners' personal records and translating bugged conversations, as well as typing and reproducing reports in German. Native German-speakers were required for this work and this was the leading factor in recruiting these émigré women who were enlisted into the ATS and attached to the Intelligence Corps. Among them was Gerda Engel, born in Breslau, whose father was a dentist. Her family was forced to flee to England in 1935 after the Nazi regime forbade Jews to hold professional jobs. During the war, Gerda was based at Latimer House and Wilton Park, where she became close friends with Susan Lustig (née Cohn), also from Breslau and born the same year as Gerda.

Susan fled Nazi persecution and arrived in England on a domestic permit in July 1939 where she obtained work in North London. On the day war broke out, her employer dismissed her, 'not wanting a German living in her house', so Susan joined the Engel family and trained as assistant in their dental practice. In 1943, she enlisted in the ATS and, after a number of other postings, met with Gerda Engel during a period of leave in London. In December 1943, Gerda, who was by now a sergeant in the Intelligence Corps, recommended her for transfer to the same secret unit. Susan had no idea what that work was, but underwent an interview and a series of aptitude tests in London. She was successful and a month later received a letter for transfer to Latimer House.

She recalled: 'It was all very exciting. I had a railway ticket to Chalfont and Latimer station and was told that I would be met there.

A very smart naval officer and his driver waited for me in a jeep outside. As I got into the car the driver said to me: "I bet you a packet of cigarettes that you'll be a sergeant by tonight." I didn't believe him. That evening, I was unexpectedly promoted to sergeant and I owed him a packet of cigarettes!'[35]

Susan spent time at both Latimer House and Wilton Park, where she was tasked with overseeing prisoners' files and card indexes. She was not permitted to speak about her work to any other personnel on site, even though they had all signed the Official Secrets Act. On one occasion she came across the papers of a former teacher from her school in Breslau. He was being held prisoner by CSDIC and she knew that he was no Nazi. She recalled how she put in a good word for him and he was soon transferred to another regular POW camp.

While working at CSDIC, Susan met secret listener Fritz Lustig and they embarked on a romance.[36] They married on 6 June 1945 with Kendrick's permission, as per army rules for serving personnel at that time. Theirs was not the only romance on the site. Several relationships became permanent and one of these was between Junior Commander Madeline Grugeon and Captain Mario Manzone of the US army. At Latimer House, Claudia Furneaux met her future husband, US interrogator Harry Lennon.

Daily Life

A glimpse of daily life for the women working for CSDIC can be found in a handful of rare unpublished reminiscences. These provide an important backdrop to understanding the life and roles of the women in particular branches of military intelligence. Elizabeth Bruegger commented: 'Life in the Sergeants' Mess was pleasant and congenial; association was very easy – several of us got together to do the *Times* crossword. We were very well fed. Service rations were larger than for the civilian population and we appointed a member of the Sergeants' Mess as catering officer. There were two or three amongst them who had pre-war experience of the catering business and we benefited from that.'[37]

In her privately published memoirs, Catherine Townshend provides some humorous touches of life at Trent Park: 'During our lunch hour, on fine spring days, six of us women walked across the fields of daffodils to a rifle range in the park where a corporal guardsman taught us how to shoot . . . We were amused to see, when censoring a prisoner's letter to his headquarters in Berlin, that he had observed us from his window and written: "Churchill is training women to fight." '[38]

At Latimer House, the women slept two to a room in a Nissen hut annexed to the old mansion and overlooking the Chess valley. Pauline Rubin recalled, 'The furniture and furnishings were adequate and we had the service of a batwoman to clean the room, do our ironing and generally look after us. Meals were taken in the officers' mess and all officers were expected to appear on time.'[39] They worked in shifts, sometimes finishing around 11 p.m., but working later if necessary. No visitors were allowed into the camp and they therefore had to provide their own entertainment. This consisted of dances, occasional cabaret and parties with games. The bar was open till late and was extremely well stocked. Personnel from the Royal Corps of Signals who were working at Latimer House and Wilton Park provided music for weekend dances and the Christmas ball.

Pauline Rubin recalled: 'Our food was adequate but rather monotonous. By comparison, American servicemen and women had daily banquet. Many items were rationed and fresh eggs, sweets, meat were a real treat. Fresh milk was doled out to women personnel only. Men had to make do with the powdered version.' Reflecting decades later, she concluded with some nostalgia, 'my army days when soldiers, sailors and airmen saluted me seem quite unbelievably far off'.

The role of women in wartime intelligence is often a hidden story, difficult to recover. The women of CSDIC never talked about their work – bound as they were by the oath of secrecy, having signed the Official Secrets Act. The unit's existence had to be protected at all cost, even into the Cold War and beyond. It would be at least sixty years before some of unit's former members broke their silence – and only after they were sure that the official files had been declassified, finally being released between 1999 and 2004. And when they could speak of it, they were modest about what they had done. They believed their contribution was not important enough to talk about. In actuality, their work was essential to the success of the eavesdropping programme and an invaluable service that helped to win the war.

By the time the files were released, the majority of CSDIC's women had already passed away. They went to their graves bearing some of the most highly sensitive secrets of a nation. Most did not live to see their story become public knowledge and understand exactly how their contribution at the three clandestine POW intelligence sites made a material difference to the outcome of the war.

8
WOMEN OF NAVAL INTELLIGENCE

Intelligence practices underwent a major change in the 1939–45 war with the establishment of tri-service intelligence units. This transformation saw the closest cooperation between the services, not only in information gathering, but in working practices on the same clandestine sites. Army, naval and air intelligence worked together at various secret locations in the UK, as has been seen with Bletchley Park, the CSDIC eavesdropping programme and RAF Medmenham (intelligence from aerial photography). This greater cooperation across the three services was a triumph in enabling the Allies to win the intelligence war against Nazi Germany. It brought a closer and more immediate understanding of the inter-service intelligence work and analysis than if each service had operated independently. It brought a realisation that information gained by one service could be relevant to another service. This chapter focuses primarily on women's roles within Naval Intelligence at the Admiralty, which liaised closely with other branches of military intelligence, including MI5, MI6 and MI14 (the latter regarding Germany and German-occupied territories). The role of Wrens and naval civilians across a range of tri-service intelligence units is covered in Chapters 6, 7 and 9.

Women supported and were an integral part of Naval Intelligence, though their roles are all too often underplayed in books on intelligence or in narrations about the Second World War. Hundreds of women carried out support roles for Naval Intelligence in the Registry and personnel department, overseeing records, carrying out translation duties and dealing with the distribution of vast amounts of signals material and general intelligence. In the Registry, women worked as temporary clerks and couriers, but also handled top-secret material and its despatch in sealed packets. Miss S. Gage, for instance, had been in charge of 'the most secret papers' since September 1941. The work of these women was a truly diverse, indispensable contribution to the overall success of British intelligence.

The Naval Intelligence Division (NID) of the Admiralty was located in a building on the corner of Horse Guards Parade in Whitehall.[1] Room 39 was like any other busy wartime office, its personnel consisting of clerks and typists who moved reams of paper around desks and compiled card indexes and files. The furious clack of typewriters filled the room during working hours and added to the sense of a hectic workload. The director of NID, Rear Admiral John Godfrey, held the post until 1942, when Rear Admiral Edmund Rushbrooke took over until 1946. Miss Joyce Cameron was Godfrey's secretary, and then Rushbrooke's. This was a position of responsibility which gave her access to the most highly classified intelligence material and knowledge of clandestine operations. One of NID's most famous officers was Ian Fleming, Godfrey's right-hand man and the brains behind many naval intelligence operations. Fleming also recruited some women to unusual jobs within Naval Intelligence, including as interrogators.

As director, Godfrey was forward-thinking in his belief that intelligence should be the role of civilians at the Admiralty, so as to allow uniformed personnel to serve on active duties. He began a drive to recruit civilians, including women, commenting that 'the next stage was to put women in men's places, but I was almost too late, for so many able women have been recruited elsewhere'.[2]

NID had around 2,000 personnel, divided into geographical departments to cover different countries abroad as well as technical material.[3] It generated vast volumes of intelligence, much of it categorised at the highest level of secrecy. NID 14, which was part of Room 39 and the personal secretariat, had responsibility for sorting the most important intelligence and despatching it to whoever needed to see it. Miss R.H. de Renault-Martin, appointed on 12 August 1942, kept the secret register. The female staff of the assistant director of NID worked as clerks and shorthand typists on aspects of security and liaison with MI5 and other security organisations.

Specialist Sections

NID 1 covered intelligence from Germany, Holland, Belgium, Switzerland, Scandinavia, Finland, Denmark, Poland, Slovakia, occupied France and the Channel Islands. It was headed by Commander Tower, whose primary assistant was Miss P. Hyde, a civilian officer who undertook secretarial duties and what was described as the 'most secret' typing. She collated material and correspondence from the British and foreign press and was aided in this by Miss S.V. Reade.

NID 1 had a small team of female civilian assistants who analysed and processed intelligence. Miss E. Hart handled intelligence on the coastal defences of the countries covered by NID 1. Miss L.M. Roome was appointed in April 1942 and worked on coastal and port defences, as well as liaising with the Free French, Dutch and Belgians. Mrs N.L. Brown and Miss M.P. Maggs liaised with the Naval Intelligence personnel who were attached to CSDIC (eavesdropping on the conversations of German POWs) at secret sites based outside the Admiralty. In addition, Brown and Maggs handled captured German documents that had been impounded by Allied forces as they advanced through Germany and extracted intelligence from them. The documents were flown to the UK in vast quantities to process for information of value to the Allies.

In some sections, like NID 3, responsible for Italy, Turkey, Greece, Balkans and the Middle East, the intelligence work was carried out primarily by male officers. The women worked as assistants, clerks and shorthand typists. The same scenario was true for NID 4, which dealt with the Far East, Pacific Islands, Indian Ocean, Kenya and Australasia.

NID 5 was responsible for producing geographical handbooks for use by the military. It was based at Oxford, under the direction of Professor K. Mason, with sub-sections dealing with different countries. Women worked in each of the sections. One section consisted of fourteen women who worked under the direction of Professor J. Myres and these women carried out all the work of the section. Eleven were draughtswomen and three were typists.[4] Two women with Master's degrees were contributors and editors to a geographical handbook: Miss M.G. Jones for France and the Low Countries, and her colleague Miss

J.B. Mitchell for Greece. Once the handbooks had been printed, the work was not finished. Draughtswomen in the Drawing Office continued to revise and produce new editions of the handbooks. Working alongside the Wrens on this were ATS and WAAF women, as well as female officers preparing and revising intelligence reports for a number of geographical regions.

Related to this work was the Inter-Services Topographical Department (NID 6), which was based partly at the Bodleian Library in Oxford. It had responsibility for investigating the existing intelligence material, maps and charts and producing reports on areas for which it was essential that topographical information should be more complete. The head was Colonel S. Bassett RN, with three women working in his section on specialist duties: Mrs H. Hughes, who was the map curator and librarian, and Miss J. McComas and Miss M. Hastings, who were responsible for photographs, town plans and maps. In addition, there were some female assistants and clerks, and women working in the temporary Drawing Section. In the Registry of NID 6, a number worked as clerical staff, telephonists and typists.

At Oxford there were women working alongside their male colleagues in wireless traffic (W/T) intelligence, the training and drafting of new W/T personnel and the analysis of W/T traffic. NID 9 was responsible for wireless intelligence. In this, Miss J. Patterson was a duty officer of W/T Intelligence. There were a number of temporary female clerks, too. NID 11 covered the photographic library. Although it was headed by a male civilian officer and his assistant, the work of the section was conducted by thirty-nine temporary civilian clerks – all of whom were women. Two shorthand typists and seventy Wrens came under the command of Third Officer O. Nepean (Wren).

The female personnel in NID became specialists in intelligence and contributed in no small part to the success of processing the vast volume of material. They worked as clerks with a naval attaché in the British embassies abroad. In Cape Town, for example, eight female coders made up the whole coding section, with two women as cipher assistants. In the NID station in Singapore there were twelve temporary female assistants processing material. An intelligence station at Kandy was run entirely by ten Wrens, with First Officer Miss J. Stewart in charge. At Trincomalee, the senior censor officer was Second Officer Miss Davidson, and she had five women on her team, all Wrens. These examples demonstrate the previously hidden roles of women in intelligence.

The Russian section of NID 16 had one female civilian officer engaged on intelligence reports about the USSR and three female civilian assistants. Miss D. Sanders was engaged as a translator, alongside Mrs J. Coombe, an expert on the Soviet navy. In addition, four male officers worked in the section, alongside a Wren second officer who was a Russian interpreter. She was attached to the section exclusively for liaison duties with the Russian Naval Mission in London, Russia being on the side of the Allies from June 1941. She liaised on intelligence matters for the British Naval Mission in Moscow and naval parties in north Russia. From July 1944, Mrs R. Gardom worked on intelligence reports and coastal defences, aided by two female assistants who sent the intelligence to the Soviet navy.

Women were assigned to roles of responsibility in naval censorship in the postal and telegraph section of outposts across the UK and abroad.[5] From September 1941, the mobile naval section for the UK was run entirely by Wrens and commanded by First Officer D. Salmond.[6] The section was divided into units, all headed by female Naval Intelligence officers.[7] The postal censorship in Belfast was entirely run by women and headed by Third Officer Miss F. Reynes. In addition to these duties, the women acted as naval advisers to local postal authorities. Across the Atlantic in New York, censorship was headed by Third Officer Miss P. Taylor, working with Third Officer Miss V. Browne. In the Levant at Alexandria, Second Officer Miss V. Snook commanded censorship at the base and acted as adviser on matters of naval censorship. Her team, which had four posts, was comprised entirely of women.[8]

Other stations abroad were run by women too, including in the Middle East, Far East, the Caribbean, Africa and Australia, intercepting cable and postal communications. The role of the Bermuda 'trappers' was 'intercepting, censoring, and examining mail. Their claim to fame in the world of espionage was finding and reading secret-ink letters and helping to solve the microdot mystery'.[9] Microdots were extremely shrunk-down photographic images of text or drawings, usually to 1mm diameter, to enable secret information to be transmitted within an innocuous-seeming document. Invisible to the naked eye, they could only be found or read using magnification of 60x or higher, and it was painstaking work to check intercepted documents to see whether a microdot was present.

Being able to name some of these female figures begins a necessary process of understanding their legacy. But one of the most hidden stories of all at the Admiralty, and still relatively unknown by the public, is that of the 'Secret Ladies'.

The Secret Ladies

The 'Secret Ladies' was the unofficial title given to a group of female civil servants who worked in Room 29 of the Admiralty, all of whom held the rank of temporary section assistant. Room 29 was only accessible via Room 30 adjacent to it, and access was restricted solely to the women in those rooms. Consequently, members from other naval sections, such as couriers, had to conduct business through a hatch in the wall of the corridor. Between seven and ten women worked in Room 29 at any time, split into shifts of 9 a.m. to 6 p.m. and 6 p.m. to 9 a.m. Two were billeted on duty at night, while the daytime number could vary. Their role was to log, distribute and file the 'Z messages' – paraphrased naval Enigma messages sent to the Admiralty direct from Bletchley Park. The Admiralty was the only service that received the Z messages directly; the other services received them from MI6 naval section.[10] The Secret Ladies logged and checked all Ultra signals (as the sources referred to them) and took them to the War Registry for ciphering. It was a physically demanding job, not only because of the volume of material being handled and processed, but also the amount of walking involved in taking the typed Ultra signals immediately to the duty captain and duty commander, and then to the Registry for ciphering. Working conditions were extremely difficult as Room 29 and Room 30 were underground, with artificial light and extremely poor ventilation. The challenges of such physical conditions were explained to a Secret Lady before she started her job so she could factor this in to her decision whether to continue after the initial interview.

The Secret Ladies were drawn from various backgrounds and occupations, with no prior training that could prepare them for their role. They had to learn on the job and visits to Bletchley Park were sometimes arranged in order to help them understand Ultra material. The official job skills required to be a Secret Lady included a meticulous attention to detail, considerable physical stamina and an acceptance that one day one might be swamped with work and another comparatively idle.[11] The nature of the workload varied each day and night, which meant that there could be periods of working at full capacity, when the ladies were stretched to the limit. On a busy operational day, up to thirty Ultra signals could be dealt with and the women had to have the ability to type quickly and accurately, with urgency.

The Secret Ladies typed the intelligence summaries that were issued twice a day by the German section and daily by the Mediterranean section. This involved producing a 'headline' intelligence summary every morning by 9 a.m. – typed and checked, and at least one copy ready for despatch by courier to the Air Ministry. This could be a challenge after a long and arduous night shift when tiredness was an issue and a rush of early-morning Ultra material was coming in and had to be dealt with. Depending on the volume of material coming in, the women were entitled to a rest period of three hours during each shift, which was taken in a room on the upper floor of the Citadel that was fitted with eight bunks in two tiers. In addition, the Secret Ladies typed up other Special Intelligence summaries, including Ultra material within those summaries, for despatch by courier to commanders-in-chief and other sections. These intelligence summaries were distributed within the Admiralty in locked boxes because they were so top-secret. The official account written after the war by one of its members, Miss Kiddy, comments that 'the Secret Lady could never justifiably complain that her job was lifeless'.

Room 29 also consisted of teleprinter operators, who were known affectionately as the 'teleprincesses'. They processed 'Z' intelligence material that came from Bletchley Park via the teleprinters, and worked in three twenty-four-hour shifts, supported during the day by two

Wrens. There were four teleprincesses initially, but by May 1944, their number increased to six to deal with the influx of work. During the night shift, they were occasionally helped by the Secret Ladies. The original four teleprincesses were already civil servants working as shorthand typists. The two who joined later were given the rank of 'temporary typist'. The teleprincesses occasionally received teleprinted material from Scarborough and HMS *Flowerdown* – both listening stations that fed information to Bletchley Park. The teleprincesses could have benefited from a supervisor to portion out the work more fairly because the less conscientious colleagues took extra time off for meals and rest, leaving the others to pick up the urgent workload.

By early 1943, there were eight teleprinters in Room 29, six for receiving messages and two for sending. This was increased a year later to twelve teleprinters, to cope with the increase in incoming messages. It was not unusual for eight or nine teleprinters to be receiving intercepted W/T traffic simultaneously. There was little time to read the incoming material, and outgoing material was in code. The volume of work was described as 'physically exacting' and it was noted that 'too much praise cannot be given to certain members of this teleprinting staff who carried out – some of them for years – an uninteresting task in the most discouraging conditions'.[12] It was as demanding as that of the Secret Ladies. For the teleprincesses, the shifts entailed long hours of standing, walking back and forth between teleprinters, against the backdrop and strain of noise all day and night, and frequently renewing the paper in the teleprinter machines.

The Secret Ladies and the teleprincesses worked in very cramped conditions and confined physical spaces. The teleprinters took up a substantial amount of room leaving little for the typists, while the papers for filing were often stacked on the floor, not always leaving enough room even for a chair for each of them. The women toiled away to keep abreast of the incoming material and not allow it to pile up too much.

Operational Intelligence Centre

The Operational Intelligence Centre (OIC) inside the citadel was the eighth section of NID, also known as NID 8.[13] The OIC was established by Commander Norman Denning in 1937, one of the first commanders to recognise aerial photography as a principal source of intelligence. It initially consisted of one male naval officer and a few clerks, and from 1939 it was headed by Rear Admiral Joc Clayton. The OIC dealt with information on the movement of enemy ships, from POW interrogations at the eavesdropping sites of CSDIC and other interrogation centres, reports from agents, signals intelligence and decrypts of enemy W/T from Bletchley Park. It was responsible for operational intelligence – for example, from German naval messages. It worked, too, with intelligence from other geographical sections within NID (like NID 1) as well as the topographical department at Oxford. By 1943, the OIC was fully developed in time for the planning and processing of intelligence ahead of D-Day. In 1944, it was receiving 600 to 700 deciphered signals a day.

The OIC was sub-divided into sections to deal with specialist naval subjects and geographical areas.[14] Section 8S, the plotting section, tracked U-boats and the position of every British ship and all convoys and transports. Located in Room 41, it worked closely alongside Section 8X in the same room. Section 8X carried out the directional finding (D/F) of U-boats. During the 'wolf pack' attacks on Allied supply convoys, plotting charts enabled a picture of the U-boat dispositions to be assembled fairly swiftly. If a U-boat was near an Allied convoy, the plotters had to send an signal immediately, giving full details of the time, length and origin of the signal that they had picked up from that U-boat. Plotters often worked on 'hunches' which were inexplicable to outsiders, but often proved correct, and these hunches only came after long experience in the job. Towards the end of 1942, the male staff of Section 8X were joined by four women who worked in new shifts of twenty-four hours on, forty-eight hours off, because of the difficulty in changing a watch during the night-time blitz.[15] The 'wolf pack' attacks by German U-boats on convoys frequently occurred across a period of twenty-four hours or longer, and continuity of personnel was required on a shift to enable the plotter to have a complete picture across the whole of an enemy attack.

The aim was to crack the dominance of the German navy and U-boats by using every source and scrap of intelligence. After an Axis signal had been read by sections 8E and 8S, the first priority was to compare it with previous intelligence material and ascertain what enemy action was intended. This enabled the Allies to gauge the nature of an attack, to prepare for it and to build a wider view of the enemy's overall strategy. Messages were analysed to such an extent that NID personnel gradually came to recognise the personality of individual commanders of German U-boats, E-boats and destroyers. The German commanders left a 'fingerprint' which enabled staff to identify the sender and receiver of signals. Experienced officers and staff, including women, were essential to achieve this depth of analytical work, and thus avoiding staff turnover was most important.

Section 8E, in which women worked, dealt with German surface warships. The work of this section proved that 'acute trained and imaginative minds working under high pressure and a maximum intensity of war fervour can get results of a super quality of accuracy and insight'. Section 8H was headed by Lieutenant Commander Frank Harrison and covered intelligence on Norway. The OIC was sub-divided further into Room 30, which dealt with German naval intelligence and came under the command of Denning. Until 1943, there had been no women working in these sections of the OIC. However, due to the drain of manpower in the wartime, women were recruited to ascertain if they were suitable for analytical work that had hitherto been carried out by male officers. Room 30 comprised three main geographical sections: 8C (Baltic), 8H (Norway) and 8K (Germany to the Spanish border). Section 8C was overseen initially by Lieutenant Clements and collected and analysed intelligence on the Baltic region. When he left in early 1943 for other secret work, Ena Shiers took over as head of the section and oversaw all of the naval material for the Baltic.

Shiers was not alone in operating in a position outside the norm for women in Naval Intelligence. Section 8K, which dealt with the region from the Elbe in Germany, to France and the Spanish border, was initially headed by Lieutenant Fenley. When he was transferred to the Submarine Tracking Room, he was succeeded by Mrs Margaret Stewart, an archaeologist by training. From 1943, apart from the occasional male worker, intelligence Section 8K was run entirely by women.

Senior Intelligence Roles

Margaret Stewart wrote up a snapshot of life inside Room 30 for the NID files. It affords an understanding of the challenges of the work itself as well as the unique trials facing the female personnel in particular.

Few personal details are known about Stewart, who was of Scottish background, married and had a degree in archaeology. In March 1943, she was posted to Section 8C, working for Ena Shiers, where she sorted and logged each day's signals for the Baltic. The work required 'a certain amount of intelligent appraisal, a facility for scientific deduction as opposed to guesswork, a trained mind, a long memory and clear concise expression'.[16] She worked steadily and methodically, but it took considerable time to sort the signals, relate them to one another and build a picture of the sequence of daily events. She delivered with accuracy, but she often fell behind with her work, losing ground, for which Denning reprimanded her. She was dedicated, but he expected personnel to work at the same pace and intensity as himself.

With Stewart concentrating on the logs, Shiers was able to carry out research and analysis of the material. As with the women of Room 29, Section 8C laboured in unacceptable working conditions, with poor ventilation in a room initially designed for seven people, but invariably containing more. Stewart found the atmosphere in the basement room so stifling that she suffered from 'thunderous headaches, a mental woolliness and an overpowering feeling of sluggishness'.

Initially, women operated in the face of a certain amount of male prejudice. Stewart commented that her presence was resented by some male colleagues because her role as 'a potential equal threatened an established monopoly'. The one exception was Denning, who was never too busy to answer questions or explain the technicalities of the job to her. The chauvinism lessened after the female officers' new roles delivered intelligence results.

After a few weeks in 8C, Stewart was transferred to Section 8K, with a new boss, Lieutenant Fenley. Section 8K carried out analysis of incoming Ultra traffic and phoned the latest dispositions to the relevant naval bases and departments. This often required a level of multi-tasking. For example, when a German convoy was being tracked as it headed eastbound in the English Channel, an interception was planned by the Allies, but, against this, a watchful eye had to be kept simultaneously on north German W/T traffic. Any sign of east- or west-bound Axis convoys to and from the Hook of Holland had to be analysed, decisions taken and conveyed to Coastal Command. Stewart logged the daily W/T traffic, but this was recorded in a different way than in Section 8C. She undertook no analysis of the data because Fenley did this. Rather than writing it down, he carried the information in his head. The most serious omission, as she saw it, was his failure to brief her on the significance of the data and where movements by the enemy might indicate new routes to be monitored. She had to learn on the job and it required intense and sharp intuition, and an extremely logical mind. She wrote about the 'endless struggle to keep abreast of the job and constant effort to maintain mental equality with men trained to do their job and with the technicalities at their fingertips'.

She soon succeeded in a way that even she could not have foreseen when she joined the team. At just a few hours' notice, Fenley was transferred one day to the Submarine Tracking Room, and Stewart found herself the head of Section 8K, in charge of all the naval intelligence from the Elbe to the Spanish border. For Stewart, there was huge satisfaction in being able to deliver outstanding work and 'of promulgating a long digest of Special Intelligence to operational commands; of bringing a forecast and sharing in the success of a reliant interception; of saving lives, and above all, of pitting one's brains against the enemy and winning'.

By mid-September 1943, Miss Lee had joined Section 8K because of the anticipated increase of planning and workload for Operation Neptune and D-Day the following year. Lee was soon placed in charge of all intelligence on harbour defence activities between Cherbourg and Le Havre. It was here that the most detailed information would be needed because the Allies intended to (and did) land their invasion forces on the beaches of Normandy. In other words, Lee was in charge of all naval intelligence in the region of the D-Day landings. Lee's role here is yet another example of an extraordinary situation, hitherto undiscovered, where a woman had responsibility for intelligence of seismic importance – in this case, the naval operation which decisively turned the tide of the war.

By May 1944, such was the success of the work at the OIC that surface ships of the German navy were incapable of interfering to any significant extent with the Allied invasion of Europe. Germany's major battleships and heavy cruisers had either been sunk or put out of action. Others were being refitted in ports or were engaged in supporting German operations in the Baltic. Trying to keep abreast of the volume of intelligence by all sections of the OIC was a constant reality; as more signals came in there was a frenetic atmosphere. Sometimes the new information required decisions to be updated and fresh instructions telephoned to the correct commands.

During 1944, everything was subordinate to the priority of Operation Neptune. There was no pause in the volume of traffic coming from sites like Bletchley Park and this meant that a twenty-four-hour watch by the section was required. Bletchley Park had pushed up the priority of all channel signals and, after the breaking of Dolphin – the principal German cipher for U-boats and surface ships – there was no delay in the receipt of traffic. Each Dolphin message had to be analysed within twenty-four hours, before the next deluge of messages arrived.

The pressure of work became so intense that some women (most of them civilians) simply slept in rotation at the Admiralty, in a poorly ventilated room with six bunks. A typical shift consisted of a morning on operational intelligence at high pressure, a noisy lunch in the canteen of the National Gallery, then the afternoon shift from 2 p.m., when, rather than being able to carry out research, there was another raft of incoming traffic for analysis. By 8 p.m., Stewart could finally return to the Operations Room to catch up on other intelligence work that had fallen behind. She frequently finished work between midnight and 1 a.m. The knowledge of the urgency of the material, their sense of patriotism and strong wartime work ethic spurred these women to work overtime, with no extra pay. They understood the significance of their intelligence work – timely information could make a difference to a decision taken by a commander.

During the critical months of 1944, as many as fifteen people worked in Room 30 as 'the nerve centre of naval operational intelligence on D-Day'.[17] The quality of intelligence produced was down to the sheer mental and physical stamina of the personnel in Room 30, the majority of them female. They were a central and formidable part of the NID workforce.

Section 17M

The work of Section 17M, which formed part of NID 12, was particularly important ahead of D-Day – and two-thirds of its workforce was comprised of women. It was responsible for a number of deception operations to fool the Germans about where the real invasion would take place – most famously Operation Mincemeat (see pp. 216–19). Headed by Ewen Montagu RNVR, Section 17M was tasked also with working on the Ultra messages from Bletchley Park, the decrypts of which were catalogued and filed by the female staff. Early in the war, these messages came in slowly, as not all German Enigma codes had been broken by the Bletchley codebreakers. But by 1942 the incoming Ultra messages amounted to over 200 messages a day and had to be prioritised in terms of importance, thus significantly adding to the workload. Montagu decided which intelligence was the most significant and to be dealt with urgently.

Joan Saunders was Montagu's chief assistant, engaged in indexing, filing and research. She worked exclusively on enemy agents' traffic and, because Montagu might not have read all the reports, flagged up items of importance at her daily meetings with him. Montagu described her with no small amount of admiration, trepidation and old-fashioned mid-century misogyny: she was, he said, 'practical, bossy, occasionally terrifying and wore a tiger skin fur coat to work in winter . . . extraordinarily good, very methodical but also frightfully alert. Very pleasant to work with, although not much to look at. I'm not lucky in assistants as regard looks.'[18] Decades later, it is difficult to get to the real character of women like Saunders through the thick veil of male attitudes to women at the time.

Saunders's assistant was Miss Boxall; she typed up Montagu's reports and notes on all aspects of the work of the section. Both women made index cards of agents in neutral ships, their names and cover names, as well as enemy ships' names and an index of important ISOS material (that is, deciphered messages of the German secret service). Mrs Fenley specialised in service traffic, primarily in relation to the Mediterranean, and Miss Trehearne specialised in service traffic and selected material for the geographical and technical card indexes. Miss McCarthy, Miss Ponsonby and Miss Hall carried out typing, filing and clerical work. Detailed card indexes had to be kept up to date with technical and military details and names of key personalities from the myriad of teleprints that were received by the section. These totalled hundreds of cards. The relevant female officers dealt with all special material that came in throughout the day and went through the night's traffic for service traffic and agents' traffic to ensure nothing had been missed by the night watchkeepers.

Three typists were central in covering the work between the morning and evening shifts and for absences due to leave or sickness. Because the work of the section was so secret and required clearance on Special Intelligence and Ultra, it was not possible to bring in people from other departments at a moment's notice. Miss Kirk was responsible for recruiting and selecting the shorthand typists for the section. With one or two exceptions, the typists were said to have done a remarkable job with great loyalty and efficiency.[19] Their work was not as interesting as that of the other officers and they were worked much harder, usually under more pressure than any other typist job in the Admiralty. They worked long hours, in bad conditions underground, with little hope of promotion and doing work normally carried out by clerical grades.

The youngest member of the section was Jean Leslie, who joined in 1941 and initially worked for Section B1b, which gathered and analysed Ultra decrypts and intelligence to be used for the running of double agents. Her job was to sort through copies of interrogation reports from Camp 020, the MI5 secret interrogation site at Latchmere House. She read enemy spies' stories and accounts to check for inconsistencies or anything of concern which she should raise with her senior male colleagues.[20]

Section 17M operated from the poorly ventilated, hot and stuffy Room 13 in the basement of the Admiralty. It was just 20ft by 19ft, with a low 8ft ceiling, and much of the available space taken up with furniture, such as large steel cupboards. These were cramped and noisy conditions, with three typists hammering full blast on the typewriters for hours. Eventually the section was given the small room next door for the typists to move into, enabling the others in Room 13 to have clearer heads for thinking. An official report on the section noted that it had only had four breakdowns among female staff and not much sickness – remarkable given the challenging working conditions.

A Measure of Success?

Women's success in their roles within Naval Intelligence is often hard to quantify because their stories are still largely obscured by secrecy. But examining some of the women's service records that are available can, with a little detective work, reveal aspects of their work and careers in intelligence. This is true, for instance, of Margaret Brentnall. In 1939, she joined the naval attaché's office at the US embassy in London. She worked for Commander E.B. Strauss of the US Navy who, from 1942 until 1943, was a naval observer in Combined Operations Headquarters in London. In April 1943 she was recommended for an interview and transferred to SOE, where she worked in U Section. She was, her service record stated, 'a very intelligent, capable, calm and practical lady'.[21] She resigned at the end of the war in Europe and spent the rest of her life as an author. She never married and lived with her sister, also a spinster. What is most striking is that Brentnall is the only woman in the photograph of the line of naval officers meeting King George VI, reproduced in Barbara Bond's book *Great Escapes*.[22] It underlines her important position within the section that she was working, even if we cannot fully understand yet the extent of that work.

Looking back at Brentnall's earlier life, it could be that her career in intelligence started much earlier. She attended finishing school in Switzerland for a year, and then spent a lot of time in the 1930s travelling in Germany, often with her sister. This included attending a rally at which the Führer was present. Brentnall was a keen and competent photographer. Between 1929 and Christmas 1938, she hiked and cycled very extensively in Switzerland, Austria and central and southern Germany. She spent a lot of time at Oberammergau in Bavaria, very close to the Austrian border, and travelled through Heidelberg, Freiburg, the Black Forest, Munich, Cologne, the Danube, the Rhine, Stuttgart, Innsbruck, Interlaken and Lausanne. She would have acquired extensive knowledge of those cities and areas and their infrastructure – extremely useful information to SOE when planning infiltrations and assessing potential escape routes. The truth of Brentnall's pre-war life may never fully emerge, but, given her subsequent wartime career, it is likely that she was gathering information for the British Secret Service. It is becoming clear that women gained expertise that made them essential to British intelligence.

On the question of the success of the women in Naval Intelligence, Section 8K head Margaret Stewart commented from her own first-hand experience that women brought to the work a conscientiousness and attention to detail which did not come quite so easily to men. Female personnel tended to be meticulously accurate and with an orderliness of mind which 'made all the difference between work done well or indifferently'. It was her opinion that a woman has a brilliant intuitive mind, whereas a man uses logic and reason. A woman is slow to change her opinions radically and she can tackle a problem along an infinite number of detailed lines of enquiry. Given time, this will lead her to a bird's-eye view of the whole situation. Hating to discard knowledge, she stores snippets of information until they might be of use, while most men have 'a natural facility for discarding irrelevant information'.

Stewart's views reflect her own times – a period in history before the liberation of women at home and in the workplace, and within branches of intelligence. Stewart was making a case for women to be present in the room precisely because they 'thought differently'; to claim that they brought the same attributes as men would be too threatening, and unthinkable in that milieu. Whether we would agree with her or not, Stewart sensed from her own experience of scrutinising the work of women and men that women brought something special and unique to the mix, needed for good intelligence.

Life for women trying to gain some parity with their male counterparts was not without friction, even for those like Stewart who had risen through the ranks to achieve some seniority. On one occasion, for example, Denning came to Section 8K and swept away that's day's analysis to revise the intelligence picture of parts of the French coast. Tempers were frayed and, for the only time in her career, Stewart defied him and argued for a continued analysis of what they had been working on, which she assessed as and knew to be the higher priority for operational intelligence. The incident resulted in temporary chaos in the operational room. Stewart wrote, 'The whole thing was absurd, illogical, almost farcical. For the first and last time in my term of service I defied the suggestion, pleading the pressure of our immediate operational work'.[23] In her report about it for the Admiralty she is ambiguous about the outcome, but the undertones make it clear that she felt Denning ignored her expertise and analysis and imposed his strategy on the team simply because she was a woman. It led her to conclude that she should have borne complete responsibility, without having to explain her actions or her decisions to Denning and others.

Stewart was a strong advocate for the complete freedom of responsibility and initiative for women who were employed alongside men in intelligence positions. She argued that if a woman is placed in a role of responsibility, it must be complete, and not overseen by men. From her own experience – often frustrated by the constraints of her day – she concluded that the minds of women and men run along parallel, but separate, lines and that women should be given a greater degree of independence in their work rather than having to defer to a man to make the final decisions. These were some of the major early challenges for women carving out new roles, beyond traditional and inherited boundaries. They laid the foundations for women to progress in the intelligence world.

What emerges from the archives is a picture of female personnel in NID who overturned conventional ideas. They showed that women's roles needn't be restricted to secretarial duties and confidential filing. Margaret Stewart, Ena Shiers and Miss Lee are good examples of this as the first women to take over high-level duties from a male naval officer for intelligence work that had hitherto been regarded as a man's job. Alongside this, the Secret Ladies analysed and distributed Special Intelligence messages. With no time for lengthy naval training, the female workforce had to learn on the job, and many women went on to achieve astonishing results as the first women in Naval Intelligence to be entrusted with operational responsibilities.

Perhaps one of the greatest compliments ever paid to women in this era was this: that it was a woman who was entrusted with the Neptune intelligence for D-Day. These kinds of stories which are now emerging from history are not only exciting, but also change our perception of just how integral women were as intelligencers.

9
EYES IN THE SKY

Aerial reconnaissance photography had been in its infancy in the First World War, but it would prove vital to the intelligence jigsaw in the fight against Nazi Germany. Multi-layered sources of intelligence were required to corroborate the information that was coming from all areas and aspects of the war, including from Bletchley Park and CSDIC. Air intelligence became an integral part of the tri-services cooperation on intelligence and, as with other intelligence units, uniformed as well as civilian women played a central role.

In 1938, MI6 recruited an Australian man, Sidney Cotton, to pioneer new methods of studying and analysing German rearmament, using aerial photography from reconnaissance sorties.[1] Cotton based his nascent unit in a hangar in the corner of Heston airfield, west of London.[2] His girlfriend, Pat Martin, was a good photographer, and as his companion on secret flights over Germany she snapped shots of military installations and sites of potential interest to British intelligence.

For the remainder of 1938 and into 1939, Cotton transformed the principles of photographic reconnaissance and instigated the changes that were required in the organisation of photographic interpretation. He was instrumental in engaging civilian women as photographic interpreters (PIs) for the highly skilled and responsible job that this analysis work entailed. He believed that they were ideal for this type of work because they were patient, paid attention to detail and were persistent in achieving results. The first women to arrive at Heston were Cynthia Wood, Mary Chance, Mary MacLean and Angus Wilson.[3]

With the volume of work increasing, Cotton relocated to the site of the Aircraft Operating Company (AOC) at Wembley in North London.

Owned by his friend Major Hemming, the site was already producing detailed reports from aerial photography of civilian flights and using state-of-the-art machinery from Switzerland to interpret the images. British intelligence needed swift results and those from missions involving military aircraft could take days to reach the desk of the intelligence chiefs. By this time, the information, particularly about the positions of Axis battleships and aircraft, was old. The operators at the AOC adapted to 'interpreting military targets instead of commercial subjects and, most importantly, their reports were delivered to the relevant HQs within hours of a photographic flying sortie rather than days'.[4]

This laid the foundations for the unit to gradually increase its workload across the war to become an industrial-scale 'intelligence-gathering factory', much like the scaled-up operations at Bletchley Park and the CSDIC bugging operation. Enemy targets were photographed, the films were developed and then sent to a number of secret air intelligence sites for interpretation. Women were very much at the heart of this intelligence work.

The First Photographic Interpreters

PIs were selected on their ability, irrespective of gender, and in mid-1940 the site at Wembley saw the first WAAF officers taking up this role.[5] One of the first arrivals was Molly Thompson, who had a degree in economics from University College London. When war broke out, she was working in the research department of the Portland Cement Company in Westminster. She volunteered for the WAAF and was posted to Wembley. She worked as a PI on aerial photographs from the coastlines of France and the Low Countries. The PIs monitored German troops amassing along the coast of the English Channel as part of the imminent German invasion of the UK. She recalled, 'As far as the interpreters were concerned you did your job, you were capable and whether you were a man or a woman did not matter.'[6]

During the Battle of Britain, between July 1940 and October 1940, an increasing number of WAAF personnel arrived at Wembley. They received training, were assigned as PIs and continued to monitor the German invasion threat. One of the ways they did this was by analysing aerial photographs for evidence of the accumulation of German invasion barges in one region. This could indicate an impending attack on England by sea.

In 1941, Danesfield House near Marlow in Buckinghamshire became vacant and was requisitioned by the Royal Air Force. It is set in its own parkland on high ground, overlooking the valley with the winding River Thames below. The site became known as RAF Medmenham and was home to the Central Interpretation Unit (CIU). Photographic interpretation was relocated from Wembley to Danesfield House and saw the arrival of fifty-three PIs, a third of whom were WAAFs. The workload increased and with it the creation of a number of specialist sections, all of which had their share of female personnel.[7]

As part of the recruitment process, women sat an IQ test which, if they passed, led to an interview. They were from diverse social backgrounds and not necessarily privately educated. Some women were older than the upper limit for conscription but made a conscious decision to put their careers on hold to serve their country. As the number of female recruits increased, the ATS personnel among them received training at the School of Military Intelligence at Matlock in Derbyshire, and were then posted to RAF Medmenham or RAF Nuneham Park. One of the early officer training units for WAAFs was the country estate of Bulstrode Park, near Gerrards Cross in Buckinghamshire.

By 1944, personnel had joined from other countries, like the United States and the Dominions. The unit at Danesfield House changed its name to the Allied Central Interpretation unit (ACIU), and a number of female US personnel were stationed at RAF Nuneham Park, too. The photographic sections at both sites were equipped with the latest automatic printing and developing apparatus to enable photographs to be developed quickly. Approximately 275 photographers and maintenance personnel were employed in the two sections. During peak times, over 1 million prints and 140,000 duplicate exposures were produced each month. Although much of this was automated, a large amount of the work still required skilled personnel.

The section produced mosaic maps of different areas needed by a particular commander of a unit. The largest mosaic constructed had to be copied onto 24″× 24″ films. This was an impressive achievement in itself, but the photographs taken by the pilots and developed at places like RAF Medmenham would have been nothing without interpretation which gave the Allies the intelligence they needed, especially on enemy targets and installations.

Specialised Sections

The full-scale interpretation of aerial photography became quite an art. The sheer volume of material needing to be processed for intelligence on a daily basis required that the work be apportioned to specialist departments. Each specialist department had its female workforce, who developed a particular expertise and who were part of the work described below. A study of each section across air photographic interpretation reveals some incredible hidden stories of the role of women in intelligence.

Constance Babington Smith, who would go on to identify the V-weapons from aerial photography in late 1943, is probably the most famous of the women who worked in this section. Beginning as assistant section officer in January 1941, Babington Smith believed that more attention should be paid to enemy aircraft, so, in her spare time, she decided to study all aspects of them, writing a brief report on her research for her own interest. After it was accidentally discovered and read by her boss, Squadron Leader Riddell, he acknowledged that the study of aircraft should be more central to their work as PIs. He asked Babington Smith to form a new section called the Aircraft Interpretation Section, which she headed – even though it was highly unusual for a WAAF officer to head her own section without oversight from a male officer.

Z Section reported on the movement of enemy shipping and kept a large index of enemy vessels, as well as cards with reference to the relevant photographs pertaining to that information. In the latter part of the war, the section was divided into Z1 (dealing with Scandinavia and East Baltic) and Z2 (all other areas). A daily airfield report was written to summarise each day's aircraft and aircraft interpretation from the movement of Axis aircraft to provide intelligence on the state of the

German air force where possible. Likewise, a daily report was compiled for German railways and transport and these were written by both women and men. Z Section also dealt with enemy balloon barrages, smokescreens and any damage and repairs to canals and bridges. Eve Holiday was assistant officer of the section because she knew a lot about shipping. Her expertise placed her as deputy to the head of the section.

The Coverage Section worked in 'watches', or shifts, across twenty-four hours, to examine incoming sorties to decide which jobs had been satisfactorily photographed and which must be flown again by the RAF. Listings of targets covered by each sortie helped those interpreters in a second phase of analysis; they usually interpreted a sortie before it was fully plotted. A Section was responsible for producing accurate drawings and silhouettes of an enemy ship from air photographs. These drawings enabled accurate, detailed models to be made of enemy ships. The section reported on German naval and merchant shipping, U-boats and pens, E-boats and invasion barges.

C Section covered intelligence on enemy airfields and was responsible for detailed information on the state and disposition of the enemy's airfields. This intelligence was vital for planning and assessing bombing operations on those sites. Information was required on all German air force bases. The PIs were especially looking for the expansion or modification of existing German airfields and the construction of new ones, to track future enemy offensive plans. This work by the PIs was detailed and required precision. It was a woman, Flight Officer Ursula Powys-Lybbe, who became head of C Section at RAF Medmenham. A professional photographer in the 1930s for the society magazine *Tatler*, she enlisted in the WAAF in autumn 1939 and initially became a photographic interpreter. Her level of expertise in aircraft, largely self-taught, meant that she was promoted to head of this specialised section and ran the whole team.

D Section, the Industrial Section, gathered intelligence on Axis industries, including power stations, powerlines and transformers that could be traced and plotted to produce a map of the enemy's electric power grid. A large board displayed the details of the production of German synthetic oil plants and oil refineries on a daily basis. Knowledge of the locations of the Nazi regime's production of iron, steel, fuel, chemicals and explosives, light metals, synthetic rubber and textiles was required to assess the massive war industry and to plan Allied bombing raids on those sites. An extensive card index was created that listed all of Germany's power plants and industries, alongside comprehensive plans of industrial towns. The Industrial Section was initially staffed by male scientists and engineers who had specialised industrial knowledge. Professional women eventually joined the section, working on interpretation and intelligence, and they included Anne Whiteman, an Oxford historian and archaeologist, Ruth Langhorne, a geographer from the University of Oxford, and Winifred Bartingale, who became a doctor.

E Section and Q Section operated closely together, with E Section dealing with the enemy's use of camouflage and smokescreens to obscure sites of importance, and Q Section responsible for identifying decoys – German use of fake structures to fool Allied bombers into bombing the wrong sites. Aerial photography was very successful in unmasking Germany's decoy system, as in the case of aerial reconnaissance over open countryside in the Ruhr, where three rectangular structures surrounded by bomb craters were soon discovered to be decoys. Through painstaking hours of analysis of an increasing number of photographs, the PIs accumulated incredible detail on the German system of camouflage. Personnel in the Camouflage Section consisted primarily of women, and it has emerged that the head of the section was a woman, Flight Officer Molly Thompson.[8]

F Section dealt with the identification of locations of enemy communications, rail, road and waterways, although the main concern for the PIs here was the movement of traffic and location of marshalling yards, depots, bridges and aqueducts. Reports were issued on the movement of enemy traffic which provided an overall picture of troops moving to a particular battlefront or the movement of armaments and industrial products needed for the running of the war machine.

G Section was one of the most important sources of intelligence, as it was responsible for detection of the enemy's wireless technology – its offensive and defensive radio systems. This included identification of sites related to the use of X-Gerät and Knickebein, the new technology of navigational beams used by the enemy to direct their bombers to targets across England. This intelligence was first discovered from the bugged conversations of German POWs at Trent Park in the spring of 1940. The PIs were tasked with working on intelligence from POWs to find the actual sites from aerial sorties. Pinpointing the navigational beams being used by German bombers enabled the British technologists, under the direction of MI6 scientist Professor R.V. Jones, to produce effective counter-measures. This led to the famous 'bending of the beams' by teams at secret sites like Alexandra Palace in North London, such that German bombers dropped their bombs slightly off target. Prior to D-Day, this section's work was vital in understanding the locations of German radar equipment around the invasion area of Normandy before the Allied landings. Knowledge of this meant that the Allied forces that landed on 6 June 1944 by air and sea did so without prior detection by the Germans. Not only did this enable a successful invasion, but it also prevented a greater loss of Allied personnel.

A number of sorties were flown solely to provide air photographs to analyse the damage to enemy sites and compile reports of the results of those missions for distribution to the relevant departments. From the photographs taken before and after the bombing raids, the PIs in K Section were able to offer a precise assessment of the damage inflicted on the enemy by Allied strategic and tactical bombing. It was important to understand the extent to which an operation had been effective. Assessment of these locations was ongoing to establish whether the Germans had cleared the bombed sites and begun a programme of repair and reconstruction on specified military installations.

L Section worked on enemy aircraft and factories to identify the amount of production of aircraft to replace German losses, but also to discover new types of aircraft and modifications to existing models. Some of this kind of information was picked up by the eavesdropping programme at Latimer House and Wilton Park, where German air force POWs liked to boast about new aircraft and compare models with older planes. This kind of intelligence was passed to RAF Medmenham to identify and corroborate from aerial photography. It forewarned British intelligence before a particular aircraft became operational. The section also looked for enemy airfields that had been recently converted from operational ones to aircraft production and this activity was monitored closely. It was essential for the Allies to assess the replacement of German losses, whether in the air, on land or on the sea, which could shift the balance of power in any war.

As the war progressed, Allied night bombing missions were carried out in which every aircraft of Bomber Command carried a shutterless camera so that night photographs could be taken. N Section analysed all types of night photographs, pinpointing fires on those photos which showed what targets had been hit, 'thus producing evidence which would not have been accessible in any other way, about the tactical efficiency of attacks and the effectiveness of weapons'.[9] The Target Section prepared illustrations and material for strategic and tactical target bombing.

The remarkable Lady Charlotte Bonham Carter (née Ogilvy) was allocated to the Ground Intelligence Section at RAF Medmenham, having already enjoyed an important and colourful career in the last war: she had served in the Voluntary Aid Detachment (VAD), then was seconded by the Foreign Office to MI5 to track Lenin across Germany before the 1917 Russian Revolution, and had even sat on the Secretariat of the conference during the negotiations for the Treaty of Versailles in 1919. The Ground Intelligence Section was responsible for all reports from ground sources, including charts, maps, telephone directories, brochures and handbooks of industry. It created a card index of its holdings, and distributed ground intelligence reports to the relevant sections. It created and cared for a reference library of guidebooks, technical books and dictionaries, as well as filing and indexing all PI reports. It produced a monthly summary of activities at RAF Medmenham for publication in the weekly intelligence summary of the Air Ministry. The work involved consulting the intelligence summaries, filing reports and editing the Monthly Interpretation Review.

One of the most fascinating sections was the Model Making Section, or V Section. Set up in August 1940 it went on to construct over 1,400 models for the three services. The range of models included meticulously accurate reconstructions of terrain, used for the planning and briefing of all large-scale Allied landing operations and almost every special commando operation. Until 1941 it consisted only of male members, but after the move to Danesfield House an increase in personnel was necessary and this was when women joined the section. The work was highly specialised and carried out by those with a professional background as artists, sculptors or illustrators.

Two of the first women to arrive in the Model Making Section were Thea Turner and Gilly Porter. Only women from the WAAF were transferred to this section, which comprised two officers and twenty-one other ranks. The women were expert at precision, able to conduct the long hours of detailed and patient work, which required single-minded concentration. General Eisenhower was quoted as saying, 'each of these model makers is worth 100 men!'[10]

The models were built to scale and the information for them obtained from maps and interpretation of aerial photographs. The base of a model was prepared using four sheets of hardboard, mounted onto the base board. Modelling material was used to build the land areas, then the surface was painted for roads and rivers, trees, hedges and buildings. As the work progressed, it was regularly checked for precise accuracy because, in the planning stages of an operation, personnel had to study the features on the model so that when they landed they knew exactly what to expect of the terrain. Once the original model was complete, plaster moulds were taken and, from these, synthetic rubber copies were cast. A model of a port would include individual dock layouts, road and rail links, precise numbers of buildings, cranes, ships and boats, all built to scale with added details of cargoes and crates. Once the model was made, it was painted in the exact colours of the real location, and the roofs were even at the same slant as the real buildings. An attacking force from land, air or sea would have a precise view of the place that they had seen as a model. Exact models of the landing places on the Normandy beaches provided essential briefing to the personnel about to mount the D-Day landings. In September 1944, the same type of model was prepared for Operation Market Garden at Arnhem.

The main task of W Section was the production of town plans from aerial photographs, so that, when field commands made a rapid advance, they understood the layout of towns and cities in enemy-occupied countries. This was especially important between January 1944 (with the Allies planning the D-Day landings for that June) and VE Day on 8 May 1945. The section produced approximately 500 town plans, as well as relief models for strategic use in the invasions of North Africa and Europe, and other tactical operations.

All operational sorties were plotted on a map by the Plotting Section within twenty-four hours of the prints being developed. In spite of photographs often being obscured by cloud, expert WAAF officers averaged around a hundred prints an hour, working first in the former library at Danesfield House, then moving into the splendid ballroom. After each photograph had been plotted on a map, the finished area was cut out, mounted on card and annotated. From this original card, photostat copies were made by the Photographic Section for distribution as necessary. The three services could request photographs of an area that was needed for their analysis and planning of operations. This was handled by the Progress Section, which despatched the correct photographs to the department that had requested them. Over 1 million photographs were handled by its personnel each month, and this averaged 350 demands a day for photographs.

The Tracing Section covered all theatres of war in Europe, North Africa, the Middle East and the Far East. It split maps of these countries into a scale of 1:250,000. After a photographic sortie was plotted, that plot was traced onto the respective area of a map, and was an easy way to keep track of aerial cover of particular geographical areas. Around two-thirds of the staff working on the prints, maps, mosaics and in Tracing Section were women.

A number of women in the WAAF and the ATS were trained as draughtswomen for map making. Some were talented calligraphists or well versed in geography, making them ideal for this kind of highly concentrated and detailed work. In fact, it was one of the female clerks (WAAF) who issued the target maps and material to the air crew ahead of the Dambusters Raid on 16 May 1943, the famous attack on the Moehne and Eder dams in the Ruhr valley. The raid disrupted Germany's ability to support its manufacture of armaments. Afterwards, aerial photographs of the damage to the dams were assessed by the Damage Assessment Section, which had taken over the largest room on the first floor of one of the towers at Danesfield House.

Curatorial Support

Behind all the hubbub and busy work of each specialist section were the curatorial and administrative staff.

The Confidential Bookroom held hundreds of documents of a secret and confidential nature, and consequently the door was locked. Any item could be consulted while under the supervision of the bookroom officer, and some items could be signed out for borrowing. The Print Library contained the reference material relating to over 80,000 sorties, which amounted to 6.5 million prints, all carefully recorded, given a reference number and filed. It occupied over 2.5 miles of shelves.

The Central Registry handled all correspondence for RAF Medmenham and constituted over 4,000 files. It was also responsible for the issue of stationery, the maintenance of a reference library of Air Ministry Orders and publications, current distribution lists for where reports were to be sent and a list of all material issued for internal circulation. Distribution was carried out by the Despatch Section, which sent out over 40,000 items every day to various Allied addresses, including material by despatch rider to every war zone, as well as by aeroplane courier services. This site operated on an industrial scale of intelligence processing. Its printers were capable of producing 1,000 photographs an hour.[11] Over 60,000 tins of film were kept in the film store, as any might contain film required for reprints at any point across the war.

The telephone network consisted of over 300 extensions, linked to all sections of the unit. A team of typists typed up reports, often running into several pages. Fine weather meant that more sorties could be flown and this increased the work, such that their in-tray was overflowing with top-secret and priority jobs. An average of 100 copies of each report were needed for the various sections and rolled off the duplicators. The teleprinters were essential for coordinating the high-priority work of operational sorties and interpretation.

RAF Medmenham and its related sites represented a vast, efficient apparatus to support the intelligence work so necessary to affect the outcome of the war.

Intelligence Results

The significance of photographic interpretation cannot be overestimated. Throughout the war, it was used to keep track of key German battleships, like the *Scharnhorst* and the *Tirpitz*. In 1941, it identified the location of the German battleship the *Bismarck*; six days later it was sunk and its operational threat removed.

A good example of the significance of RAF Medmenham for operational intelligence was its role in the first joint Anglo-American invasion, Operation Torch, in North Africa in November 1942. Ahead of the landings, photographic intelligence was absolutely essential in the planning and briefing of the invasion forces, which were being led by General Eisenhower. Specialist photographic sorties, coordinated from Gibraltar and Malta, were carried out and the films rushed across to RAF Medmenham to develop and to construct accurate scaled models and topographical reports. Eisenhower's planners needed as much detail as possible on the invasion area, including the heights of buildings, details of defences and positions of Axis communications (like pylons and telephone posts) and the location of enemy airfields. A map would not accurately reflect the requisite level of detail and markers by which parachutists could assess their landings. On the other hand, a replica model – to scale – could include all buildings, farmhouses, defences and even the location of barbed wire and telephone poles.

The photographic intelligence for Operation Torch was headed by Douglas Kendall, who assigned two women, Dorothy Garrod and Sarah Churchill, to work on the operation, alongside the male army, navy and RAF officers. In her professional life, Garrod was an archaeologist and, before the war, was professor and director of Archaeology and Anthropology at Cambridge University.[12] In the 1930s she had led archaeological expeditions to Iraq and Palestine, and then, from around 1934, had worked as a nurse in northern France and the Rhineland in Germany. Her professional skills were required at RAF Medmenham because as an archaeologist she was used to studying landscapes in intense levels of detail – a necessary skill for constructing a model of the invasion sites of North Africa. Garrod recommended that one of her archaeology students at Cambridge, Elspeth Macalister, should join the section too.

Sarah Churchill (married name Oliver), an actress by profession and second daughter of Winston Churchill, began at the site as a plotter. She went on to become a PI and was skilled at relating locations on photographs to printed maps. There is a wonderful story about Sarah Churchill and Operation Torch. On 7 November 1942, the day before the invasion, she took forty-eight hours annual leave and visited her father at Chequers, the British prime minister's country residence. Sitting by the fire at 1 a.m., with her father pacing the room, Winston suddenly said to her: 'At this very minute, under cover of darkness, six hundred and forty-three ships that are carrying our troops on the great enterprise, are approaching the shores of Africa.'

> 'Six hundred and forty-four,' said a voice from the armchair.
> 'What's that?'
> 'I've been working on Torch for months.'
> 'Why didn't you tell me?'
> 'I was told not to mention it to anyone.'[13]

It is a great example of how assiduous those working in intelligence were to keep their work a secret – in this case, even from the prime minister.

Terror Weapons

Arguably, RAF Medmenham's most significant work was in identifying the secret weapon development site at Peenemünde on the Baltic coast.

Intelligence on Hitler's secret weapons programme would be the urgent focus of all intelligence operations across the war. The threat to London and the rest of England of the V-1 ('doodlebug', flying bomb) and V-2 (rocket) weapons was serious and, if not sabotaged, could have cost the Allies the war. Reconnaissance missions had been flown in 1942, but it had not been possible for RAF Medmenham to positively identify the V-weapon site from analysis of the aerial photographs. After the corroboration of the secret V-weapons programme from the bugged conversations of Hitler's generals in captivity at Trent Park (see p. 149), in spring 1943 the RAF flew a number of new sorties over

Peenemünde, the aerial imagery of which provided evidence beyond any doubt that this was the secret experimental site, and it was bombed on the night of 16/17 August 1943. Ahead of the raid, a model of Peenemünde was made at RAF Medmenham, and reconnaissance flights afterwards provided the necessary photographs for PIs to assess the extent of the damage.[14] Huge areas of the living quarters had been destroyed and over 700 German scientists and workers killed. The site was made non-operational for over nine months.

The hunt for intelligence on the V-weapons continued. Constance Babington Smith was instructed to keep analysing the air photographs of the experimental site. She worked on areas around the hangars and buildings, and finally, in November 1943, using her Leitz magnifying glass, she saw something outside a building that could be a testing site. The small cruciform object was only just visible from its white reflective outline and shadow on the ground. It was 'less than a millimetre in length on the aerial photo . . . Measuring it, she calculated that its wingspan was about twenty feet'. She had found the flying bomb.[15] Babington Smith demonstrated amazing defiance of initial opinion dismissing what she had found as 'ski sites' by arguing that the images revealed launch ramps for the V-1. She was almost certainly taken seriously because of her expertise and position as head of the Aircraft Recognition Section. With the knowledge of what exactly to look for, the PIs were able to re-examine the latest aerial imagery and identify V-1s on the ground that had previously been missed. The ACIU went on to compile vital intelligence on the size, shape and method of firing the V-weapons and the locations of the mobile ramps.

Then came confirmation that Hitler had moved his factories and vital industries underground to prevent destruction by Allied bombing. This led to a new race for intelligence. Babington Smith and her team were tasked with monitoring aerial imagery about German factories concealed below ground or within mountainsides. Sometimes this knowledge came via the eavesdropping programme at the three CSDIC sites or from captured German plans which revealed the underground structures. Once known from other sources, reconnaissance missions could be flown over the sites and the results analysed by the PIs at RAF Medmenham. This enabled Allied intelligence to locate entrances to tunnels and underground factories as well as to work out the height of a hill under which a factory was built. Over 400 underground factories were discovered by the PIs in a special army section called B6.[16] It was a huge undertaking to keep abreast of these new Nazi structures and identify them as targets for Allied bombers to make them non-operational. Failure to do so could tip the balance in Germany's favour and Hitler could win the war.

The battle against the flying bomb, the German rocket programme and the atomic bomb lasted the whole of the war. By its end, more than 3,000 sorties had been flown and over 8 million photographs had been interpreted and plotted at RAF Medmenham, more than 1.2 million of which concerned the V-weapons alone.[17] The ACIU supported strategic and operational intelligence which, along with other tri-services intelligence sites, shortened the war and saved lives.[18] Babington Smith was one of the women who contributed in no small measure to that huge success. With the European war over, she continued her work on photographic interpretation, attached to the USAAF Intelligence in Washington DC, for the Pacific theatre of war.

Over 800 women worked at aerial photographic interpretation units in Britain and overseas, and, as one historian of the Medmenham operation stated, 'they could be proud of the part they have played in one of the Second World War's greatest achievements':

> From a few lumbering aircraft and a handful of civilians in 1939, photographic reconnaissance and interpretation had become the major provider of intelligence used in virtually every wartime operation. Unusually for those times, women had carried out the same work as men, were chosen for a particular job solely on their capabilities and played a decisive part in winning the war.[19]

It had been a huge success in contributing to strategic and operational intelligence. Techniques and expertise acquired by this unit across the war laid the foundations for the advanced development of aerial photography across the Cold War and up to today.

10
DOUBLE CROSS AGENTS

In the first two years of the war, British intelligence adopted a policy of trying to block the infiltration of enemy spies and agents by capturing them as soon as they landed in Britain, thereby limiting their activities on British soil. This strategy was very successful: during 1940, over twenty-five German agents were landed on Britain's shores and captured.[1] MI5 quickly conceived that it might also be possible to 'turn' some Abwehr spies after their capture and use them to work for British interests: they would send information back to their Nazi handlers on conditions in wartime Britain, as was their original task, but in line with MI5 and MI6's goals of strategic deception against Germany. German intelligence would be none the wiser and its handlers would believe that their spies were still working for them.

A new committee was established to oversee these activities, meeting in London in utmost secrecy for the first time on 2 January 1941. It was called the Twenty Committee after the Roman numerals XX, standing for 'double cross'. The committee was to 'exercise a steady and consistent supervision of all double agent work' for MI5 and MI6 who wanted Double Cross activities to be on a professional footing.[2] It operated under the auspices of MI5, with 'C' (the head of MI6) directing operations of the agents abroad.[3] Although historically there was frequent tension between the two intelligence agencies, in terms of the Double Cross System they had a close, cordial relationship of cooperation.

Double agents were not only German nationals who been captured and secretly 'turned' to work for the British, but also men and women who had been approached by the Germans to work for them against Britain, but who then informed the British authorities; they were given dispensation to seemingly work for Germany while secretly working for

British intelligence. They communicated with their German handlers using traditional spycraft – secret ink, wireless transmissions, courier or personal contacts. Some double agents were shared by MI5 and MI6 for deception purposes, but MI6 also ran a number of its own for the purposes of counter-espionage as well as deception. 'C''s representative on the Twenty Committee was Frank Foley, an intelligence officer who had served in intelligence since the First World War, and formally on the payroll of SIS from 1923.[4]

Although final decisions rested with MI5 and MI6 on an agent's mission or the standing down of an agent, the Twenty Committee oversaw the daily work of double agents by a section of MI5 known as B1a. The committee was chaired by Professor John Cecil Masterman, a fifty-year-old ex-Dean of Christ Church, Oxford, and Section B1a was headed by Colonel T.A. Robertson, nicknamed 'Tar' as per his initials, who was answerable to the Twenty Committee. He selected the first five case officers and handlers, all of whom were male. They were Billy Luke, two lawyers Ian Wilson and Christopher Harmer, Hugh Astor (son of Lord Astor) and Cyril Mills of Bertram Mills Circus.

No women served on the Twenty Committee, but behind the scenes they were involved in positions of authority and responsibility in the Double Cross System. They were double agents themselves, or handlers of double agents, and they signed counter-espionage reports.[5] Two women are particularly prominent in its history – Mary Sherer and Mrs Susan Barton, who were appointed to work with the five male case officers.

Susan Barton was the first woman recruited to Double Cross. It was a cover name: her real name was Gisela Ashley. Originally Austrian, she had married a British man, then divorced him after she discovered he was homosexual. She then lived with playwright Gilbert Lennox, also an intelligence officer. They wrote stage plays together and she worked on a casual basis for British intelligence. In 1939 she moved to The Hague under diplomatic cover for SIS to spy on the Germans via the German naval attaché there, whom she successfully befriended. The Venlo incident of November 1939, in which two SIS officers (Sigismund Payne Best and Richard Stevens) were abducted on the German–Dutch border in a German sting operation, necessitated her swift return to Britain for fear she may have been compromised by Stevens during interrogation by the Gestapo.[6] On her return to England she was posted to Section B1a where her vivacious personality was said to have brought an important antidote to the male-dominated chauvinistic world around her.

Another central female figure in Double Cross operations was twenty-nine-year-old Mary Corrie Sherer, who had been recruited to MI5 as a secretary in 1936. She was soon posted to Malta, but at the outbreak of war returned to England and worked for a while in sabotage for MI5 officer Victor Rothschild. She transferred to the Double Cross System as MI5's first female agent runner. With a military background as the daughter of a brigadier and having grown up in the Indian Raj, Sherer chose to dress like a general and 'often wore a red jacket with epaulettes . . . and walked with a long, martial stride, swinging her arms'.[7] She was a tough, resolute character who smoked filterless Kent cigarettes and enjoyed a gin. She could hold her own in the male-dominated world of British intelligence and was highly vocal in persuading her male colleagues that women could become successful double agents. She reassured Robertson, who constantly worried that the double agents might be working for the Nazis as triple agents, that the Nazis were good double-crossers but they lacked the patience to set up a carefully worked out system of deception.

Declassified files reveal the existence of at least seven female Double Cross agents. These were Gelatine, Bronx, Treasure, The Snark, Ecclesiastic, Penguin and Gleam.[8] There may have been more female double agents: there is a single reference to an agent code named Josephine, and two entries in a war diary for Redhead.[9] Nothing further is known about them, including their original names. Penguin, Gleam and Ecclesiastic appear only fleetingly in official files or books, and their personal MI5 files have also not been released.

Known also as special agents, the double agents were selected for 'aptitude for this kind of work and not because he holds a particular job in a certain ministry'.[10] While this report used a male pronoun, the criteria were true for women too. The recruitment of female special agents for the Double Cross System began initially for the purpose of letter-writing and feeding deception material to the Germans. Some were run for a short period only; others were considered for the job but not taken up. Many had started their intelligence career with SIS or MI5 in the 1930s and transferred to the Double Cross after 1939. The Twenty Committee acted as a clearing house for the deception information going out via these agents. The ISOS messages (deciphered messages of the German secret service), where they related to the work of the double agents, were made available by 'C' to the committee.[11] In total, around 120 male and female agents worked for the Double Cross System.[12] How and why each of the female Double Cross agents named above were recruited will become apparent.

Gelatine

As we have seen (p. 83), Friedl Gärtner was already working for SIS by the time she arrived in England in April 1938. With SIS consent, she had been in touch with the German secret service before the outbreak of war, but the precise nature of her work in this respect has not been released.[13] Her MI5 file notes that she worked for her brother-in-law, Ian Menzies, and Dennis Wheatley on unspecified research work.[14] She successfully penetrated the National Socialist German Workers' Party in the UK and tracked the Russian spy Anna Wolkoff who, as we have seen, was based at the Russian Tea Rooms in London. When war broke out on 3 September 1939 Gartner, having a German passport, was classified as an 'enemy alien' and subjected to travel restrictions. Later that month, a request was sent to New Scotland Yard asking for her to be released of restrictions under the Aliens Act so she could travel freely in the UK in her work for British intelligence.[15] That work was to be as a highly successful double agent for the British, with the code name 'Gelatine'.

On New Year's Eve 1940, Stewart Menzies – 'C', the new head of MI6 – held a party at his home of Little Bridley, an Edwardian house in extensive grounds in Worplesdon, Surrey.[16] Among the guests were his brother Ian, their mother Lady Hartford, who was renowned for entertaining with glamour and style, and Gärtner. That evening Gärtner was first introduced to Dusko Popov, a thirty-year-old lawyer of Yugoslav nationality, who was pro-Allies and had arrived in the UK during December 1940. He had been recruited by the Abwehr in

Belgrade six months earlier in August and reported this fact immediately to the British embassy. Popov was – to use spy language – a walk-in. The Germans believed him to have excellent contacts in England and provided him with an extensive questionnaire about military and economic matters to direct his espionage. They thought he would form a German spy ring in England, and so he would – though they would never find out that it was secretly controlled by the Twenty Committee. 'C' himself was to recruit Popov as double agent 'Tricycle' to penetrate Abwehr circles in Lisbon.[17] Such was the closeness of Popov to the Menzies family that he would be godfather to Ian Menzies's first child.

That New Year's Eve, Gärtner was introduced to Popov as Gerde Sullivan – or at least that is the name he uses for her in his memoirs published in 1974. He was immediately taken in by her huge, expressive eyes; she was flirtatious and 'the most glamorous creature I had set eyes on since arriving in England'.[18] The role given to her by Menzies was to educate Popov in the ways of British high society and introduce him to socialite parties, which she duly did. He commented, 'all doors were open to her . . . Never before in my life had I had such a dominating passion for a woman.'[19] Over the course of the next year they embarked on an intense relationship. He was given cover as a businessman in an office on the sixth floor of Albany House, near Piccadilly Circus. Susan Barton was assigned as his secretary and she mixed his invisible ink and prepared code messages and the content of the letters to be sent to his mail drops; Tricycle copied the letters in his own handwriting before they were finally posted to the Germans. His German spymaster was a man called Major Ludovico von Karsthoff, head of the Abwehr in Lisbon. Karsthoff was working under an assumed name: his real name was Major von Auenrode. He gave Tricycle the cover name 'Ivan', and letters went back and forth between them.[20]

By early 1941 the Twenty Committee was looking to increase the number of double agents, and in February Robertson and Maxwell Knight, the head of MI5's M Section, discussed potential recruits. Knight suggested Gärtner, who was already employed by his department. A few days later Knight and Robertson met Gärtner with Masterman at a flat in Grosvenor Square to discuss plans for Tricycle to take her cover story to Lisbon.[21] MI5 believed that Gärtner would be a perfect double agent because the Germans already trusted her; she had worked for them before the war for no payment on account of her (alleged) loyalty to the Fatherland.[22] The Germans knew that she had been a secretary to Dennis Wheatley and that her sister had made a very successful marriage to Ian Menzies. The question was whether the Germans would engage her to mix at parties to gather gossip for them from circles within Britain.

On 7 March 1941 Bill Luke and Robertson met Tricycle at 18 King's Court, Chelsea to discuss how he could best introduce Gärtner to his handler without arousing suspicion. Tricycle came up with a cover story that he had met Gelatine in England and formed an attachment because they were both pro-German. He would then drop into the conversation with his handler that she was prepared to work for the German secret service in the UK. She would be valuable to them because she had impressive high-level contacts in US diplomatic and military circles, as well as British circles.

Gärtner accompanied Tricycle to the airport in a chauffeur-driven car for his mission to Lisbon to feed information to Karsthoff in person. They held hands on the back seat and there seemed to be a tenderness between them. Tricycle followed through with the plan in Lisbon.[23] He told Karsthoff that he had met Gärtner at a dinner at the Yugoslav embassy in London. His job of introducing her to the Abwehr was made easier by the fact that they knew about her through several internal cables which commented on how useful she could be to them. The groundwork was already in place for Tricycle to achieve a positive result, but, even so, Karsthoff conducted rigorous background checks. To reinforce the stories about Gärtner, Tricycle mentioned to Karsthoff that her father had been a member of the Nazi Party; at her apartment, Tricycle had noticed a photograph of her father wearing a small medallion on his lapel with a swastika on it. Karsthoff checked with the German secret service and found the facts to be true. It was enough to convince him to take on Gärtner as an Abwehr double agent. She was given the codename 'Yvonne' and instructions to write to a German contact called Maria Ganzalves de Azevedo at a cover address in Lisbon.

Tricycle had succeeded. Gärtner became MI5's double agent Gelatine.

Gelatine received training in writing and the use of secret ink – a solution of ammonium chloride crystals dissolved in a wine glass of water.[24] A report in her personal file noted that the nib should be sucked before writing so the solution ran freely, then the paper left to dry. Gelatine wrote with a steel nib on one side of the paper. It was agreed that she would not initially write more than one letter to Lisbon every ten days, the contents of which (often unspecified in the files) the Double Cross wished her to pass on. MI5's Section B1a would give her around £25 per month to cover the expenses of her flat,[25] but told her to ask for money from the Germans to finance her lifestyle and extravagant entertainment at home – this was the 'inevitable heavy expenditure' of working for them. The Germans paid Gelatine around £238 every three months, approximately £100 less than their male agents received.[26] Getting the Germans to inadvertently pay for MI5's double agents was a shrewd idea, all part of a plan called 'Plan Midas'. Gelatine received a 5 per cent bonus from MI5 on money which she received from the Germans; she kept the bonus and MI5 put the salary towards the running costs of its Double Cross operations. This financial arrangement was agreed by the double agents.

Gelatine worked for British intelligence out of idealistic motives, because of being born in Austria. In one report, she was described as 'an ideal, social drone, intent on having a good time. She would want to go on living her life on the winning side. She would go to no great risks to help the Germans now, but she might have at one time if German victory seems likely.'[27] However, it is worth noting that she was recruited because of her familial connections to the head of SIS, Stewart Menzies, and it is probable that she would not have betrayed the British if the Germans were winning the war.

Knight thought that Gelatine could be used effectively in connection with the arrival in the UK of Hitler's deputy, Rudolf Hess.[28] Hess had bailed out over Scotland on 10 May 1941 on a mission to broker peace with Britain, had been captured and was being held at the behest of MI6.[29] At a meeting at an undisclosed location in the countryside, Knight suggested to Bill Luke that Gelatine could feed information to the Germans via the social circles in which she associated on the effect the Hess incident had had upon people of influence in the country.[30]

Luke expressed concern over the idea of involving the subject of Hess because the policy would have to be 'dictated from the highest sources' (MI6) before MI5 could send out any information via Gelatine. Luke was of the opinion that the information Gelatine gave to the Germans should be solely of a political nature, as she would be party to such chatter being sister-in-law to the brother of the head of MI6. Gelatine thus inadvertently found herself at the centre of the developing policy discussions about war-altering information.

Gelatine often worked in conjunction with the famous male double-agent 'Balloon', recruited by Tricycle in 1941.[31] Balloon, whose real name has not been released, was British, thirty-four years old and employed in a company which dealt in arms.[32] He had been educated at Cheltenham, then Sandhurst Military Academy and left the army in disgrace due to some kind of financial irregularity over cheques. The Germans paid their male agents more; for Balloon this amounted to sums of between £325 and £360 every three months.[33]

Gelatine was allocated a new British handler, Susan Barton, and began to sign her letters to the Germans 'Mabel', sending them to a new cover address in Lisbon.[34] She fed deception to the Germans – snippets of gossip like 'Lord Beaverbrook refused to join the War Cabinet if it included Sir Stafford Cripps. Cripps is very popular with the public'; 'I heard that General Wavell would hand in his resignation should he not receive sufficient reinforcements and supplies this time'; and 'The working classes here take every opportunity to humiliate rich people.'[35]

Some figures within Double Cross began to question Gelatine's suitability as an agent. On 12 March 1942 Masterman received a telephone call from Victor Cavendish-Bentinck (chair of the Joint Intelligence Committee) in which Cavendish-Bentinck raised concerns about Gelatine. He described her as an intelligent woman, 'yet with the mentality of a night club hostess and having a terror of the Germans winning the war'.[36] His comment reflects a stereotypically misogynist attitude of the era, but he was not the only figure who was critical of her. Wilson reported that the Germans took such little notice of Gelatine that it would be better to let her case die.[37] He suggested she should be sent back to Maxwell Knight, concluding that 'She will never be of the slightest use to us in obtaining her own information.'[38]

Menzies, 'C', did not allow the Twenty Committee to stand Gelatine down: she was an MI6 double agent and, as such, he had the final say over her future.[39] She was part of Menzies's own inner circle and, more, 'C' believed in her. Soon, too, she would prove her worth.

Gelatine was involved with double agents Mutt, Jeff, Dragonfly and Balloon in Operation Omnibus, a major deception plan executed between 31 May and 30 June 1941 to fool the Germans into believing there was an imminent invasion of the coastline of German-occupied Norway.[40] False reports and messages were given to the Germans about the special training of troops in Scotland, an influx of refugees there from Norway and recruitment adverts asking for fishermen with a knowledge of the Norwegian coast. The deception continued after the German invasion of Russia in Operation Barbarossa on 22 June 1941, in an attempt to keep German forces occupied elsewhere so that they could not reinforce the Russian front.

Later that year Gelatine sent a letter to her Abwehr contact in Lisbon saying that she had recently attended a cocktail party in London at which she had met a major from the War Office. He had informed her that he was always busy and worked late into the night just before a significant military operation. He told her that he had been present at the raid on the Lofoten Islands (the first being in March 1941) and was shortly going abroad again. He hinted at the best strategic place for the British to invade Norway. Gelatine's letter also mentioned fishing in the southern fjords. The intention was to divert the attention of the Germans towards defending a different part of the Norwegian coastline ahead of the next raid. Gelatine's deception supported a successful raid by British commandos on the island of Vågsøy on 27 December 1941 in Operation Archery.

The success of operations Omnibus and Archery in 1941 demonstrated that it was possible to deceive the Germans about the location of an invasion.

In early 1942, Tricycle was sent to the United States to work closely with the FBI. His trip nearly blew Gelatine's and Balloon's cover. The Twenty Committee received information that he had been compromised and the Germans suspected him of working for Allied intelligence.[41] The Abwehr did not suspect Gelatine, even though Tricycle had introduced her to them.[42] The Twenty Committee needed to know whether Gelatine and Balloon had been betrayed, and in the interim decided not to send her letters of 9 and 10 May 1942 to Lisbon.

A meeting of a few members of the Twenty Committee took place on 12 May 1942 to discuss a response.[43] It was decided to increase and improve the traffic being fed to the Germans by Gelatine and Balloon so the Germans believed them to be German agents. False information that Tricycle had only been working as an agent for Allied intelligence since his trip to America was successfully fed to the Abwehr. It worked. The Germans concluded that Balloon was not working for the British and was one of its own most outstanding agents. This meant that Gelatine and Balloon were able to continue their operations.[44]

With Gelatine and Balloon cleared of any suspicion, MI5 planned further specialist deception for autumn 1942 to protect the invasion of North Africa (Operation Torch). Plans Solo 1 and Overthrow were implemented by the Twenty Committee to trick the Germans ahead of the landings. With the previous success of Plan Omnibus in Norway, the Twenty Committee believed deception could work again. The Germans had underestimated the Allies, erroneously believing that they did not have sufficient naval resources to mount a successful assault on North Africa.[45] Gelatine and others had provided false material on this to their German handlers so the invading forces could maintain an element of surprise – the Germans believing it would not happen and thereby ensuring more chance of success in the invasion.

How many times could the Germans fall for such trickery? Susan Barton, Section B1a's expert on the German mindset, urged her male colleagues to create ever more elaborate future schemes.

Bronx

In October 1942, another female agent, Elvira Concepción Josefina de la Fuente Chaudoir, joined the Double Cross System. The twenty-nine-year-old was already an MI6 agent. The daughter of a Peruvian merchant, she had fluent French, English and Spanish, and a basic level of Italian. Between 1919 and 1934 she lived with her parents in Paris. In 1934 she married Jean Chaudoir, a Belgian stock exchange representative of a gold mining firm in Brussels, but she soon found life dull in Belgium.[46] Unconcerned about leaving behind a life of financial security, she returned to Paris in November 1938 and rented a flat on her own. In the spring of 1939, she travelled to Italy and by the summer was staying in Cannes in the south of France, touring casinos with Romy Gilbey, the wife of a gin manufacturer, Quintin Gilbey. With war in Europe imminent, Chaudoir and Gilbey decided to travel to England. Like all civilians entering Britain, they were interrogated by British intelligence (MI9b) to check they were not enemy spies.[47]

For the next two and a half years it is not known what work Chaudoir carried out in England, but in 1942 she was turned down by SOE for reasons not given in her personal MI5 file.[48] Neither is it known whether MI5 or MI6 had her under surveillance. She lived the high life at weekends, attended parties hosted by Lord Carnarvon and spent weekday evenings at the bar in the Ritz Hotel or gambling at poker tables. Moving in these circles meant that eventually MI6 noticed her, and she was asked to meet a gentleman at the Connaught Hotel. He was Claude Dansey, deputy head of MI6, and a man who believed that 'every man has his price and every woman is seducible'. He proposed that she return to Vichy France, live with her parents again, mix in high society and send back political intelligence as a SIS agent. It is perhaps surprising that Dansey sought to recruit her, given that he was averse to sending female agents behind enemy lines, believing them to be untrustworthy.[49] But, even he had to concede to the louder argument within MI6 that women behind the lines were valuable to the secret service. In the end, Dansey did not consider Chaudoir's espionage mission to be risky because living with her wealthy influential father would place her above suspicion in the circles in which she would be mixing. Dansey secretly hoped that the Germans would pick her up as a double agent. Her motivation in working for the British was 'for love of adventure and excitement and in the hope of getting money'.[50]

In January 1942, she received her first instruction in codes, trained by Beau Baschwitz, a Belgian agent and SIS officer from the First World War.[51] She was found to be quick to grasp the essentials of the training but inclined to be careless. She received instruction in the use of invisible ink, and SIS assessed her to be 'intelligent and [with] a quick brain but is probably rather lazy about using it'.[52]

In the months immediately before her mission, Chaudoir frequented the Hamilton Bridge Club and the Ritz Hotel with her friend Romy Gilbey and bragged to her about working for the British Secret Service.[53] She said that she was shortly to be sent to Vichy France to pass on codes to British agents there. The gossip was mentioned by Gilbey to a friend, Miss Monica Morrice, who was an acquaintance of Sub-Lieutenant Burnett RNVR, an interrogator at Cockfosters POW camp at Trent Park. Burnett was concerned by Chaudoir's indiscretion and commented to MI5 that Chaudoir was pretending to be a secret agent. Her claims must have continued because a few weeks later SIS wrote to MI5 a memo which ended: 'You will probably be interested in finding out what grounds the lady had for making this rather sensational claim.'[54]

Consequently, Chaudoir received a visit from an officer of Special Branch, on behalf of MI5, and was told to cease her statements about working for the British Secret Service. She was not told the source of the information, nor that it had come via MI5.

MI5 continued to be concerned about her and wrote to Kim Philby at MI6 asking if Chaudoir was employed by SIS.[55] Philby replied on 3 May that she was not employed by SIS or SOE, not wishing to reveal to MI5 that she was an SIS agent. Later that year, when Masterman was considering Chaudoir for the Double Cross, he asked whether she had double-crossed SIS and given away its methods in secret ink. It is clear that, by now, SIS had finally admitted to MI5 that she worked for them.[56]

Given Chaudoir's indiscretion, it is perhaps surprising that SIS continued with her mission to Vichy France. Preparations were made behind the scenes for her to slip into high society there. One of the ways this was achieved was to notify the Peruvian consul general, Mr Benavides, who was a friend of the family and the military attaché, that she intended to come to Vichy France because the war looked as if it would be a long affair and, with little prospect of a job, Chaudoir did not want to be cut off from her parents.

With the cover name 'Cyril', SIS sent her to Vichy France in July 1942 where she began to mix in casinos and at parties in the hope that she would be contacted by the German intelligence service. At a casino in Cannes she was approached by a French collaborator, Henri Chauvel, who invited her to lunch.[57] Over their meal he expressed pro-Axis views and discussed England. He was keen for her to meet his German friend, Helmut Bleil (aka Biel, and nicknamed 'Bibi'). Chauvel told her that Biel was a secret agent working for Hermann Goering, head of the German air force, and that Biel changed his name every day. It was some considerable time before she met Biel, which she did in Cannes. Chauvel and Biel both accepted her cover story that she was in the region on a personal visit. They did not suspect her of being a British agent. Biel asked her to gain economic and industrial intelligence from England and to penetrate SIS to pass information back to the Germans.[58] He agreed to pay her a salary of £100 a month. Little did he know that she was, in fact, already working for SIS against him.

Ten days after the first meeting, Biel reappeared and provided Chaudoir with instruction in German techniques of secret ink writing. Her salary would be paid from a bank account in Switzerland, which she could purport came from her separated husband as part of a settlement.[59] Chaudoir was assessed by British intelligence to be the kind of character who would not take risks unless paid.[60] The Germans would treat her with caution initially because of her need for money, but once they paid her properly it was a clear indication that they trusted her. With this trust established, Chaudoir was due to travel back to London via Lisbon sometime during October 1942. She kept a diary of her time in occupied France during 1942 but its whereabouts, if it has survived, is unknown.[61]

From Lisbon, Kim Philby was working as head of counter-espionage for MI6 in the Iberian peninsula, where his officers were tracking German agents and spies. Whether Chaudoir met him in Lisbon is not noted in her MI5 file, but he was monitoring the Peruvian consul general, Benavides, who had met an important German agent in Nice.[62] Chaudoir had kept up regular contact with Benavides, and Philby asked MI6 to question her about him on her return to Britain. Chaudoir had been due to travel back to London with Benavides, but unexpectedly he had left ahead of her. MI6 asked MI5 to exempt Chaudoir from interrogation or any examination of her papers on entry into Britain, and for them to 'expedite her journey to London', where she would be met by an MI6 officer.[63] This instruction to MI5 reinforces the view that she was in fact a double agent for MI6.

For a short period, Chaudoir conducted Spanish translation work for the BBC. She maintained contact with SIS via Dansey and offered to visit her sister in Italy for MI6, but gave no hint as to whether her sister would be willing to pass information to SIS/MI6.

After her return to Britain, Chaudoir was enlisted into the Double Cross System and given the codename 'Bronx' by her case officers Christopher Harmer and Hugh Astor, after the cocktail she drank when she met them. She became a letter-writing agent and wrote to her German handler in Lisbon via two cover addresses given to her by the Abwehr. It was noted that she received letters from the Germans in a type of ink only used for her. She was a gambler and frequented the Hamilton Club and Crockfords in London, often playing for high stakes. SIS and MI5 tracked her movements and acquaintances, and tapped her phone calls to ensure that she was not a security risk or double-crossing them. It was discovered that she had relationships with women which, as homosexuality was illegal, caused some concern because she could be open to blackmail. It was concluded that she displayed no evidence of pro-German sentiments and was a reliable agent.

She continued to receive occasional bonuses and a salary of £100 a month from the Germans.[64] But debts continued to mount from her extravagant lifestyle and gambling, and she turned to her parents for help with the cost of food, clothing, dentistry, medicine and (in her words) 'amusements'.[65]

Meanwhile, MI5 was having its own discussion about Bronx's finances and tried to negotiate with Bronx via case officer Harmer that she hand over a portion of the money received from the Germans to help MI5 with the costs of running her case.[66] Bronx did not agree and argued with Harmer that she would have been quite happy to accept £20 a month from British intelligence for her work. It was finally agreed that she would accept no expenses from MI5 and could keep her salary from the Germans. Much to Harmer's annoyance, Bronx discussed her finances over lunch with Dansey. Harmer believed it was none of Dansey's business to be interfering in MI5's financial arrangements with her. He noted how Bronx's case was being 'supervised by Dansey in this indirect manner and I am informing Major [Frank] Foley who I know is not very happy about his [Dansey] having a great deal to do with Bronx'.[67]

The continued interference of Dansey in the running of Bronx caused friction and irritation with MI5 during 1943. Using the pseudonym 'Mr Masefield', Dansey lunched with Bronx on 24 February 1943 and remarked to her that MI5 was not handling her case in the way he would have done.[68] He told her that, when he ran agents, he did not expect them to start giving up useful information to the enemy for a considerable period of time, but rather to build up specific contacts with confidence first. For a senior SIS figure whose name is largely absent from declassified intelligence files, these comments provide a rare glimpse into Dansey's modus operandi and thinking.

Throughout 1943, Bronx continued to receive money from the Germans for communicating in secret writing.[69] They organised a questionnaire for her to answer about preparations in Britain for gas warfare. She replied with a glowing account of preparations and said that England was far better prepared than the Germans in this respect, and the Germans believed her. Masterman described her as a very competent letter-writing agent for MI5.[70]

Penguin

The real identity of 'Penguin' is still unknown and her personal file is not declassified.[71] She was born in London on 9 June 1905 of British parents, and educated in England, France and Italy. She spoke the languages of these countries fluently. She had three children, but had separated from her husband in 1937 when she went to live in France. After the outbreak of war in 1939 she held various positions with the French Red Cross until June 1941, when she was informed that she could no longer be employed by them. She managed to obtain visas to enter Spain and Portugal and on 24 October 1941 arrived in Lisbon, where the Abwehr were constantly watching for new contacts to send to England for espionage. Penguin crossed paths with an Abwehr recruiter, Werner Schiebald, who proposed that she return to England and devote her energy to spreading peace propaganda for Germany. She agreed to 'work' for the Germans but refused to carry propaganda material back with her.

She arrived back in England on 14 March 1942. Details of her career as a double agent are patchy and thin, but it seems likely that at this point she was in touch with British intelligence, told them about Schiebald and was taken on as a double agent for the British. By the end of May she received a postcard from Schiebald inviting her to correspond with him. The communication hereafter appears patchy and eventually she wrote to him that she was employed by Censorship (which was in fact a purely notional job). At the end of August 1942, Schiebald replied that he had a friend who was 'crazy' to get in touch with her and suggested that she should travel to Lisbon. Penguin replied that this was not possible. At the end of December, MI5 put into operation a plan for opening up communication with Schiebald through the postal service, but no response was received. No further information is available currently about Penguin after December 1942 and it is assumed that she was closed down by MI5, although this cannot be said with certainty and she may have continued to operate.

Redhead

Another new channel for the Twenty Committee had opened up in Lisbon in 1942. Known as 'Redhead', her original name is not given in the files. She was a Belgian woman who could be of potential use to the Double Cross, being a mistress of the German Counsellor in Lisbon and known to be in contact with Weber of the Ribbentrop bureau.[72] Her supposed source of information would be the Belgian Legation, with whom she was on friendly terms. Her bona fides were unquestioned by 'C''s representative for Lisbon, Kim Philby, but, in spite of that, Cavendish-Bentinck decided a week later that Redhead should not be used and this was agreed by the Twenty Committee.[73]

The Snark

Maritza Mihailovic, codenamed 'The Snark', was another female agent used by the Twenty Committee.[74] She was a Roman Catholic, born in a small village in Yugoslavia and one of many children. Her father was a carpenter.[75] She had had no schooling and started work at the age of ten, looking after children in the village. She spent twenty years with one family in Zagreb, and in 1935 came to England as a cook/housekeeper, having seen an advertisement in a newspaper; as she could not read or write English, she had asked her boyfriend to reply on her behalf to the job agency in London. Her first position was with a family in Scarborough, where she stayed from May 1938 to January 1939. It was here that she learnt German from the other maids in the household. Then she took up employment with a doctor and his wife – refugees from Vienna – living in Kensington Park Gardens, until the couple departed for the United States.

In December 1940, Mihailovic made an unsuccessful attempt to return to her mother and sister in Yugoslavia, but difficulty in obtaining the necessary visas delayed her in Lisbon and then Madrid. There, a German-Yugoslav agent, Mirenad Jevrenovic, made contact with her and suggested that she return to England for the Abwehr. He required her to write to him fortnightly from England with details of air raid damage, factories and industry, location of military barracks, the food situation and morale among the poorer classes. She agreed, partly for fear of the Germans and because the Spanish police had threatened her with internment if she did not leave the country. However, she immediately reported the approach by them to the Yugoslav Legation and British authorities in Madrid.

Jevrenovic introduced her to two other members of the Abwehr, Friedrich Knappe, who ran an organisation there for despatching Abwehr agents overseas, and Helmut Lang, the liaison officer between Madrid and Bilbao. She also began receiving instruction by Dr Lanschk of the German secret service in the use of secret inks. She was given a small, unspecified sum of money and asked to sign an agreement that she would work for Germany. Later, in questioning by the British, she said she had no intention of fulfilling her mission for the Abwehr.

Mihailovic arrived back in England by ship from Lisbon on 4 July 1941.[76] She was arrested straightaway on suspicion of being an enemy agent and held in Holloway Prison. British intelligence looked to 'turn' her to work for Double Cross and secured her release. During her interrogation, she offered to pass information to the British if she overheard material; she talked about men who she believed were German spies in Lisbon.[77] She told her interrogators that she acted stupid so that people said things in front of her because they thought she did not understand. She was asked if she wanted to work for the British and she said that it had always been her intention to do so.

MI5 noted on her personal file: 'She is a remarkable intelligent woman, quick on the uptake and apparently very independent.'[78] However, Cyril Mills (of Section B1a) was inclined to believe she was not suitable as an agent; he assessed her to be quite incompetent and found it difficult to comprehend why the Germans would have selected her for a mission.[79] She was given an initial cover name 'Kissmequick' by MI5.[80] Double Cross's agent runner Mary Sherer deemed it unsuitable and changed it to 'The Snark', taken from the poem by Lewis Carroll 'The Hunting of the Snark'.

Susan Barton became The Snark's main handler and initially met her at a rented property in Barnet (Roseneath, 3 Gallen Lane). The Snark even spied on the other tenants of different nationalities and passed details about them to Barton.[81] Barton moved her to Flat 19, Rugby Mansions, an MI5 safe house in Kensington under constant surveillance, where the phones were bugged and the post monitored. The Snark was considered trustworthy by Sherer and she was given a position as housekeeper in accommodation that chiefly housed members of the Yugoslav Legation in London. She wrote fairly regularly to the Germans, to a contact address in Madrid, and signed her letters 'Carmen'. Later she was given a new address in Lisbon and told to sign off her letters 'Sylvia'.

The Snark's lack of a formal education showed in her letter-writing. Sherer wrote: 'Both her German wording and spelling is absolutely atrocious as in parts quite unintelligible, but as she herself says the people on the other side know that she's not very good at it. I suppose we better leave it as it is.'[82] The letters were general in content, then were overwritten by messages in secret ink, which gave intelligence to the Abwehr that had been approved by MI5. The Snark practised writing in secret ink and her attempts were analysed initially by the Scientific Section of MI5 to ensure they were correct. The report, partially quoted here, said: 'The brown letters fade and the background becomes lighter after a little time. This is a phenomenon with which we are well acquainted. The screed is somewhat irregularly written, no doubt due to writing too much with one dip of the stick. We find the same difficulty and get over it by dipping the stick more frequently. I regret there was a little accident during the development and the signature of the writer was burned. Trust this is not important.' Samples of The Snark's letters that use invisible ink survive in her file.

Replies from a German contact, Carlos Ramos, were slow. The Snark sent a letter to him in September: 'I have not heard from you for a long time. Have you forgotten me? Why don't you write? I am very sad. I am well. Please write soon.'[83]

Barton met with The Snark frequently and, in spite of the slow response of the Germans in corresponding with her, Barton wrote about her: 'Every time I see her, I impress upon her how essential it is to keep her mouth shut about her experiences and her connections with us. But the more I see of her the more convinced I've become that properly employed she could be very useful to us. But this quite apart from her main work of writing letters.'[84]

By March 1942 a situation developed in Lisbon in which The Snark's letters were being intercepted by an SIS agent who was (unknown to SIS) actually double-crossing SIS and was really working for Germans. He passed to SIS enough damning evidence about her for her to be arrested, except she was working under the control of MI5 who were monitoring her loyalty. It turned out that the SIS agent was double-crossing the Germans on his own initiative, in the hopes of receiving substantial sums of money. For nine months The Snark received no letters from the Germans, and it was thought that they no longer valued her as an agent. Eventually a letter arrived containing a new cover address, but still the Germans were slow to correspond with her. It was decided that The Snark would write a final letter and would be dropped unless they replied.[85]

They did not reply, and The Snark was faded out as an MI6 double agent; Foley reported that no further traffic was required from her.[86] However, her work for MI5 and MI6 was not over. She was assigned by Barton to spy on her colleague Lily Sergueiev (Sergeyev), aka 'Treasure', whose loyalty and reliability as a double agent were under question.

Treasure

Nathalie Lily Sergueiev was a French citizen of Russian origin, born in Petrograd (now St Petersburg) on 25 January 1912.[87] She had lived in Paris most of her life, where she had gained a considerable reputation at one time as an artist and latterly as a journalist. In Berlin in 1933 she met a German journalist, Felix Dassel, and remained in contact with him. In 1937 he asked her to go to Spain to cover the Civil War. At the same time, he intimated that he wanted intelligence reports from her, admitting that he was a member of the Abwehr. Sergueiev refused to comply and severed connections with him.

In November 1940 she applied to the French Red Cross to be repatriated and eventually returned to Paris the following month. Her country was under Nazi occupation and she was determined to work against the Germans. She believed that the best way to do that was to be taken on as a German agent and then work against Germany as a double agent for the British. She made contact with Dassel again, suggesting that she could undertake a mission abroad because of her language qualifications. Further, if he was ever in Paris, she would like to see him. About ten days later she received a letter saying that he had arrived in Paris. They met at a restaurant, Maxim's, and during the conversation he asked what she thought of the British, to which she replied that she considered Britain had badly let down France, and she had no love for that country. He asked if she would be willing to work for German intelligence service against the British. She accepted. She did not hear from Dassel again for some time. After nearly six weeks, she wrote to him to say she believed the Germans no longer wanted her services. She received a reply and was invited to Berlin where she began to receive training.

Her first mission was intended to be to Syria, but this fell through; then Australia via Russia, which also did not transpire. Sergueiev persuaded Herr von Winter, who had taken her over from Dassel, to send her to England because of her knowledge of English and because of her connections to a lecturer at Cambridge University. Winter assigned her to Major Emil Kliemann of Luft I, Paris (the Luftwaffe intelligence service). Kliemann was already the handler for Double Cross agent 'Dragonfly'. Kliemann organised Sergueiev's training, which included instruction in secret ink and wireless transmission. In the spring of 1942 she was in Paris receiving further instruction in writing in secret ink from a woman called Yvonne Delidaise. Details of the training she was being given by the Germans are vague in her MI5 file, but that does reveal that she had at least three rounds of training in secret ink writing.[88]

Before she left Paris, Kliemann supplied her with some pellets to use for secret writing. She was to heat one of these in a clear flame and, once melted, to take a wooden toothpick and dip it in the liquid. When that was dry, she was to redip it and continue doing so until all the liquid was absorbed and a new pellet had formed on the end of the stick. She was to take a sheet of paper with a non-shiny surface, and rub the paper evenly with cotton wool. On the side she rubbed she was to write her own cover letter in ink or, preferably, pencil. Her letter in invisible writing was written on the same side of the paper but at right angles to the visible text. It was her decision whether to use a code in her letter, but this was considered unnecessary by her handler.

The Germans gave Sergueiev a questionnaire to acquire information about the locations of military headquarters in London; exact addresses of buildings destroyed in German raids on railways and junctions; modifications to coastal defences; restricted areas; industrial centres; the situation of food supplies generally in England; and if she travelled to Cornwall she was to locate modifications to the transatlantic telephone cables which started from there. First, she needed to obtain the necessary visas from Madrid because she would be travelling to England via Spain and Gibraltar. Between January 1942 and June 1943, she received 3,000 francs a month from the Germans, plus expenses for travel into the unoccupied zone in connection with gaining her visas. Kliemann gave her a valuable diamond ring and a brooch. MI5 tried to work out whether this was a gift or payment for work. Kliemann in fact doubted that she would succeed in getting into England and being taken on as a British agent. If she did, he said he would send her a wireless transmitter camouflaged in an electric portable gramophone so they could communicate. He explained the dangers that her work involved, asked her to invent a cover story and warned her that if she should 'turn' as a double agent against the Germans she could consider the lives of her parents at risk.

Sergueiev arrived in Madrid on 25 June 1943. During this first week she called at the British consulate and passport control office to fill in a form for a British visa. She handed herself in and explained to the British passport control officer, Kenneth Benton – in actuality an SIS counter-espionage officer working undercover – that she wished to work for the British. Sergueiev was one of a number of 'walk-ins', to use that spycraft phrase again, who presented themselves to Benton and his wife Peggie, who were both working for SIS in Madrid. (For more on the couple's SIS careers, see Chapter 19.) Sergueiev outlined her background and explained to Benton how the Germans had recruited her for espionage against Britain. She remained in Spain for a few months during which time Peggie Benton, who was running 'watchers', was tasked with placing surveillance on Sergueiev to check she was not double-crossing them.

On the night of 5 November 1943 Sergueiev left by plane from Gibraltar for England, carrying false documents in the name of Dorothy Tremayne. On arrival in England, she was interrogated for five days at the Royal Patriotic School (RPS), a Victorian building in south London given over to a military intelligence branch to screen refugees and civilians coming into the country. Colonel Robertson assigned Mary Sherer to be Sergueiev's case officer, and she was the one responsible for conducting checks on her background. Sergueiev handed over the diamond ring and brooch that Kliemann had given her and these were placed in the B1a safe. Sherer assessed her as having great potential as a highly valuable double agent ahead of D-Day, if carefully assigned to a gullible German handler and given a wireless transmitter in Europe. Sherer gave her the codename 'Treasure'.

Robertson agreed with Treasure that MI5 would pay her a salary of £50 a month; any money which she received from the Germans as a salary would be handed over to MI5.[89] However, if she received bonuses from the Germans, she could keep 10 per cent of them. Guy Liddell described her as 'very intelligent and co-operative'.[90] But that perception was to change in light of what seemed to MI5 a fairly inconsequential matter: Sergueiev's dog Babs.

Babs could not be brought to the UK without six months' quarantine. During their discussions in Madrid, Kenneth Benton had assured Treasure that, if she left for England without her dog, Babs could perhaps be smuggled out by sea and reunited with her later. But the British authorities instead sent Babs to Algiers in the care of Treasure's sister.

This was hugely upsetting for Treasure. Sherer wrote: 'Treasure is very upset about the absence of her dog and has seriously threatened that if the dog does not arrive soon, she will not work anymore. I think this can be dealt with but it will remain to be seen. I didn't quite know what we can do to help, because if we have the dog sent over here officially it will have to go into quarantine, which from Treasure's point of view would be as bad as having it in Gibraltar.'[91] In addition, Treasure had fallen ill and was taken St Mary's Hospital, London, on 29 December 1943, where she was diagnosed with kidney stones. Doctors told her that her condition was so bad that if she did not have an operation she would die within six months. She continued to be depressed by her illness and the separation from her dog. Masterman described her as 'an intelligent but temperamental person'.[92] He and other MI5 officers found her difficult and, perhaps, lacked sympathy for her personal problems.

Three weeks later, in January 1944, Treasure received a letter from her sister that Babs had been run over. She was devastated and spoke about the circle of loneliness that was closing all around her. She described how 'In three months England has killed all my enthusiasm although it survived three years of the German yoke . . . I would like to say "Mariya [Sherer], laugh, cry or scream"; I would like to see her face express something. To me, she seems almost an automaton.' This was not an ideal relationship between agent and handler.

For MI5 there were other far more pressing concerns: they had just had to liquidate double agent Dragonfly after he was compromised. Fortunately, Dragonfly's case did not blow Treasure and she continued to be run successfully.

Ecclesiastic

A new Double Cross agent was recruited by SIS during 1944. She was Olga Zemanova, twenty-two years old and of Czech nationality, and she was given the codename 'Ecclesiastic'.[93] She was described as intelligent and a woman who utilised her feminine charms with great success, with a 'certain amount of patriotism', motivated by 'financial reasons' and wanting to 'keep her head above water by working for allies'.[94] She worked for a while on targeting Italian diplomats for the Polish intelligence service.

1. Memorial to Edith Cavell, near Trafalgar Square, London. Cavell ran a clandestine organisation that aided British and French POWs to escape from Belgium in the First World War. She gathered intelligence for the Allies and was arrested by the Germans on 12 October 1915 on charges of espionage. She was shot at the execution ground of Tir National, Brussels. Her defiance and heroism inspired women to take up resistance and intelligence activities for the remainder of the war and beyond.

2. Countess Gabrielle de Monge, who headed the Service de Monge escape line in the First World War to rescue Allied soldiers and aid their escape from German-occupied Belgium. It also collected intelligence for the British. Gabrielle de Monge is pictured here outside Château Conneux, the home of Thérèse de Radiguès.

3a. A miniature message sent by an agent of La Dame Blanche, which operated behind enemy lines in Belgium. During the First World War the network collected vital information for British intelligence (SIS) on the movement of German troops and armaments being sent to the front line. Tiny messages were hidden in household items, like the inside of a broom handle, to be collected from a dead letter box by another agent.

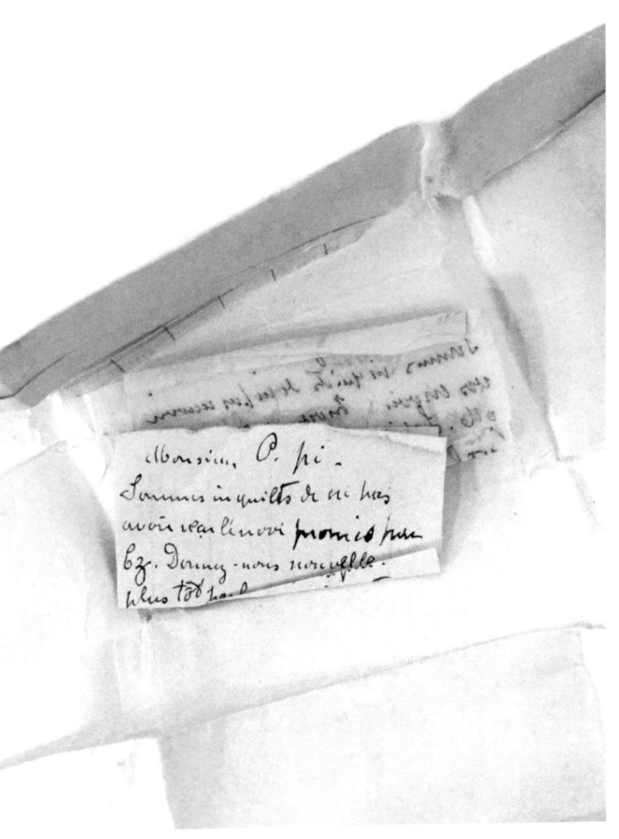

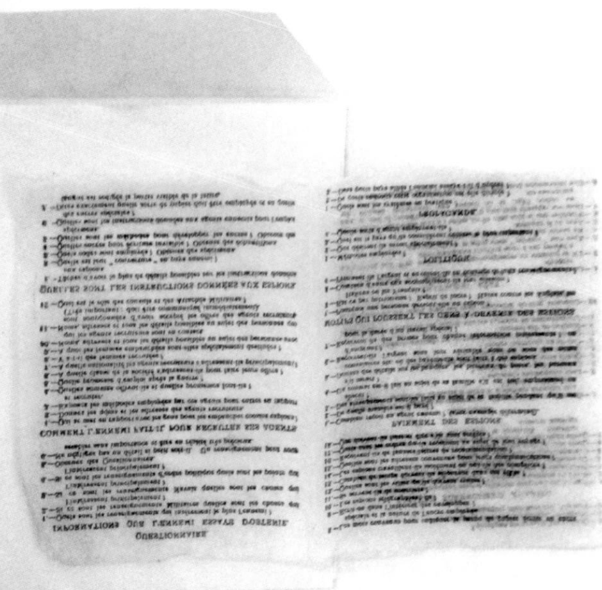

3b. An example of a printed micro-message containing intelligence. These were sent across La Dame Blanche and were impossible to read with the naked eye. They were hidden inside minuscule envelopes and were part of the spycraft of the First World War. La Dame Blanche was later recognised as being 'the most successful single British human intelligence operation of the war'.

4. Thérèse de Radiguès, who headed Platoon 49, an observation post for La Dame Blanche. In 1918 she was one of four women designated to take over the leadership of La Dame Blanche if the male leaders were arrested by the Germans. When Belgium was occupied again in 1940, she was co-founder with Walthère Dewé of the Clarence Service, the successor to La Dame Blanche. Then aged seventy-five, she again conducted intelligence work behind enemy lines.

5. The château at Conneux, the home of Thérèse de Radiguès during the First World War. From here she conducted her clandestine operations for La Dame Blanche and was one of over 3,000 Belgians who risked their lives as agents.

BEWARE

—OF—

FEMALE SPIES

Women are being employed by the enemy to secure information from Navy men, on the theory that they are less liable to be suspected than male spies. Beware of inquisitive women as well as prying men.

SEE EVERYTHING
HEAR EVERYTHING
SAY NOTHING

Concerning any matter bearing upon the work of the Navy

SILENCE IS SAFETY

6. Poster warning of female spies being used by the enemy in Britain, especially against men in the Royal Navy. Vernon Kell, the head of MI5, was so concerned that a successful German espionage network was being established in the UK that he drew up a list of possible suspects and circulated it to chief constables around the country.

7. Senior staff of the MI5 Registry with SIS Assistant Director Lieutenant-Colonel Maldwyn Haldane (front row seated) on the roof of MI5 headquarters, 1918. The Registry was the hub of operations and responsible for the custody of documents, the filing and preparing of papers, the preparation of adequate indexes to the records and the overseeing of the engagement and control of the staff. By 1917 it had become so large that it had to subdivide into several sections.

8. 'Midge' Holmes with her daughter Prudence in the Austrian mountains, 1930s. In the 1920s and 1930s Midge was an SIS 'secretary' in the British passport control office in Vienna, but this was a cover for running MI6 spy networks across Europe. During the Second World War she joined SOE in London and, as an expert on the country, became a senior figure in its Austria section. She went on to despatch secret agents into Austria.

9. Joan Osborne worked in the British Legation in Vienna from the early summer of 1939. She was known to be working for MI6 and, in 1940, was attached to the Political Intelligence Department in Whitehall, working on aspects of Czech and Polish intelligence. She helped with the research and compilation of weekly political intelligence summaries. At the end of the war, her work took her back to Austria.

10. Vera Atkins, WAAF intelligence officer and agent handler. She became deputy head of F Section, the French section of SOE. She believed in the ability of women to become highly suitable agents. At the end of the war, she interrogated Nazi war criminals to establish the fate of all her missing agents.

11. An assassin's pen, issued to some SOE agents, including women. The pen could be quite elaborate and ornate, but it concealed a sharp dagger. Such an item was found in the jewellery box of Margot Morse, one of the 'Baker Street irregulars' who worked in utmost secrecy for SOE.

12. Jane Archer (née Sissmore), MI5's first female officer who trained as a barrister in her spare time. By 1929 she was in sole charge of MI5's department for Soviet espionage in the UK and she went on to interrogate the Soviet defector Walter Krivitsky. Her subsequent career with MI6 was disrupted when double agent Kim Philby moved her aside, fearing that her interrogation skills might unmask him as a Soviet mole.

13. Section 17M, Naval Intelligence Division, in Room 13 of the Admiralty. The section executed Operation Mincemeat, in which a corpse, dressed as an officer of the Royal Marines, was floated off the coast of Spain carrying fake invasion plans. Seated, first left, is Helen Mary Brown (née Sullivan); on the back row, third right, is Joan Saunders; to her right is Juliette Ponsonby, and to her left is Patricia Trehearne.

14. The mansion house, Bletchley Park, Buckinghamshire, late 1939–early 1940. A couple of the original wartime huts are visible, as are bicycles by the main door and a few (as yet) unidentified personnel. By January 1945, three-quarters of the workforce at the codebreaking site were women.

15. The Quiet Watch, Hut 6, Bletchley Park. Messages were handed to the Quiet Room to try to unravel if the Watch was unable to break a code. The Quiet Watch was an essential part of the codebreaking process, ensuring that as much as possible was done to break every message. Helene Aldwinckle (née Taylor) is sitting on the far left.

16. Mrs Olive (Catharine) Milne Myler, MI6 spy and radio ham. She is pictured here at her home in Knowle in North Devon, working for MI8 as a voluntary interceptor (VI). She was one of only three female VIs in the Second World War and sent her intercepts to Box 25 at Arkley, North London. She was the only woman awarded the BEM for this intelligence work.

17. The White House, Wilton Park, Buckinghamshire. The site was the headquarters of MI9, the department of military intelligence responsible for escape and evasion and Q gadgets; and HQ also to MI19, which interrogated German POWs and bugged their conversations for vital intelligence.

18. Catherine Townshend at her desk at Wilton Park. In 1942 she became head of MI19(e), the department responsible for setting up and maintaining the highly classified 'M Rooms', which housed the eavesdropping equipment. She recruited secret listeners to the three clandestine sites outside London to record the conversations of German POWs for intelligence.

19. Dawn Rockingham-Gill at MI19 headquarters at Wilton Park. She was personal assistant to the head of MI19, Lt Col Arthur Rawlinson. MI19 processed intelligence from eavesdropping on the conversations of Axis prisoners of war, here and at its sister sites of Trent Park and Latimer House.

20. The Naval Intelligence Section, Latimer House, 1943. The Wrens at this site were interrogators and, as such, were the first known female interrogators used in wartime. The team often enjoyed cocktails of pink gin on the terrace.

21. Caryl Rosemary Baring-Gould, WAAF in Air Intelligence at Latimer House. In another groundbreaking first, she and her female colleagues analysed the intelligence coming out of the M Room and ensured it reached the right intelligence commanders and departments. Caryl also interrogated Adolf Galland, Germany's ace pilot. After the war she served as section officer in IS9's station at Wassenaar, near The Hague.

22. Constance Babington Smith, photographic interpreter at RAF Medmenham, Danesfield House, Marlow. She headed the Aircraft Interpretation Section at Medmenham, and went on to identify the V-1 sites from aerial photography brought back by RAF pilots on reconnaissance missions.

23. Z Section of RAF Medmenham, on the steps of Danesfield House. Z Section reported on the movement of enemy shipping and kept a large index of enemy vessels, as well as cards referencing the relevant photographs.

24. Nora Littlejohn of B2 Section, RAF Medmenham, where she analysed aerial photographs for intelligence purposes, including in identifying V-weapon sites.

25. Helroise Hawkins, WAAF officer in the Model Making Section, or V Section, RAF Medmenham. The section constructed over 1,400 models. These were used in the planning and briefing of all Allied landing operations, including D-Day. Eisenhower said, 'each of these model makers is worth 100 men!'

26. A rare photograph of the founding members of the Comet Line, July 1941. The Comet escape line ran from Brussels down to the Pyrenees via Bayonne, then over the mountainous terrain into Spain. It was used to smuggle Allied escapers and evaders out of Nazi-occupied Europe, to be flown back to the UK.

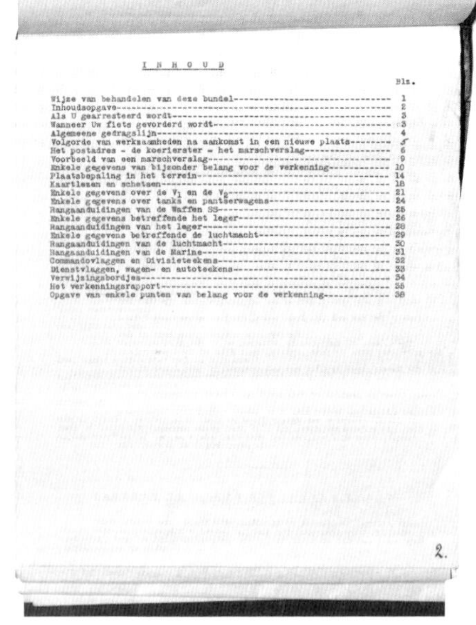

I N H O U D

	Blz.
Wijze van behandelen van deze bundel	1
Inhoudsopgave	2
Als U gearresteerd wordt	3
Wanneer Uw fiets gevorderd wordt	3
Algemeene gedragslijn	4
Volgorde van werkzaamheden na aankomst in een nieuwe plaats	5
Het postadres - de koerierster - het marschverslag	6
Voorbeeld van een marschverslag	9
Enkele gegevens van bijzonder belang voor de verkenning	10
Plaatsbepaling in het terrein	14
Kaartlezen en schetsen	18
Enkele gegevens over de V_1 en de V_2	21
Enkele gegevens over tanks en pantserwagens	24
Rangaanduidingen van de Waffen SS	25
Enkele gegevens betreffende het leger	26
Rangaanduidingen van het leger	28
Enkele gegevens betreffende de luchtmacht	29
Rangaanduidingen van de luchtmacht	30
Rangaanduidingen van de Marine	31
Commandovlaggen en Divisieteekens	32
Dienstvlaggen, wagen- en autoteekens	33
Verwijzingsbordjes	34
Het verkenningsrapport	35
Opgave van enkele punten van belang voor de verkenning	38

2.

27. The 'cookery book', a plain, blue, linen-covered book, written in Dutch, with a label that reads in translation 'Recipes, Domestic Science School'. In reality it was an intelligence handbook belonging to an unnamed female agent who worked in Holland for Room 900, a top-secret section of MI9. She reported to Airey Neave of MI9/Room 900 immediately after Arnhem, between October 1944 and May 1945. The first page of the book contains a warning about its secret nature. The table of contents deals with spycraft and provides a series of instructions on how to identify key military targets in enemy country, including Hitler's V-weapons and naval units.

28. Monica Washburn (née Paterson), who worked for MI6, pictured here in Paris around 1945–46. She had had a career with SIS in Izmir, Turkey, from the 1930s. After the war, she transferred to Paris for an intelligence role with the Supreme HQ Allied Powers Europe (SHAPE), where she ran the library at its headquarters near Fontainebleau. From there she was posted to MI6 headquarters in London.

WEEK - I - SAW - A -
MEN - UNLOADING - A - LORRY - FULL - OF -
FOOD - STUFFS - IN - TO - AN - OLD - EMPTY - HOUSE
NEXT - TO - THE - CHURCH - AT - ROEHAMPTON -
I - HOPE - YOU - WONT - MIND - READING - MY -
ARTICLE - IN - SUNDAY - GRAPHIC - AS - IT - WAS -
ESSENTIAL - THAT - I - SHOULD - GET - THE -
REPUTATION - OF - HATING - GERMANY

29. Sample of secret ink from a letter written by female Double Cross agent Bronx. Her real name was Elvira Concepción Josefina de la Fuente Chaudoir. Her most important contribution was to Plan Ironside, in convincing the German secret service that the Allied landings were due to take place in the Bay of Biscay, rather than the Normandy beaches. Resultingly, on D-Day the Germans held back the 11th Panzer Division in the Bordeaux area.

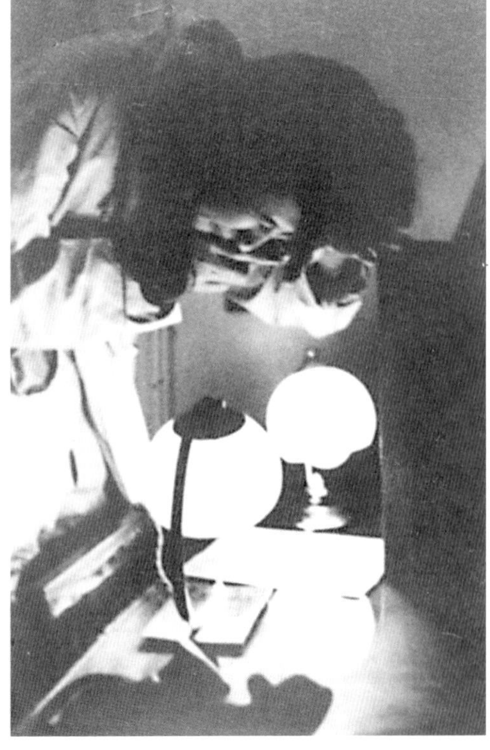

30. MI6 double agent Ecclesiastic, whose real name was Olga Zemanova. Of Czech nationality, her British handler was 'Klop' Ustinov, the father of actor Peter Ustinov. The photograph was taken in Lisbon by her German handler, Franz Koschnick. One of her roles for MI6 was to target the chief of the Abwehr in Lisbon in order to gain German aircraft industrial intelligence.

Ecclesiastic's British handler was 'Klop' Ustinov, the father of actor Peter Ustinov.[95] In 1944 she was placed in Lisbon as the mistress of Franz Koschnick, an Abwehr officer who was desperately short of intelligence on the Allies. SIS believed that his need for intelligence could be used to its advantage and positioned Ecclesiastic under civilian cover to work as a secretary in an office staffed by British RAF personnel. This job convinced Koschnick that she had access to technical air intelligence. Koschnick required her to develop contacts and friendships with British and Dutch aircrew flying between Portugal and Britain to secure information from them on the damage caused by V-1 weapons. He unwittingly fed her deception to the Germans, including misleading claims about the damage that German bombs had caused to central London. But the material that Ecclesiastic passed to him was beyond his expectation, including details about a new aeroplane and various letters printed on authentic Air Ministry notepaper which she had photographed for him. The letters contained aero-technical information. This had been prepared for her by Flight Lieutenant Charles Cholmondeley of MI5.

Koschnick photographed her in action, providing her with a copy, and this rare photograph is reproduced in the official MI6 history. He remained infatuated with her and considered leaving his wife, but Ecclesiastic had no intention of marrying him. In April 1944 she received a new assignment after the cover office in Lisbon was closed down by SIS. She remained in the city and targeted the chief of Abwehr responsible for German aircraft industrial intelligence. Further details of her clandestine work are difficult to ascertain since her personal file has not been declassified and therefore there is currently only a patchy picture of her work. Nevertheless, it appears that she did indeed achieve results for MI6.

Operation Triplex

Triplex, or XXX, was a joint operation by MI5 and SIS which used a number of the double agents to covertly copy the contents of diplomatic bags as they passed in and out of neutral countries' London embassies. It remains one of the most closely guarded secrets of the

Second World War, revealed in detail by Nigel West and Oleg Tsarev.[96] Triplex was managed for SIS by David Boyle and for MI5 by Anthony Blunt. Unknown to MI5 and SIS, one of the Cambridge Five – Anthony Blunt – was secretly passing Triplex information to the Russians.

At least one of the Double Cross agents, 'Josephine', was believed by Guy Liddell to have been used for Triplex.[97] While her precise role in the operation is unknown, it is likely she was copying the material in the Yugoslav diplomatic bags. The Triplex material reveals the codenames of MI5 assets inside London diplomatic missions, and these names were passed to the Russians by Blunt and the others. One of them was double agent 'Duck', who was working out of Spain. It was not possible to assess Duck's achievements but it seems that she was working in connection with diplomatic reports and signed for telegrams.

Blunt gave away information on 'Rumba' who was used in a section of the Ministry of Information in Latin America and was acquainted with its diplomats. 'Plover' worked as the secretary typist at the embassy in Argentina, then transferred to Gibraltar. Information was leaked on 'Hale', a secretary typist in Colombia who looked to be stationed there long term. She was willing to pass information at her disposal, although her information had not been of too much use. 'Lemon' was working out of Sweden and she was described as an invaluable agent who gave information on various attachés.

Towards the end of the Second World War, Blunt asked for a full list of the double agents working out of various embassies and agencies involved in Triplex. He was given a list, but was also told that British intelligence tried to avoid keeping such documentation and he was to destroy it. Blunt did not comply – and instead passed it to the Russians.[98] One of those was a forty-three-year-old Spanish woman working in the French Independent Agency as a senior typist and secretary. The Spanish authorities had not allowed her to return to Madrid because she had worked for the Republican government during the Civil War. She had been working for British intelligence since around 1943. It was commented that she would probably continue to help British intelligence after the war and until a change of government allowed her to return to Spain. She was seen as a rather frivolous woman but a satisfactory agent.

It is not possible to ascertain, on current information, whether Blunt betrayed the real names of the above agents. Their files have not been released into the National Archives.

Special Agents and a German Invasion of the UK

MI5 put in place contingency plans in the event of a German invasion of Britain. Codenamed Plan Hegira, it made provision for its double agents to be evacuated immediately to Wales to avoid them falling into enemy hands.[99] It allowed also for the evacuation of their wives and children. The case officers were each allocated to a particular double agent and family to escort personally to Wales, and this included ensuring that all documents were burnt and wireless apparatus destroyed. The accompanying case officer was to be carrying not less than £10 in cash, petrol coupons for 20 gallons, a revolver and two pairs of handcuffs.

Orders were given to MI5 case officer John Marriott concerning the wife of double agent 'Snow' that, 'As it is of vital importance that Mrs Snow should not fall into the hands of the enemy, you must be prepared to take any step necessary to prevent this from occurring.'[100] Parallel orders were given for the wives and families of other double agents; their work affected the women connected with them, whether those women were aware of their husbands' work or not. MI5 officer Cyril Mills was instructed in a similar vein to protext double agent 'Stork' and his wife and baby. Arrangements were even made for Cyril Mills's Bertram Mills Circus and its animals to be evacuated to North Wales.[101]

Robertson noted to Maxwell Knight that 'C' had a special interest in Gelatine and wished her to be specially looked after in case of invasion. SIS gave instructions for Gelatine to be moved to Wales, accompanied by Susan Barton. Barton made it clear that she would escort her to Wales but did not wish to be left in charge of her. Christopher Harmer was to take over with Gelatine and ensure she burnt all documents.[102] Plan Hegira mentions 'Michael', a female agent who was to be put on the suspect list for immediate arrest in the event of a German invasion; reasons for this action are not given and her file has not been declassified. Of The Snark and Penguin it was noted – again without explanation – that they were not to be moved; they would be allowed to continue their normal occupations and stay at their residences, but all steps were to be taken to ensure they were not captured.[103] Plan Hegira was updated periodically, with instructions issued that Bronx was also to be sent North Wales, although travelling first via one of MI5's addresses in Hendon.[104]

The relationship of the female Double Cross agents with their German handlers was developed over a long period of time and required patience. The Double Cross operation was part of the slow intelligence war that would later yield results. Susan Barton believed in the value of the female special agents beyond the role of letter-writing and she, in the end, would be proved right. From 1943 the war was entering a critical phase with the planned invasions of Sicily and Normandy. The double agents, male and female, were about to assume a new importance.

11
DOUBLE CROSS DECEPTION

Throughout 1943 deception operations against Nazi Germany were dramatically escalated to support the Allied plans for the invasion of Sicily and Italy that summer. British intelligence believed that advance deception and false intelligence fed to the Germans would increase the chances of Allied successes and minimise casualties in the landings. The Germans anticipated a landing somewhere in southern Europe, but had not established where that would be. The challenge for British intelligence was to feed enough material to the enemy for them to think that an invasion was to take place in Greece rather than Sicily. Behind the scenes, British double agents continued to build up the relationship of trust with their German handlers. Tricycle, Gelatine and Balloon fed important information to the Germans, which could not be verified or discredited, on British defences, production and technology and political gossip.

While plans for invasion deception were being discussed by the Twenty Committee, the Germans were trying to gain intelligence on Britain's atomic programme.[1] Ironically, they used British double agents to gain information about the wider British armament programme, believing them to be loyal German agents. Gelatine was given a detailed questionnaire by her German handler to establish the progress of uranium development in the UK. MI5 and MI6 knew about this and, consequently, Gelatine's British handler gave her rumours to spread back to the Germans.[2]

Meanwhile, Bronx had received a questionnaire from the Germans about the Vickers Windsor four-engine heavy bomber and the Bristol Blenheim light bomber, to establish whether these aircraft were yet in production.[3] The Germans wanted to know the names of other aircraft and their specifications, the types of engines (including development by Rolls Royce and jet propulsion) and whether Frank Whittle's turbojet engine was being produced under US licence. The questionnaire was a good indication of the kind of intelligence the Germans were trying to acquire on Allied armaments and provided an opportunity to feed false intelligence back to the Germans.

Since its beginnings in 1941, the Double Cross System had progressed to be used for counter-espionage activities as well as deception. It had five supplementary aims which formed the core of its work: to control the German espionage service; to detect and apprehend enemy agents; to gain knowledge of the German intelligence service system and personalities; to gain evidence and an understanding of enemy intentions; and to gain assistance for code and cipher work.[4] It had evolved into a sophisticated programme that would reap rewards for British intelligence and make a material difference to the intelligence war.

Ahead of the invasion of Sicily in summer 1943, the Twenty Committee planned a new covert operation with Section 17M, the section within Naval Intelligence 12 (NID 12) responsible for naval deception and the handling of special intelligence from ISOS.[5] Its head, Ewen Montagu, served as the NID representative on the Twenty Committee. The aim of the new major deception was to fool the Germans about the location of the invasion in southern Europe by floating the dead body of an officer of the Royal Marines off the coast of Spain. In his briefcase chained to his wrist would be papers that included fake invasion plans. It was a work of total fiction that took some of the most creative minds in intelligence to write the script. It was codenamed Operation Mincemeat and would be one of the most audacious naval deceptions of the war. The unknown element was whether the Germans would fall for it.

Operation Mincemeat

Section 17M set to work in meticulous detail on Operation Mincemeat to ensure that nothing was left to chance. By the planning stage, the section had fourteen members, two-thirds of whom were women.[6] The female secretarial team was nicknamed 'the Beavers', the youngest of whom was eighteen-year-old Jean Leslie. The first priority was to acquire a corpse and preserve it until the operation was set to go. British pathologist Sir Bernard Spilsbury and coroner Bentley Purchase were consulted by Section 17M. In St Pancras mortuary was the corpse of thirty-four-year-old Glyndwr Michael, an unemployed labourer of no fixed abode who had committed suicide with rat poison. He was about to be given a new identity and the starring role in Operation Mincemeat. The details of his new identity were to be worked out by Montagu, Flight Lieutenant Cholmondeley and Joan Saunders. They decided on 'Major William Martin of the Royal Marines', born in 1907. It was not only a matter of creating a new identity but of crafting a whole personality, even his likes and dislikes, and a full family background so as to be more convincing to the Germans. They spent the days discussing and slowly compiling a portfolio of the man. In the evenings they went off to the Gargoyle, Montagu's club in Soho, where over drinks they continued to build up their imaginary hero.

Major Martin was given identity papers and a card to show he was a member of the Naval and Military Club in London, with a history of mounting debts, as confirmed in a fake letter from his bank asking him to pay off his overdraft. The fictitious paperwork and his apparent extravagant lifestyle were necessary to hold his cover story. Joan Saunders noticed that Major Martin lacked a love life and it would be more realistic for him to have a girlfriend. The women of Section 17M created 'Pam', a pretty young fiancée, a holiday snapshot of whom – actually MI5 clerk Jean Leslie – was placed on his body. Miss Hester Leggett, who headed the secretarial team, has been credited with writing the fictitious love letters purporting to be from Pam, but in reality it was probably a combined effort by a number of women.

On 3 April 1943, the body of Major Martin was clothed in the battle dress and flashes of the Royal Marines by Montagu and Cholmondeley, with assistance from the coroner.[7] A briefcase with the forged documents, including invasion plans suggesting an Allied assault was soon to take place on Greece and Crete, was strapped to the wrist of the corpse. The body was placed in a specially manufactured airtight container to prevent deterioration and loaded onto submarine HMS *Seraph*. The submarine left the port of Greenock in Scotland and headed for Spain.

At 04:30 hrs on 30 April 1943, the body was launched into the ocean from HMS *Seraph* near Huelva, off the coast of Spain.[8] As had been hoped, it was picked up by a Spanish fisherman, who passed it to Spanish naval headquarters. The Spanish naval authorities refused to hand over the briefcase to the British consul and instead sent it to Madrid where the three letters were opened and photographed. The envelopes were then resealed to look untouched and passed to the British naval attaché. The photographed versions were despatched to the Germans with a request for strict secrecy. The German intelligence service in Portugal finally heard about the documents and were summoned to a conference on 12 May. In the interim period between the body's discovery and the conference, a post mortem by Spanish authorities concluded death by drowning. On 2 May 1943, Major Martin was buried at Huelva and his funeral attended by Spanish naval and military officers.

On 12 May, at the Admiralty in London, Juliette Ponsonby picked up the day's decrypts from the teleprinter room. Bletchley Park had intercepted a wireless message sent by General Alfred Jodl, chief of the Operations Staff of the German forces, responsible for all planning and strategic operations. His message, copies of which were despatched across the German High Command, was to confirm that an enemy landing on a large scale was projected in the near future in the eastern and western Mediterranean. This was the moment that Ewen Montagu knew that the Germans had been duped by Operation Mincemeat. The Germans were convinced that an invasion was planned for Sardinia, rather than Sicily, and dispersed their troops accordingly. A whole Panzer division was moved from France to the Peloponnese and a communications headquarters at Tripoli was established in mid-May 1943.[9] Verification of this was received back in England via Special Intelligence and Ultra decrypts.

Operation Mincemeat was also supported by Bronx, who informed her German handler that an Allied invasion of France was to take place in September 1943. Her messages were part of Operation Cockade, which was a series of deceptions designed to relieve pressure on the Allied landings in Sicily. It also had the effect of aiding the Russians on the Eastern Front by diverting attention towards other alleged attacks by the Allies in Western Europe.

Documents captured by the Allies at the end of the war confirmed that the Germans had fallen for the fictional invasion plans. Operation Mincemeat was 'a small classic of deception, brilliantly elaborate in detail, completely successful in operation'.[10] An appendix to a report on the operation ended with the words: 'MINCEMEAT swallowed whole.'[11]

The Double Cross System was proving so successful that by the end of 1943 it had become more powerful and better equipped than before. The Twenty Committee was confident to tackle the biggest deception of all: uppermost in the minds of its members was whether a similar ruse to Operation Mincemeat could deceive the Germans ahead of D-Day.

Dangers

In the period leading up to D-Day, the Double Cross was always in danger and, as Masterman admitted, 'was not far from failure just before the period of our greatest success'.[12] By 1944 Allied preparations for D-Day and the largest amphibious invasion in history faced real intelligence dangers, despite Double Cross's strength. These emanated from German spymasters and intelligence officers in the Iberian peninsula who began to realise that Germany was going to lose the war and came over to Britain to impart information to their agents.[13] In April 1944 Heinrich Himmler replaced Admiral Canaris as chief of the German secret service. The Twenty Committee's concern was that Himmler's efficiency and ruthlessness could unmask weak spots in the Double Cross during the crucial period before D-Day. But Double Cross held up, and no investigation was ever undertaken to check on its agents.

There were other difficulties too, in relation to double agent Treasure. Her handler Mary Sherer had concluded that Treasure was of little use to the department without a wireless transmission set. On 1 March 1944 Treasure was sent to Lisbon to secure a transmitter from her Abwehr handler, Kliemann, to enable her to communicate with him from England.[14] The mission received approval at the highest level from the head of MI6. Ahead of her visit, she alerted Kliemann by secret letter that she would be in Lisbon. Her cover story was that she was working in the Occupied Territories Section of the Ministry of Information's film division, which produced documentaries on the history of war to counter German propaganda. She met him and his Abwehr officers several times in Lisbon, and he asked her to report on such matters as the exact location of Eisenhower's headquarters, provide information on new aeroplanes, make observations in the Bristol area and inform him whether the Americans were sending invasion barges there, and, if so, how many and when. This would give the Germans an idea of the extent of invasion plans by the Allies. He agreed she could have a wireless set.

Treasure arrived back in the UK on 23 March and provided MI5 with a full description of the men she had met in Lisbon. She brought back with her £1,200 in cash and a diamond bracelet worth £300, given to her by the Germans for her excellent work. Undisclosed secret sources revealed that she was highly regarded by the Germans and was not suspected of having double-crossed them.[15] The wireless set was sent to her via the diplomatic bag, and was installed in the furnished flat at 39 Hill Street in Westminster provided for her by MI5. She started transmitting to the Germans, who had agreed to contact her on Tuesdays, Thursdays and Saturdays at midday and 10 p.m. If she needed to communicate with them, she was given two slots of a half hour per week to do so to maintain security and remain undetected.[16] She spent weekends in Bristol and informed Kliemann that she had not observed any troop movements of importance anywhere in the south-west. This reinforced the Germans' view that the invasion would be mounted from Kent and the south-east of England.

But Treasure was struggling. Distressed by the death of her dog and by the response of British intelligence, she threatened to betray the whole double agent network to the Germans, including her part in it, as revenge.[17] To manage the threat, MI6 confiscated her radio transmitter and continued to transmit messages as if they were her. Mary Sherer struggled to know what to do with her and reported to MI5 that Treasure was being very unreasonable.[18] The two women had not really bonded, and Treasure believed Sherer to be entirely unsympathetic to her situation. The difficulty for MI5 was that Treasure was indispensable, because ciphers used by her and 'Brutus' had already enabled GC&CS to break an extremely important group of telegram traffic.[19] It was reluctant to cease her activities because of the valuable cryptographic material that was being obtained from her work. Guy Liddell, head of counter-espionage at MI5, commented: 'We see no particular object in having a showdown with her at this moment'.[20]

The Twenty Committee pressed ahead with plans for its D-Day deception, focusing almost exclusively on strategic deception.

D-Day Deception

The main deception for Overlord was codenamed Plan Bodyguard and designed to mislead the Germans that the D-Day invasion would take place at Pas-de-Calais in northern France.[21] At the forefront of Plan Bodyguard were the male agents Garbo, Tricycle, Brutus, Mullet and Tate.[22] Strongly supporting their male colleagues were the female agents Gelatine, Treasure and Bronx.[23] Garbo was running an organisation of fake German sub-agents with great efficiency and panache, leading the Germans to believe that he had a real network of agents. Brutus built up a false order of battle for D-Day which the Germans believed. Gelatine was thought to be useful for peace negotiations after D-Day, although the minutes of the Twenty Committee's discussions do not specify how.[24]

Bronx's most important work was immediately prior to D-Day, in Plan Ironside, to convince the Germans of an attack at Bordeaux rather than the Normandy beaches. The plan was put into action in the second half of May 1944. The Germans expected her to report on any sign of British troop movements that might signal the start of an invasion. She was given a code to indicate where the landings would take place and asked to send a telegram asking for a sum of money to pay her dentist.[25] The amount requested would indicate to the Germans the location of the invasion. If a landing was to occur in northern France and Belgium, she was to ask for £70, for both northern France and the Bay of Biscay £60, solely the Bay of Biscay £50, Mediterranean £40, Denmark £30, Norway £20 and the Balkans £10. In case of multiple invasion points she was to wire a message such as 'send £30 plus £80, and the rest as soon as possible'. She improved her credibility with the Germans by extending her code to include not only her dentist, but payment for her doctor and physician.

As part of Plan Ironside, Bronx sent a series of carefully timed telegrams to her German handler in Lisbon, knowing they would take about fourteen days to reach the Iberian peninsula. The first asked for £70 to be sent to her to pay for medicine. This was the code that an invasion was expected against northern France and Belgium on an undetermined date. The following day, she sent a second telegram asking for £50 urgently to pay her dentist, to be paid within a fortnight of the first remittance. Her message to Lisbon, translated, thus was: 'I have definite news that a landing will be made in the Bay of Biscay in about one month, i.e. about 15 June.'[26] Bronx told them that the information had come from an intoxicated friend, an officer who had been informed that an airborne attack on Bordeaux would happen on 15 June. That fictitious date was nine days after the real invasion of Normandy. Bronx strengthened the story by telling the Germans that the officer was worried about his security breach the following day and had asked her not to tell anyone.

The Germans believed Bronx. They immediately authorised a payment of £50 in addition to her regular payment of £100 per month. The extra money was believed to be a bonus because of the value of the Plan Ironside material, or in recognition of the general excellence of her traffic at that time.[27]

Bronx's communications deceived the Abwehr that the Allied landings were due in the Bay of Biscay rather than the Normandy coast.[28] The result was that on D-Day the Germans held back the 11th Panzer Division in the Bordeaux area and did not send it to reinforce forces in Normandy. It prevented a larger disaster and loss of life for the Allied forces during the landings. It was a magnificent strategy: the Germans continued to believe Plan Ironside well after the first landings took place on the Normandy beaches on 6 June 1944. This fact was verified by a number of sources: Special Intelligence, captured documents and statements by German generals at MI19's clandestine bugging sites. Plan Ironside split German troops before D-Day and saw troops retained, not only in the Bay of Biscay, but north of the Seine for a prolonged and vital period.

After D-Day, Bronx and other double agents continued the strategic deception by hinting at a second invasion, informing the Germans that the landings in Normandy represented a small force compared to the vast armies waiting to invade in a second wave at a different location, probably Calais. Bronx passed false information to the Germans about liners repeatedly crossing the Atlantic with US troops, suggesting that these reinforcements were part of an Allied global strategy.

By mid-July 1944 the Twenty Committee considered using Bronx for political deception because it had been struggling to find suitable traffic for her. Her lack of training and interest in technical matters made her unsuitable for gathering that kind of intelligence from the Germans; however, she and Gelatine were considered by British intelligence to be the only special agents at that time who could undertake political deception.[29] That deception could take the form of misinformation regarding Britain's relationship with its Allies or the movement of political figures. To build up Bronx's status in the eyes of the Germans, MI5 suggested that she should start supplying political scoops from Foreign Office plans as well as propaganda. Her socialite circles were extended to include new Spanish and US diplomats as well as British government officials and British aristocrats who might be considered by the Germans to be pro-peace with Germany.

Rocket Deception

Of concern to British intelligence before D-Day was patchy information coming from a number of secret sources about Hitler's secret weapon programme, the development of V-1 and V-2 rockets, but it had not been possible to corroborate the intelligence. The importance of understanding at what stage the Germans were with these weapons could not be overestimated. A successful attack with a new and unknown weapon could mean a change in the course of the entire war and the obligatory cancellation of the Normandy landings.

As we have seen, in the spring of 1943 British intelligence was able to decisively confirm the precise location of Germany's secret experimental site at Peenemünde, first through the bugged conversations of German POWs and Hitler's generals at three clandestine sites outside London, and then from analysis by RAF Medmenham of the images provided by new reconnaissance flights (see pp. 185–6). The bombing of the site on the night of 16/17 August set back Hitler's V-weapons by nine months, but did not halt their development indefinitely, and the first V-1 landed on London on 13 June 1944. Consequently, the special agents of the Double Cross assumed a new importance: their deception work was now focused on Hitler's V-weapons.

The Germans had no reliable way of verifying the impact or damage inflicted by the V-1s, and later the V-2s, on England. The Twenty Committee turned this desire for information to its own advantage. It directed its special agents to report to their German handlers some accuracies in the V-weapon damage to maintain credibility, but to downplay the results. The agents were not necessarily to pinpoint accurately for the Germans where the V-weapons had landed. Occasionally they reported a hit on London, whereas in fact the Germans had not succeeded. The purpose of this misinformation was to force the Germans to shorten the range of their weapons so they fell on less populated areas outside Greater London.

This new strategy was not without controversy. Although approved by the Chiefs of Staff, civilian departments in the areas which might be hit by the V-weapons attempted to block the plan.[30] An agreement was made with Chiefs of Staff and the Cabinet Office to feed information to the Germans to lead them to believe that they did not need to shorten their range in cases where doing so would mean the V-1 would fall on the south and east of London, rather than central London. In parallel to this, Bronx, Gelatine and Treasure also misled the Germans over how much knowledge British intelligence had of its secret weapon programme. In turn, the Germans prompted Bronx to supply intelligence on the state of British development of radio-controlled rockets.[31]

As a result of the double agent reports sent back to the Germans, the technological calculation for the weapons were adjusted. The Double Cross System had to decide what information to leak to the Germans to ensure the agents were not 'blown'. The director of Military Intelligence reported that scientific analysis revealed that if Double Cross deception work had not moved the main point of impact of the rockets outside the Greater London area, then 1,300 more people would have been killed, 3,000 more seriously injured, 7,000 more slightly injured and some 23,000 additional houses damaged.[32]

V-2 Weapons

Paris was liberated on 25 August 1944. The threat from Hitler's V-weapons, however, had not diminished. By September 1944 the Germans started the V-2 attacks on England. A similar deception to the one used for the V-1s was adopted for the V-2s by the special double agents of MI5 and MI6. Gelatine assisted in the implementation of a plan for misleading the enemy about the effect of the V-2, passing on false details about the weapon's impact on London.[33]

Kliemann, the Abwehr handler for Treasure and a number of male double agents,[34] was captured in Paris and brought to England as a prisoner of war at one of MI19's sites where the conversations of POWs were being bugged.[35] He was reluctant to give up intelligence in interrogation, but after several weeks in captivity provided considerable material to MI19 about his relationship with double agent Dragonfly, revealing his identity. To safeguard Dragonfly's cover, MI19 led Kliemann to believe that Dragonfly had been arrested in December 1943, but there had been insufficient evidence of espionage for the British authorities to charge him. In an ironic twist, Kliemann suggested that British intelligence ought to run Treasure and Dragonfly as double agents.[36] Guy Liddell commented in his diary: 'He has no idea that they have been run as such over a considerable period and he himself is the sucker.'[37]

With Kliemann in custody, Treasure returned to France and served as an officer in the French ATS. From there she continued to work for Double Cross as per Masterman's plans made for her a few weeks earlier.[38] Because the Twenty Committee continued to run her radio as if they were her, the Germans believed she was still working for them in England and that her spymaster, Kliemann, was in Paris. She sent reports to the Germans that their V-2 attacks on England had inflicted serious damage on Camberwell, Mitcham, Sidcup and Edmonton. Intercepted messages (ISOS) confirmed that the Germans had taken the information verbatim from her report of 25 October 1944 and incorporated it into their High Command communiqués.[39]

Of the traffic of Treasure and Brutus, Masterman concluded it 'was of the greatest assistance to those watching the activities of the French network'.[40] Of the success of the whole French network, 30 per cent was, in his words, 'due solely to Treasure and Brutus'.[41]

One of the last activities undertaken by Treasure was to report to the Germans on V-2 incidents in Battersea.[42] She never came to terms with the death of her dog and continued to cause security anxieties. By the end of 1944 she had finished writing her memoirs, giving details of her experience and modus operandi with the Double Cross, and made it known that she was intent on publishing them.[43] The problem facing MI5 was that the memoirs could be published in the United States and MI5 had no jurisdiction there to prevent it. If they emerged, Double Cross would be blown at a time when it was still operational. Other factors came to the fore, the GC&CS indicated it had no further interest in her and she was discontinued.[44]

In anticipation of the final stages of the war, Bronx was despatched on a mission to Madrid on 19 December 1944, carrying a Peruvian diplomatic passport with a Spanish diplomatic visa.[45] She was primed to tell the Germans that she had a new post as an assistant to her father in the Peruvian embassy in Madrid. The Twenty Committee sent her there to try to meet face-to-face with her handler Bleil (aka Biel), who claimed to be attached to the German embassy in the capital.

As late in the war as March 1945, the Germans remained anxious for information on V-weapon landings in England. They asked Gelatine to find out whether England had a method of warning against V-1s, V-2s and aeroplanes controlled from a distance, and, if so, how the warning system worked.[46] She was mixing again in social, political and diplomatic circles in London, and sending the Germans high-level gossip from cocktail parties as part of the ongoing deception being fed to them. Importantly, Gelatine and the other double agents deceived the Germans into thinking that the V-2 rockets had failed and it was not worth Germany investing in their further production.

The Far East

The Twenty Committee ran double agents in the Far East, but their personal files have not been declassified and an assessment of their work is not possible. A few of their names are known from the minutes of the Twenty Committee, though.[47] One female double agent working against the Japanese was 'Gleam', who dealt with traffic from Ceylon.[48] It is not clear where she was living, and it was not necessarily in the Far East, because intelligence from her was handed to the Japanese via German agents in Stockholm.[49] The Twenty Committee expressed concern that passing intelligence via Stockholm would lead to delay before the deception material was received by the Japanese. To prevent her being compromised, her handler had to ensure that her messages were not too similar to those of other double agents.[50] Such work became increasingly important when, in the autumn of 1944, MI5 received evidence via its Double Cross agents that Japanese diplomats in Europe had been instructed by Tokyo to increase intelligence activities in that arena.[51]

Double agents also worked in Delhi, India, and they were used for tactical deception connected to the British units in India (14th Army and the 15th Corps), and for strategical deception outside Burma with the Japanese. One of their briefs was to build up the Allied order of battle in India to seem of greater strength than in fact was the case. Double agents in India included 'Owl' and 'Marmalade', who were of Japanese origin. 'Brass' and 'Oatmeal' were controlled by SOE and Inter-Services Liaison Department (a branch of SIS).

Towards Victory in Europe

The special double agents continued to be run until the end of the war and, in some cases, beyond May 1945. The fact that the (known) female double agents were not blown and held their cover at critical points in the war is a testament to their success. It raises the question of why more women were not taken up by Double Cross. It is possible that there were many more female agents, but their files have not been declassified.

These women continued to deceive their German handlers even in the final stages of the war. Ecclesiastic continued to be run, with Flight Lieutenant Cholmondeley suggesting that she could be used to plant a deception document on the Germans about V-2 – which she did.[52] For reasons not explained in the minutes, she became uneasy about her own security; there are some pages missing, perhaps explained by the fact that she was an MI6 agent and part of her work remains classified today. She had dealings with a Czech double agent, 'Ostro', of Hungarian parents, living in Lisbon. But nothing in his MI5 file has revealed anything of Ecclesiastic's work.

SIS used Ecclesiastic to target another Abwehr officer, thirty-four-year-old Friedrich Blaum.[53] He was a sabotage expert who manned the Madrid desk, and brother of Dr Rudolf Blaum, head of the Abwehr II branch in Portugal. From ISOS messages it was suspected that he was organising German sabotage activities in France. Ecclesiastic was sent to charm him and glean information on his work. Ustinov, her British handler, reported on 9 January 1945 that she 'was continuing to work on him [Blaum] in the direction of softening his belief in victory . . . even two prolonged kissing bouts at his flat, one of which lasted 35 minutes, have not had the desired effect'.[54] Blaum did not fall for her, and in February 1945 the Abwehr gave him a new assignment in Italy.

Towards the end of February 1945 Masterman held a meeting with Guy Liddell, Herbert Hart and John Marriott to discuss the future of Section B1a. Liddell, Hart and Marriott were keen to stand down Gelatine and Bronx. It had been a relatively quiet period for the two double agents, though they had been with continuing the rocket deception, which had already succeeded in moving the rocket landings approximately 6 miles to the north-east of their intended London target.[55] Gelatine had received a letter in the beginning of January 1945 giving two new cover addresses to correspond with the Germans, who were clearly still duped about her real loyalties. Masterman strongly objected to these agents being stood down, feeling that they could be useful in future circumstances not yet known. Liddell noted in his diary, 'J. C. [Masterman] was very obstinate about getting rid of any of our B1a agents.'[56]

Masterman was soon proved right in keeping the agents on active service. The following month, March 1945, Bronx received a letter from the Germans asking her to telegraph them about any new Allied invasion plans by landing or by parachute. They issued her with a new code, parallel to the one she had received before D-Day: if a new landing was to occur south of Sweden, she was to ask for £30; Norway £40; Denmark £50; the German Bay (as the files term it) £60; landing *and* parachuting in the German Bay £70; parachuting west of Berlin £80; or parachuting west of Berlin *and* landing in the German Bay £100. Of all the female agents, Bronx was seen by the Germans as their most important. She wrote her last letter to the Germans on 5 May and received two letters in return on 7 May. Gelatine wrote her last letter on 30 April and received a final reply from the Germans on 25 May 1945. The following month, MI5 informed her that she was no longer required.

The remarkable work of the Double Cross held up until the final capture of Hamburg on 3 May 1945. The Germans were still believing deception about anti-U-boat minelaying only eight hours before the city fell to British forces.

It is not known what happened to the majority of female double agents after the war. They may have continued to work for British intelligence or been stood down. It was proposed to try to keep some of the double agents, both male and female, in the field in the event that in future a German intelligence service came to life again; if so, the Germans would most likely try to contact the same agents, either for propaganda matters or because they were seen to be favourable to the German cause.

Elvira Chaudoir (Bronx) was considered for post-war intelligence work as 'potentially one of the best B1a agents for post-war use' because she had presented herself to the Germans not as a pro-Nazi but a mercenary, and she could therefore survive the defeat of Nazism. She continued to move in influential circles where she could maintain contact with the Abwehr that was primarily largely anti-Nazi. She sent a letter to her German handlers offering to work for them even after the Allied armies occupied Europe, provided they continued to pay her an annual salary of £1,200.[57] It is not clear whether they took her up on the offer. After the war she lived in Beaulieu-sur-Mer on the French Riviera and ran a gift shop.[58]

MI5 sought to gain British nationality for Friedl Gärtner (Gelatine), who had held a German passport for her cover work. In spite of her wartime service to British intelligence, and an application robustly defended by Maxwell Knight, she was not given preferential treatment. The Home Office refused to speed up her naturalisation on grounds of first needing to process more than 15,000 other applications. Gelatine left MI5 and married a US diplomat, Donald Calder.

Mary Sherer left MI5 and met Phyllis McKenzie, who had worked for British intelligence in New York in the war. They lived together in Rome and in 1947 opened the Lion Bookshop on Via del Babuino, near the Spanish Steps.

Assessment of the Double Cross System

Masterman recognised that 'the use of double agents in time of war is a time-honoured method, both of deception and of counterespionage'.[59] What was the legacy of Double Cross?

British intelligence successfully ran and controlled the German espionage system in the UK after the fall of France in 1940. In the early days, opportunities were wasted by an understandable excess of caution. Had intelligence officers realised from the start that the Germans did not draw from other sources or agents in England, the Twenty Committee could have acted more boldly and offered a better service than it did. Double agents had to be built up. It was a slow and laborious task. The years 1941 and 1942 saw a period of recruitment, experimentation and development of double agents that led eventually to stabilising the organisation and putting it on a professional footing. Masterman commented: 'Only long experience taught us the extent to which the Germans depended on our controlled agents and taught us the gullibility and the inefficiency of some branches of the Abwehr.'[60]

With the implementation of numerous deception plans, the British double agents successfully influenced enemy policy and operational intentions. Double Cross created a complete espionage system that was under the control of British intelligence, and thereby also controlled sources of intelligence to the Germans from the UK.[61] It contributed to the success of Overlord and impaired the German success with V-weapons, and, as Masterman concluded, 'we were surely entitled to feel that the Double Cross System had done its full share in the saving of many thousands of lives'.[62] The rocket deception operations perpetrated by the agents had meant that the Germans landed their V-weapons 5 miles further west each week.

Success, which was secured by both female and male double agents, went yet further. Double Cross assumed a new and greater importance in counter-espionage work.[63] The long-term rewards included providing MI5 and MI6 with information on Germany's own methods of intelligence gathering, as well as details of its personalities, and methods with codes and ciphers. It enabled MI5 and MI6 to penetrate the German secret service and receive operational intelligence about the enemy. It revealed what the Germans needed to know of the British, as well as being an opportunity to mislead the Germans.

The system established the enemy's confidence to such a degree that it limited other enemy espionage activities in the UK, as the Germans decided against diverting money and resources to other espionage operations. Enemy resources were therefore concentrated on the British double agents. Between 1940 and 1945, the money paid by the Germans to maintain its system, including the British double agents, was staggering – amounting to over £85,000.[64] And so the biggest irony of all was that the whole of the British Double Cross System that undid the Germans so effectively was being unwittingly funded by them. The female double agents were instrumental in making that happen.

12
THE BAKER STREET IRREGULARS

In the summer of 1940 the war was tipped enormously in favour of Nazi Germany. How could the small island of Britain stand up to the military might of the enemy? Hitler's troops occupied much of Western Europe. Britain was next on his agenda for invasion, and soon it was battling for its very survival in the skies over southern England in the Battle of Britain. Prime Minister Winston Churchill sanctioned a new clandestine organisation 'to set Europe ablaze' and it was called the Special Operations Executive, or SOE.

SOE endorsed unorthodox methods of warfare and from its headquarters at 64 Baker Street in London planned for 'ungentlemanly warfare' and active resistance against the Nazis.[1] Across the war, thousands of women and men were recruited by SOE as agents, couriers, wireless operators and saboteurs to disrupt and incapacitate the enemy's war machine. Churchill ardently supported SOE and revelled in its disruption to production, defences and communications in Germany. There was no blueprint for this avant-garde organisation, which emerged from a combination of Section D of SIS, MI(R) of the War Office and the propaganda department of Electra House. The public face of the organisation was the innocuous sounding Inter-Services Research Bureau, a name which masked its true work.

Major-General Colin Gubbins, formerly of the 24th Guards Brigade, became head of SOE in 1940, and he recognised that women would be vital in carrying out highly confidential and top-secret work for his organisation, including behind enemy lines. The women were enlisted as civilians or into the WAAF and ATS. They were also drawn from the FANY, which was a volunteer corps of the British army. It consisted solely of women, with their own uniform, whose duties in the First

World War initially consisted of nursing wounded soldiers and running hospitals.[2] Their roles expanded from 1939 and they became agents, radio and teleprinter operators, secretaries and intelligence officers. Recruitment was carried out using trusted personal networks and, once selected, the women underwent an intensive four-month training programme at a site in Norfolk and later at its new headquarters at Chicheley Hall, Newport Pagnell, in Buckinghamshire. They served all over the UK, as well as abroad with F Section of SOE in France, in North Africa and with Force 136 in the Far East. All signed the Official Secrets Act.

Some of SOE's women enlisted in the FANY as their cover unit and were sent for SOE training alongside male agents at Thame Park, a former Cistercian abbey in Oxfordshire. Phyllis Bingham was responsible for interviewing well-educated young women for recruitment into the FANY. She conducted the interviews at headquarters in the vicarage of St Paul's Church in Knightsbridge. Gubbins, who was a family friend, had first recruited her by inviting her to report to Baker Street. She and her friend Peggy Minchin arrived at SOE headquarters and entered a mysterious world of frenetic activity and hush-hush work. They both served SOE, although Minchin's exact role is still unknown because there is no personal SOE file for her.

Well-educated women were the mainstay of the signals department at the Baker Street headquarters, where they prepared SOE's poem codes.[3] This was a relatively simple cryptographic method which only entailed the agents to memorise a prearranged poem, rather than carry a code book.

Hundreds of women worked for SOE, but only a few are well known, and these are primarily the female agents who were dropped into France with F Section.[4] Before turning to them, one of the most underrated roles was that of the women working on clerical and secretarial duties in the registries of SOE.

The Registry

Female secretaries have been overlooked in the history of intelligence organisations, but they were essential to the efficient administration of data and records that enabled the work to be effective. They had oversight of the most top-secret data of all – agents' records and plans of missions abroad. Women played a crucial role in the registries of each SOE section, at the main Registry at Baker Street and across all administrative duties in SOE sections. Many started as secretaries, then distinguished themselves such that they achieved promotion to officer rank with an accompanying salary increase.

Marguerita 'Margot' Morse was one of the women whose wartime careers began as a secretary, but who went on to become the great organiser at SOE's Registry in Baker Street. She was the hidden hand behind its planning and administration. As with so many of the women serving in intelligence, Margot never disclosed anything. She signed the Official Secrets Act and it was believed that she was working for the Department of Transport, but this was far from the truth. In reality, she had been recruited into SOE. She was born in Purley, Surrey, on 16 March 1914 and educated at the City of London College, Moorfields. She enlisted in SOE towards the end of November 1940, working in the Air Operations Section, in charge of records and statistics. She soon became the lead Registrar at SOE, serving as secretary of the London HQ of the Balkans, Middle East and Russia, and worked closely with Gubbins. She had oversight of all SOE's sensitive material, including agents' records. Her managerial skills were soon needed by the registries of other sections, as noted in her SOE file: 'The present need of many departments for a senior woman officer to assist with the re-organisation of their registries has become increasingly urgent . . . most anxious to arrange for Miss Morse to continue assisting various registries during the next three to six months.'[5]

Gubbins tasked her with the reorganisation of a number of registries.[6] Her efficient dealing with the other secretarial staff was characteristic of the effectiveness that made her so valuable to SOE. Her exceptional skills led to promotion from secretary to officer on 14 February 1944, serving as a civilian in the equivalent military rank of staff lieutenant.

In August 1944, thirty civilian secretaries were transferred to work at EMFFI (the organisation of operations undertaken by the French Forces of Interior). For this it was thought necessary to appoint a senior female officer to take charge of their welfare and administrative duties. Margot was proposed in view of her 'experience and calibre'.[7] On 23 October 1944 she transferred to Section X, the German and Austrian section of SOE, ahead of arguably this section's most important operations in the final stages of the war. (The pivotal role of the other female intelligence officers in Section X operations is covered in Chapter 13.) During her time with Section X, Margot was involved with Operation Periwig, a clandestine campaign to create the illusion of a well-equipped anti-Nazi movement preparing for a coup in Germany and in collusion with the British.[8] It was, in fact, incredibly well-planned and believable propaganda.

Margot's intelligence career continued after the war, working as an operative at home and abroad for the Security Service, MI5. She travelled widely with Mobil and Zonta (an organisation that promoted the interests of women) and this was most likely her cover. She never married. Her work included liaison with the SIS station in Washington. During the Cold War, in the 1970s, she travelled into Russia by coach and, on her return journey, was detained for eight hours of questioning at the Finnish border. Although only 5ft 5 ins in height, Margot was a confident, brisk, no-nonsense woman who, on occasion, could be terrifying to those who met her. She was a founding and active member of the Special Forces Club (SFC) in London, a club that treats equally its membership of men and women and closely reflects the ethos of SOE.[9]

A Necessary Workforce

The background and education of the women who joined SOE was varied. Many had completed a secretarial training course in a college and/or they had fluency in languages, but not all of the women had attended a public school. The main route for their recruitment into SOE was through the Ministry of Labour and National Service, although some were transferred direct from MI5 where they were working as secretaries. The application form for 'temporary employment in Government Service', sent to the Ministry of Labour and National Service, served as a screening process. It asked about background, family and education, knowledge of languages and foreign countries, and skills (such as whether they could ride a bicycle, ski, fly an aeroplane or swim). The recruitment officer at the ministry identified potential women from the application forms and sent their details to Miss D. Furse at the Inter-Services Research Bureau. Furse was SOE's female recruitment officer at Baker Street. She invited the women for an interview, during which she did not reveal anything of the true nature of the work. It was Furse who identified the type of work within SOE for which a particular female applicant might be suited.

Women played a necessary role across all SOE's operations and theatres of war, not only as agents behind the lines but as couriers, forgers of papers, despatch riders, coders and packers of parachutes ahead of a clandestine drop. Female couriers were discreet and could move around enemy territories without suspicion, proving ideal replacements after the arrest of a male courier. The female wireless operators carried out the same level of operational work as the men. Women distinguished themselves in code and cipher work across the war, an important role because they linked the whole chain of operations, without which missions would have struggled or failed. There are too many examples to cite, but Margaret Elizabeth Panting is a figure described by SOE as 'one of our best women in codes and ciphers'.[10] She was employed in North Africa until April 1944 as a decoder and instructor of foreign personnel in the use of ciphers. British, born in Kuala Lumpur, she enlisted in SOE in May 1942 as a FANY in the rank of lieutenant. From May 1944 until her demobilisation in the summer of 1945 she worked in Algiers. She was considered to be of a strong constitution, showing fortitude after the death of her husband and with her parents imprisoned by the Japanese. After the war she took up unspecified work for MI5.[11]

Women were posted to various of SOE's Special Training Schools. Barbara Keeley was one of them.[12] She started her wartime career in June 1940 as a secretary with Room 055A at the War Office (MI5's section for counter-espionage), from where she was transferred to SOE that same year. She was posted as a secretary with D Section at SOE's Station IX. This was located at the Frythe, near Welwyn Garden City, the estate that was then the clandestine home of the real-life 'Q branch' of gadgets. Run by scientists Professor Dudley Maurice Newitt and

Major John Dolphin, Station IX tested machines and weapons for SOE. By 1943 the workload had increased significantly, and so had the number of secretaries arriving to work there. Keeley's efficiency in a very technical department was appreciated and she was recommended for a pay rise on a level with junior officers, with a salary of between £330 and £400 p.a.[13] The recommendation stated: 'The work of a secretary in a technical department is particularly difficult, but she has succeeded in familiarising herself with the technicalities of our work to a remarkable extent.'[14] She continued at the Frythe until posted to Algiers and then India on SOE operations.

From 1942 women were permitted to train as agents for operations behind the lines. Miss Furse looked to recruit women who might be suitable for such operations. These prospective female agents were sent to SOE's Special Training Schools (STS) where they underwent a period of training of between four and six months. Training as a W/T operator typically took three months. At the STS, the women's characters and skills were tested to the limit and an assessment made about their suitability for work in the field or other duties. The woman officer responsible for sending male and female agents into the field in France was Vera Atkins, who became deputy head of F Section.

Vera Atkins and F Section

Vera Atkins is a good example of the extraordinary contribution that women made to secret operations. Born on 15 June 1908 to a British mother, Hilda Atkins, and Romanian father, Max Rosenberg, Vera studied at the Sorbonne in Paris and subsequently lived in Romania for a few years. Her family already had a long history of working for British intelligence in South Africa and SIS in Romania since the turn of the twentieth century.[15] She frequently accompanied her father as a translator during a period when he worked for SIS spymaster Thomas Kendrick. This meant that Vera already had connections to the world of the British Secret Service and it is possible, although cannot be verified, that she herself worked for SIS in the 1930s. In 1931, when her father's health deteriorated and he had to go into a sanatorium in Vienna, she and her mother lived for a short time in the city too.

Vera came to England in 1931 to take up a secretarial course at the Triangle College. After her father's death in 1932, she returned to Romania, where the family estates were sold and she obtained a position in one of the oil companies there as a foreign correspondent dealing with their English and French correspondence. She came back to England in October 1937, where it was not easy to obtain employment, but she worked for a time in the London offices of the Pallas Oil Company.[16]

In September 1939, Atkins applied to serve in the Land Army, but was not accepted because of her Romanian nationality; neither was she permitted to join the British Red Cross, and so found a role helping evacuees in Winchelsea in Sussex. But Atkins's knowledge of Europe from her extensive travel in the pre-war period, as well as her fluency in a number of languages, would make her a valuable recruit to SOE. Knowing this, in March 1941 Major Humphreys (a friend of the family) put forward her name for a post which she only knew in advance as 'special confidential work' in his office. On 4 April 1941 she joined SOE as a WAAF officer.

Atkins was sent to work for Colonel Maurice Buckmaster, the head of F Section (France), with whom she forged a close and successful working relationship. She immediately showed an aptitude for the job and was placed in a highly responsible position in Buckmaster's section, overseeing the training and despatch of male and female agents overseas for their clandestine missions. Her duties as an intelligence officer included advising on the current political events in France, as well as responsibility for passing to the BBC the various messages that agents in the field would hear and upon which action was taken – including the D-Day action messages.[17] Importantly, too, she inspired her agents with a feeling that their requests would be met, whatever difficulties might arise during their service with SOE. She was instrumental in building up the *esprit de corps* which existed between SOE headquarters and officers in the field. On the agents' return to the UK, Atkins was waiting to greet them at the airfield and subsequently conducted their intelligence debriefings.

By 1942 Atkins was serving in a more senior role as an officer of F Section, but receiving a salary of £285 per annum, equivalent to that of a high-grade secretary. It highlights the inequalities between male and female officers and was something which Buckmaster recognised and tried to rectify. He made a formal request for Atkins's salary to be increased to £325 per annum to match her rank as an officer.[18]

Atkins believed in the talent of women and their ability to be highly suitable agents, as well as being able to move more freely in occupied territory than men.[19] On 25 September 1942 she sent the first female agents into France: Andrée Borrel and Lise de Baissac.[20] In total, F Section sent around 470 agents into France by Lysander plane or by putting them ashore from boats. They formed circuits behind enemy lines, with couriers who carried messages for the network and radio operators who communicated with London. Before agents left for their mission, they were unknowingly tested by Marie Christine Chilver (aka 'Christine'), codenamed Agent Fifi, to see if they held up under subtle security questioning.[21] Agent Fifi was a good example of an *agent provocateur*.

Among the women dropped into France with F Section were Noor Inayat Khan, Violette Szabo and Odette Sansom. Inayat Khan (aka 'Madeleine'), from an Indian Sufi background, was the first female wireless operator sent from Britain to link up with the French resistance. She was betrayed and executed in Dachau concentration camp on 13 September 1944, along with three other SOE colleagues.[22] Odette Sansom, codenamed 'Lise', joined SOE in 1942 and worked as a courier behind enemy lines in France with the Spindle circuit.[23] On 16 April 1943 she was arrested by Hugo Bleicher, a brutal Abwehr officer, and transported to Ravensbrück concentration camp, but survived. Sansom became the first woman to be awarded the George Cross by the UK. Cecile Pearl Cornioley (née Witherington) was a courier behind the lines in France who went on to command 3,000 men after D-Day, and survived to tell her story years later.[24]

Marguerite Diana Francis Knight (aka 'Nicole') was born in Paris to a British father and a Polish mother. She was trained by SOE in April 1944 and was parachuted into France on 6 May as a courier to a resistance circuit in the Côte-d'Or and Yonne departments. She carried coded messages and radio sets in her suitcase through the German lines. A British officer who worked with her later reported:

> She took her place on the staff exactly as one of the men. She marched with them and took her turn at sentry duties with them, always a volunteer. On one occasion she marched 35km by night with a sabotage party. When there was almost total lack of rail and road communication, her work as a courier by bicycle was invaluable. She was quite fearless and undertook work on roads known to contain enemy barrages with a nonchalance which was the admiration of all.[25]

She cycled through the villages of Burgundy under the guise of a twenty-four-year-old 'peasant girl' on a score of hazardous missions, carrying false identity documents and collecting intelligence on German strong points. On another occasion she walked 30 miles in the dark to aid a sabotage team in blowing up a German troop train. She was described as a 'sensible and courageous girl, [who] show[s] lots of good sense and intuition in most dangerous and awkward situations. Determined, wise and eager, one of our outstanding girls.'[26] Returning to England in November 1944, Knight was later awarded the Croix de Guerre and an MBE.

The personal risk to SOE agents was very real, as networks were betrayed and agents arrested, subjected to severe interrogation and unspeakable torture, and killed by the Gestapo. Many of the female agents who were dropped into occupied France were captured and transferred to Ravensbrück concentration camp, where most were shot and from which many did not return. Their exact fate was unknown until after the war.

Countess de La Rochefoucauld

Countess Yvonne de Mirmont de La Rochefoucauld was a French civilian who worked for F Section.[27] In 1940 she was working in a French hospital when she was arrested and imprisoned by the Germans. She was released the following year and immediately joined the resistance in Normandy, attending to many wounded airmen in the area in her professional capacity as a doctor. In January 1943 she was recruited by the Robin circuit, working as a courier and liaison officer, and transported arms and explosive switches for the network. She returned to her flat in Paris, where she sheltered British escapers and one of SOE's W/T operators, 'Justin' (aka Captain G.A. Cohen). She helped him in his decoding of wireless messages, keeping watch for German patrols and raids during his transmissions. In July 1943 she allowed herself to be arrested during one of his transmissions, enabling him to escape back to England.

She and her husband, Count de La Rochefoucauld, were both arrested and severely tortured, but did not betray their friends. The Count died in a Nazi prison camp. Countess Yvonne endured seven months in a condemned cell at Fresnes prison, during which time she was chained and taken out once to Vincennes to be shot, but the guards brought her back to the prison. Her supreme endurance prevented her from divulging any secrets. She was transferred to Ravensbrück concentration camp where, in early 1945, she was used as a human guinea pig and injected with ten different serums. She was due to be hanged with other women there, but instead the authorities injected her with typhus and left her to die. Due to her terrible treatment, she lost the sight in her right eye and hearing in her right ear. The Swedish Red Cross arrived two days before the camp was liberated by the Allies and removed some of the prisoners, including Yvonne, who took eight days to come out of a coma in a hospital in Sweden. For her bravery, the British rewarded her with the King's Medal for Courage.[28]

Christine Granville

Krystyna Skarbek (aka 'Christine Granville', a name she later legally adopted) was the first female agent to be commissioned in the field by SOE.[29] She was despatched undercover to Poland by SOE two years before Vera Atkins sent her first female agents into France. Born in Warsaw in 1908, Granville was the daughter of Count Jerzy Skarbek and Countess Stefania Skarbek; her maternal grandfather was a prominent Jewish banker. In 1938 she married Polish author and later diplomat Jerzy Gizycka, and the following October the couple travelled to England where she offered her services to the British to fight Nazism. She spoke fluent Polish, almost perfect French, good English, a little Italian, Hungarian and some Russian. She would prove vital to SOE in terms of her knowledge of languages and expertise on Poland.

She was first introduced to SOE officer Major Taylor by Lord Robert Vansittart (Foreign Office) at the home of Evelyn Stamper at 46 Lexham Gardens, in west London.[30] Journalist Fredrick Voigt was there that day too. Granville already knew him, having met him in Vienna in the 1930s.[31] He was already working undercover for SIS. Stamper and Clara Marguerite 'Midge' Holmes, whose SIS work was covered in Chapter 5, had lived at 46 Lexham Gardens since the early part of the war. Holmes then moved with her daughter to De Vere Gardens in Kensington, from where she despatched SOE agents until 1945.[32] It appears from Granville's SOE file that Holmes, the SIS expert on Austria and Hungary, and known to her agents as 'Clara', was her handler.[33] Granville can be firmly placed within the circle of those important SIS secretaries who were handling Austria and Hungary for SOE.

Poland was cut off from the West due to the German occupation, and subject to great brutality by the occupying forces. Granville was eager to help her country. She was an expert skier and a great adventurer, very smart in appearance, with excellent contacts in Vienna from the 1930s.[34] She was well placed to smuggle reports from Vienna and Poland. SOE believed that getting Allied propaganda into the country would help support the building up of a resistance movement in Poland. Granville was initially placed on a six-month trial to ascertain her usefulness and paid £250 a month, via an account in the name of Frederick Voigt.[35]

On 22 December 1939, Granville returned to Poland via Budapest, under the cover of being a journalist. Her mission was to set up lines of communication for passing propaganda into Poland and to begin smuggling it in. She gathered intelligence that the Germans planned a large offensive in the West. She returned to England during 1940, having successfully set up propaganda links in Poland. One SOE officer described her as 'absolutely fearless'.[36]

During 1940, she stayed in Poland for five weeks and covered the whole country on foot and by rail and cart. Between June and October she was in Budapest, having tried to cross back into Poland and then being arrested by the Slovaks. They interrogated her and took all her money, rather than handing her over to the Gestapo. She denied any knowledge of English and returned penniless to Budapest. There, she set up observation posts on the River Danube on Hungary–Romania–Germany borders. Information continued to flow to her station in Budapest from Poland, and the intelligence was taken to England by courier.

On one occasion, during the severe winter of 1940–41, she walked for six days through a blizzard in temperatures of -30°C. The results of her operations were of the highest importance as she transmitted back intelligence in the spring of 1941 about Germany's decision to attack Russia in the summer of that year, in what became known as Operation Barbarossa.

During the course of her wartime career, Granville carried sabotage material into occupied Europe, as well as smuggling secret mail and large sums of money into Poland. The route that she took over the high Tatra mountains was arduous, but that was where her skiing prowess came into its own. In the spring of 1941, she was arrested in Budapest with an assistant and was brutally interrogated by the Gestapo. She displayed great coolness, was released and kept under strict surveillance. With the help of the British Legation, she was smuggled into Yugoslavia in the boot of a car and, during 1941, went to Istanbul. From there she continued to work successfully on behalf of Britain and Poland in the Polish Section as a courier. From Istanbul she carried out similar work in the Middle East and Syria.

By 1944, Granville was the only trained W/T operator in SOE with both a knowledge of Hungary and availability for a mission.[37] She went on to set up fifteen illegal frontier crossings into Poland and Hungary and rescued Polish officers by aiding their escape into Yugoslavia. In the spring of 1944, she attended a special course in subversive work, including parachute training, and became the first woman to receive parachute training in the Polish Section in the Middle East.

In June she was transferred to North Africa where SOE Algiers required her services for a mission into southern France. On 6/7 July, she was parachuted into the Vercors in southern France as a liaison officer working with the Maquis network. With the codename 'Pauline', she was temporarily attached to F Section of SOE. She remained on the remote Vercors plateau throughout the greater part of the Allied attack. Within a week, she reported that she had done the preparatory work subverting Polish troops who had been conscripted into the German army and that the possibilities of destabilisation within the German army were considerable. On 17 July her work was considered so important that another officer was sent to help her. At the end of the month, she travelled for three weeks on foot, finally crossing into northern Italy to make contact with the only Italian partisans in the Italian Alps.

On 13 August 1944 she again revealed great courage after the arrest of a senior British officer, his second-in-command and a French major by the Gestapo at Digne. For three days and three nights she tried to assemble a corps to attack the small German garrison at the barracks, even offering to lead it herself. The risks of such action were too great and so, on 17 August, she decided to visit the Gestapo. Revealing herself as a British agent, she convinced them that US troops were closing in and the Allies were focused on the safety of POWs. The Gestapo could have shot her; instead she negotiated the release of the prisoners just hours before they were condemned to be shot dead. For her nerve, her coolness in a life-and-death scenario, her devotion to duty and high courage, she was recommended for the immediate award of the George Medal.

In November 1944 she returned safely to England and was enlisted into the WAAF in readiness for the final missions of the war. In 1945 she was due to be infiltrated back into Poland from Italy, but this operation did not materialise. Instead, in mid-March she received a letter telling her that there were no proposals to send female personnel into Germany for the final stages of the war, nor any plans to use female operators in the Far East. An unnamed SOE officer wrote to her, giving her a say in her future: 'Knowing your dislike of office work, I do not suppose that any form of secretarial work would be of any interest to you, and this rather limits the possibility of finding something for you to do. In view of this, we would be most grateful to know of the plans you have yourself thought of and in what way we can assist you in furtherance of these plans.'[38] Such an offer showed the extraordinary regard with which she was held by SOE.

After the war, Granville applied for British naturalisation, which was granted. Tragically, having survived such perilous missions across the war, she was stabbed to death in the Shelbourn Hotel in London on 15 June 1954, aged just forty-four. Her grave is in St Mary's Roman Catholic cemetery, Kensal Green, North-West London.

Virginia Hall

American-born Virginia Hall is another female SOE agent who has been widely celebrated for her achievements.[39] After an accident in Europe in 1933, her leg was amputated below the knee. She had ambitions to become a diplomat but having a disability barred her from such service; she appealed directly to US President Franklin Roosevelt, but to no avail. With good humour, she viewed her artificial leg as a companion and named it 'Cuthbert'. Determined and courageous, she distinguished herself in wartime operations for SOE in France and did not allow her physical limitations to affect her operations for F Section. In fact, she believed that her disability would make her less suspicious as a spy in occupied France.

By the time she joined SOE in 1941, she already had nearly a decade of experience in intelligence work. After studying French and economics at George Washington University, between 1931 and 1938 she studied and worked in a number of European countries, including France, Italy (where she spent three and a half years), Austria (two years at the diplomatic school), Poland, Turkey and Estonia. She was fluent in German, French and Italian, with a working knowledge of Russian. Among her accomplishments were horse riding, sailing, shooting, mountaineering and skiing. From 1938 she worked undercover in Europe as a journalist for the US Foreign Service. She was employed at the US embassy in Warsaw, at the US consulate in Smyrna, then Venice and Tallinn. In London she was based with the military attaché at the US embassy, engaged on coding and decoding.

On 19 May 1941, having received training with SOE, Hall signed the Official Secrets Act. Initial instructions for her duties in enemy territory were plain and simple: 'We are not asking her to do anything more than keep her eyes and ears open.'[40] But, her work would soon assume a greater importance.

On 23 August, Hall was despatched on her first mission into Vichy France on liaison and intelligence work.[41] Under the codenames 'Marie' and 'Philomène', she became a vital link between SOE in London and various operational groups in the field, as well as maintaining contact with agents.[42] She was to provide intelligence about conditions in France, develop various contacts for resistance opportunities in enemy-occupied France and act as a channel for transmission of instructions to F Section agents. Almost every F Section agent sent into France from 1941 was in touch with her. She helped them with false papers and cover stories when they were in difficulty.

Hall's intelligence reports were passed to SIS by F section.[43] This demonstrates that in spite of the frequent tension between SIS and SOE there was also cooperation. The reports commented on unrest among the peasantry in the south of France as well as continued and unwanted interference by the Vichy government in their private affairs. British intelligence was keen to ascertain the state of morale within enemy-occupied countries and whether the population would undertake resistance activities. Hall passed on information about increased German motor torpedo boats and their positions and shipments still being made from Marseille to North Africa.

In November 1942 she aided the escape of several Allied prisoners from Castres. That same month, with the Gestapo hot on her heels, she had to make a swift exit from France. She visited a man whom she knew in Perpignan to arrange guides over the Pyrenees for herself and three male escapers she had picked up en route and whom she believed could be useful to SOE. They trekked over the difficult terrain at night, aiming to board the 5.45 a.m. train to Barcelona, but arrived too early at 4.30 a.m.[44] They were arrested by the Spanish authorities and sent to jail.

Hall was released on 2 December 1942 through the efforts of the US consulate in Barcelona and returned to London on 19 January 1943. She provided SOE with a full update on the current situation of the networks and personalities behind the lines, including details of her collaborators in Limoges, where she had hidden uniforms, and having given 30,000 francs to the network for expenses and instructions on how to get across the Pyrenees. She also told SOE about Lilias, a forty-year-old woman, who was acting as a courier for her between Lyon and Limoges.

Hall's Couriers

Lilias had worked for the prisoners-of-war escape line in Paris since 1941, finding accommodation, food and clothing for them, but the SOE networks and agents were threatened with betrayal. Lilias was at risk from one of the most treacherous agents in France at that time, British agent Harold (Paul) Cole. In 1940 Cole started to work for MI9, the branch of British military intelligence that aided Allied airmen and soldiers in escaping enemy-occupied territory. Initially, he genuinely brought airmen and couriers from Paris and Lille to Vichy France and Spain.[45] On 6 December 1941 he was arrested by the German authorities and it is clear from his personal MI5 file that at this point he was turned to work for the Abwehr as a double agent. He gave away everything about the escape lines to the German secret service and even sent bogus airmen to penetrate the homes of helpers and guides.

About a week later, on 14 December 1941, Lilias received a visit from Cole who said he had come on behalf of the 'intelligence service'.[46] He was accompanied by a man whom Lilias knew to be the head of the Gestapo in Lille. Cole wanted to hand her over to the Germans, but she managed to escape. Lilias sent a report of her escape to London, but this does not appear to have survived in SOE or MI9 files.

At the beginning of January 1942, Lilias fled to Lyon, where she changed her name to Mademoiselle Deschamps and hid in a convent. She sent a message to London asking to be exfiltrated but, for unknown reasons, her request was ignored. Alone and without support, she was defenceless and kept asking to be connected with British intelligence. She was eventually put in touch with 'Marie' (Virginia Hall) and began working for Hall, SOE and the resistance movement.

Lilias lived in fear for her life. In a statement to the War Office she said that the traitor Cole, although by then in jail, knew she was in Lyon and the Gestapo might start hunting for her again. She wrote: 'I beseech you to call me back to London. You have promised shelter to those who have helped you. I have done my duty to England . . . and I'm still ready to do my best for her and her Allies. I beg you not to destroy my faith in her. Trusting you will grant my request, yours faithfully Lilias.'[47]

Virginia Hall last saw Lilias on 8 November 1942, the day before Hall left for the UK. She had handed Lilias 7,000 francs and documents to pass to another member of the network. Once back in London, Hall informed SOE that Lilias must be running out of money and they should find ways to help her. But at this point she disappears from the records.

Another woman who aided Hall was Madame Landry, who secured all kinds of fake papers and ration cards for people in the network.[48] Hall's network also made good use of her two sisters in Paris as a means of communication. Landry had no inkling of Hall's real work or for whom she was working, but trusted her and conveyed verbal messages for her to people across France.

On 15 May 1943, Hall returned to Spain by air, undercover as a foreign correspondent for the *Chicago Times*. Her brief was to undertake any clandestine work necessary in the region, secure safe houses and look for suitable persons for possible future recruitment. She took verbal and written messages between Bilbao and Madrid for 'HX' (aka David Babington Smith, an RAF intelligence officer) who had taken over from agent DH18. Hall organised escape routes in Spain for refugees of the French resistance before returning to England.

Once back in England, Hall was impatient to return to the field and volunteered for a further mission to France. After receiving training as a W/T operator, she was landed on the Brittany coast on 21 March 1944 as organiser and W/T operator, with a roving mission in central France as a lieutenant to an agent, 'Aramis/Lassot'. Her role was to set up a large and a small W/T set in each safe house. She inaugurated a new circuit in central France and supplied it with arms and explosives. This circuit became a powerful factor in the harassment of, and disruption to, enemy troops in the area.[49] She organised the receptions of arms and weapons for resistance groups and was particularly important in this respect in the Haute-Loire district ahead of D-Day. She cycled long distances in mountainous country to find dropping zones, visiting her contacts and carrying out W/T operator work. The British awarded her an MBE for her work in the field.

Women of Distinction

By 1944, fifty women, a mix of SOE and Free French, had been despatched into France as active agents.[50] Their missions were incredibly risky – SOE headquarters already knew that the agents in France had been compromised. Exactly why Buckmaster and Atkins continued to send their agents into France remains the subject of debate. Many female agents disappeared. After the war, Atkins vowed to find every missing agent and confirm their fate (see Chapter 20).

The women of SOE distinguished themselves with exceptional bravery in the field, with three awarded the George Cross and two the George Medal. A senior SOE recruiting officer, Captain Selwyn Jepson, went so far as to say that, in his view, 'women were very much better than men at the work. Women have a far greater capacity for cool and lonely courage than men.'[51]

Of course, Jepson's assessment cannot be substantiated one way or the other. But one thing that SOE's history does demonstrate is that bravery is not gender specific. Male and female agents, couriers and W/T operators risked and in some cases gave up their lives equally behind enemy lines. Much more important is to understand their legacy and what each agent, woman or man, achieved for SOE.

13
SECTION X

Historically, women have appeared only fleetingly in histories of SOE, and for over seventy years the majority of them have been hidden and nameless. With the release of thousands of personal SOE files, as well as operational histories, it is now possible to make an assessment of the contribution of women to Special Forces. The records show that the female agents of F Section in fact made up only a small percentage of SOE's women who served in the field abroad. Different geographical sections were established within SOE to serve particular enemy-occupied countries and women were at the heart of them, serving in operations in other parts of Europe and the Mediterranean, the Middle East and the Far East.

Emerging now is the extraordinary full story of three women who were close friends of Vera Atkins and who were SIS 'secretaries' in Vienna in the 1920s and 1930s. They were Midge Holmes, Elizabeth (Betty) Hodgson and (as we saw in the previous chapter) Evelyn Stamper. Thus far, they have received no attention for their senior roles in Section X, the German and Austrian Section of SOE. Their primary role was to organise and oversee the penetration of agents and SOE operations into Austria via Switzerland or Italy.

Holmes, Hodgson and Stamper were fluent German-speakers and MI6's most experienced specialists on Austria because of their intelligence work in Vienna in the 1920s and 1930s for the SIS head of station, Thomas Kendrick (see p. 87). They had travelled extensively through the region, were regular visitors to the ski resorts and took trips to Czechoslovakia, Hungary and other parts of Eastern Europe. After the arrest of their boss, and with charges of espionage still hanging over them, they arrived back in England and were assigned to D Section of SIS, a forerunner of SOE.

Being a woman in intelligence in this period had its personal challenges. Holmes, a widow, had a teenage girl to bring up on her own and support financially. That daughter, Prudence, was evacuated to Canada in the early part of the war along with other British children – an experience that was to affect her for the rest of her life. But this did make life less complicated for Holmes and enabled her to travel around the UK delivering lectures about the Nazi threat. She made several long and often tiring journeys to France, carrying large cases of camouflaged black propaganda material for her contacts, who passed them to smuggling lines across the frontiers into Austria and Germany.[1] After the German occupation of France in May 1940, it was too dangerous for her to return there. She instead provided important briefings to British intelligence on her extensive knowledge of reliable and unreliable elements inside Austria, ahead of SOE plans to infiltrate agents in the region. Her work at this time was described as being 'of the greatest value for this organisation [SOE] in a difficult task of penetrating Austria from neighbouring countries'.[2]

Betty Hodgson was also engaged on propaganda work for the Joint Broadcasting Committee (JBC). The JBC was subsidised by the Ministry of Information at a not insignificant cost of £2,000 a month and had a studio and two recording vans. It broadcast programmes that included talks, music, jazz and classical songs, pretty much like a traditional wireless station, but with propaganda interspersed in some of the programmes. With some governments overseas declining to air any programmes from official British channels, the outreach of the JBC made an impact. For example, it was estimated that of the twenty-one stations broadcasting in fifteen Latin American states, JBC occupied twenty-five hours of air time per week. In November 1940 Hodgson took over as the controller of the JBC from Miss Hilda Matheson, the first controller, who had died the previous month.[3] Matheson's family had found a cache of what were described as 'secret papers' and contacted an appropriate (unnamed) government department. Whatever was in those secret and sensitive papers, Hodgson was the trusted officer who dealt with them. Between 1940 and 1941, as the new controller, Hodgson was engaged on overseeing propaganda content for radio broadcasts as well as printed material by journalists and correspondents.

The careers of Holmes, Hodgson and Stamper were about to take an even more important direction. Their expertise in matters relating to Austria and Eastern Europe and their experience of secret intelligence gained during their years in Vienna in the 1930s arguably made them indispensable for a new section of SOE. They were transferred to Section X on its establishment in 1941 and became trailblazers for SOE.

Section X was tasked with establishing channels of communication into Germany and Austria and building up a network of agents for subversive activities there.[4] It was headed by Major Ronald H. Thornley, who, from his office at 64 Baker Street, liaised with the Foreign Office and 'C', head of MI6.[5] He had worked in Germany up to 1939 and was already aware that anti-Nazis in the country were not prepared to conduct subversive activities against the regime. Thornley therefore sought not to create an organised resistance in Germany, but to focus on sabotage, which was considered an equally valuable weapon against the German war machine. Thornley was under no illusion about the difficulties of penetrating Austria which, since its annexation by the Third Reich, had remained largely isolated. The only way he could hope to establish contacts there was from northern Italy, usually via Switzerland. Even then, it proved difficult to accomplish, other than through neutral Vatican channels or isolated individuals.[6]

Holmes, Hodgson and Stamper supplied agents, intelligence and documents and infiltrated agents into the region. Sub-sections in the field were run out of Switzerland, Istanbul, Cairo and Sweden.[7] Propaganda was distributed to encourage the demoralisation of German troops, Catholic resistance, the misrouting of consignments heading for Germany from Sweden and Switzerland and the derailment of trains and sabotage of brakes on German rolling stock. Special literature was prepared to encourage a run on German banks. Stamper was responsible for handling Austrian contacts and operations into Austria. Holmes was her assistant, who was also responsible for code communications.

Agent Recruitment

The three women became the primary organisers and handlers of missions into Austria and Germany. One of the first challenges facing them was the recruitment of suitable agents to send there. It was recognised that Germans and Austrians in the UK – primarily Jews fleeing Nazi persecution – had left their homelands in the 1930s and lacked up-to-date knowledge of the situation on the ground. Attitudes towards the use of these émigrés would change in 1944, but until then Section X had to source agents from elsewhere.

It looked to MI9, the branch of military intelligence responsible for enemy prisoners of war. In 1941 MI9 was processing German POWs for CSDIC, commanded by Thomas Kendrick, the pre-war SIS boss of Holmes, Hodgson and Stamper. Special arrangements were made for MI9 to supply Section X with regular sight of documents that could be relevant to SOE operations. To facilitate this, SOE constructed a questionnaire about the kinds of useful information that could be gained from the interrogation of POWs at Trent Park and how this could also be a way to spot recruits as possible agents. In this way, MI9 became a source for agent recruitment for Section X.

While a cooperative relationship existed between SOE and MI9, and also between Section X and the German Section of MI5, the same was not true of SIS/MI6. In spite of pre-war SIS intelligence officers transferring to SOE during the war, there were tensions between SIS and SOE. MI6 was unable, or unwilling, to give SOE any assistance or channels inside Germany. Thornley met with members of MI6 in early 1941 and was told that it would be futile to start a German Section in SOE because the task of penetrating Germany was impossible.[8] The official history of Section X makes explicit reference to this: 'From the very earliest days until the end of the war, we were very disappointed by the meagre assistance we received from C . . . We were gravely handicapped in neutral countries by a lack of information concerning the German counter-espionage, which was our constant enemy.'[9] Ironically, on several occasions during operations, Section X was helpful to MI6 in apprehending and handing over a number of valuable German secret service agents. The head of MI6, Stewart Menzies, sent a letter of thanks and appreciation at the end of the war for this assistance – but, during the war, offered no help to the German and Austrian Section of SOE. It is probable that MI6's lack of support stemmed from a desire – and necessity – to keep SOE operations separate from its own, so as not to jeopardise SIS networks deep undercover behind the lines. But, operationally, it was still unhelpful to Section X.

Although infiltrating agents into Germany was difficult, this did not prevent Section X from planning such activities. The decision was taken to establish channels into Germany from neutral countries bordering Germany or via German-occupied countries. This proved problematic because these countries were focused on resistance within their own borders rather than operations in Germany, meaning that SOE was reliant on its own representatives operating undercover in neutral countries.

One of its earliest missions was Operation Champagne, which was centred on a POW who had been turned by MI9.[10] He was Richard Kuehnel, born in 1916 of a Sudeten German father and a German mother, a Roman Catholic who had belonged to the Hitler Youth. In June 1941 he was pulled out of the sea after the sinking of the German meteorological observation ship SS *Lauenburg*. Once MI9 had identified him as a potential recruit for SOE, he was interrogated by a member of Section X, thought to have been Holmes or Stamper, and turned to work for the British. He was SOE's first German agent. Kuehnel was trained in demolition, taught a simple code and the use of simple secret inks for communication. Holmes and Stamper planned an operation to send him undercover to Hamburg to organise sabotage and subversive political activities among the ship builders in order to disrupt the production of ships and U-boats. His cover story was that he was an escaped German POW who had fooled the British into believing he was an anti-Nazi, which had led to his release from a POW camp to work in the docks at Dundee, from where he was supposed to have escaped.

On 7 April 1942 Kuehnel left Aberdeen aboard a fishing vessel, aided by the Naval Section of SIS. An SIS agent in Norway reported back that Kuehnel had made it to Bergen in Norway. His mission took an unexpected turn when the Germans flew him from Bergen to Berlin on 23 April. After nearly three months of silence, Kuehnel sent a message to London on 2 July that he had not been posted to Hamburg but was back in Bergen.

Bergen was an important U-boat base for the Germans. Kuehnel began to organise subversive activities in Norway, including the sinking of U-boats. SOE could not verify these actions until MI9 sent a copy of an interrogation report from one of its other POWs, a German U-boat machinist captured on 20 August 1942. This POW told the interrogators how a U-boat had been sabotaged when it returned to a port in Norway. SOE now believed this was the work of their agent Kuehnel.

A period of three months passed with no contact from Kuehnel. On 10 October he sent a second message to London to say he would be sinking U-boats. The following month, he sent a garbled message giving partly correct information. He was never heard from again and his fate is unknown.

SOE's work in Scandinavia was disrupted during 1942 after Major Threlfall, Section X's representative in neutral Sweden, was 'blown' in August. Miss J. Forte was despatched to replace him as head of Section X operations in Sweden; with no personal SOE file, however, no further details about her are known. She led initiatives to send agents into Germany from neutral Sweden, but her work was hampered during the summer of 1943 by a number of police investigations and arrests of SOE agents. She began the laborious task of rebuilding this network and, by September 1944, had smuggled subversive propaganda into Germany and enemy-occupied Norway via her channels in Sweden.[11]

SOE Operations from Switzerland

On 4 September 1941 Betty Hodgson was sent undercover to Switzerland to head SOE operations there. She was posted to the British consulate in Zurich as a 'secretary' – a front for her clandestine work for SOE.[12] She was chosen for this posting because she had 'worked with C for some years in Vienna and is eligible on linguistic and other grounds'.[13]

The first report which she sent back to headquarters in Baker Street advised that penetration of Austria and Germany from Switzerland would prove extremely difficult.[14] Two months later, in November 1941, she received from London the first batch of itching powder which she was to send to SOE's collaborators in Switzerland for smuggling into Germany for use on the clothing and bedding of German troops. A few months later she received confirmation that itching powder had been successfully introduced into the clothes of German crews on ships.

Hodgson oversaw the increased dissemination of black propaganda literature to her clandestine contacts. The first W/T set was sent from Switzerland into Austria in Operation Aquavit in April 1942. The following month saw the success of five separate acts of sabotage, including derailments of trains in towns in the Ruhr region of Germany. Agents were successfully distributing propaganda after bombing raids in north-west and west Germany.

There was limited success in Austria at this time, with Hodgson receiving reports in June 1942 of sabotage at an aircraft factory near Vienna. By the summer of 1942, she succeeded in infiltrating black propaganda into Austria by developing certain Catholic lines, utilising her knowledge of Austria and Austrians from the 1930s. From London, her female colleagues were coordinating sabotage and passive resistance in Germany. The first successful drop of an SOE agent into Germany (Krotzky) took place on the night of 16/17 February 1943, though he was arrested by the Gestapo in April. Over the summer of 1943, SOE lines in Hamburg suffered losses and one group of agents had to be evacuated and the lines rebuilt. In spite of such challenges and setbacks, Section X's representatives in different European countries persisted in infiltrating enemy territory.

Hodgson had a measure of success in establishing new contacts in Austria from Switzerland. But in October 1943 she was gravely compromised by the indiscretion of one of the members of her network. On 26 October she was informed that her anti-German activities had been divulged to the Swiss authorities and that an order was out for her arrest. She had been betrayed by the careless talk of her chief helper, Karl Gerold, who worked for Swiss military intelligence against Germany and whom she had recruited to pass intelligence to the British.[15] Placed in an embarrassing situation by the Swiss authorities, he had no alternative but to confess to Swiss military intelligence about Hodgson's clandestine activities in order to protect himself. His actions had serious consequences for SOE operations being run out of Switzerland because Hodgson – Section X's representative and head of operations there – had to flee the country. It was a dramatic and hazardous escape, alone, across Nazi-occupied France. She was smuggled over the Pyrenees into Spain with the help of MI9's secret escape lines, successfully exfiltrated from Europe and returned to London.

In January 1945, Hodgson was tried *in absentia* by a Swiss court on charges of working against a foreign power from Switzerland, disobeying regulations and crossing the frontier without permission.[16] She was sentenced to two years in prison and forbidden entry into the country for five years. The Foreign Office sought to have her sentence quashed, but ultimately recognised that her having conducted espionage in Switzerland made that problematic.

After Hodgson had been compromised, penetration of Austria from Switzerland remained difficult for the duration of the war, but this did not prevent Section X from making other attempts. Neither was it the end of Hodgson's career with Section X. She was about to be despatched to head SOE operations in Italy.

Section X Agents: Italy and Yugoslavia

As Allied commanders prepared for the amphibious landings on the beaches of Normandy on D-Day, Section X stepped up their planning to penetrate Austria for the final stages of the war. It was essential to build up resistance groups, and to have reliable contacts and safe houses once Allied forces moved into Austria. But coded messages received by Section X in February 1944 from left-wing contacts in Austria indicated that subversive activity was virtually impossible. This did not deter SOE from making preparations. Plans were already in train for Operation Clowder, in March 1944, which would penetrate Austria from Slovenia. In readiness, Holmes and Stamper began the preparation of agents' cover stories, documents and identity papers, alongside similar work for MI9 and MI6. The initial objectives – of establishing five secret lines across the frontier into Austria without the knowledge of the Germans – were achieved. Allowing for occasional interruptions in the German offensive, there was no insurmountable difficulty until the snow of the winter of 1944–45.

Hodgson was despatched to head Section X's operations in Italy. With Austria too distant from England for SOE to parachute agents directly, they were sent to a holding place in Italy and despatched from there.[17] Section X also sought to infiltrate agents into Austria from many directions to stir up Austrian resistance to the Nazis and establish a base of support after the Allied liberation of Austria. It was thought to be feasible to link up with Slovene and Italian partisans, who could operate within striking distance of the southern frontier of Austria. The task of missions from Italy was to establish links with Italian partisans in the southern foothills of the Carnaric Alps and to organise courier routes into Austria between the Ploeken and Brenner passes.

In April 1944 Hodgson and Major Darton attempted to recruit new agents from POW camps in Italy whenever likely candidates were reported by MI9 as being available. Only a few proved suitable. There was a lack of trained W/T operators, too.

Five men were formed into a group with a view to being dropped to join partisans in Yugoslavia for penetration into Austria. Because they had been in the Middle East for so long, Hodgson sent them on courses to fill them in on the current conditions in Austria. They were despatched on the night of 12/13 June 1944 with blank documents to be filled out by the Yugoslav partisans. The situation in Yugoslavia was complicated and fraught with dangers. The partisans did not always trust those who were sent to them and could kill them on arrival. It made for incredibly risky operations for those agents dropped in. When partisans refused to complete the documentation, this led to delays in operations and requests for documents to be sent out from London. By the time this had been done, the Germans had begun a thorough clean-up of the district they were in. The men had to be evacuated from Yugoslavia and sent back to SOE.

An attempt was made to drop a party of three agents, known as the Temple Party, on 14/15 July 1944, but they had to return after the plane was given the wrong recognition signal for pinpointing the landing zone. A second attempt was made, but was hampered by bad weather. Increasing difficulties in getting SOE agents into Austria from Yugoslavia led to delays. In addition, the Yugoslavs were holding up operations by insisting on agent documents being sent to them in advance for approval before they would issue the relevant permits for the men to be dropped to them. The Germans also became very active in that part of the country. There were arrests of agents, so that operations were held up until it was ascertained that there were no further repercussions.

There were successes in establishing contacts in Austria and plans were made to penetrate deeper into the country and carry out sabotage on a large scale. A party was dropped on the night of the full moon in August 1944 and, as Hodgson later wrote in the official history of the section, they had 'a lively time up there and did some excellent work, with the local partisans and in paving the way for the penetration of Austria by agents who are to follow later'.[18]

Hodgson was joined in Rome by Captain and Mrs Wise, whose task was to keep in touch with the various activities of the local Austrian colony in Italy. The couple had been working together for many years on a card index for SOE of reliable people who would be of use to British intelligence, and SOE specifically, after the German collapse. In order to bring this card index up to date, it was essential to interview as many Austrians as possible for the latest information. The couple had high-level connections to the Vatican as well as to the Austrian branch of the Roman Catholic Church. They were installed in a flat in Rome and Captain Wise visited prisoner-of-war camps to interrogate the men. The card index was of enormous value in providing contacts and safe houses for men dropped into Austria during this period. They were able to contact important figures in Vatican circles to arrange for a letter to be sent from a cardinal (unnamed in the files) to Bishop Pawlikowski in Gratz and Cardinal Innitzer in Vienna, urging them to take a stand against Nazism.

From the summer of 1944 and into 1945 a number of groups were despatched by Hodgson into Austria from Italy – too numerous to detail here. They included Austrian socialists and some communists. There were challenges and setbacks, with problems in sourcing aircraft; the Poles and Italians were given priority, with no planes left for SOE for their own missions. Once, when a signal was received from agents saying 'we are surrounded and cannot last another 48 hours', Hodgson was not given an aircraft to send in supplies and arms. These particular agents were evacuated eventually by Lysander, with some of their party making their way through Yugoslavia, where they met considerable opposition from the Yugoslavs. It was a constant struggle to arrange flights for SOE's operations in Italy. When aircraft were finally available, this often coincided with bad weather and a drop was not possible.

Further, many supplies were lost or damaged in a drop; often they were dropped at the wrong place, somewhere within a 40-square-mile area, and so could not be recovered. The difficulties in sending in supplies became acute and Section X laid on one drop after another. Eventually it decided to shift its strategy and concentrate on blind drops directed to Austria and not to send any more men into the country from northern Italy or Yugoslavia.

Challenges for Section X would soon increase with a new German attack in northern Yugoslavia on 27 November 1944, which aimed at clearing the partisans in the region. This made SOE/partisan operations virtually impossible, but did not deter the female officers from planning new ways to penetrate Austria. The section had already begun to recruit Austrian Jewish refugees living in the UK.

The Émigré Jewish Agents

The close circle of women who ran Section X had the foresight to begin the recruitment of émigrés. Already in the British Army's Pioneer Corps, thousands of émigrés – the majority Austrian and German Jews who had fled Nazi persecution – were 'digging for victory', engaged on forestry work and construction of defences around Britain.[19] Their aim was to fight the Nazi regime and, from 1944, Holmes and Stamper provided them with another opportunity to do that.

The two women began to interview a number of Austrian men for SOE's long-term plans to infiltrate Austria in blind drops from Italy. These interviews were designed to ascertain whether these Austrian émigrés would be willing to be parachuted back into Austria. Holmes recalled: 'We had lunch with them in a lovely country house on the north side of the Hog's Back in Surrey.'[20] Following a successful interview, Holmes and Stamper oversaw the men's training and despatched them on their missions from De Vere Gardens in Kensington. On one extraordinary occasion, Holmes despatched Eric Sanders (original name Ignaz Schwarz), who had fled Vienna in 1938 and later joined the Austrian Section of SOE – he recognised her immediately as the woman who had issued him with the fake visa that had allowed him to escape Austria and saved his life. Holmes and Stamper handed out the agents' kit, paying meticulous attention to detail, as Holmes recalled later: 'We even checked the inside of their pockets to ensure that there were no clues as to where their clothes had come from.'[21] Holmes also had use of her own pigeon to communicate with personnel behind the lines.

The first party of émigrés was dropped on 30 July 1944 in the neighbourhood of Mantua, in Operation Ice Cream. Michael O'Hara (original name Friederich Berliner) was the last to parachute from the plane and on his descent heard rifle shots. Thinking these were directed at him and that the reception committee had been attacked by the enemy, he manoeuvred himself away from the landing point as best he could and hid. In fact, his group had successfully met up with the reception committee and made their way to Bolzano. For seven weeks there was no news of O'Hara and Holmes and Stamper feared the worst, until news came of him through an OSS (Office of Strategic Services) party that had arrived inside the German lines, north of Rome.

A short time later O'Hara made his way through enemy lines and arrived in Rome. He was extremely anxious to get back to his original party as soon as possible and immediately volunteered for a blind drop direct into Austria – the first offer by an émigré for such a hazardous undertaking. Betty Hodgson, who was stationed in Italy, made all the arrangements. His mission would prepare the groundwork for another party of émigrés to be dropped after him that would include George Bryant and Frank Kelley (original name Otto König). Hodgson understood that despatching O'Hara into Austria was vital preparation for the success of Section X's other imminent missions there.

In September 1944 Eric Sanders was sent to Italy as radio operator to émigré SOE agent Theo Neumann. Neumann was not Jewish but a Social Democrat from Vienna who, as a member of the exiled Austrian Social Democrats living in London, had been contacted by Holmes and Stamper to ascertain if he would be prepared to be dropped back into the country. Neumann had maintained contact with anti-Nazis in Austria and it was thought that this could prove useful for SOE in trying to link up with underground resistance in the country. Neumann and Sanders were part of a detachment that consisted of Michael O'Hara, John Miller (Hans Wirlandner), Hans Hladnik and Hermann Faltitschek.

Sanders recalled:

> Neumann and Hans Hladnik frequently disappeared for a day. We learned that they successfully smuggled themselves into a German POW camp, mixed with the prisoners as if POWs. It was such a risky operation, but they recruited two POWs who were reliable anti-Nazis who could be dropped ahead of us as a reception committee. I was responsible for training the first of the anti-Nazi men in radio, coding, de-coding and fieldcraft.[22]

However, significant obstacles had to be overcome before Hodgson could send the men into Austria. Considerable time was spent in finding suitable drop zones and there were delays because of the onset of bad winter weather.

On 7 February 1945 O'Hara was parachuted blind, with no reception committee, at a point west of Graz in Austria to make contact with the Social Democrat underground movement. He reached the area safely to find that the majority of underground leaders had been arrested or called up for the German army. He was forced to make a hurried departure because of the vigilance of the Gestapo, travelling south towards the Yugoslav border and joining a group of partisans. By March 1945 O'Hara was on the run again. As he tried to cross the Drava River into Yugoslavia with a small group of partisans, they were ambushed by a German patrol. There is little doubt that he was believed to be a spy and was shot by the SS in Maribor.

Back in Italy, the group that included Eric Sanders waited for O'Hara's safe return before they could be dropped into Austria as part of a group called the Dilston Party. After O'Hara went missing in action, feared captured, together with a sudden German attack in North Italy, made any operations too dangerous, so Sanders and his party did not go into action. The group was assigned to interrogate enemy prisoners of war in a camp north of Bari, a port city on the Adriatic coast. Through these interrogations, Section X gained a good understanding of the conditions and possibilities for further clandestine work inside Austria – necessary for SOE's operations during the final stages of the war. POWs were recruited by Betty Hodgson to go back into Austria and were given wireless training to prepare them for their missions.

During my interviews with Sanders over a period of twenty years, he said that he never knew the exact fate of O'Hara, his friend and colleague. This had a profound emotional impact on him for the remainder of his life. It was only with the declassification of the Austrian SOE files that the fate of O'Hara became known. With it came conclusive confirmation that 'Clara' Holmes, the woman who had saved him in Vienna, was the same woman who sent Sanders into action for SOE. That kind of closure was terribly important for him.

In March 1945 Section X's team in Italy received orders to move to Siena. Hodgson remained temporarily in Rome with Captain Woodhouse, an air liaison officer, to despatch agents as part of the groups codenamed Electra, Eveleth and Ebensburg.[23] Hodgson subsequently transferred to Siena, where work concentrated on getting the remainder of the agents and 'turned' POWs into Austria as quickly as possible. What followed was a disaster: the new pilots operating the Halifax planes for the blind drops proved to be most inexperienced in night flying. Their navigation was erratic and they dropped agents in the wrong place. Out of a total of five drops of parties in March–April 1945 only one arrived at the landing zone. Agents in all five operations lost their kit, including their W/T equipment, because it was not dropped behind them.

In 1943 Anton Walter Freud, grandson of Sigmund Freud, was headhunted by SOE whilst serving in the British Army's Pioneer Corps (having fled Nazi-occupied Vienna in 1938). After SOE training, he was kitted out for his mission by Holmes and Stamper at the same Kensington address as Sanders a few weeks earlier. In April 1945 Freud was parachuted into Austria with Hans Schweiger, an Austrian ex-lawyer who had good contacts in Austria. They were to go into action on the same night as a second group of émigré agents consisting of George Bryant, a Viennese lawyer, Frank Kelley (Otto König), Fred Warner (Manfred Werner) and Eric Rhodes. The operational briefing for both groups was the same: to contact the local population and establish whether they would cooperate with the Allies; to carry out acts of sabotage on railways and communications; and to establish a British presence in the area ahead of the Russians and take the strategic air base of Zeltweg in southern Austria.

Freud was dropped at the wrong height, landed safely but was separated from his colleagues and survived on his own behind enemy lines in southern Austria.[24] Wearing a long greyish gas cape, he blended into the populace, looking not dissimilar from the local woodcutters as he made his way along the Mur valley, heading for the strategic Zeltweg aerodrome. He decided that he was going to take its surrender for British forces, which had been part of the original mission brief. With the help of a local woman, he was taken to the mayor's office in Scheifling, the nearest town to Zeltweg, where he gave the mayor little option but to surrender the airfield to him or the approaching Russian forces. After several meetings and negotiations with local Nazi dignitaries, Freud singlehandedly took the formal surrender of the airfield for the British. It was a resounding success for Section X and in particular for the women who had sent Freud into action.

The second group that had been parachuted into the region alongside Freud's, consisting of Warner, Rhodes, Bryant and Kelley, landed several miles away from their dropping zone and even from each other. They survived on their own behind enemy lines, evading Nazi patrols that were looking for parachutists in the area. Warner finally arrived on the outskirts of the village of Weissenbach, where he was given shelter by an elderly couple, a young woman and her two children. They did not betray him. One of their friends linked him up with local partisans. Warner received news that Zeltweg airfield had been taken for the British and he was taken there to be reunited with Freud and his other comrades.

The group then moved to a nearby castle across the river, belonging to Princess de Croy, the Belgian aristocrat who had aided British intelligence operations in the First World War, including the smuggling of messages, and again in this war. De Croy enabled Bryant to set up radio contact with SOE headquarters in Siena from within the castle. This was exceedingly risky for her, with terrible consequences had she been caught by the occupying forces. She also sheltered civilians who needed help, among them women who had been raped by Russian soldiers. To date, de Croy's work in support of SOE has been another hidden part of women's history in intelligence.

The above profiles of the male émigré SOE agents and their missions shine a light on the legacy of the women who sent them behind enemy lines. Hodgson and Holmes – the prominent Section X women who despatched these male agents – were experts on the region from their SIS work in the 1920s and 1930s, and they were the brains behind all these operations into Austria, Yugoslavia and Hungary. Theirs was an important, and hitherto relatively unknown, contribution to the history of SOE.

The Istanbul Station

Section X sought ways to penetrate Austria from Turkey. In 1941, Eric Gedye, another member of the pre-war SIS circles in Vienna, arrived undercover in Istanbul to direct Section X's operations from there. Gedye (codename 'D/H98'), a newspaper correspondent, had worked as an agent for Thomas Kendrick in the 1930s and was closely connected to Holmes, Stamper and Hodgson from those days.[25] The same was true for Gedye's secretary and mistress, Mrs Alice (Litzi) Lepper. Gedye and Lepper were tasked with running SOE's resistance and sabotage operations into Austria from Turkey, including the targeting of transport and communications systems.[26]

Alice Lepper was originally Austrian, born Litzi Mehler in 1910, the daughter of a prosperous Jewish Viennese businessman. As a Jew in Vienna, after the Anschluss in March 1938 she was at risk, so a marriage of convenience was arranged with John Harper Lepper, military attaché at the British Legation, to protect her. Lepper and Gedye, whom she would go on to marry after the war, fled to Prague in March 1938, where they worked undercover for British intelligence, Gedye as a journalist and she as his personal secretary. After the annexing of Czechoslovakia by Hitler in March 1939, the couple fled again and worked for a time in Palestine. With the formation of SOE's Section X in 1941, they were a perfect choice to direct infiltrations in Austria. As a report stated, Alice 'has quite exceptional qualifications for the Austrian work she is engaged upon [with SOE]; she has spent over

25 years of her life in Austria'.[27] Her SOE symbol was 5009; pseudonym Miss Pearson, with a codename given by her colleagues as 'Lepperova'.[28] Her cover in Istanbul was as assistant to the correspondent of the *Daily Express*. She was a fluent speaker and writer in German and English, with excellent knowledge of French and some Russian.

Between June 1942 and July 1943, working as Section X's representatives in Istanbul, the couple carefully concealed coded messages and found ways to smuggle them into Austria. Since the 1930s, Gedye had maintained good connections with Austrian revolutionary socialists in exile and, because they were so well organised, they were deemed to be the best elements for SOE to send back into Austria to work against the Nazi regime. By September 1944 Gedye was successfully infiltrating a flow of agents and couriers from the Middle East into Austria. Lepper carried out his secretarial work but also had a number of her own contacts and agents.[29] This meant that, when Gedye was absent from Istanbul on clandestine work, she was fully qualified to run operations on his behalf, including the handling of his agents. This led Gedye to petition on her behalf for her promotion from secretary to officer, with increased remuneration.[30] It was noted that 'she has worked very hard and is exceptionally well suited to her job'. As an expert on Austria, nearly all questions which came up on Austria were referred to her.

One of the ways the couple smuggled propaganda into Austria and Germany from Turkey was via tinned fish. The tins were opened, their contents replaced by soft soap concealing sabotage instructions and propaganda in a waterproof bag, and then resealed. Gedye later claimed to have managed to get up to 1 million copies of various publications into Austria and Germany from Turkey via all kinds of methods, including in fish tins.[31] Fresh fish that were caught could also prove useful for clandestine messages of a different, rather humorous kind. Gedye and Lepper organised fish bound for Germany to have thumb-size celluloid strips stamped with anti-Nazi slogans slipped into an incision in their bellies. Some of the fish would certainly end up on the Nazi top tables, and the saboteurs' hope was that the military leadership would be unnerved to discover upon cutting into the fish that even their dinner was fighting against them.

The couple established communications by W/T as well as running couriers and sending coded letters to reliable oppositional groups inside Germany and Austria. Although their efforts in propaganda proved particularly fruitful, infiltrating Austria always remained much more difficult and largely inaccessible from neighbouring countries. They tried to recruit suitable workmen, secretaries and governesses who were leaving the Balkan countries to work in Germany and Austria and who could be sources of intelligence for SOE. Working with them for a short time was Mary Vischer, who had been born in Antwerp in 1910, the daughter of an Anglican chaplain to the Mission of Seamen. She was educated in England and Scotland and, after secretarial training in London, took up a post in Romania with Shell/Bataafsche Company. On the basis of her Romanian experience, Vischer was recruited to the Balkan Section of SOE, and subsequently served at SOE's HQ in Cairo, before being transferred to the British Legation in Istanbul.[32] SOE Cairo was very active in engaging women, some of whom linked up with X Section (for penetration of Austria) and others for operations across the Middle East. Many of the female personnel in Cairo worked on ciphers and covered the vast regions of Egypt, Palestine, Syria, Trans-Jordan, Iraq, Turkey, Persia and Malta. After Cairo, Mary Vischer transferred to F Section until the end of the war, working for Vera Atkins, with whom she had certainly crossed paths in Romania in the 1930s.

There are some insights into female agents who worked for Lepper and Gedye because they have a fleeting mention in SOE files. They included Tamara Danailova, a Bulgarian who worked as a clerk in an Istanbul firm. Her codename was 'Dinner'. She was recruited by Gedye via her brother, who worked for Gedye in 1941 from Palestine, and collected local information which she passed to one of Gedye's main agents, Hans Sailer. For her work she received £75 a month and continued it until January 1944.[33]

Another female agent was Mrs Nowak (aka 'Blitz'). She was about thirty years of age, of Greek/Turkish origin, and her profession was tailoring. Blitz was living in Istanbul with an Austrian by the name of Hochleitner and anxious to travel to Vienna to obtain a divorce from her first husband so she could marry him. She provided a perfect one-off opportunity for Gedye and Lepper to smuggle messages into Austria.

She was recruited as a courier and given presents for two socialists in Vienna – parcels that had letter codes hidden in them. Blitz delivered the parcels and brought back messages from the socialists. For her work she received living and travel expenses while away and £150 on her return to Istanbul.

Frau Pinkowa was a sixty-five-year-old Austrian émigré, a monarchist and not Jewish. Her codename was 'Otto'. She decided to return to Vienna, where she owned property. Although she refused to take any despatches into Austria for British intelligence, she agreed to provide a safe house for twenty-four to forty-eight hours for any agent sent into Austria by Lepper and Gedye. Grete Reisner (aka 'Tomson') was an Austrian nurse, not Jewish, aged forty-five. Lepper and Gedye discovered that she was just returning to Austria because she had a dependent child there under the age of sixteen. She refused to carry anything into Austria, but memorised double transposition codes and the location of cover addresses for two socialist contacts in the country.

The work out of Istanbul used any opportunity to infiltrate subversive propaganda into any part of Austria and Germany. They organised the drops of anti-German leaflets from the tops of buildings onto the streets below. Some Turks were aware of what was going on and, on one occasion when Lepper gave a taxi driver her address, he said, 'Oh, you mean the secret house.'

There was also penetration work from Turkey into the Sudetenland, lands comprising former Czechoslovakia inhabited primarily by Sudeten Germans and annexed by Hitler in October 1938. This region was one that fell within the expertise of Gedye from his pre-war work for SIS and he oversaw the penetration of the Sudetenland for Section X. SOE's work there included sending agents to establish large-scale resistance work among the Social Democrat party.[34] It proved just as difficult as Austria. All men between the ages of sixteen and sixty were either in the German army or conscripted into the Nazi war effort. The Sudeten Social Democrats appeared to have been terrorised and denounced by the Czechs in their bitter animosity against the Sudeten Germans as a whole, such that initiating any resistance movement proved virtually impossible. The remoteness of the Sudetenland made it challenging for airdrops too.

Even though it is not possible to gain a full picture of SOE's activities in the region, declassified files make reference to one of the female couriers, Marenka Koenigova, the wife of Agent HC 3 Zdenek Koenig. All that is known is that they had a seventeen-year-old daughter living in the Sudetenland and Koenigova travelled to see her daughter or frequently tried to send parcels to her. Although Koenigova was reluctant to work as a courier in the long term because of the risks, she agreed to pass information to the British on potential couriers inside the Sudetenland for smuggling parcels and propaganda across the area.

Lepper and Gedye, working as a successful couple, first for SIS, then for SOE, played their part in ensuring propaganda reached the Nazi regime, yet also ran agents, much of the details of which remain secret.[35] Their story does nevertheless provide a snapshot and a rare insight into clandestine work in the region that has so far been unacknowledged in histories of SIS and SOE. And, at the heart of this, was Lepper herself – a strong, confident and highly competent female agent-runner. That she was highly valued by the organisation for which she worked is suggested by a curious item which she kept in her possession. As a souvenir of her Istanbul days, Alice Lepper kept a silver ashtray inscribed 'To Lepperova from Some Other Evacuees Istanbul 1942.'[36] 'Some Other Evacuees' was a play on the acronym SOE.

Final Stages of the War in Europe

In the final stages of the war, until May 1945, agents continued to be despatched from Switzerland and undertook propaganda activities in Austria. Three women whose first names only are given in the files as Jutta, Selma and Agnes were given a crash course in sabotage and sent behind the lines into Germany by agent handler 'Charles' (real name René Bertholet). Jutta, Selma and Agnes took black propaganda with them to distribute secretly through contacts in Germany as well as to Austrian anti-Nazi Catholic priests. The personal risk for agents was ever present. In April 1945 Selma offered to go into the Vorarlberg region in western Austria on a mission, the details of which are still unknown. It was successful but ended fatally.[37] She was shot dead while trying to escape from an Austrian frontier guard who caught her on her way out.

In May 1945, Frau Wanda Roggenbrod, known only as 'Mrs Bread', was working for Section X from Basel. With the unconditional surrender of Nazi Germany, Section X sought to build a network of 'Codford' agents for purposes of economic warfare. Little is known about Mrs Bread, except that she was potentially useful for Codford because she had contact with key figures in the region. In spite of having been an ally, Russia was emerging as the new threat in Europe and so Section X ran secret agents from Switzerland to gain intelligence on the Russians. Mrs Bread kept SOE in touch with the Trotskyists in Switzerland and they brought reports to her about Russian-occupied areas of Germany.

Another Section X female operative was Magda Hay, described as a Czech Hungarian who, on 2 September 1944, received a visit from a stranger whose identity is not given in the files.[38] He was carrying German documents and asked her for shelter. To persuade her that he was genuine, he was obliged to tell her the whole truth. He confessed to being an English parachutist who, between 2 a.m. and 3 a.m. the previous night, had been dropped by mistake into Czech territory, near Poseyen. He should have parachuted into Austria and was expected in Vienna. He requested Hay to help him over the frontier. Hay wrote a letter in invisible ink to Switzerland, posted around 6 September, then arranged his transport to Vienna. Hay was arrested by the Gestapo on 13 September and taken to Vienna, where she was confronted with the parachutist and accomplices who had also been arrested. She denied any knowledge that he was English; he had allegedly signed a statement betraying her, although whether or not he actually did so is not known. The Gestapo released her and there was no further news of him. Afterwards, she gave a description of him to X/A2 of the Austrian Section of SOE.

At the end of the war, the duties of SOE agents and personnel were not over. Many were involved in the denazification process in Austria and Germany and the restoration of democracy.

The Contribution of Section X

The history of Section X was beset by difficulties and ordeals, yet also had many achievements. Penetrating Austria remained a challenge for the duration of the war, but the persistence of Section X personnel has to be applauded. The work required the most experienced experts with knowledge of Austria and Austrians – including women who already had decades of experience in intelligence work for SIS in that region of Europe. They faced the geographical challenges of organising missions behind enemy lines and the lack of an existing subversive network within Austria, which made the problem of mobilising any resistance there extremely tough. There was also the problem of finding agents who had experience of post-Anschluss Austria or who had a high enough standard of confidence to go back into the Third Reich. The complications of providing regular air support from the RAF, especially in winter conditions, proved largely insurmountable and was the biggest barrier to particular Section X missions. It was also clear from one of the missions that the Austrian people were apathetic, lacking in patriotic spirit and scared of Nazi reprisals.

In spite of the challenges, there were successes, as shown by the mission of émigré agents like Walter Freud, who managed to secure the strategic Zeltweg aerodrome for the British instead of it falling into Russian hands. From London HQ there was complete success in sending masses of fake documentation into the field for the agents, largely prepared by Captain Harvey (FANY) of Section X.

Holmes, Hodgson and Stamper each received medals at the end of the war. The citation for Holmes's MBE read: 'Through her expert knowledge of Austria and Austrians, she has rendered most valuable assistance in recruiting suitable agent personnel and then briefing them for their work in the field. In addition, this officer has made herself into an expert on the writing of letters in code and successfully used this knowledge to maintain a vital link between this HQ and agents overseas.'[39]

Hodgson was awarded an OBE and went on to write the official history of Section X in Italy.[40] Stamper went on to write the history of SOE in the Balkans.

Throughout her life, Holmes remained vague about her career with SIS and SOE. 'The work was sometimes very dull routine,' she once said. 'One could not have excitement all the time.' It was a realistic appraisal of what working in intelligence often comprised. Holmes, like thousands of others who served in SOE and its intelligence roles, experienced moments of drama, high tension and excitement, but also accepted that routine, mundane work was an essential part of their intelligence operations.

To date, a light has been shone by historians on some of the courageous agents of SOE, but what has remained largely unnarrated is the immense legacy of the expert women behind the scenes, women such as Holmes, Stamper and Hodgson, who were the driving force behind SOE's success.

14
SPY SWAP

On 29 May 1943 the Foreign Office in London gave consent for a forty-nine-year-old British agent, Baroness Mary Miske, to be exchanged for an Axis prisoner of war in custody in England.[1] Miske was an SOE operative and working out of Istanbul for SOE/SIS man Eric Gedye (aka 'DH 98') and Captain J. Craig (aka 'DH 18').[2] During a clandestine assignment in Budapest in early June 1942, she was arrested, accused of espionage by a German-Hungarian tribunal and sentenced to death. Held in prison for fourteen months, Miske was at the centre of negotiations in exchange for thirty-six-year-old Hungarian-born spy Eugene Wieser. He had been accused by the British of conducting espionage for Germany on UK soil. Miske must have been important enough to British intelligence to be the subject of the only known spy swap of the Second World War.

Baroness Miske was born in Ustje in Russia to a German father, Wilhelm Wolters (Walters), and a British mother, Julia Walters (née Miller).[3] Her parents died abroad in unknown circumstances and so Mary was raised by her mother's sister and received her education from a governess. She met Hungarian diplomat and aristocrat Baron Eugene Jean Paul Miske (Miske-Gerstenberger) on a visit with a friend to the Hungarian Legation in London to enquire about travelling to Budapest. She married him in Vienna on 4 June 1931.[4]

From 1933 to 1939, the couple lived in Trieste while Baron Miske was serving as consul general at the Hungarian consulate. In 1939 his job led them to move to Munich, then to Istanbul in October 1941. A short time after their arrival in Istanbul, and unbeknownst to her husband, Baroness Miske was first used as an agent by Commander V. Wolfson, the British assistant naval attaché in Istanbul.[5] She started to meet secretly with British friends while her husband was out and never talked politics with him; if discovered, her clandestine meetings could jeopardise his own status as a Hungarian diplomat.

By the beginning of 1942 Baroness Miske was asked by Gedye to work as an agent and courier for SOE's missions from Istanbul into Hungary, Bulgaria and Romania.[6] She agreed and was given the code-name 'Fruit' (aka 'AH 64' and 'Zed'). Her immediate handler was Salvet Lufti Tozan (aka 'AH 6' and 'Pants').[7] Hungary and the Balkan countries of Bulgaria and Romania were on the side of Germany in the war and fought with German forces against Russia. For political reasons, German forces did not occupy Hungary until March 1944, but nevertheless Hungary was still a legitimate target for SOE, as well as the ongoing penetration of the region by SIS for intelligence and counter-espionage. Miske carried letters to anti-fascists in Budapest and made contact with members of the Hungarian upper classes who were thought to be anti-German.[8] It was undercover work that actually placed her husband at risk because of his job as a diplomat, but still she did not disclose her work to him.

Reading between the lines of declassified material, it is probable that Miske was an agent of SIS and that is why she was deemed valuable enough to be the subject of a spy exchange. Her work in SOE went beyond the traditional activities of sabotage and propaganda. She was primarily engaged in counter-espionage – the domain of SIS – which is confirmed by a cipher sent from Istanbul: 'Fruit's detailed and useful information on Hungarian counter-espionage follows by [diplomatic] bag.'[9] Her case is therefore an example of how the boundaries between SIS and SOE occasionally became blurred, in spite of the best efforts of Claude Dansey, deputy head of MI6, to keep the two rival organisations separate.

There are other relevant connections, too, regarding Miske's circles that could place her with SIS. As far back as 1931, it is possible that Baroness Miske had contact with spymaster Thomas Kendrick in Vienna, in the year of her marriage there to Baron Miske. It is perhaps no coincidence that she was recruited to SOE in Istanbul by Gedye, who had been operating from Vienna into Hungary in the 1930s as one of Kendrick's closest agents. For most of the 1930s, Miske was living in

Trieste, her occupation given as 'housewife', at a time when Kendrick was running agents into Italy to monitor the Fascist dictator Benito Mussolini and conducting surveillance on Italian Fascists. Kendrick's agents were also the primary source of Italian intelligence for SIS during the Abyssinian War, which lasted from October 1936 until February 1937.[10] Miske would have been valuable because she was fluent in English, Italian, French, German and Hungarian. Kendrick sent Marguerite Holmes, one of his SIS secretaries, into Italy from Vienna to gain secrets from Italian naval officers for SIS – and Holmes and Miske ended up working for the same section of SOE in the Second World War, both with links to Gedye. Holmes may have crossed paths with Baroness Miske at social events in Italy in the 1930s.

Agent Fruit

In January 1942 Miske was despatched on a mission into the Balkans that was clearly about counter-espionage, rather than sabotage activities. She secured intelligence from Laszlo Bekeffy, who was also an SOE agent.[11] Bekeffy was already known to Miske because she had worked with him in an undisclosed capacity between 1932 and 1934. In the summer of 1941, before she arrived in Istanbul, Bekeffy asked her to distribute anti-German leaflets for an illegal propaganda organisation. Together they produced and distributed several leaflets, mainly of traditional anti-German songs and poems.[12] The work was small-scale and quite amateurish.

During Miske's mission in the spring of 1942, Bekeffy informed her that the Hungarian government had agreed to mobilise 700,000 troops by 1 March 1942 in support of Nazi Germany's offensives in Europe, of which 500,000 soldiers would be sent to Bulgaria for a possible attack on Turkey or for use against Russia.[13] The remaining 200,000 military personnel would be sent to occupy parts of Serbia. In return, Hitler agreed to recognise Regent Miklós Horthy's eldest son as a rightful legal successor to the Hungarian regency. Bekeffy reported to Miske that there were no plans by Hungary or Germany to revise the Transylvanian frontier in Hungary's favour. Furthermore, two Hungarian men had visited Berlin to meet with Hitler and had informed him of reports of an attempted putsch against Horthy. Miske took the information back to Istanbul and this provided British intelligence with an up-to-date perspective of potential ongoing military action in the Balkan countries.

Miske gathered snippets of information from casual travellers whom she met on the journeys between Hungary, Romania and Bulgaria, including three German diplomats who said that they could arrange for her to stay at the Park Hotel in Svilengrad (Bulgaria), but they themselves decided not to stay in the city and returned to Sofia. She does not name the diplomats in her debriefing to SOE, but one was the German military attaché for Turkey, another was personal secretary to Ribbentrop and the third was apparently of no importance. During her stay in Svilengrad she discovered that the chief of the Gestapo unit there was Lieutenant Horvath, a Viennese man. Intelligence taken back to Istanbul included identifying Dr Korda as the head of the German Secret Police in Hungary. He was working under the cover of being a representative of an automobile factory that employed 157 men. All this enabled British intelligence to build a picture of key personalities in the Axis command and secret service and to monitor them. Horvath did not suspect Miske of being a spy and offered to escort her to the Turkish railhead in his Wehrmacht motor car. This meant that she crossed the border without being searched. She observed the procedures there, that all travellers crossing the border in either direction were thoroughly searched by this Gestapo unit. He was aware that she could be the target of recruitment by the British and warned her that she should not stay in Turkey for more than three weeks because Istanbul was full of British agents. He advised her to talk to no one and said that he expected to receive military orders to move his unit into Turkey around 10 or 15 March.

Miske arrived back in Istanbul on 8 February 1942 with messages from her various contacts. She explained how she had met a German agent named Volochoff at Giurgiu (Romania), who suggested that she should work for him in Turkey. She had last seen him in Sofia three days earlier on 5 February. Before leaving Budapest, she said that she was approached by the Secret Intelligence Service (MI6) to work for them, but admitted that she evaded the request and left before anything definite was said.

By April 1942, Miske was back in the field, working for two months out of Zagreb, the capital of newly autonomous Croatia.[14] A message was received in Istanbul that she had arrived safely and was staying at the Hotel Esplanade.[15] She was to send SOE as much information as possible by cipher and secret ink on the political situation in Croatia, particularly on the relationship between the Italian and German diplomatic missions. She was to collect intelligence on the Croatian army, the Croat government and neighbouring governments. She attempted to make contact with friends in Zagreb. While in Hungary she made social contact with a Mrs Buday, whom she met several times. Two reports on their liaisons were sent to Istanbul, but these reports have not survived in the files.[16] It was hoped that Buday would be a useful channel in the future, but events soon intervened.

Another female agent in touch with Miske and part of her circle was Kuelfoldi Hirek. She was 'ZED/2' and little is known about her precise operations in the network.[17]

Arrest of Agent Pants

The undercover work was fraught with danger. While Miske was in Zagreb, her handler Pants (Salvet Lufti Tozan) was arrested on the Hungarian–Romanian frontier after a search of his baggage revealed incriminating documents and letters from the British in Istanbul.[18] Those letters were addressed to four people – all of whom were arrested by the authorities and executed by order of the military court. Pants was taken to Budapest, court-martialled and sentenced to be hanged.[19] This was commuted to twelve years' imprisonment. His wife left for Berlin to see if she could secure help to get him released. At his trial he took off his shirt in order to show the presiding general the deep scars and wounds on his back, but the general said, 'I'm not interested, please dress yourself.'

With Pants in custody, Miske returned to Budapest on 3 May 1942 and called Árpád Szakasits, editor of the Social Democratic Party's newspaper *Népszava*, from a public telephone box because she had a letter for him from Istanbul.[20] She went to his office, where he read the letter and asked if he could reply. She answered 'yes'. It was agreed between them that if he had an urgent message he would write to her at her husband's country estate in Kőszeg, Hungary. Miske was about to spend three weeks there with her husband. She promised to visit Szakasits before returning to Istanbul. A week later, before she left for Kőszeg, she arrived at the Auto Club in Budapest for a meeting with Count Andras Bethlen, the oldest son of the ex-premier, who was chief editor of a newspaper. She had two highly confidential letters for him. He reassured her that she should not worry, but hand the letters over to him because she could trust him as they were friends. She gave him two letters.

After this meeting, Miske and her husband went to their country estate. Three weeks later they returned to Budapest because he was due to return to Istanbul. As they packed their belongings, two men arrived at the hotel and ordered the baroness to accompany them to the nearby Hadik barracks – the headquarters of the Hungarian counter-espionage organisation and military security.[21] She was searched and three letters were discovered hidden on her, one for the general secretary of the Social Democratic Party in Budapest and the other two for editors of newspapers in the capital. These three figures were soon arrested. Miske appears not to have followed instructions given to her by Istanbul SIS station that she should not deliver the letters personally, nor keep them on her person if she was unable to arrange their delivery. The situation was grave because the authorities suspected Miske of being a British Secret Service agent since at least the beginning of the war, possibly longer.[22] They were furious that she had abused her husband's position. Although Baron Miske had no part in his wife's activities, he was forced to resign as Hungarian consul general. News of Baroness Miske's arrest swiftly found its way to headquarters in London, but there was little they could do.

Interrogation of 'Fruit'

Miske was transferred to the infamous Conti Utca prison, known for its brutality, and here she suffered terrible treatment from the Hungarian soldiers and guards. She was taken into a room where head of the investigation Lieutenant Colonel Fothy, investigating judge Captain Bodo and other military investigators took part in her cross-examination. She was asked if she had brought any letters to Hungary.

'Yes,' she replied. 'Several.'

'Were these for newspaper editors?'

'No,' she replied. She was marched into another room where three letters were laid out on the table; the letters were addressed by her in Budapest.

One of the men shouted at her, 'Here are the letters! The proof that you have committed high treason. How could you do such a thing? A Baroness, your husband a Consul general. Of course, you are British, that's why.'

Miske explained that she had brought several letters with her to Hungary but did not know their contents. This was said to be true, according to her SOE file. She was taken into the next room where a very sick-looking man with a black beard was leaning on the table. His hands were shaking and his suit was in such a state that he had clearly worn it for several weeks. At first, Miske did not recognise him. As he turned his head, she saw that it was Szakasits. They admitted to knowing each other. In her handbag were found the names of Count Palffy and General Andorka. She was questioned as to where she got them and replied that she had been given the names by Szakasits. (He denied this in his own interrogation, not wanting to incriminate them.)

Fothy shouted, 'You a Baroness . . . bringing letters to this filthy communist.' She answered that as far as she knew Szakasits was general secretary of the Social Democratic Party and chief editor of the *Népszava*. He continued, 'He is a dirty communist and you are a traitor!'

Miske was removed to the Maria Theresa barracks and held in solitary confinement. This did not break her will. On 8 June she was brought back to Hadik barracks for further interrogation. She was questioned about receiving letters from Mrs Buday. She admitted that Buday spoke to her in English but denied any letters. She was asked whether she had met other figures in Istanbul and the names of suspected traitors were given to her, but she denied knowing them.

Three days later, on 11 June, Miske was taken to Conti Utca prison, the political branch of the military prison, where she was placed in a cell with several communists and Serbian girls accused of a communist plot. At night she heard the terrible screams of women and men being tortured, and during the day she witnessed many young girls forced to crawl on their elbows and knees because their hands and feet had been badly beaten. One of them was twenty-year-old Vera Pavlovic, who told her that Pants was in the same prison and had been tortured. On one occasion, Miske saw him through the window, during the men's parade, and she thought he looked like a walking corpse.

At 8 a.m. on 15 June 1942 Miske was led into a room for her trial before four generals who were to sit in judgement over her. The main investigating judge was Captain Bodo. The same questions were put to her as during her interrogations, and she gave the same answers.

The first witness was Count Andras Bethlen, who said that one of her letters was found mysteriously in his letter box, but that he had never met Miske. This was untrue because he had met her in the Aero Club in Budapest. Szakasits was brought in as another witness. A letter addressed to him, originally delivered by Miske, was found in the office of his lawyer, to whom it had been passed for safekeeping. In Miske's defence, her lawyer argued that the British were not in the habit of reading other people's letters and that it was obvious that Miske had no idea of the contents of any letters that she carried. The lawyer pleaded her innocence, stating that Miske was simply the person who delivered the correspondence, but was not privy to its contents.

It was an unfair trial. The four generals concluded that Miske was guilty of high treason and sentenced her to death.[23] One morning, she was taken with eleven other prisoners to be shot, but at the last moment she and a Turk were returned to the barracks. Miske was informed that her sentence had been commuted to life imprisonment on the intervention of Horthy, the Hungarian regent. She remained in Conti Utca prison until 25 June, during which time she became quite ill. Her husband gave money to the commandant to have her moved to the prison hospital, where she was given a room on her own. Conditions were barely better than in the prison.

After two and a half months in the hospital, Miske was transferred to the Maria Nostra jail for women, near the town of Szob in central Hungary. Run by nuns, it had been converted from a convent to a prison by the Nazi regime. Miske was kept in solitary confinement for over a year.[24] Her cell measured only 8ft × 5ft, with a wooden bed and blankets; an electric light burnt day and night and she was forbidden to turn her eyes from the light or hide under the blanket. Daily wake-up at 4.30 a.m. began the prisoners' routine of slopping-out duties, a procedure which she found distasteful and upsetting. She was not allowed books or magazines, but she was loaned a copy of the New Testament by one of the nuns. Ten to fifteen minutes' exercise were permitted a day but it was forbidden to talk in the exercise yard. The diet was sparse and monotonous, consisting of bread and water, cabbage soup and rotten, often dirty, beetroot, with a little milk on Sundays.

It was at Maria Nostra jail that she met fifty-year-old SOE agent 'Max' (aka Irma Piesz, also known as 'Zed'), who looked after Miske while she was ill and in the prison hospital. During this time, Miske heard her story, just as news was also filtering back to SOE headquarters in London. They received information from a reliable Polish source that the Hungarian authorities had arrested at Budapest station a smart woman, dressed in fox furs, who came from Istanbul. Although the identity of the woman had yet to be established by Baker Street, it turned out to be Piesz. Taken to the Hadik barracks, the authorities found a stash of microfilms in her fur stole's head. These had been destined for Gedye in Istanbul, although the Hungarian authorities did not know this. At her trial she was sentenced to twelve years' imprisonment. Piesz had not been tortured, but was in bad health.

One day Piesz was unexpectedly transferred to the hospital unit at Budapest prison, along with a Serbian communist girl. Three weeks later the girl returned to the Maria Nostra jail and told Miske that Piesz had been visited by a man named 'Otto', who informed her that SOE agent Laszlo Bekeffy, with whom Miske had worked, had died in prison in April. Miske never saw Piesz again: a week later the nuns told her that she had died following an operation.

These were incredibly dangerous and unpredictable times. It was not possible to guess what the authorities might do next. Illness placed Miske's life in danger. In the middle of July 1943 Miske was taken to a sanatorium in Budapest where she was placed under surveillance by the Hungarian secret service, most of whom had received SS training in Germany. On the day of her release, her entire belongings were searched again. She learnt that her former handler Pants was very ill, but after some months in hospital he was set free and returned to Turkey. Szakasits was set free after two months' imprisonment, probably because he was too powerful a political personality in Hungary, and only jailed because he had received a letter urging him to form a people's front with liberals and peasants.

By that point, Miske had heard that she would be released. In the early summer of 1943 her husband had been permitted to visit her and told her that she was going to be exchanged for a Hungarian prisoner. He informed her that he could keep his job as consul general and receive promotion, but he would have to divorce her – he would remarry her after the war.

The Spy Exchange

In August 1943 Baroness Miske was exchanged for Eugene Wieser, who had been declared *persona non grata* by the British authorities.[25] His employment in the Hungarian embassy in London had been cancelled on 20 May 1940 as he faced accusations of spying against Britain for the Germans.[26] He was arrested and interrogated at the Oratory School. From 27 July to 2 September 1940 Wieser was held at Camp 020, the secret MI5 interrogation centre at Latchmere House. He was transferred to internment camps in Huyton, near Liverpool, then to one on the Isle of Man. His continued detention was deemed essential by MI5, who had credible evidence from a source inside the Hungarian Legation that he had strong pro-Nazi sympathies and was a Gestapo agent.[27]

In the early part of the war he went on a short mission as a courier to Budapest and stayed in Berlin secretly, before returning to London. While at the Hungarian Legation in London he purchased large quantities of wireless apparatus from the US which he claimed was for his club, the Royal Aeronautical Society. One piece was an essential part for a transmitter to enable the sending of messages. He sent much of the equipment to Hungary in the diplomatic bag. MI5 established that he had also been instrumental in the export of wireless apparatus direct from the US to Hungary. He appeared to be in command of sums of money far in excess of anything he could have earned in his official salary as an assistant.

When arrested, papers and rough notes written in Hungarian were discovered at his home. These covered the RAF, bomber strength and the performance of particular types of British aircraft. It is clear from his MI5 files that his mail had been being opened and monitored for some time, too.

After release from internment, Wieser was transferred to the airport in a vehicle with the blinds drawn down. He was not permitted to communicate with anyone before boarding the plane. As his plane touched down in Lisbon for his repatriation to Hungary, Miske was being driven to Istanbul because a direct journey to the UK was not possible. Arrangements to repatriate her to England straightaway were complicated by the fact that she was not a British national, although the divorce from her husband made it simpler for MI5 and the Home Office to issue temporary travel papers to Istanbul. During her short time in Turkey, officers found her indiscreet and were concerned that she was contacting former German friends. The British officers found her to be 'demanding, insulting, and telling all she knew, clearly in hysterical condition', and said she should be put 'in a safe place where she can no longer pester hardworking officers'.[28]

Miske travelled on to Palestine, where she was admitted to hospital for a few weeks, and then to Cairo. She remained under the care of the War Office, Middle East department (Force 133), and for a few months stayed at the American School of Oriental Research in Jerusalem. At the end of 1945 she was able to take a flight to England.

Security Concerns

Once in England, Miske took up an undisclosed job at the War Office.[29] She pressed the authorities in Britain to be allowed to return to Hungary to rejoin her husband. Theirs had been a divorce of convenience. Baron Miske approached the British Military Mission in Budapest for permission for the baroness to enter Austria to stay with relatives at Schloss Meiselberg, near Klagenfurt, in the British zone of occupation, until conditions in Hungary improved. The Russians were exercising a reign of terror and it was considered unsafe for the baroness to travel there. She stayed for a time with her old friend Countess Helen de Fours.

On 15 May 1946 the British Military Mission pressed the Soviet authorities to grant clearance for her entry into Hungary, in spite of ongoing concerns over her health. But she suffered a mild stroke and was admitted to the Royal Free Hospital in Hampstead, London. She was discharged, but her right hand was paralysed and she had difficulty walking. SOE feared she might become an expensive liability for them to support and pressed for her return to Hungary. A permit for her to enter Austria was granted and, on 22 July 1946, she left London by air for Vienna to track down her husband and be reunited with him. One Foreign Office report states that she was flown to Vienna by special bomber.[30] Miske soon learnt from a British soldier that Baron Miske had tragically committed suicide because he could not bear to watch Austria and Hungary suffer under the iron fist of the Russians.[31]

Miske's presence in Austria began to cause security concerns for the Allied intelligence organisations working in the Allied occupied zones. She proposed to live in Graz with her stepson, Jeno Miske, but the security services believed she would come into close contact with a large circle of Hungarians and pose a security risk because she knew too much about British intelligence.[32] Her connections with British officers and intelligence officers past and present would make her a target for recruitment as a penetration agent. In view of this, it was urgently requested of London to have her removed from Austria and returned to the UK. Perhaps in an attempt to discredit her, it was suggested that her behaviour had become hysterical and unreasonable after she received the news of her husband's death.

MI5 raised the matter with Kim Philby at SIS and argued that the reasons being given for her removal from Austria seemed not to be valid: 'The fact that she would doubtless come into close contact with a large circle of Hungarians does not seem to me to be sufficient grounds for saying that her presence in Austria constitutes a security danger, any more than any other ex-SOE agent would be who could be contacted by some other intelligence service.'[33]

Amidst these security issues were ongoing worries over Miske's nationality. Philby replied to Mr R. Reed at MI5 that he had received documents which he was asked to pass on to Miske. He had read them and one was a copy of a declaration made by her at the Hungarian Legation in Warsaw in November 1933 in which she gave her date of birth as 17 February 1892, which contradicted the date on other British documents.[34] Further, now that her husband was dead, if she renounced her Hungarian nationality she would revert to Russian nationality because she was born in Ustje and could not claim British nationality. Although her mother was British, born in Newcastle upon Tyne, her father's birthplace was not known, and there was a presumption that he was German. Miske, under her maiden name Mary Walters, had been issued with a British passport by the United States consul general in Budapest in 1919 and he had accepted her British nationality. But, when she came to renew her passport in April 1925, the British vice consul in Budapest investigated and concluded that she was not entitled to hold a British passport. She was advised to apply for British naturalisation.

The situation was soon to become far more complex in the triangle of espionage, nationality and loyalty, and it became a headache for the British intelligence services.

Second Arrest

On 13 May 1947 Miske was arrested for a second time on charges of espionage, this time while in the Russian zone of occupation of Austria.[35] Europe was two years into the Cold War, marked by a severely strained relationship between Russia and the West that at points bordered on 'hot'. Miske had entered the Russian zone region illegally, in spite of advice from her colleagues and friends not to do so. A hard-faced woman came to the house where Miske was staying with a letter from her stepson, Jeno.[36] Miske saw that it was not his handwriting. The woman suggested that the letter had probably been dictated by him, shrugged her shoulders and walked over to the open window.

For the first time since she left England, Miske felt fear.

The woman gave a sweep of her hand and grinned, remarking to Miske, 'What a beautiful view'; in fact she was signalling to two burly Russian men on the street below. Within minutes the door was flung open and the two Russians stormed in.

Miske remained defiant and shouted at them, 'How dare you! Take your hats off when you speak to me. And leave my room!' But she knew they had come to arrest her.

The long drive to Budapest gave her time to think and for her fear to grow. The fifty-two year old, now grey-haired, blind in one eye and partially lame in one leg from her previous captivity in Gestapo prisons, was facing incarceration in Russia. Her thirty-two-year-old stepson was apprehended by the Russians at a different address, also on suspicion of spying.[37] They were interrogated separately at 33 Vilma Kiralyne Street, a Russian interrogation centre in Budapest.

To divert attention from the charges of espionage that were being levelled against her, Baroness Miske told her interrogators a long and complicated story about having been the wife of a Hungarian diplomat in Turkey, but she did not admit to having worked for the British. The Russians were reluctant to release her because she would reveal too much about the interrogation centre and transferred her to a prison in Baden.

It took time for news of Miske's arrest to reach the British authorities. It came after US intelligence had taken in Vera Feodorovna Takach and Mikhail Fillipovi Denisov, two Soviet agents who had just defected to the West, who confirmed that Miske and her stepson Jeno had been arrested by the Soviets and were being held in prisons in Baden.[38] The news caused alarm in SIS headquarters and a letter was sent to the attaché at the US embassy that Miske's 'knowledge of British intelligence activities was considerable and she was regarded as a security risk'.[39]

The Foreign Office intervened on behalf of one of its experienced spies and asked its representative in Moscow to make representations to the Soviet authorities as early as possible, saying that 'His Majesty's government was prepared to take action on her behalf in 1943 when an exchange of prisoners was arranged.'[40] In view of her age, it was emphasised that 'the release of this lady as an act of clemency would be viewed with satisfaction'.[41]

Soviet Prison

Later, Miske spoke about the horrors of her nine years in a Soviet prison. She was held in a rat-infested cell, the light was never switched off and the floor was covered in mould; there was no heating, and only an iron bedstead. For her, the bravest of the internees were nuns who had been arrested and brought to the prison, some of whom died at the hands of their Russian captors: 'In all my years in prison camps, I never saw such bold defiance as those 180 women displayed. They did nothing they were told to do. They refused to go to the bath house and had to be forced there. When their lice-ridden clothes were pulled off them for the weekly bath, they refused to dress and marched back to their quarters stark naked through the snow.'[42] As part of their resistance to the guards, the nuns sang hymns and were consequently subjected to hours of Soviet propaganda blasted through loudspeakers that were switched on at 5 a.m. and only switched off at night.[43] One evening the women heard mournful wailing that lasted well into the early hours of the morning. Miske recalled, 'Nobody told us what it was. But in our bones, we knew – Stalin was dead.'[44]

Nine years in a Soviet prison and labour camps in the Vorkuta region of the USSR could not break Miske's spirit. She remained defiant. The Foreign Office continually bombarded Moscow with requests for her release. At first, Moscow denied she even existed, but the Foreign Office had collected evidence from ex-prisoners who had met her in various prisons and was able to prove that the Russians were holding her. The Russians ignored letters or replied that they were investigating. Finally, in 1956, they released her, when Premier Bulganin and President Khrushchev made a visit to England and met Her Majesty Queen Elizabeth II.[45]

Return to the Foreign Office

Thirteen months in Gestapo prisons and nine years in the Soviet penal system did not deter Miske from working for British intelligence again. Back again in London and living at 185 Ladbroke Grove, she took up work with the Foreign Office at 12 Carlton House Terrace for the Information Research Department (IRD).[46] Prior to her employment, the Foreign Office conducted a vetting procedure via MI5 who responded: 'We have nothing to add to this and do not consider that her proposed employment as a clerk/librarian will constitute any substantial risk to security.'[47] The IRD was a secret department of the Foreign Office during the Cold War for anti-communist propaganda. Miske worked for the IRD for nine years, though during this period she also suffered a nervous breakdown – the past could not easily be erased. Her stepson was also released by the Soviet Union in 1956, applied for a visa and came to live in the UK.

Declassified files have shone a light on the incredible courage and sacrifice of a female spy whose career in the clandestine world of espionage for British intelligence spanned the 1930s, the Second World War and into the Cold War. Baroness Miske's importance within SIS saw her at the centre of the only spy swap of the Second World War. She had always worked in clandestine operations, first attached to SOE but primarily for SIS. Her patriotism and loyalty to Britain meant that, in spite of her horrific treatment at the hands of the Germans and Russians, she was prepared to use her new-found freedom in 1956 to work again for British intelligence.

Miske's story is an example of how women excelled in intelligence operations. Her case also demonstrates how the demarcation lines between SOE and SIS were often difficult to disentangle. Like Miske, some agents worked for SIS but were nominally attached to SOE. Traditionally, it has been unclear whether SOE operatives were 'spies'. Clearly, some were spies, others not.

It is unequivocally clear that Miske conducted intelligence work and this blurs the lines in what has traditionally been understood to be the domain of SIS rather than SOE. When SOE was established in 1940, its primary role was understood to be sabotage, disruption of enemy capabilities and propaganda. Today, its operatives are often depicted in popular culture and books as spies. How far was this true? Were they spies?

Further examination of SOE's women will demonstrate that Miske was not a lone case . . .

15
SOE AND INTELLIGENCE

SOE's presence behind enemy lines afforded an ideal opportunity to gather intelligence but, as one report suggested, it had 'only a secondary role in the collection of intelligence . . . that is to say it is natural in the course of receiving reports from our various agents, items of intelligence invariably occur from time to time. This [intelligence] goes straight to SIS to disseminate to relevant departments.'[1]

However, a deeper study of the contribution of women to SOE shows that, in fact, they were engaged in intelligence gathering and, rather than this being a secondary role, it was their primary mission. Declassified personal SOE files reveal a more nuanced understanding of SOE and intelligence. They show that female SOE agents did undertake intelligence duties and that these were the focus of their main duties rather than a subsidiary role. This new understanding provides a deeper appreciation, not only of the roles of women but also of the history of SOE.

SOE's F Section is the one most fully researched and written about by historians, but SOE's women were operational in other occupied countries. They undertook missions as dangerous as those in France, including intelligence duties, as can be seen from declassified files in the National Archives. Revelation of their clandestine activities cements these agents' involvement with some of the most important intelligence ever gathered for the Allies from behind enemy lines.

SOE and Denmark

From the beginning of SOE's operations in Denmark, women were clearly involved in the country, not only as secretaries but also in intelligence work. Two secretaries were posted to Copenhagen, and a secretary placed in each of Frederikshavn, Aarhus and Kolding.[2] Between 1941 and 1945, fifty-seven agents were sent to Denmark. Files do not reveal how many of these were women; nevertheless it is possible to gain an insight into women's contributions in the country.

Denmark had been occupied by German forces since 9 April 1940. It was a country unaccustomed to war, and one that had gained a relatively high level of social prosperity. The Danish people did not initially grasp the necessity for resisting the occupying forces. This led to a number of challenges for SOE operations that were unique to the country. Its geographical division between the mainland and various islands made communications more difficult.[3] The long passage across the North Sea and the coast of West Jutland which was unsuitable for landing agents on made clandestine communications between Britain and Denmark almost impossible.

In the early part of the war, SOE could draw on only a small number of Danish men in Britain who were suitable for recruitment for special operations. However, there were also factors that favoured SOE. Its early contact with Danish military intelligence led to all clandestine activities in the country being controlled by SOE, with little of the friction with SIS that took place in other countries. At the request of Danish military intelligence, all intelligence from the country was apparently handed to SOE rather than SIS as it was believed that only one secret organisation should operate in such a small country.[4] (It is not possible to tell whether this was in fact the case because SIS does not release its files.)

In spite of its slowness in coming to resist Nazi occupation in the early days of the war, Denmark did finally organise a resistance movement. A large number of successful operations were carried out against a variety of targets that caused grave difficulties for the Germans. Sabotage activities in Denmark were rigorously planned and widespread. Many successful attacks took place on armament factories, radio installations, ships, railways and rolling stock, military and Gestapo headquarters, airfields, shipyards, stocks of rubber and industrial installations.[5] But there is no report of the use of secret ink, nor did the Danish Section of SOE use pigeons. The action carried out by SOE in

Denmark escalated in the years 1944 and 1945, with 127 attempted sorties, of which 93 were successful in 1944. In 1945, for example, SOE managed to drop into the country 4,157 containers of special supplies and 468 packages, whereas the previous year it had only succeeded in dropping 1,642 containers and 73 packages.

As seen in Chapters 7, 9 and 11, Germany's secret weapons programme had been disrupted by the bombing of Peenemünde by the RAF on 17/18 August 1943, following corroborative intelligence gathered from the bugged conversations of German POWs and Hitler's generals in captivity. But the threat from Germany's V-1 and V-2 programmes remained as the secret development sites or the factories where the parts were being made were moved. One woman at the heart of V-1 intelligence operations in Denmark was thirty-eight-year-old Jutta Graae. During the autumn of 1943, she arranged for secret drawings of German fortifications and weapons to be smuggled out of the country. She acquired the first sketches of the V-1 site from the Baltic island of Bornholm, where German experiments had taken place, and forwarded these to London. One of her couriers, who is unnamed, was carrying a copy of these sketches when he was intercepted by the Gestapo and arrested. It was a dangerous moment for Graae, too, as she was compromised by his arrest. The Gestapo began a thorough search for her and she was forced to escape to neutral Sweden.

On 8 November 1944 she arrived in the UK, carrying urgent operational information for British intelligence, the nature of which is not disclosed but may have related to the V-weapons.[6] Behind the scenes, SOE, who knew she was coming over, made a request to MI5 that she should be brought in by the 'side door', meaning that she was not to be interrogated at MI19's Royal Patriotic School, which screened foreign civilians entering the UK to ensure they were not Nazi spies. Graae had been working with British intelligence since the German occupation of Denmark in April 1940, when she had immediately offered her services to establish a resistance movement behind enemy lines. She was one of the first Danish people to take the initiative and reach out to a British intelligence organisation. How she did this is not revealed. Her personal SOE file states that her record of service was too lengthy to reveal in detail and 'no one has a more honourable name in the entire Resistance

Movement . . . she had been one of our grandest fellow workers for about three years and deserves very well of the "old firm" '.[7]

Graae became the principal liaison between the first SOE agents parachuted into Denmark and their Danish contacts, as well as the link between SOE and the intelligence department of the Danish General Staff in Copenhagen. Here she prepared intelligence reports that were forwarded to London by W/T and courier mail. After the first clandestine W/T contact was established between Denmark and London, Graae placed her flat at the disposal of the operator and gave him the necessary assistance during his transmitting to England.[8] At considerable personal risk, she carried codes and W/T sets to other places from which transmissions took place. She arranged for the collection of reports intended for London and, on numerous occasions, acted as a courier between the Danish General Staff and Allied representatives in London. Her work extended to acting as a confidential courier for the chief of the Danish underground movement, as well as being active in the formation of the Danish Freedom Council. Preliminary meetings of this clandestine body were held in her home.

By 1943 the Danish General Staff had evacuated to Sweden and Graae herself had had to flee. She became personal assistant to Colonel Northern Topps, the Danish director of military intelligence there. Her work involved the collection, analysis and coordination of intelligence emanating from Denmark which was sent to London. Graae was in frequent contact with Allied representatives of intelligence organisations and arranged meetings between chiefs of various sections of Danish intelligence and the relevant Allied representatives.[9] She furnished the Allies with copies of all intelligence material emanating from Denmark, including counter-espionage operations.

Graae was formally enlisted into the Danish Section of SOE in January 1944, was paid a gross annual salary of £285 and continued to operate in Sweden with the Danish Mission.[10] In her application she gave the names of two referees working in SOE. They were Captains Truelsen and Junker, who were based at 166 Chiltern Court, Baker Street. She went on to marry Captain Junker. Her alias was 'Storeyrstinden' and her code '7442'. A document in her personal SOE file containing a reference with the prefix CX – used uniquely by SIS/MI6 on its correspondence – suggests that she may have been an SIS agent attached to SOE.[11] Her primary role continued to be intelligence duties.[12]

Because of her knowledge and expertise of Danish operations, Graae had been urgently called back to London by SOE by December 1944, using the Danish Mission as a cover. The application for her transfer to London said this was 'owing to great increase in traffic in Intelligence sub-section'.[13] It is clear that she was bringing with her information on the enemy that was too sensitive to send via any other means and was to be passed to British intelligence without delay. Her transfer to London from the Danish General Staff did not occur swiftly enough for SOE because another urgent memo was sent, requesting her arrival as soon as possible, in which she was described as wholly reliable and discreet, 'her sense of security and discipline is unimpeachable'.[14]

Graae was well informed of all SOE's activities in the field in Denmark and conversant with the identities and codenames of most of its representatives and its intelligence network in the country. Her expertise in intelligence obtained since 1940 and knowledge of SOE's activities in Denmark, as well as her liaison skills with the Danish officials, made her of great value to SOE. She was given the responsible role because she was the right expert for the job. Her work with SOE, and probably for SIS too, is just one example of the Special Intelligence activities undertaken by women in Denmark.

Graae's Replacement in Denmark

After Graae was forced to flee to Sweden in October 1943, twenty-one-year-old Varinka Wichfield (later Mrs Muus) was sent to Denmark to replace her. Varinka, who had a Danish father (Joergen Wichfield) and an English mother (Monica Massy-Beresford), became secretary to the chief agent of Allied propaganda in Denmark in the intelligence sub-section and 'one of the outstanding female members of SOE's organisation in Denmark'.[15] Owing to the ill-health of her boss, she took part in policy and intelligence meetings with leading Danish politicians and high-ranking military and naval officers.

She remained undeterred by her mother's arrest by the Gestapo for involvement in the underground resistance movement in Denmark.

Her mother was sentenced to death, later commuted to penal servitude for life. She was sent to a German concentration camp where she later died. In spite of this tragic personal blow and the risks, Varinka continued with SOE and had many narrow escapes from the Gestapo herself. In August 1944 she married Major F.B. Muus, DSO, the chief organiser for SOE in the field in Denmark from 1943. SOE scrutinised the possible security risks in having an officer's wife, also technically an 'enemy alien', in the intelligence sub-section, but the situation was sanctioned in view of the fact that her husband was earmarked for duties overseas.

In December 1944 Varinka Muus was forced to escape to Sweden and on 2 January 1945 arrived in England. Incredibly, in spite of the known dangers, she was determined to be trained as an agent and sent back into occupied Denmark. SOE requested of MI5 that she should not go through the usual interrogation procedures on arrival in the UK, but was to be exempt on 'special grounds' because she was 'urgently required for operational reasons'. She underwent training and, as noted in her personal file, 'physically appeared to be hardly strong enough to take the course, however soon proved that she possessed good mental control and determination, was able to at all times think for herself, and owing to her light weight, made extremely easy landings on her three descents'.[16]

Her strongminded character was picked up during training. She was described as 'ruthless if her plans were interfered with',[17] and it was noted that she would unconditionally follow the orders of a person whom she admired and was prepared to sacrifice everything for a purpose she considered worthwhile. In spite of her previous work in the field, she never tried to impress others with her special knowledge of life behind enemy lines. She took an interest in the welfare of the other students.

Varinka's file does not reveal details of her mission or whether she did indeed go back into Denmark. What is known is that in May 1945, with Denmark liberated, she was given authorisation to proceed to Copenhagen for undisclosed work with SHAEF, probably undertaken as a civilian rather than in uniform.

Many of the women remain nameless, but Graae and Muus are examples of the incredible sacrifice made by women behind enemy lines and those who risked their lives to bring intelligence out of occupied Europe. Their contributions were essential for the wider Allied operations because Denmark was a vital link in German communications to its occupying forces in Norway. Consequently, a close working relationship was developed between SOE in Denmark and Norway where, again, women were central in support of SOE's activities.

SOE in Norway

The Norwegian and Scandinavian Section of SOE operated from a number of centres, with their operations being coordinated from Baker Street, Stockholm and SOE's North Sea base at the remote seventeenth-century Lunna House in the Shetland Islands. The duties of the female personnel in the Norwegian and Scandinavian Section of SOE were primarily as secretaries across these three centres.[18] The Shetland base provided SOE with a link between the UK mainland and German-occupied Norway for its clandestine missions, which despatched over 500 agents into Norway. The special operational route was known as the 'Shetland Bus'.[19]

Norway was of strategic importance to Nazi Germany because from there Hitler could mount attacks on Britain from air and U-boat bases and disrupt vital Allied supply lines at sea. Norway also had the heavy water production plant at Vemork (Telemark), which was absolutely essential for Hitler's atomic bomb programme. The site was earmarked for a number of SOE sabotage raids to destroy it, in raids with the commandos, which included Operation Grouse in October 1942;[20] the unsuccessful Operation Freshman the following month; and Operation Gunnerside, the attack on the night of 16/17 February 1943 that successfully destroyed the production plant.[21]

Other major SOE and commando activities in Norway included Operation Claymore, Operation Wallah and Operation Archery. Operation Claymore was a raid on the Lofoten Islands on 4 March 1941 which was designed to destroy fish-oil-producing facilities needed for the German war machine.[22] In July that same year, Operation Wallah was instigated to establish a base in northern Norway from which to attack German naval traffic along the coastline.[23] Operation

Archery was a raid on the islands of Vågsøy and Måløy, the aim of which was to destroy key German installations and defences, oil tanks and ammunition stores and take prisoners for interrogation.[24]

Six awards were given to personnel for their work in the Norwegian and Scandinavian Section of SOE, one of which was awarded to a woman. Joan Maud Armstrong's citation for an MBE stated that for over four years she was in charge of all the papers connected with SOE's activities in the Scandinavian region. The task was described as one of 'considerable magnitude, and of great responsibility'.[25] Her work involved the building up and control of the resistance movement in Denmark and Norway, as well as the administration of SOE in Stockholm. She collated and coordinated all the political and economic information and material for SOE concerning Sweden, Finland and the Baltic States. Her citation ended: 'She has contributed in no small measure to the work which Scandinavian region of SOE has been able to achieve on behalf of the Allied cause.'

As with so many women, their particular roles are shrouded in secrecy or not mentioned in files. Occasionally there is a glimpse of women working for British intelligence, but with no details on their work. Lily is one example. Her surname is not currently known, but she was a German woman working in the German consulate in Stockholm who passed intelligence to the British.[26]

SOE and Belgium

Women were integral in support of SOE in Belgium, although details remain sparse. However, one woman we do know something about is Mary Millicent Kozlowska (née Lee-Graham), who was an intelligence officer in SOE. Like Midge Holmes, Evelyn Stamper and Betty Hodgson, Kozlowska was valuable because she had a particular expertise in a country then under German occupation – in her case, Belgium. Kozlowska was British, born in Ealing in June 1912. She was educated in a French convent until the age of seventeen and then undertook a degree in French, which she could speak as a native, followed by a commercial diploma. She had a considerable knowledge of France from 1921 to 1939, having worked as a secretary at a cotton company in

Lille, then in technical translation in a factory there and from 1937 to 1939 as manager for various wine merchants anywhere between Bordeaux and Paris and in commercial exhibitions in France.

During 1939 and 1940, having no official occupation, she travelled monthly to Belgium, something she had done since the mid-1930s. She was very familiar with Brussels, Bruges, Charleroi and Tournai. It is possible, even likely, that she was already undertaking intelligence work for the British at this time. She formally enlisted on 4 June 1941 and attended officer training for the WAAF at Loughborough, working initially as a flight officer in WAAF, T Section, Air Operations. By the autumn of 1941, SOE was in urgent need of experienced officers with knowledge of particular countries to support its operations behind enemy lines. The reason given for Kozlowska's transfer to SOE was shortage of qualified officers due to mounting air operations. On 5 November 1941, she signed the Official Secrets Act and worked at Baker Street under the alias Mrs Mary Cameron. Her commission as a flight officer into SOE is stated as being in intelligence.

Kozlowska held 'a very responsible job in the Belgian Section of SOE'.[27] As an intelligence officer she was engaged in the gathering and collating of intelligence on paramilitary organisations, the clandestine press and living conditions and morale in Belgium. Her duties included the clothing and equipping of agents prior to their despatch into the field to Belgium. She acted as the liaison officer with the intelligence section of the Belgian government, in which she did, as her SOE file stated, 'a first-class job'. Kozlowska's duties were described as very exacting and carried out 'with energy, common sense, and tact'.[28] She is an example of the hidden female figures who worked behind the scenes, but were instrumental to the success of operations in the field.

Mary was married to Stanislav, a Polish man, and continued to work for the Belgian Section even though she had given birth to a son. In fact, Kozlowska's boss petitioned for her to be promoted from secretary to officer, not only due to her skills but precisely because she was married and had a child to maintain. The officer wrote, 'I think that the advancing pay for promotion to Section Officer would give her more finances . . . This officer is eminently suited to her present work and will be very hard to replace.'[29] So, contrary to general understanding, some women of expertise who were indispensable to British intelligence could – and did – continue their roles even while raising children. Furthermore, SOE considered how to provide the right kind of financial support to enable Kozlowska to continue her job and not worry about money – indicative of a more flexible approach. But hers was not the only case of such support, as the case of Midge Holmes previously demonstrated. It underlines how intelligence work was defined by the right person for the job, irrespective of gender, marital or family status.

Within Belgium itself, there was no shortage of Belgians willing to aid the Allies in repelling the oppressor and frustrating the fighting capability of the occupying forces. Belgian-born Denise Leplat was one such example. Leplat was anxious to work for the resistance. At the age of just seventeen she was recruited by SOE as a courier between Liège and Brussels.[30] She used her real name, but had a cover story that she was paying weekly visits to her grandmother in Brussels. Every Monday, she took the train to Brussels, carrying messages for the SOE network. As a young female, she was barely noticed and had little difficulty in travelling without being stopped. She hid her messages in a magazine which she read on the train or inside a shopping basket. She was never told whether the messages were coded or in plain language.

Assistance was given to Leplat by Lucy and Jeanne Rouffingnon, two sisters who lived in Brussels. They helped considerably by allowing agents to transmit from their house and they found other safe places where agents could transmit to London. This network was fortunate in not suffering any arrests, but this did not make their work any the less dangerous.

When agent André Wendelen was parachuted in near Liège in 1942, it was Denise Leplat's father who was named as the local contact. Father and daughter both supported SOE behind the lines. Wendelen's W/T operator, Jean Brilliant, was living at their home at this time in 1942. He conducted eighteen transmissions from a room on the second floor of the house. Leplat was on guard duty on the evening when the German field police arrived at the house. To alert Brilliant, she tapped the central heating pipe which ran from the front door through the ceiling into the room where he was working. He immediately hid the set, together with his codes, in a space under the floorboards, and hurried down to the kitchen to start washing the dishes. He was not arrested, but Leplat had to find a new safe house for him. The Germans continued to use mobile listening apparatus in cars and drove several times around an area, hoping to catch those transmitting from clandestine radio sets. On one occasion, Leplat gave a danger signal to Jean Brilliant, who cut the transmission. They scattered, but she later learnt that he had been arrested.

The situation in Belgium became even riskier in 1943 with the intensification of Gestapo searches to hunt down the resistance and those helping the Allies. German search teams boarded trams or stood at street corners to stop people and conduct random searches. Fortunately, women were rarely searched thoroughly and could pass through occupied territory more easily than a man. Leplat suspected that she was being watched by an *agent provocateur* and might have been denounced by someone. She went into hiding in the country for six weeks.

In spite of the risks, Leplat continued the work. During 1943 and 1944, in addition to acting as a courier, she prepared the charges before a sabotage operation. The day before one such attack, she received a telephone call from one of the leaders, known to her as 'Freddy', to make a rendezvous that night to prepare the charges. When this work was completed, she carried the charges in a sack, concealed in a basket at the front of her bicycle, to the chief of the team who was to carry out the attacks. On one occasion she took part in a sabotage operation. Armed with revolvers, she went with André Wendelen to the point on the railway where the sabotage was to be carried out. He placed the charges on the line while she stayed a few yards away to cover for him in case they were interrupted. They had enough time to walk to a nearby village before the explosion was detonated and they pretended to be lovers. Nobody suspected them and the operation was successful. In 1944 several members of the network with whom she worked were denounced and arrested but she managed to escape arrest.

SOE agents continued to monitor events on the ground and pass back intelligence to London, especially on the location of the German V-1 mobile launch sites, the state and locations of the German fighting forces and their supply lines.

Operation Amelia

Within weeks of D-Day, the Allies had expected to liberate Belgium, but the advance through Normandy and northern France was frustratingly slow. By the beginning of August 1944 the Allied forces had yet to liberate Paris. There were bitter and hard-fought battles before Paris finally surrendered on 25 August 1944. Even though the Allied advance was sluggish, preparations were being made by SOE to provide relevant support from the resistance movement for Allied forces once they crossed into Belgium.

On 5 August 1944, a twenty-one-year-old British woman arrived at USAAF 179 Harrington in Northamptonshire to prepare for her mission into Belgium. She underwent the final checks to ensure she had no English labels in her clothes or used bus or train tickets in her pockets or the wrong brand of cigarettes: these were all items which could give an agent away. She was handed a cyanide pill, concealed it in her lipstick and boarded the B-24 Liberator.

Elaine Marie Madden (aka 'Alice') was about to parachute into Belgium for Operation Amelia, with a male chief in the field called 'Odette/Brabantio' and a W/T operator Jacques van de Spiegle (codenamed 'Foxtrot'). She had enlisted into the FANY, one of the main covers for female SOE agents, and was issued false identity papers in the name of Hélène Marie Maes. During the flight she and her companions ate corned beef sandwiches and took the opportunity to catch some sleep. As they approached the landing zone in Belgium, the B-24 Liberator dropped to 600 ft. It was just before 1.30 a.m.[31]

The green light indicated it was time to jump. Madden insisted that she should be the first to exit the plane to show the men that she was not afraid. As she was about to jump into the darkness, the despatcher swiftly picked her up, kissed her on her lips and threw her out of the plane.[32] As she descended, she felt exhilaration, mixed with fear and excitement. She landed and hurried to bury her parachute. Containers of equipment and packages were released behind her. Her two colleagues parachuted down behind her. Since she was less likely to be stopped than Foxtrot, she carried his radio in a brown suitcase.

The following day, her first task was to link up with André Wendelen, who had already been operating with Mary Kozlowska. He was waiting for Madden at the Central Café on the north-west corner of the main square in Ciney. As instructed, Madden entered the café and asked the waitress for Delphine. An older woman appeared and led her out of the back room to Wendelen. He was immediately concerned by Madden's grey-and-white tweed suit, expensive handbag and shoes that had not been seen in Belgium for four years. She was highly conspicuous in enemy territory. It seemed incredible that the final checks at the Special Training School at Beaulieu had allowed her to go behind the lines in such an extravagant outfit. He reprimanded her for the lapse in security, and she left the café in drab clothes, looking less like a model from Harrods. She learnt an important security lesson within the first forty-eight hours in Belgium. She had been lucky that her appearance had not given her away.

With that mistake behind her, Madden heeded at least one warning from the training at Beaulieu – that overconfidence could be fatal for any agent. She must always be on her guard, with no room for complacency. The secret police were everywhere. No one knew how Hitler would react to defeat in particular countries and how long it would be till the Nazi regime collapsed.

Wendelen and Madden operated from an apartment in Brussels close to the capital's smart shops and expensive apartments, but only a few minutes from Gestapo headquarters. The Gestapo probably would not suspect that anyone would operate so close to them. Madden became a fast courier for Wendelen, who was acting as the liaison and point of communication between the Belgian government-in-exile and Belgian state security (Sûreté de l'État). He held together the disperate resistance groups in Belgium, particularly in the Ardennes region.

During the first week, Madden made contact with Denise Leplat, who was based in Liège. Leplat sourced safe houses for Foxtrot and recruited people to be his protection force when he transmitted from them. They could alert him to the roaming German radio detection vans. Most of Leplat's close trusted network were women.

On one occasion, Madden was aware of being followed by a typical Gestapo type, wearing a standard issue coat and Homburg hat.[33]

Fortunately, on this occasion, she was not carrying the radio, but had a pistol hidden among the vegetables in her basket, having failed to pass the weapon to a contact earlier that day. She hopped onto one tram, then another, but was still being pursued. She alighted at some smart shops and casually browsed the window displays. Looking at the reflection in the glass, she could see her tail waiting and watching in the doorway a few shops away. She entered the lingerie shop and went into the changing room to try on a couple of items. Quickly thinking how she could escape him, she decided to change her appearance. She wiped off her make-up, swept up her hair and put on a scarf, slipped off her jacket and left the basket with the gun under the chair. She stuffed tissue paper that had been wrapped around the lingerie into her shoes to alter her walk and removed her stockings, shoving them inside her bra to increase her chest size. The change of appearance worked. The woman at the counter made no comment as Madden walked out of the shop with two other women and blended into the crowd. She walked down the road, and only once dared to glance in a window. She could see that her follower was still waiting in the doorway, his eyes fixed on the lingerie shop. She descended into the metro station and was free.

Back at the apartment, Wendelen had been growing concerned about her safety. He was impressed that she had managed to lose her follower.

In the coming weeks Madden travelled between Brussels and the Ardennes, concentrating attacks on Belgian railways to prevent Axis forces from transporting military vehicles by train from Germany into occupied Belgium and onwards to the fierce fighting on the front line in France. Heavy installations constructed by the Germans in Belgium were to be sabotaged by removing major central parts, which were hidden and kept safe but not destroyed so they could be reinstalled easily once the Allied forces arrived. Sabotage activities included the disruption of enemy telecommunications by cutting telephone lines and telegraph cables; interrupting supply lines by destroying lock gates on waterways to prevent the movement of enemy munitions; and damaging enemy aircraft, airfield installations and aviation fuel dumps.

V-weapons

There was another dimension to Madden's mission that proved to be extremely significant. She was tasked with collecting the highest-priority intelligence on the V-weapons and flying bombs from agents in the field to send back to London. Detailed instructions were given to agents in Belgium (and France) on what to identify and the kind of information needed. It was explained to agents how, at some time prior to launching a V-weapon, the bomb was fuelled with petrol and the rocket propulsion unit on the trolley was filled with hydrogen peroxide. British intelligence needed to know where this was carried out – whether one filling station was being used to serve several launching sites, and what materials were used to fuel the bomb and provide rocket propulsion, as well as complete details of the design of the trolley, with a sketch or photograph, if possible. It was thought that the launching trolley might be transported separately from the rocket unit or other component parts and even disguised inside a skeleton crate sent by rail or road. The bomb might be transported in one piece, in which case agents were to identify this by its length of 22 ft and diameter of 3 ft. Instruction was given that the warheads might be transported separately: they were described as truncated cones 47 inches long and with a minimum diameter of 28 inches. How was any of this guarded?

Agents were instructed to pass back information on whether the waggons transporting V-weapons could be attacked by rifle or motor fire from a distance of about 100 yards; where depots and filling points were located and what kind of transport was allowed to use them; and whether any foreign workers were employed on the site. The information would give the Allied air forces potential targets to hit, but also an opportunity to recruit foreign workers for passing back information from these places.

Knocking out the V-weapons was essential to prevent the destruction that they could wreak on London and elsewhere. The V-weapons were powerful enough to affect the outcome of the war. If their launch was not prevented, Germany could have won the technological war. It remained a close call until as late as February 1945.

A mass of reports were sent daily to Madden and Wendelen, some of which were accurate, while others turned out to be not so useful.

Wendelen bribed a German worker to provide details of the movement of the weapons and then he and Madden organised saboteurs to destroy the railway lines that transported the V-weapons to the Belgian coast.

The ongoing collection of intelligence behind enemy lines gave information to the Allies in the various battle areas, especially on German troop concentrations between the Somme and Loire rivers, their headquarters, and petrol and ammunition. Details were to be collected from agents in the field on sightings of new wireless aerials installed for enemy communications or renewed activity around a headquarters, including the movements of enemy troops and the timings of such movements. Madden carried messages and weapons (including revolvers) between Brussels and the Ardennes, travelling considerably in the latter. She recruited a protection team for Foxtrot and was in charge of the *service de protection* for him.[34] She carried his transmitting set and found safe houses for the network.[35] She encoded the messages for Foxtrot so he could transmit the intelligence in them to London within as short a time as possible. He could only transmit on air for a maximum of 10 minutes, otherwise he risked being picked up by the mobile D/F vans which were often disguised as bakery vans.

'The only regret that I have,' she commented, 'is not having arrived sooner [in Belgium] and being able to work more.'

'Monsignor Bernard'

During the autumn of 1944 Madden was informed of a new task, to act as companion to an agent while he waited for exfiltration to the UK. She knew him as Monsignor Bernard, whose codename was 'Patron'. At his safe house, Château d'Halloy in the Ardennes, just north-west of Ciney, they spent hours playing cards and walking the grounds, discussing contemporary matters. In response to his questions, she was honest about the Belgian royal family, who she felt were not demonstrating enough leadership in the war. She wondered who Bernard was, and thought that he must be an important figure to be hidden in the castle. After a time, he was moved and, as before, Madden carried arms, messages and cash for the resistance between Brussels and the Ardennes during August 1944.

On 3 September, tanks of the Guards Armoured Division finally crossed the border into Belgium, beginning the liberation of the country. That day, André Wendelen finally admitted to Madden the identity of Monsieur Bernard: he was Prince Charles, the younger brother of King Leopold III of Belgium.[36] In the end, he was not exfiltrated from Belgium because he was about to become Prince Regent. He served as Regent from 1944 to 1950 while the Allies investigated whether King Leopold had betrayed them by surrendering too soon to German troops in May 1940.

Madden met him again at a liberation cocktail party for members of the resistance and tried to hide her embarrassment at having been rude about the royal family during her time as his keeper. He was gracious and relaxed towards her. She nervously asked him, 'How should I address you?'

He replied, 'Just call me Bernard.'[37]

Special Forces

Brussels was liberated from the east, but late autumn 1944 still saw parts of Belgium under German occupation and facing a harsh winter of starvation and further intense fighting. Antwerp was bombarded by V-1s and V-2s, and neighbouring Holland was under German occupation. In anticipation of the liberation of the rest of Belgium, and Allied forces moving into Holland, a new SOE-type group was formed called the Verstrepen Group.

On 30 October 1944 Madden was one of only two women assigned to the Verstrepen Group, a specialist unit of the best W/T operators, with her old W/T colleague Foxtrot among them. Retaining her rank as cadet ensign, Madden was despatched to Antwerp as a coder-secretary as part of an attachment of British Special Forces. The unit handled coded communications between five operational zones in Belgium and the country's Secret Army. Under a new codename, 'Helene', Madden again worked with the resistance and provided tactical intelligence for the Canadian First Army. During this time, she met one of the most experienced W/T operators, Michel Ghislain Blaize (aka 'Mitten'). He was a Belgian SOE agent in the field and was handling the W/T communications for the head of the Secret Army. On 31 March 1945 he and Madden married. For security reasons they needed the approval of SOE, which had been reluctantly granted, with it also being noted internally that SOE should not make a habit of approving marriages between agents.

At the end of the war Madden was awarded a Mention in Despatches as she had undertaken her duties in the field 'fearlessly and displayed a great devotion to duty in performing her many and varied tasks'.[38] She enjoyed her time with SOE and did not wish to give up the secret world. She applied to the US equivalent, the OSS.

Two days after her wedding, on 2 April 1945, she was redeployed for new clandestine duties with SAARF (Special Allied Airborne Reconnaissance Force), a joint Anglo-American unit for special operations in Germany in the final stages of the war. These were the last days of Hitler holed up in his bunker in Berlin. The SAARF's special operations within Germany were designed to fill the vacuum during the final collapse of the Nazi regime by using its own agents behind the lines. The Allies were trying to secure Berlin for the West, in a race with the Soviet forces who, it was feared, might take the whole of Berlin. The groups were modelled on SOE teams of two agents and a W/T operator. The aim was to send 120 teams of agents into Germany. One of their roles was to negotiate the safe passage and liberation of Allied POWs.[39] Their safety was of deep concern, especially due to the death marches in which the Germans forced POWs to walk hundreds of miles in poor health and with little food. Many died along the way.

A new training programme was conducted jointly by SOE and the OSS at the Old Clubhouse, Wentworth, in Surrey. Madden was one of a small number of former Belgian SOE agents who received training there and was then assigned to a Belgian team. She and her colleagues were flown back to Belgium ahead of their secret missions into Germany. Parachuting agents into Germany was fraught with danger at this stage of the war. The first team of six in Operation Violet were French; all were captured by the Russians and interrogated on grounds of being revolutionaries.

Madden went into Germany by truck as part of Operation Bluebell, a mission to help with the liberation of the concentration camps or to enter a camp shortly after liberation to rescue SOE's Belgian agents or establish their whereabouts. Madden spent time working in relief efforts in the concentration camps of Buchenwald, Dachau and Flossenbürg. The work had a profound impact on her health. At the end of it, she returned to the UK totally exhausted and began to suffer nightmares, unable to erase the horrific scenes in the camps from her memory.

Olga Jackson

The night of 4/5 August 1944 saw several separate missions setting out from Tempsford aerodrome. Madden was not the only agent to be parachuted into enemy territory; there was also thirty-five-year-old Olga Jackson (née Thioux), who was originally from Belgium. Born in Liège on 6 January 1909, during the 1930s she was the first Belgian woman to undertake a professional parachute jump in Belgium.[40] Precisely when she came to England before the war is not certain, but on 26 January 1938 she married Major Thomas Jackson of the Royal Artillery in the City of London.[41] She enlisted into the FANY as a cadet ensign, then rose to the rank of lieutenant.

During SOE training, her instructors recognised that she was unable to work well in a group, and her training report noted: 'She will nearly always get her own way. Her charm and sense of humour should make her attractive to many men for she is very feminine and willing to take instruction and advice from those whom she respects. Her main weakness is her inability to plan on a large scale.'[42] She was determined and unscrupulous, yet 'might go far in a lone propaganda mission'.[43] She was given the name 'Babette' for operation in the field.

Jackson's mission in August 1944 was a lone assignment, with no other agents, and conducted jointly on behalf of SOE, the Political Intelligence Department (PID) and the Belgian intelligence service. Hers was a different mission from Madden's. Exiting the plane, she jumped a few seconds too soon and was separated from her packages. She reached Brussels and, as arranged, stayed with a brigadier of the Belgian police.[44] Clear instructions were given to her that her role was not espionage, which could jeopardise her own safety and risk the entire mission, but to demoralise a number of senior German officers and officials who occupied key positions in the German administration in Belgium.[45] The highest-ranking officer on her list of targets was General Alexander von Falkenhausen, head of the military government in Belgium.

Jackson made suitable contacts and established a centre for gathering information on the private and public lives of the men in whom she was interested. Her activities were initially limited to particular towns and cities.[46] In these places, she made contact with the mistresses of German officers and sought to bribe the women into aiding the process of demoralisation of that officer.[47] Methods included the use of sex workers against the officer being targeted or exploiting his weaknesses if he had a propensity towards excessive use of drugs or alcohol. 'Prostitutes, waitresses, barmen and even doctors were to be contacted and instructed in ways to spread defeatist feelings against their German clients.'[48] By encouraging the target's vices to excess, it was believed he would neglect his duties. Another tactic was to seek to convince a German officer that the war was lost, ask who he thought would protect him when Germany falls and question if he might like to consider desertion. This strategy required careful thought and the seeds of desertion needed to be planted cautiously. If the German officer did decide to desert, he was connected to the resistance network, who could provide him with civilian clothes and temporary shelter.

Jackson's role was considered a success. On 4 February 1945, she was loaned to the Intelligence Section of SHAEF for a short time on undisclosed duties as an intelligence officer. Colin Gubbins, the head of SOE, wrote in the citation for her award of a Mention in Despatches that she 'deserves high praise for the courage she has displayed in undertaking this important mission'.[49]

Jackson and Madden were the only female agents currently known to have been dropped into Belgium with SOE. But an incident occurred during the final stages of the war which has marred their SOE record. Part of the file has been redacted; however, one comment has not been blanked out and reads: 'both Madden and Jackson have frankly been a bloody nuisance ever since the liberation'.[50] Another source explains the circumstances.[51] Madden, and a lieutenant who was escorting her, had failed to link up with one of the resistance groups and had strayed into an area of crossfire with the last resisting Nazis. The pair were arrested by US officers and suspected of being traitors or German spies. Madden petitioned her case and asked to speak with her senior officer. He in turn vouched for her over the telephone and she was released. Jackson, meanwhile, was involved in some kind of road accident which wrote off the army vehicle she was travelling in and she tried to obtain another one via unauthorised means. This action tarnished her reputation within SOE.

However, these two incidents should not eclipse the important operations which Madden and Jackson carried out for SOE behind enemy lines. In the end, they were among the brave women of SOE who risked their lives to gain intelligence for the Allies.

Women, SOE and the Far East

At the end of 1944 and in early 1945, in anticipation that the war would continue longer in the Far East, hundreds of SOE women – the majority of them experienced in SOE's operational methods – were transferred from the European theatre of war to India, where they served as secretaries, typists and cipher clerks, but not as agents. By July 1945, the total number of female personnel as support staff to SOE in the Far East numbered 723.[52] Of those, 449 belonged to the FANY and 274 were civilians. Over half were engaged on signals, and during 1945 they were responsible for a staggering 1,422,356 cipher groups going in and out of the field from approximately 183 operational W/T sets across south-east Asia. There were over fifty W/T sets in Burma alone. The cipher women worked in twelve-hour shifts, sending and receiving messages across twenty-four hours a day, seven days a week and every day of the year. It required a lot of concentration to ensure that no incoming or outgoing messages were missed. Without the female personnel in the Far East, Force 136 would not have been able to carry out its operations. A great deal of the work was concerned with Burma, as this was the country where SOE conducted its largest operational commitment in the war against Japan. Much of the rest of the Far East was covered by the US equivalent, the OSS.

A Diverse Legacy

Thousands of women were engaged in secret work for SOE in the war. The precise number is still not known as not all their personal files have been declassified. Some operated in the field and lost their lives as agents; others worked behind a desk in Baker Street or in SOE section headquarters around the world. They were all part of the hidden hand and apparatus behind the success of SOE – a necessary work force.

There have been some surprising discoveries, as in the case of SOE's female interrogators – a role not undertaken by uniformed female intelligencers until the Second World War. One of those SOE interrogators was Mrs Anne Delves (née Todd), who began her career as a secretary in North Africa for the organisation. In November 1944 she transferred back to the civilian staff at Baker Street to fill a vacancy in a new section for the interrogation of agents, run by Colonel Woolrych.[53] Prior to the war, she had worked in a reserved occupation for the National Central Library in London, evacuating in the early part of the war to undertake the same confidential work at Bourne Lodge, near Hemel Hempstead. Vera Atkins, senior officer in F Section, is another example of the female interrogator. Her interrogations of numerous Nazi war criminals took place at the end of the war and often, though not exclusively, in Germany.

SOE made good use of the fact that women could move around enemy territory with relative ease. No wonder, then, that there is at least one example of a male SOE officer who was recruited as a spy and saboteur in Norway who dressed as a woman to move through the German lines. He was Major Malcolm Munthe MC, formerly of the Gordon Highlanders. He established a network of 'friends' in Norway whom he called the 'Red Horse' and led operations in the country against the heavy water plant. After a dangerous escape, he went on to head SOE activities in southern Italy and participated in the Anzio landings. It was while he was in Italy that he dressed as a large woman to smuggle a radio transmitter past German lines.

While SOE was not established initially as an intelligence-gathering organisation, it developed that dimension because of the very nature of its missions deep within enemy-occupied countries. SOE's agents became a most valuable source of eyewitness accounts of life behind the lines and an indispensable source of intelligence. It is now possible to firmly conclude that women undertook intelligence duties as spies and agents in all countries where SOE was operational, including Italy, the Balkans, Greece and the Far East. It is a rich legacy.

16
NOAH'S ARK

In July 1941, MI6 headquarters in London received a coded message from behind enemy lines in France: 'N1 arrested this morning, network intact, everything continuing, best postpone parachuting next moon, patrol leaves for Paris tonight, confidence unshakeable. Regards POZ 55.'

SIS sent back a message, 'Who is taking over?'

Poz 55 replied, 'I am.'

N1 was the codename for Commandant Georges Loustaunau-Lacau (aka 'Navarre') who had led the Alliance, a clandestine network in France that passed intelligence back to MI6 in London. Importantly, it covered the gaps that the Ultra material from Bletchley Park and other sources could not reach. With Navarre behind bars for a second time, Marie-Madeleine (aka POZ 55), his second-in-command, took over as successor. She was a twenty-nine-year-old mother of two who believed that victory over German occupation was possible. For over a year she had risked her life for the Alliance, but MI6 was unaware that she was a woman. After taking control of the network, she decided to keep her real identity hidden, believing that MI6 would remove her as leader because of her sex. She was probably correct, given Dansey's reservations about female agents. Ironically, she was heading one of MI6's most important and far-reaching spy rings in German-occupied France and Vichy France.

The Alliance was established in June 1940 during the early weeks of the German occupation of France. In London, exiled French General Charles de Gaulle had declared that his country was not lost – French men and women were to take up arms. But there was no appetite for another war so soon after the bloodshed of the First World War. The majority of the population believed it could live satisfactorily under the

Nazi regime. Others were more realistic about the impact of occupation and bravely took up resistance.

Since Western Europe was largely lost to the Third Reich, Britain needed intelligence from behind enemy lines. The US was not yet in the war, the air war hung in the balance and Britain had to hold on to supremacy at sea. It was imperative that communications and supplies from the United States to Britain were protected for Britain's very survival. Vichy France was a French state, unoccupied by the Germans until 1942, and headed by Marshal Philippe Pétain, who collaborated with Nazi Germany. As such, it was a dangerous place for Allied agents and spies to operate in.

The situation for MI6 was serious. Its intelligence officers and agents had been compromised by the Venlo incident – the abduction of two SIS officers – on the German–Dutch border the previous November. The situation necessitated the recall to London of European SIS officers across Europe in case their names had been revealed during the officers' interrogations. It left MI6 struggling to gain intelligence from these countries. The German occupation of Western Europe in 1940 had then virtually obliterated MI6's presence in those countries. Intelligence was vital. Marie-Madeleine and Navarre became important in this respect.

Born Marie-Madeleine Bridou in Marseilles on 8 November 1909, she had been raised in the Far East, where she had lived a life of luxury. Her father was a leading figure in the shipping company Messageries Maritimes. She married an officer, Edouard Meric, in 1929 and they had two children. The marriage did not last and by 1938 she was working as a secretary for Navarre's underground magazine *L'Ordre National*, which specialised in reports on German rearmament. Navarre was a hero of the First World War and an anti-fascist. By June 1940, as German military units approached Paris, Marie-Madeleine closed down the magazine. She and Navarre, with several of their friends, met in the western foothills of the Pyrenees and the Alliance intelligence circuit was born.

June 1940 to July 1941

From its foundations in June 1940 to Navarre's arrest in July the following year, the clandestine headquarters of the Alliance was located in the Hotel des Sports, Pau, along the northern Pyrenees and approximately 50 miles from the Spanish border. The network operated in Vichy France as well as German-occupied France. Vichy France was the diplomatic centre and, as such, the source of power and where all foreign embassies were located after the Germans occupied much of France. It was therefore one of the best places to gain intelligence from diplomatic and military circles. The Alliance divided itself into zones to cover Vichy France through to Spain, as well as Switzerland and Italy. Posts in Marseilles observed activity in the Mediterranean; others covered areas in North Africa. The Alliance was an MI6 network which had its own MI6 liaison officer. He was Kenneth Cohen RN, alias Keith Crane, of SIS.

Whenever the Alliance headquarters were compromised, a new location was found in Pau. Navarre acted as the formal head of the network until his arrest, but focused his efforts primarily on North Africa. He handed the direction of the entire intelligence operations in France to Marie-Madeleine. During all of this, her children were either in a boarding school or being cared for by relatives and this enabled her to run the network.

As Easter 1941 approached, Marie-Madeleine collected her eleven-year-old son from a nearby Jesuit school where he was a boarder. As a mother, her conscience struggled with the desertion of her children and she decided to tell him that she was involved in secret work. She gave no specific details but told him broadly of the struggle and his face lit up. She told him that she was doing her duty for France and if she did not write to him it was to protect both of them because many people depended on her. She drove him to Toulouse and across the south of France, touching base with informants en route and renting new rooms from which to operate.

On 22 June 1941 the war took a new direction when Hitler attacked Russia in Operation Barbarossa. British intelligence dropped more agents and wireless operators to the Alliance in France. The network had over a hundred patrols, with a wide web of agents and couriers. Meanwhile, Navarre was busy with a plan to encourage an internal revolt from Tunis to Agadir to seal off the Mediterranean to prevent access by Axis troops. Supported by Prime Minister Winston Churchill, this action would be followed by a number of surprise attacks by local troops. The Mediterranean had to be secured for the Allies for vital communications with the Middle East and all naval transport around the Cape. It was hoped that revolt, followed by liberation, would come from within North Africa itself. This did not happen and in November 1942 the Allies mounted Operation Torch, an invasion of North Africa. It was while Navarre and others were planning the revolt from a secret location in France that police officers burst into the premises and arrested them. They had been betrayed. Pension Welcome, the headquarters of the Alliance in Pau, was raided and had to be closed down. Marie-Madeleine evaded arrest and went into hiding. Navarre was moved from the prison in Pau to other Gestapo prisons and eventually to Mauthausen concentration camp, which he survived. Marie-Madeleine commented later, 'We were shattered by the magnitude of the disaster.'[1]

When it was safe to do so, she returned for a brief visit to Pension Welcome; an elderly lady there promised her that she would not give the network away and would cover for Marie-Madeleine by saying that she had left for the Riviera. The Germans raided various premises and found Marie-Madeleine's notebooks in which she had written down the codenames of her agents – their real names were not in the books. She had made the decision to change their codenames from groups of letters and numbers to the names of animals. The Nazis therefore called the network 'Noah's Ark'.

Marie-Madeleine continued to move between occupied France and Vichy France, building up and running the Alliance as the Gestapo placed her on the wanted list. She arranged safe houses, money for operating the network and dead letter boxes where intelligence could be left securely. Gradually, a network of radio operators working from safe houses was built up. Posts covered regions from Paris to Brittany and northern France. Money was often in short supply, which led Marie-Madeleine to run the network on loans and her own personal funds, which became exhausted.

The Gestapo intensified their searches, utterly determined to break up the network, but, each time they succeeded, Marie-Madeleine started up again. She moved between various safe houses, travelling in different disguises as secretary, nurse and charwoman. Refusing to be defeated, she established another secret headquarters in Pau, from where she coordinated the writing and receiving of messages in invisible ink, and the coding and decoding, with a young woman, Josette, acting as her courier.

Network Revival

In the midwinter of 1941, a courier arrived at the British embassy in Madrid from France with the diplomatic bag.[2] The consul opened the seal and out stepped a beautiful woman – the quintessential female spy, an image immortalised by Mata Hari after the First World War. The reality was rather different. Cold and cramped, Marie-Madeleine had been cooped up inside the bag for nine hours, hidden inside an old car that had taken the final stage of the journey on a train over the Pyrenees. A British intelligence officer, Jean Schoofs, who was also being smuggled into Spain, had periodically opened the bag so she could breathe fresh air.

The contact at the British embassy in Madrid was Mr Richards, a pseudonym for MI6's man Major Eddie Keyser.[3] Marie-Madeleine had much secret information to impart to him face-to-face, the nature of which has not been not disclosed. She was with him when she received news of the betrayal of the Alliance network in occupied France and Vichy France. Fourteen months of hard work was gone.

The network had to be rebuilt. Richards gave her a new set of codes and instructions to establish new links between Marseille and Madrid as a priority. He then arranged for her to be moved out of Spain in the diplomatic bag again and dropped in the middle of the countryside in France to continue the clandestine work. She went on to build up a network of over 3,000 informers, couriers and agents, scattered all over France and Vichy France. She was astute in being able to discern what intelligence was needed by the Allies. MI6 supplied her with wireless operators.

During 1942, Marie-Madeleine had an agent in Italy called 'Pelican' (Petru Giovacchini), who sent back details of the flight times of the Italian squadrons to be flown to North Africa to reinforce the Afrika Korps. She coded the information and sent it to MI6 and consequently the planes were intercepted by the Allies. This action deprived German General Rommel of the air support he needed to advance on Tobruk. Reports were coming in, too, from all over France, on German air defences, the location and identification of German divisions in Normandy, intelligence maps and details of German troop movements to the Russian front.

That same year, French General Henri Giraud escaped German captivity in the fortress Königstein, near Dresden. He was sheltered by Princess Marie de Croy, who had worked with Edith Cavell in the First World War and was working again for British intelligence and the Belgian resistance in this war, and possibly with deep connections to SIS (p. 12). After Giraud's escape, Richards sent Marie-Madeleine a coded message asking her to make contact to find out his intentions. Giraud wanted to help the Allies from within France, but Richards deemed it more important for him to assist with resistance activities in North Africa.[4] On the eve of the Allied landings there in November 1942, Marie-Madeleine smuggled Giraud out of France to North Africa.

Betrayal

Arthur Bradley Davies (aka 'Bla'), an agent sent to the network by British intelligence, turned out to have been the traitor who was working for the Nazis and who by the beginning of 1942 had blown the Alliance network in occupied France. Richards issued orders that Bla was to be liquidated.[5] The problem for Marie-Madeleine was how to find Bla's hiding place in occupied France. But during 1942 Bla was captured by her agents and interrogated. He refused to give up any information and soon found himself directly facing Marie-Madeleine. During her intense interrogation of him, he finally provided details of how he had infiltrated the network and how the Abwehr had tasked him with hunting her down. There was no compromise for traitors and British intelligence sent a message that he was to be executed.[6]

Marie-Madeleine had not seen her son and daughter for over a year and she missed them. Intelligence duties and resistance activities took a toll on the women who undertook espionage and had a family as they had to spend long periods away from their children. Marie-Madeleine's children believed that she was in England and she did not wish to upset them by visiting them fleetingly and immediately disappearing again. Just prior to sending them for safety to Switzerland, where her mother had a chalet, she asked her courier Monique Bontinck (aka 'Ermine') to collect them and walk them past the window so she could see them. The children knew Ermine because occasionally they had stayed with her. Marie-Madeleine recalled, 'they looked thin and pale, and utterly lost and helpless. I had a feeling of being buried alive. Their departure for Switzerland plunged me into the depths of despair.'[7]

In early 1943, German General von Paulus suffered defeat at Stalingrad in Russia. From France, the Alliance continued to send intelligence to London on German shipping and troop movements. Securing intelligence for the Allies came at a cost as members were rounded up and shot. Some of the key workers disappeared and the network collapsed yet again in Lyon and Marseille.

On 5 February 1943 there were a number of other arrests, including Giovacchini, the man who had reported on the Italian air squadrons going to North Africa. Arrested too were 'Hummingbird' (Michele Goldschmidt), 'Ewe' (wife of an agent codenamed 'Moufflon') and 'Mouse' '(Madeleine Crozet). They were horrifically tortured for weeks by Klaus Barbie, the 'butcher of Lyon'. They suffered electric shocks all over their bodies and their breasts were burnt with cigarettes, but they refused to betray the network, continuing to claim not to know anything about it or its leader. Marie-Madeleine later remarked how these women went 'unflinching to the military tribunal that was to condemn them to death . . . These great French women had accepted martyrdom to preserve the secrets that meant life and liberty to their comrades.'[8] Marie-Madeleine described it as a terrible year, admitting that some of her agents were irreplaceable. The whole of the sector in Vichy France also collapsed after another betrayal, and there were further arrests in March 1943.

Marie-Madeleine restarted from Paris, but her own chances of survival in France were slim. She was too valuable, knowing the network so intimately, and the Gestapo were still on her trail. It was time for MI6 to exfiltrate her from France.

The Old Owl

At MI6 headquarters in Broadway Buildings, Claude Dansey – whom the Alliance called 'the old owl' – had become increasingly concerned over the safety of the network's leader. Marie-Madeleine had led Alliance for two and a half years but Dansey still did not know that she was a woman. On the night of 17/18 July 1943, she was picked up by a Lysander from an airfield near Meaux and flown to England. She was desperately tired and strained, but immediately regretted leaving her friends and network in France.

Mr Richards (Major Eddie Keyser) greeted her off the plane, and she stayed overnight with Major Bertram and his wife, Barbara, at Bignor Manor, near Chichester in Sussex.[9] The Bertrams were a very ordinary couple; nothing marked them out as recruits into the Secret Intelligence Service from 1940 to 1944. Bignor Manor was a secret SIS safehouse, a despatch and meeting point for spies and agents being flown in and out of occupied Europe. Barbara Bertram was no mere bystander to her husband's activities but was actively engaged in sheltering SIS agents. She cooked the meals before their departure on missions and, with the FANY drivers, checked their belongings to ensure their clothing had no British labels or markers which could give them away.

From Bignor Manor, Marie-Madeleine was taken to an MI6 flat in London. The following day, she finally met Dansey, who arrived promptly at 11 a.m. He took both her hands and exclaimed, 'So this is the terrible woman who has had us all scared! I've often wondered what you were like, Poz. It's good to have you safely here.' 'Not for long,' she replied.[10] She immediately told him that she wanted to return to France at once. He refused – he had received news of further arrests in the network. He reminded her that she had led the Alliance for two and a half years; the average survival for a leader in the field was six months. He thanked her for everything that she had achieved and explained that she could coordinate the Alliance more efficiently from London. He indicated that MI6 would probably need her back in France just before D-Day. For the rest of 1943 and into 1944 Marie-Madeleine coordinated the Noah's Ark from London.

After the bombing of Peenemünde, reports continued to arrive from the network informing MI6 of the V-1 installations at sites in France that, if operational, could methodically destroy most of Britain's large cities. Marie-Madeleine sent gifts to her agents: soap and other presents for the men, and stockings, underwear, jumpers and Ceylon tea for the women. But her sense of frustration about not being sent back into the field grew. When she met Dansey again for lunch, she petitioned him to be allowed to return to France. He resolutely refused because the Nazis had intensified their efforts to destroy the network. There was news of how the Gestapo were setting traps and ambushes. Gestapo officers arrived at the house of 'Ladybird' (Madame Berne-Churchill), a doctor, who sheltered Marie-Madeleine's agents. While she was busy convincing them that they had come to the wrong place, Noah's Ark agents escaped out of a back window with secret papers. It was a close shave. Afterwards, Ladybird fled into the night to warn the rest of the network.

On 16 September 1943 key members were arrested, including Commander Leon Faye (aka 'Eagle', and Marie-Madeleine's second-in-command), a number of radio operators, the head of operations, the head of security and a courier. As a result of the interrogations of these members, the Gestapo made further arrests of members in Paris and elsewhere. From London, Marie-Madeleine issued orders for the network not to contact other sectors within France to avoid compromise. Her agents were shot by the Gestapo; others were found hanged in various locations, including one agent in a bank with two machine pistols around his neck. This was designed to terrify the network.

The transmitters of the Noah's Ark fell silent across France. Colonel Ehringer (head of the Abwehr III F in Dijon), declared at a private banquet, 'The Noah's Ark that we have been fighting since 1940 has been destroyed.' The French traitors who infiltrated the network each received 100,000 francs from the Germans. Sectors in Normandy and Brittany were decimated. Marie-Madeleine erased over 400 names from her chart and was emotionally devastated. 'I saw their twisted, agonised mouths crying out for help,' she wrote, 'I was dying of grief.'[11]

That autumn 1943, there were no further flights by Lysander to the network. But, in spite of heavy casualties, Marie-Madeleine knew it was not time to stop. Intelligence was needed on 'Fortress France', the country that had been heavily fortified by the Nazis. That intelligence began to flow again, with messages about the movement of U-boats and details of German aircraft and their numbers. As a result, photographic reconnaissance missions were regularly despatched by the RAF to supplement and verify the intelligence coming in. There was more on the V-weapons, including a secret message from 'Grand Duke' (Captain le Comte Helen Charles des Isnards) that the Germans were on the point of completing installations under bomb-proof cupolas between Calais and Boulogne, with rocket-shells with a firing range of 100 miles and 1,000 guns concentrated on London.

In January 1944 parachute drops resumed again. Dansey was still reluctant to send Marie-Madeleine back to France because the third leader in the field, Jean Sainteny (aka 'Dragon'), had been captured. He said that she could not return until he could guarantee her security and that she would not be arrested within a week. Finally, preparations were made for her to go back into France with false papers identifying her with the nevertheless unlikely sounding name of Mrs Flying Fish. To increase her chance of survival, Dansey insisted that she change her appearance. To make her look older, she wore round black-framed glasses, put on a hairnet and used a set of false teeth. The unflattering disguise worked.

Dansey's conversation with Marie-Madeleine immediately prior to her departure reveals something of his enigmatic character, a character that has been elusive to historians studying the history of MI6. It demonstrates that he had connections, embedded deep in France, and maybe even within the Gestapo itself. He said to her, 'My dear child, should you be arrested you must make no attempt to defend yourself as head of the network, because then there is no way out except by taking the cyanide [pill]. And as I know you will not betray anyone, you must be quite cynical about the whole thing. Say that I sent you to France to report on the Communist Party. They know who I am. They'll be very interested indeed and they won't kill you.'

She asked, 'And the network? And usual name?'

Dansey replied, 'As for the network, you say it's smashed and nothing is left and that your job now is not to gather information for use against Nazis, but simply to prepare for future action against the Russians. Believe me, they'll all put themselves under your orders when you mention my name, with all my titles of course.'

Marie-Madeleine responded, 'The Gestapo will never swallow a story like that.'

He replied, 'If they don't believe you, you'll send a message on one of your transmitters and I'll answer them – in my own way. Believe me, Poz, I've never made this offer to anyone before.'

She then asked, 'Why make it to me? I'm not British.'

His reply displayed an honesty and openness, 'You're a woman and I'm ashamed of seeing you all these years doing things I couldn't do myself.'[12]

As they parted, he placed a souvenir into her hand: a rabbit's foot – the traditional mascot for good luck.

Return to France

Ahead of D-Day, the Allies carried out intense bombing of the railways in France. Sea routes were used to drop agents in and take them out, as well as picking up intelligence from couriers to take back to England.

On the eve of D-Day, 5 June 1944, Marie-Madeleine dined with Kenneth Cohen and his wife and the acting head of the Free French Special Services. The dinner was interrupted by the occasional sound of a V-2. That same night, de Gaulle sent a written message to the Alliance recognising the importance of intelligence during the landings: 'At this moment when the forces of liberation are coming to drive the enemy from our country, let me remind every intelligence agent that his first duty is to stay in the place he has gloriously chosen and to gather and transmit the information that is a vital importance to the progress of operations up to the very last minute.'[13]

A legal document had been drawn up to incorporate the Alliance into BCRA, the French intelligence service, to make it easier to work together and clarify the command chain in the field after D-Day. A few days later, Cohen saw Marie-Madeleine off on the night flight in a Hudson. She was due to land near Aix-en-Provence, but the reception committee was not at the drop zone because of security fears and the flight returned to England. She left again for France the following evening and made a successful landing, sheltering in a village near Nangis in north-central France. Intelligence reports and correspondence awaited her and she spent several days going through them: urgent V-1 and V-2 reports, as well as new material on German troop movements. A few days later she was informed that six agents had been caught and shot – a reminder of the dangers still prevalent from the Gestapo. She moved to a safe house between Aix-en-Provence and Marseille for several days.

The Gestapo raided the flat where she was staying, looking for 'Grand Duke', who they thought was the head of the network. He was not there, but Marie-Madeleine was arrested and taken to the local prison. The Gestapo did not realise who she was. She quietly reached for her cyanide pill in case it was needed, and, in her own view, she was saved because of her failure to show any fear.[14] She was taken to a nearby prison, from where she made a daring, but painful, escape in the middle of the night, by squeezing naked through the bars of the open window of her cell, with her dress in her teeth.[15] She ran across fields, evading the German roadblocks that had been set up. When she arrived at the farm belonging to Grand Duke, she collapsed. There was concern for her health and wellbeing, especially given the toll that over two years of heading the network had taken on her.

While she was sheltering there, a flood of intelligence came in from the network. Some of the information related to German troops being moved to the front line in Normandy. The work was too important and she knew she must carry on. She pushed through her fatigue and exhaustion and travelled to Marseille to make contact with members of the network.

The importance of continuing, against the odds, could not be overestimated. Intelligence was needed to win the war. One of the major contributions of the Noah's Ark network was to provide MI6 with information about Germany's U-boat bases at Brest and Saint-Nazaire and sightings of U-boats at Bordeaux. From 1944, crucial details about Hitler's secret weapons were gathered. The Alliance patrols sent intelligence on German trading with Spain for iron ore needed for German industry. They provided eyewitness accounts of the German work to camouflage military and other secret installations and changes to the U-boat bases. From the north came information on the number of Messerschmidt planes in certain airfields, as well as details of phoney airfields and the location of German units around Paris.

In collecting this intelligence, the risks were taken equally by women and men. Women played a central role in those successful intelligence coups for MI6.

The Women of Noah's Ark

Women accounted for around a fifth of the Noah's Ark network and succeeded because of the Nazis' stereotypical view of women as wives and mothers whose roles, as they saw it, were confined to domestic duties at home.[16] The strong and courageous women of the network ran safe houses and acted as couriers and were able to use their good looks to charm their way out of difficult situations.[17] Others contacted the wives and families of the arrested agents to provide financial aid. Denise Centore, niece of the composer Germaine Tailleferre, was secretary at the headquarters. She was a historian and very methodical in her work for the underground.

Jeanne Berthomier ('Seamew') worked as a civil servant in the Ministry of Public Works in Paris, which gave her access to top-secret material. She transported smuggled intelligence summaries and messages in the hem of her cloak. 'Shrimp', whose real name was unknown, was based at Saint-Nazaire, where she was employed to mend the vests of U-boat crews. She passed information to the Alliance on which U-boats were in the base for repairs and when those U-boats were heading back out to sea. The intelligence was passed to MI6.

Jeannie Rousseau ('Amniarix') became a member of a sub-network called the Druids and brought astonishing intelligence on the V-weapons. Her family had moved to Dinard after the occupation of Paris. Hitler placed Field Marshal Walter von Reichenau in Dinard to oversee the site where Wehrmacht troops were quartered and the headquarters set up to organise the invasion of Britain. Reichenau needed a translator and so the bright young Jeannie, who spoke five languages and had been educated at the École Libre des Sciences Politiques, where she graduated with the highest marks for her year, became his interpreter. At the headquarters where she worked, German commanders and strategists spoke openly about their plans.

One day, the German authorities sent officials to arrest her because in their view she seemed to be the only possible source of a leak to the

British about plans in the Dinard area. (She was not.) Her colleagues at headquarters protested that she was incapable of espionage and she was released from Rennes prison. She then moved to Paris where she obtained a job as translator and interpreter at a German army headquarters, located in the Hotel Majestic. There she met German officers with whom she had worked in Dinard. They trusted her, as did others around her, and open discussions took place in the office about supplies from French industrialists being sent to Germany for Hitler's secret weapons programme. Rousseau took it all in.

In spring 1943 Rousseau travelled to Vichy France and met Georges Lamarque, a former acquaintance from university. They exchanged stories on what they were doing, and he told her about the Druids network which he was running for British intelligence. Rousseau joined.

Back in Paris, she was invited by the German officers to parties, where she overheard them talking about the secret weapons programme on the Baltic coast. She was almost invisible to them in the room, but occasionally she interjected, commenting that the weapon was too fantastic to be true. Then one day, a German officer pulled out of his briefcase a number of drawings of a huge rocket and a map of the testing site at Peenemünde. He talked about how personnel entered the site, its security and what passes were needed. Rousseau committed the information to memory. Afterwards, she went to Druids headquarters and told all she knew, even though she did not understand the technological details that she was handing over, only that it was top-secret and probably important.

Rousseau was just twenty-three years old when her report on the V-weapons was sent to R.V. Jones, the head of the Scientific Section of MI6.[18] Known as the Wachtel Report, it gave details of a 'stratospheric bomb', its launch speed and fuel, the sound it made during launch – as 'deafening as a flying fortress' – and the claim that 50–100 bombs would suffice to destroy London. Jones later asked Marie-Madeleine in a face-to-face meeting in London where the report had come from and she replied, 'From the most remarkable girl of her generation.'

It was due to Rousseau that MI6 learnt about Colonel Wachtel and his formation of a new Flak regiment of 220 men that included his chief technical adviser, Major Sonnenfeld. This regiment was to oversee the deployment of V-weapons on London and major cities in England. Jones received three independent reports on the V-weapons, including the Wachtel Report; all were received after the Allied bombing of Peenemünde in August 1943. However, it underlined the continued threat of these weapons and how intelligence on them continued to be needed to stay ahead of the game. General Dwight Eisenhower said that 'were the Germans able to perfect these new weapons six months earlier, it was likely that our invasion of Europe would have encountered enormous difficulties'.[19]

Jones later wrote that Rousseau's reports 'stand brilliantly in the history of intelligence; and three concentration camps (Ravensbrück, Königsberg and Torgau) could not break her'.[20] Rousseau was arrested in Gestapo raids across northern France in April 1944 and sent first to Ravensbrück concentration camp. Fighting to stay alive there, she had no idea how significant her reports were for averting a German victory. During the final months of the war, she was rescued by the Swedish Red Cross and survived.

Monique Bontinck (aka 'Ermine') was Marie-Madeleine's young assistant and courier. She joined the network in 1940 as an anti-Nazi who wished to resist the Germans. She had grown up in northern France, hearing tales from her Belgian grandfather about the German occupation of Belgium in the First World War. In occupied Paris in the summer of 1940, she met Edmond Poulain, a young lawyer in the Alliance, and they soon became engaged. In 1941 he was arrested by the Gestapo and sent to Fresnes prison. He managed to smuggle a message out to Marie-Madeleine petitioning her to save his fiancée from the Gestapo. Ermine was fearless and often undertook reckless missions without the knowledge of Marie-Madeleine. Poulain did not survive. Ermine went on to marry another member of the network, Ferdinand Rodriquez. In spring 1945, MI6 negotiated a prisoner swap in which Rodriquez was exchanged for an Abwehr officer called Berthold Schulze-Holthus, who had been caught in Persia. After Rodriquez's release, he travelled to England, was promoted in the Intelligence Corps and returned to Paris on special duties.

Odette Fabius, the thirty-two-year-old daughter of a wealthy Parisian lawyer and wife of a rich antiques dealer, wanted more than a life in intellectual and high society circles. She joined the Noah's Ark and became a full-time courier. She was ambitious, so Marie-Madeleine taught her how to code and decrypt messages. Fabius had a daughter and occasionally hid secret material in her daughter's suitcase when they travelled. But Marie-Madeleine felt that Fabius liked the drama of being a spy more than she cared about security aspects of the network and never included her in her closest circle.

Marie-Madeleine, with other women of the network, was sheltered in Lyon by Baroness de Mareuil ('Wasp'). It was here that she received news that her agents in Marseille had all been captured. Poignantly, she wrote, 'In my network, no woman ever faltered, even under the most extreme kind of torture. I owe my freedom to many who were questioned until they lost consciousness, but never revealed my whereabouts.'[21]

She believed that survival was not enough – victory had to be achieved. The network must carry on and provide what intelligence it could to the Allies. The headquarters was relocated to the home of Madame Berne-Churchill ('Ladybird'), who aided a British radio operator, Frederick Rodney, to find a hilltop to transmit messages to London. He had been silent and not transmitting for so long that MI6 feared he and Marie-Madeleine had been liquidated. Berne-Churchill was tasked, too, with organising welfare and providing financial help for the families of arrested agents.

The extraordinary work and sacrifice of the Alliance continued until the Allies had fully liberated France. It was an intelligence network that had 'waged a relentless and unremitting fight in France from 1940 until her liberation in 1945'. But it came at huge cost. Around 500 women and men of Alliance died in the Allied cause, enduring torture and death in horrific circumstances in concentration camps or being executed by firing squads.

For four years, Marie-Madeleine had led the Alliance with great organisational skills. She was a commander from whom the whole of the network took its orders; a competent and strong woman whose network was highly valued by SIS.[22] During the tough, challenging times of the war, she had thought, 'We were bound to perish. What could we really achieve against the most powerful military machine in the world and the combined wealth and enslaved economies of a dozen exploited nations? Faced with such odds, had I the right to involve my unfortunate friends in a venture that could end only in our possibly pointless slaughter?'[23]

But, in fact, they did make a difference, fighting back with the only invisible weapon they had – intelligence. It was a slow game and one with high stakes for them personally and for the Allies more widely. They provided a source for intelligence upon which SIS came to rely and contributed in no small way to the overall intelligence picture for the Allies.[24]

The French Memorial

In recognition of the resistance movement in France, de Gaulle commissioned a dedicated memorial called the Compagnons de La Libération. There are 1,038 names enshrined on it – 1,032 men and 6 women.[25] It does not include Marie-Madeleine or any of the women of the Alliance. Those memorialised were from resistance groups other than the Alliance, including the Free French intelligence network. Emilienne Moreau (Moreau-Evrard) of the Brutus resistance network, founded in 1941 by Pierre Fourcade, was one woman memorialised. Moreau served in intelligence operations for the British in the First World War, too.

The Compagnons was opened again in 1958 to include Winston Churchill, and in 1962 for George VI. But there is still no commemoration of the women of the Alliance. It has been suggested that this was because of de Gaulle's sexism and low opinion of female resisters.[26] However, this view fails to take into account that not a single agent of the Alliance – male or female – has been commemorated on the memorial. It is more likely that the absence of their names has more to do with the Alliance being an SIS/MI6 network. That most secret of intelligence services does not release the names of its operatives.

The Alliance was the only MI6 network to survive intact in France until the end of the war.

17
THE CLARENCE SERVICE

After Belgium fell to the Nazi 'Blitzkrieg' in spring 1940, Walthère Dewé, who had headed La Dame Blanche intelligence network for SIS in the First World War, sprang into action. Dewé's close friend in the revived organisation was Hector Demarque (aka 'Clarence') and Dewé named the network after him. Dewé recalled the old guard, including seventy-five-year-old Thérèse de Radiguès, who had served in La Dame Blanche as commander of the observation post Platoon 49.[1] She became a founding member of Clarence and one of its most senior figures. Serving in the rank of captain, she was a strong and courageous woman. The first meeting of the committee of the Clarence Service took place in her home at 41 Avenue de la Couronne in Ixelles.[2] She was one of four prominent women on the Directorate (the committee that ran Clarence).

Enlistment in Clarence was voluntary, an oath of loyalty was sworn, and military ranks given. Operating from headquarters in Liège, where Dewé lived, it modelled itself along the same lines as La Dame Blanche and as an espionage network for MI6. From the London end, it was overseen by Lieutenant Colonel Frederick John Jempson (codename 'Page'), who in 1944 was promoted to head of the Belgian section of MI6.[3] His personal secretary was Lieutenant Ruth Clement Stowell (née Wright), who rendered valuable work for Clarence, not only as his secretary but in the organisation and maintenance of effective intelligence services between Britain and occupied Belgium and Luxembourg. She trained the agents being parachuted into Luxembourg.[4]

Across Belgium, observation posts were set up to gather intelligence on the German army, defences, train movements and military installations. British military intelligence officers could not base their coordination between the Clarence Service and MI6 in Paris, as they had in the First World War, because France was also under German occupation. Links had to come direct from England; and a direct connection with London proved difficult until MI6 organised a parachute drop of radio transmitters into Belgium in January 1941.

In spite of her age, de Radiguès was extremely active for Clarence. She used the pseudonym Madame Frère. Believing that she could do even more for the intelligence service, she requested new assignments and was placed in charge of the department for safe houses and meeting places. She oversaw the research of, arrangements for and use of shelters for hiding agents who had been compromised, as well as organising safe meeting places for Directorate staff. She ran her own agents, among them her daughter Marguerite. François de Radiguès comments, 'my grandmother was a strong character, fiercely patriotic, and a fearsome figure to be reckoned with'.[5] Her citation at the end of the war said that, in spite of her great age, Thérèse de Radiguès carried out the tasks in a truly remarkable manner.

Laure and Louise Tandel

Women distinguished themselves in their service for Clarence as agents, couriers and through taking charge of safe houses. They understood the risks if caught by the Gestapo. Madame Blaise acted as a courier for mail as far as Jura, from where it was taken to contacts in Switzerland. A number of women, like the Tandel sisters, had already risked their lives in the previous world war; they did not hesitate to offer themselves again when asked by Dewé.

Louise and Laure Tandel lived together. Laure, born in 1875, was a year older than her sister, born in 1876. Their citations for service for Clarence are identical. Laure had been the headmistress of a girls' boarding school and retired in 1935. She and her sister were recruited by Dewé on 1 June 1940 and operated until liberation by Allied troops on 15 September 1944. Laure used the pseudonym Mademoiselle Esther Julie Latour.

The sisters used their home as a radiotelegraphic and radiotelephone transmission site. Their devotion and discretion made them ideal for operating this site as a place of contact for agents who had parachuted into Belgium and a haven and meeting place for important agents of the Clarence network. They offered shelter and food to parachutists sent by MI6 in London (the latter known to them as the 'Page Service') on missions to set up transmitting and receiving stations for communications. They were responsible for informing the Clarence committee when parachutists had arrived safely. At the start of August 1941, a new agent was parachuted into Belgium called 'Marble' (aka Paul Jacquemin), a civil engineer/geologist and expert on mines. He was sheltered by Laure and Louise Tandel. Thanks to his transmissions, contact with SIS was established after the silence since the arrest of parachutist Jean Lamy. Another agent, codenamed 'Student' (Paul Godenne), was parachuted into Belgium on 10 September 1941 and stayed with the Tandel sisters.

In addition, the sisters personally recruited military intelligence agents for Clarence. Among them was principal agent Paul Janssens, recruited in June 1941. He served until liberation and headed the sector of intelligence gathering around Saint-Ghislain. Another was Albert Sohngen, who entered Clarence on March 1943. He provided intelligence on the coastal areas occupied by the Germans, giving precise and detailed plans of all German labour efforts for an attack or defence, as well as information on the location of dummy or camouflaged forts and minefields. Another of the Tandels' recruits was André Didier, who entered the service at the same time as Albert Sohngen. Didier went on a mission but did not return. He was arrested by the Germans on 20 January 1944 and transported to Germany on 12 August.

Importantly, the Tandel sisters provided valuable military intelligence for MI6. As agent handlers, they received intelligence from their agents on details of German troop movements around Brussels and the region; they also dealt with intelligence on aerodromes and the movement of boats on canals in the region of Lessines–Ath–Grammont. Both women were recommended for promotion to the rank of lieutenant and awarded medals.[6] Like so many women and men behind enemy lines working for these secret networks, they carried out their missions, regardless of the perils.

Women of Clarence

Thousands of agents worked for the Clarence Service during the war, though it is difficult to confirm how many were women. One inspirational and brave woman was Clotilde Lucie Coppens, who entered the Clarence Service on 1 July 1942. Born in March 1890, she lived at 59 Avenue du Parc in Brussels. She distinguished herself by enabling the organisation to use her home for meetings and the daily running of the Clarence Service. Totally devoted to the cause, she recruited other members of the family and her friends into the network. From the beginning, she was a courier and ran a dead letter box. Every week in her house, a count was recorded of the number of couriers working in all sectors of the Clarence Service.

Antonina Grégoire (aka 'Beatrice') worked with the Belgian resistance. She was university educated and an active communist. From October 1942 to October 1943 she operated as deputy of one of the resistance groups. From October 1943 until 1944 she was responsible for an intelligence section of the Belgian resistance army that gathered intelligence for sabotage and assassination.

Alice Cheramy stood out for her courage and efficiency as a liaison officer. Born in April 1907 in Farciennes, she was from a modest background and worked as a domestic servant and maid. After the occupation of Belgium in 1940, she moved to the south of France with the family who employed her, then returned to Brussels when the couple separated. Cheramy moved to Ixelles with Yvonne Meeus and her four children. Cheramy was recruited to the Clarence Service in June 1943, with the codename 'Mireille'. She was responsible for liaison and operated as a courier in the Brabant region. She always managed to escape from difficult situations to deliver the documents that she was carrying. At the end of the war, she was designated agent first-class by the network's head, Demarque.

Jeanne Claessens was the headteacher of a boys' school in Fouron-le-Comte. Within the Clarence Service, intelligence and information was collected and sent to her. She acted as a courier for this material, passing it to two priests at Val-Dieu Abbey. They were Father Etienne, a travelling agent and courier, and Father Hagues, who transmitted the intelligence from Claessens to London.

Maud Mary de Cort, born in Hackney, London, in May 1886, was married to a Belgian. She had a daughter, Mary, born on 23 February 1931; nevertheless, she did not hesitate to operate as an agent for Clarence and was recruited at the end of May 1940. She used the codename 'Marie Thérèse' and operated in the region of Gand. She regularly provided information on the military occupation in the region. From April 1943 she allowed radio transmissions from her home and provided a safe house for agents. The location was found by the Germans and they raided her house on 29 March 1944. She was arrested, along with all the occupants, and the equipment impounded. Imprisoned until 2 September 1944, she displayed a defiant attitude, 'facing with cold blood and courage the numerous interrogations that she had to undergo, and revealing absolutely nothing of the many secrets that she knew'.[7] After her release, the Clarence network promoted her to the rank of second lieutenant due to 'the importance of the risks incurred, the long duration of her clandestine activity and magnificent attitude in front of the enemy'.

Gestapo Dangers

The Clarence Service was vulnerable to the same risks as other clandestine organisations. Above all, its members feared raids by the Gestapo. Dewé knew that the total commitment of families to Clarence was more dangerous than in the last war because of the brutality of the Gestapo who would show no mercy to the women and men arrested. All knew that they would be executed if caught.

On 22 July 1941 Mrs Dieudonnée Dewé (née Salmon) suffered the first raid by the German field police (Geheime Feldpolizei, GFP), but her husband was in hiding at the time. The raiders found no compromising material; they interrogated her, but she gave nothing away. Dewé remained under suspicion and had to move frequently between safe houses. The police returned in August, September and October and on each occasion Madame Dewé kept calm, not giving away the network or losing her nerve during the long interrogations. She was quick-witted in giving the Germans false leads.

These were dangerous times. Parachutist Jean Lamy had been captured after transmitting messages for MI6/Clarence. Beaten up and tortured, he was taken to St Gilles prison, but during six months of intense interrogations he never betrayed the names of its members that he knew. Condemned to death on 10 January 1942, he was transferred to Germany on 26 February but survived. He returned home on 12 May 1945, but died a few years later as a result of his treatment in captivity at the hands of the Germans.

In June 1944 the Germans intercepted one of Dewé's messages that gave away Thérèse de Radiguès's identity. He decided to go to her house to warn her personally and was there when an Abwehr officer arrived and asked the maid whose overcoat was hanging in the hallway. She answered that it belonged to a gentleman who was waiting for de Radiguès in the small salon. Her grandson François de Radiguès explained what happened:

> The Abwehr officer entered the salon, opened a briefcase and realised that it contained interesting papers. He then called the Gestapo on Avenue Louise, who sent a car. They stopped Dewé and let him in through one door of the car. He left through the other door and ran. He ran to the crossroads of the Avenue de la Couronne and the Rue de la Brasserie. He jumped on a tram coming from the Place Saint-Croix, but the light turned red and the tram stopped. Dewé got off and resumed his run. The Gestapo officers shouted Halt! but wanted to take him alive. At that moment, a Luftwaffe officer who was walking up Rue de la Brasserie drew his Luger and fatally shot Dewé at close range.[8]

The Gestapo arrested de Radiguès. At the prison, she feigned senility and was released by the commandant.

After Dewé's death, Hector Demarque took over command of Clarence. Thérèse de Radiguès continued to work for the network until the liberation of Belgium in September 1944. She was an inspirational force and an example within Clarence as one of its principal leaders.

Intelligence for MI6

During its operational period, the Clarence Service sent 872 radio messages and 163 reports, including photographs, sketches and maps.

Much of the photographic intelligence was sent on microfilms. Ninety-two couriers operated between Belgium, France, Spain and London. The photographs survive in the Imperial War Museum, London, and provide an overview of the sites that were photographed, including ports, military installations and suspected German radio communication positions. Messages that were radioed back to London gave details of train movements and the transportation of German troops and weaponry. One message stated that fifteen loaded wagons passed through Montzen on 27 July, en route for Utrecht. The report continued, 'Little movement of troops during the week ending 30 July 1944. Some departures from Flanders are reported, and a few withdrawals from the Ardennes, destined for Königsberg; the whole not exceeding 5000 men.'[9] The report also related information that ten trains of infantry passed through Montzen for Givet, and the same in reverse. This was vital eyewitness intelligence from behind enemy lines.

Part of another message stated that, on 31 July, a transport of German infantry and artillery was destined for beyond Amiens. A consignment of no more than twelve trains began to move on 1 August and transported SS Adolf Hitler troops and a few light tanks to a region beyond Givet, in the Ardennes region of northern France. In other messages, exact time periods were given. In an intelligence briefing for the period after 25 August 1944, it was stated that, on 27 August, between 2 p.m. hours and 2.50 p.m. on the coast, work was upcoming for the defence of the Grand Duchy of Luxembourg.

The race continued to locate the V-weapon installations and mobile sites, highly important intelligence for the Allies. Agents of the Clarence Service were briefed to report on any aspect of the V-1s and V-2s, including their movement and locations of manufacture of their components. One report stated that 'the launching of V-1 bombs is confirmed by several sources. About ten trains carrying these bombs passed through Montzen, Hasselt, Baisieux, Herbesthal, Liège and Givet between 22 and 29 July 1944. The carriages, special and new, are all attached at Klagenfurt and Villach; or they return empty. One of them was destined for Boisleux, another for Doullens.'[10]

The network was primed to look out for any unusual structures being transported by rail or road. On 27 August 1944, between 3 p.m.

and 4 p.m., a train was spotted conveying V-1s for the German air force, thus confirming that Klagenfurt was a station where trains were loaded with these weapons. It seemed a V-1 factory was close to the town. The message went on, 'Mysterious works, often including a 50-metre-long concrete track, by 10 to 50m wide, are in progress in the woods and near a reservoir. Located at one of the two woods about 1 km north of the border post of Abeele, south of Poperinge.' This provided important locations for aerial reconnaissance, and for urgent bombing.

Stay-Behind Agent

The extraordinary bravery of the women of Clarence has remained hidden, largely because they worked for an MI6 network. Glimpses of their selfless sacrifice and hard work for Clarence are coming to light. This is the case for Ghislaine Marie de Moreau d'Andoy, born in 1908 in Namur, who was recruited by Thérèse de Radiguès and joined Clarence on 10 May 1940. She operated under the name of Pauline Cornil from her home address, Château d'Andoy in Naninne, and in the rank of warrant officer. She was listed as having no profession. Moreau gathered together the first nucleus of agents in the sector of Namur. She took command of a sub-section of the sector until the liberation of the region. Her network gained intelligence for MI6 on military, economic and political matters, acted as couriers, ran dead letter boxes and set up observation posts. Her brother was head of the whole section around Namur until his arrest in August 1944, after which she continued her work. She showed initiative in organisation and gaining intelligence from the agents in her sub-section, in anticipation of the combat along the Namur–Meuse front.

To date, Madame de Moreau is the only female agent known to have acted as a 'stay-behind' agent – that is, a 'sleeper' agent who remains in the field when all other operatives have been withdrawn and who can be reactivated at any time. Moreau accepted her new role and remained deep undercover for the Allies during the German offensive in the Ardennes, led by Field Marshal Gerd von Rundstedt.

The story of Clarence is another example of the selfless sacrifice of women and men behind enemy lines who knew just how important it was to send intelligence to the Allies. These women, with their devotion and courage, were indispensable to the success of the intelligence network for MI6 in Belgium. The Clarence Service ran from the German occupation in May 1940 until Belgium's liberation on 15 September 1944. It provided reliable technical information about Germany, including continuous intelligence on the V-weapons programme, the removal of uranium salts to Germany and enemy troop movements and communications.[11] After the war, 1,547 resistance fighters were recognised as having taken part in it. Fifty-two members lost their lives and are named on a special memorial in Liège; among them are women who died in Ravensbrück concentration camp.[12]

In his high praise of the network, Dansey, who was not a man prone to flattery, concluded that Clarence was the most important among the networks supplying military information in all of occupied Europe because of the quality and quantity of messages and documents it provided.[13]

18
MI9 SECRET AGENTS

SIS and SOE were not the only secret organisations to send agents behind enemy lines. MI9, the branch of military intelligence for escape and evasion, had a top-secret section called Room 900. Known also as the Intelligence School (or IS9), Room 900 trained its own agents and infiltrated them into occupied territories in operations that were completely distinct from those of SOE.[1] Some of the agents, male and female, lost their lives in action. Their operations remain so hush-hush that the files have not been released, even more than seventy-five years later. Scant references appear occasionally in War Office files.

Room 900 was founded in the summer of 1941 by Brigadier Norman Crockatt, the head of MI9. Knowledge of Room 900's existence was highly protected and its operations physically segregated from the rest of MI9. It was practically unknown to staff at MI9's headquarters in Beaconsfield, Buckinghamshire.[2] It was controlled by SIS (MI6) from its headquarters at Broadway Buildings from a small room that in peacetime was used by staff to make cups of tea.[3] Initially the section was overseen solely by Jimmy Langley, who had escaped from Dunkirk in May–June 1940, until the arrival of Airey Neave, a British officer who had escaped from Colditz Castle in 1942. The section had no more than four officers working for it at any one time. The majority of Room 900 files remain classified and this is almost certainly because of it being part of MI6.[4] It is an example of the blurring of the lines between the different secret service organisations.

The end of 1942 and all of 1943 was a bleak and dangerous period for British intelligence as it faced the consequences of the Gestapo breaking up its escape lines across Western Europe. The helpers, informers, couriers and their immediate families were arrested and endured torture, with many dying at the hands of the Nazis. They were shot on the spot or sent to concentration camps. It is difficult to establish how many civilians died working for the escape lines because their names have never been released by the British Secret Service, in order to protect their identities forever.

SIS, SOE and MI9 were all beset by betrayal and the decimation of their covert networks. This was one of the few areas of common ground between these organisations that were more used to inter-service rivalry than cooperation. Against this backdrop of betrayals and the compromise of the MI9 escape lines in Western Europe, from 1943 onwards Room 900 (IS9) sent its own agents behind enemy lines. Among them were women of extraordinary courage whose heroism remains largely unknown and thus have not been celebrated like the women of SOE.

Agents of Room 900

Potential recruits for IS9 missions were interviewed by Langley and Neave in a first-floor flat at 5 St James's Street which belonged to the Secret Service and was where Langley lived. Only a handful of agents seem to have been trained and sent into the field, but numbers cannot currently be verified due to the lack of declassified files. Neave trained and debriefed the IS9 agents from his own flat. It was work that he undertook with his wife, Diana (née Giffard), whom he married in 1942. Not long after their marriage, Diana was walking down one of the restricted corridors of Broadway Buildings when she stumbled across her husband. A look of complete surprise crossed both their faces as they said to each other, 'What are you doing here?' Both were working for MI6 and neither had told the other.

Diana had been talent-spotted by a Foreign Office scout for intelligence work.[5] During the war she was undertaking undisclosed work with Polish agents and liaison with the Polish government-in-exile, thought to have included propaganda work.

By 1943 the couple had moved into a flat in Elizabeth Street, Pimlico, that belonged to Diana's aunt. It was here that IS9 agents were given final instructions for their mission. The drab entrance to the building obscured the elegance found inside. It was hoped that the comfortable surroundings would facilitate a feeling of security and relaxation for agents ahead of their dangerous missions. While Neave spoke with them in the sitting room, Diana served drinks to calm their nerves. After the briefings, the couple took the agents for a meal at the Café Royal, where they could remain inconspicuous among the intelligentsia. It was Airey Neave who subsequently accompanied the agents on their journey to the airfield for their flight into occupied territory. The missions for IS9 were usually flown out of RAF Tempsford in Bedfordshire, with final checks for the agents conducted at the nearby Tempsford Hall.

Airey Neave believed in the ability of women to make first-class agents and actively supported their recruitment. On one occasion, he wrote to Captain Delloye of the Belgian secret service-in-exile in London, recommending that Delloye recruit female agents. In the final stages of the war, it was believed that the Germans might place all Belgian males over the age of eighteen in camps to prevent them assisting the Allied armies during the invasion of Europe. Neave urged Delloye to 'make good use of the opposite sex, women make good guides and I think attract less attention at all times than men when passing controls'.[6] He concluded by asking Delloye if he had any suitable women in mind, but Delloye's reply appears not to have survived in the archives.

Neave's view of female agents contrasted with that of MI6's deputy chief, Claude Dansey. Dansey was initially opposed to any women being dropped behind enemy lines. He oversaw the separate MI9 and MI6 escape lines in order to be in control of both and avoid any compromise of MI6 operations. But even Dansey relented on the question of female agents once Mary Lindell appeared on the scene and insisted on being sent back into France with Room 900.

Mary Lindell

Mary Lindell (aka Marie Claire) was the first woman to be trained by Room 900 and dropped back into France. Her brief was to establish an escape line and run agents for IS9. British-born Lindell was forty-five years old, married to a French aristocrat, Count de Milleville, and known to be a woman of steely nerve who revelled in daring adventures. She had enjoyed a pre-war life in Parisian high society and had been decorated for her work as a nurse in the First World War.

With France under occupation in 1940, she volunteered as a nurse but also undertook to smuggle escapers and evaders to Marseille to be exfiltrated by the Pat Line escape route (see p. 345) into Spain. The occupying German authorities placed restrictions on movement around the countryside and this initially hampered her work. As a member of the French aristocracy, she believed her name would provide an *entrée* into top military circles among the Germans, and she sought favour with General Otto von Stülpnagel, the supreme commander of German-occupied France. He agreed to a meeting, during which she gained his sympathy with tales of needing to help babies to be reunited with their parents on the Riviera. He issued her with travel permits and petrol coupons to undertake her charitable work. She used the freedom to secretly work for MI9.

In 1941 she was caught by the Gestapo and arrested for aiding the escape of British officers. She spent nine months in solitary confinement in Fresnes prison, south of Paris, but it did not break her spirit. Respect for her as the holder of a Croix de Guerre from 1916 was thought to be the reason why her sentence was not longer.[7] Lindell was released and travelled to Lyon to see the US vice consul in the hope of help. He issued papers for her under the guise of her being a governess. This enabled her to cross the Pyrenees into Spain in late July 1942. She was determined to continue working for the British and arrived, unannounced, at the British embassy in Barcelona. The embassy sent a telegram to Room 900 that Lindell wanted to restart her network for MI9. Neave and Langley agreed, not yet having told Dansey. Lindell was flown to London and was interviewed by Neave and Langley in a flat above Overton's restaurant in St James's Street. They found her forthright, with strong views and utterly determined to be sent back into France. The only person they had to convince was Dansey, who conceded on his principle of not sending female agents behind the lines.

Lindell began several weeks of training and, on the night of 21 October 1942, Neave escorted her to RAF Tangmere and saw her off. He found the experience difficult, as he commented: 'I did not doubt that Mary had the boldness and capacity to lead a réseau, but the thought of sending a woman on such a dangerous task was unpleasant . . . There was the possibility that they [women] would be subjected to the most degrading methods of torture, if captured, which distressed many intelligence officers of my generation.'[8]

Lindell was dropped by Lysander near Limoges in south-eastern France, with identity papers as Ghita Mary Lindell. Nothing was heard of her for several weeks. The Gestapo had regretted releasing her, and subsequently rounded up her network and issued a death warrant for her. Had Dansey known that she was high on the Gestapo's wanted list, he probably would not have authorised her mission.

Lindell set about re-establishing her network around Ruffec, not far from where a number of RAF and US pilots had been shot down and were in hiding. She established new headquarters for an escape route into Spain, but, against the advice of MI9, she did so without a wireless operator.[9]

A short time later, she visited the US vice consul in Lyon and requested further funds for her work. On the journey back to Ruffec with a French guide, they were accidentally struck by a car. Lindell was left with life-threatening injuries – a serious head injury, injuries to her arms and legs and five fractured ribs. Local French people smuggled her to a farmhouse and it was feared she would not survive. After preliminary medical treatment, she was secretly moved to the hospital at Loches, in the Loire valley. The Gestapo had heard rumours of an injured agent and began searches of hospitals. They arrived at Loches hospital, but did not find Lindell, who had been taken down into the hospital cellar and hidden behind a stack of wood.

By Christmas she was still gravely ill, but, in spite of this, she was about to undertake her greatest mission – rescuing the only two surviving commandos of Operation Frankton, known as the 'Cockleshell heroes'.

The Cockleshell Heroes

At the end of 1942, a section within Room 900, known as IS9(X), briefed a party of twelve Royal Marine commandos in escape and evasion ahead of their covert night mission, Operation Frankton. The mission had been authorised as part of Combined Operations under Vice Admiral Lord Louis Mountbatten and involved the men placing limpet mines on the hull of German cargo ships in the port of Bordeaux. Under cover of darkness, on 1 December 1942, the men and their equipment were loaded into submarine *Tuna* and sailed down the Irish Channel towards the French coast. They would not be able to return by submarine afterwards, so they were to escape via Ruffec, 70 miles north of Bordeaux, with the aid of Lindell and local helpers.

On 6 December, the submarine arrived at the mouth of the river and the five teams of the original twelve men separated and began to canoe down the Gironde estuary. Only two teams managed to reach the German ships; the journey took them five days and nights. Their colleagues either drowned or were captured by the Germans, interrogated and shot under Hitler's Commando Order of 18 October 1942, which stated that 'No Quarter' – that is, no clemency – was to be given to captured members of the Allied Special Forces. It was a war crime.

Major Herbert Hasler and William Sparks were the sole survivors of Operation Frankton and succeeded in attacking six German ships, damaging five and sinking one. The mines had been timed to explode after the men made it back to safer territory.

Disguised as peasants, Hasler and Sparks escaped from the area and were safely passed through a number of farmhouses by helpers of the escape line.[10] They arrived in Ruffec on 18 December, entering the Hotel des Toques Blanches and ordering a bowl of potato soup and two glasses of red wine. Hesler slipped a 5 franc note to the woman to pay their bill, concealing a scribbled note that they were English soldiers and needed to escape. She questioned them as she was suspicious about their identity, but eventually agreed to provide them with overnight accommodation and said she would find help. She disappeared and made contact with two of Lindell's people in Ruffec.

At Room 900 in London, it was weeks before confirmation was received about any survivors from Operation Frankton. Lindell was still in hospital, regularly visited by her son, Maurice de Milleville. He had received a coded message: 'Two important parcels of food waiting', meaning two escapers needing help. Lindell instructed him to contact one of her guides to evacuate Hasler and Sparks in the back of a closed baker's van.

On 19 December Hasler and Sparks crossed the demarcation line into Vichy France and to the safety of a farm owned by someone from Lindell's organisation. They were hidden there for weeks until, on 7 January 1943, they met personally with Lindell. She was still extremely unwell, but had discharged herself from hospital to be able to escort Hasler and Sparks herself.

Before her accident, she had been unable to establish a route into Spain and now sought ways to get the two commandos out of France. She smuggled herself across the border at Annemasse into Switzerland, where she elicited the help of a trusted ally of the Swiss intelligence service. She asked him to help exfiltrate Hasler and Sparks out of France, which he did via the Pat Line, the MI9 escape line between Marseille and the Pyrenees. She then returned to Switzerland for urgent medical treatment.

At the end of March 1943 Hasler and Sparks were escorted over the Spanish border to Perpignan. They arrived in Madrid and were repatriated to England by MI9. Their escape was a huge success for Room 900.

Lindell continued to help Allied airmen and soldiers with no let-up. After further hospital treatment in Switzerland, she chose to return to France to concentrate her efforts on an escape line from Ruffec. She operated with a new identity as Comtesse de Moncy and successfully established a frontier crossing point for evaders at Andorra. Between October and December 1943 her escape line rescued ten servicemen and brought them safely into Spain. But Lindell was still on the Gestapo's wanted list and they finally caught her on 23 November 1943.[11] A large sum of money could not bribe them to release her. She attempted an escape from a train that was transferring her to Paris and was shot in the head and back as she tried to flee. It was a German surgeon in the hospital at Tours who saved her life.

In February 1944 Lindell was taken to the SS section of Dijon prison for eight months and held in solitary confinement, with no food for 22–26 hours at a time.[12] For three of those months she was chained by the hands and feet. Three times she was taken out to be shot, then sent back to her cell. On 26 July she was transferred to Saarbrucken concentration camp, then Neue Bremme and on to Ravensbrück, where she was subjected to hard labour. Because of her medical training, the commandant put her to work in the camp hospital, but she suffered from food deprivation and bouts of pneumonia. When she was liberated at the end of the war, she weighed just 33 kg.

Neave later wrote: 'Her career, as an Englishwoman defying the Germans by sheer pertinacity and daring, was almost without precedent . . . [She was] one of the most colourful agents in the history of Room 900.'[13] Lindell was awarded the Croix de Guerre by the French and Mentioned in Despatches by the British.

Mary O'Shaughnessy and the Pat Line

Mary O'Shaughnessy, who knew Lindell, was another woman who helped Allied escapers in France. O'Shaughnessy's work is known because of the testimony of an RAF officer whom she helped to escape from France. Prior to the war, she worked as a governess to a French family.[14] When the Germans occupied France in 1940, she remained with the family for a time because the children's father was away fighting in the French army and their mother was ill. O'Shaughnessy had taken her father's nationality and had an Irish passport; thus she avoided internment in France because Ireland was neutral during the war.

During a period of helping in a French hospital in Angers, she nursed Sergeant Hillyard (from a bomber squadron), who was injured after being shot down and captured by the Germans on 18 June 1940. He underwent surgery in a hospital close to where he was captured and had to have his right arm amputated. He was then relocated to the hospital in Angers. From August 1940 O'Shaughnessy visited him every Sunday and smuggled in civilian clothes. On 21 October Hillyard walked out of the hospital in those clothes and met O'Shaughnessy at an agreed rendezvous in the town. He stayed with her for two days outside Angers, after which she hid him for a week in another house. This was the beginning of her work in aiding Allied servicemen to escape occupied France.

On 31 October 1940 Hillyard left the town with an unnamed Frenchman and was taken by train to Tours. He received help from a number of guides of the Pat Line who brought him to Marseille on

3 November 1940. Founded by a British soldier, Ian Garrow of the Seaforth Highlanders, the escape line had been operating since May–June 1940. After Garrow's arrest by the Germans in October 1941, the line was headed by Patrick Albert O'Leary, a Belgian whose real name was Albert-Marie Guérisse. The Pat Line ran to Marseille from Paris, via Lyons, Amiens, Lille or Limoges, then from Marseille across the Pyrenees to Barcelona and Gibraltar.

Hillyard was given shelter by a well-known MI9 operative called Revd Caskie. Hillyard was successfully smuggled out of France and back to the UK via Gibraltar on 23 February 1941. A copy of his escape report provided MI6 with special intelligence of what he had seen behind enemy lines. Escapers who were rescued by people like O'Shaughnessy were a vital source of intelligence material for MI6. It is believed that O'Shaughnessy helped around twenty-five escapers and evaders for MI9, using all her money to pay bribes to Frenchman to help her.

The work for MI9 was fraught with danger and she was arrested in 1944 as she tried to leave France after being betrayed to the Gestapo by a French traitor, Lucien Dousset. She was taken to Mont Lue prison, tortured and beaten, before being transferred with 500 French women by cattle train from Paris to Ravensbrück concentration camp. In January 1945 she was sent to the Jugendlager, a sub-camp of Ravensbrück, where the selections for the gas chambers took place. The camp was closed in late February–early March 1945 and O'Shaughnessy was transferred back to Ravensbrück. She was released through the efforts of Count Bernadotte, the Swedish diplomat who negotiated the release of POWs and Jews from concentration camps in 1945. He reached Ravensbrück in May to collect 300 French prisoners and, while there, enquired if there were any English people in the camp. He was told there were none, but he persisted, knowing that there were, having been given a list of missing English persons by a friend.[15]

O'Shaughnessy was released and finally reached England, desperately ill and weighing only 4 stone. For her self-sacrifice and bravery, she was awarded the Croix de Guerre and the US Legion of Honor. MI9 sent a letter of thanks, acknowledging the horrific injuries she had suffered from the Gestapo and for which she incurred heavy medical expenses for several years after the war. In 1946 O'Shaughnessy was asked to give evidence in the trial of some of the Ravensbrück camp staff at Hamburg and again in April 1948 at the trial of war criminals of the Jugendlager camp. O'Shaughnessy was among the few British survivors of Ravensbrück.

The Cookery Book

A glimpse into the spycraft of female agents in other parts of Europe can be found in the Walter Pforzheimer collection at Yale University. It is a plain, blue-grey linen-covered cookery book, written in Dutch. It is inconspicuous; it can be rolled up and tucked under one arm or placed in a bag. A handwritten label on the front reads, in translation, 'Recipes, Domestic Science School'. But it contains no recipes.

The first page gives a warning about its secret nature. The table of contents deals with spycraft and provides a series of instructions on how to identify key military targets in enemy country, including Hitler's V-weapons and naval units. It gives detailed instructions on how to identify V-1 and V-2 installations and their apparatus. The Pforzheimer cookery book belonged to an unnamed female agent, almost certainly working for IS9/Room 900 in Holland and reporting to Airey Neave in the months immediately after Arnhem, between October 1944 and May 1945. It was given to Walter Pforzheimer by his second cousin, Jack Charles Bottenheim, an MI9 officer who was dropped behind the lines in the southern Netherlands in autumn 1944 and was then assigned as Neave's Dutch liaison officer to the IS9 station in Wassenaar. It is copy number 40, suggesting that a few copies were printed, and they were explicitly intended for a female audience. The cookery book offers a rare insight into one way that women operated clandestinely behind the lines to gain intelligence.

SOE operations in Holland were particularly disastrous because of Dutch double agent Christiaan Lindemans (aka 'King Kong'), who betrayed the escape line from Holland to Spain.[16] He passed information to Lieutenant Colonel Hermann Giskes, the head of the Abwehr in Holland. Giskes caused major problems for the agents of the Dutch Section of SOE, one of whom was picked up by the Abwehr and made to transmit back to London under German control. Although the agent adopted the agreed 'mistakes' in his radio transmissions to alert SOE that he had been compromised, it was unfortunately believed to be human error. Consequently, SOE continued to send in its agents and they were immediately captured.[17]

Of the fifty Dutch agents parachuted into Holland with SOE, forty-seven were caught and executed by the Germans in what became known as the Englandspiel (or Engelspiel). Giskes controlled fourteen SOE agents in Holland, two of whom escaped and returned to England to alert the authorities. They were immediately imprisoned in Brixton prison because it was thought, incorrectly, that they had been 'turned' by the Germans. In spite of these disasters, MI9 was determined to succeed where SOE was failing and sent the first and only known woman to be parachuted into Holland by Room 900. She was Dutch-born Beatrice Terwindt (aka 'Trix' and 'Felix') and it is possible that the cookery book belonged to her.[18]

Although MI9 had a strict policy of not overlapping with SOE, Holland proved to be the exception because an escape line from Holland through Belgium could not be set up without the help of SOE.[19] Room 900 had no radio contact with Holland and could not communicate with its helpers and therefore relied on help from SOE. It was SOE's Dutch Section that agreed to train Terwindt and drop her into Holland for IS9. Plans to parachute her into the country in December 1942 were postponed because of the betrayal of the Maréchal family in Belgium and the subsequent swift departure of Peggy Van Lier, Georges d'Oultremont and Edouard d'Oultremont – all of whom were working for the Comet Line from Brussels to Spain.[20] Neave feared that Terwindt might be recognised in Holland and considered whether she should undergo surgery to change her appearance, but decided against such radical action. Against the backdrop of treachery and betrayals, Terwindt was parachuted into Holland for IS9 on 13/14 February 1943. Prior to departure, her mission was cleared by SIS/MI6.[21]

IS9 and Holland

Terwindt was to start a new escape line for MI9/IS9, called the Felix Line.[22] She was born in Arnhem in 1911.[23] By the late 1930s she was working as a stewardess for the Dutch airline KLM on its European routes. Due to the war she instead became a secretary for the airline at Schiphol and then in The Hague.

On 20 February 1942 she left Holland, aided by a number of Catholic priests, evaded arrest at various German checkpoints and crossed into Switzerland at Collonges. Because she had no papers, the Swiss authorities interned her in Bellechasse prison. She was released on 30 April 1942 with no explanation, taken to a place in Geneva with other Dutch refugees and given a replacement Dutch passport. On 2 July she left Barcelona for Bilbao, then Madrid to obtain the correct exit visas to fly to Lisbon. She met MI9's man Donald Darling ('Sunday') and offered to help evacuate RAF personnel from Holland. Darling told Neave about the proposal, and Neave met Terwindt in London and found her 'eager to return to Holland'.[24] She could be valuable for IS9 because she spoke several languages, including Dutch, English, French, German and Italian. On the night of 13/14 February 1943, Neave accompanied her to Tempsford aerodrome and reflected: 'Those journeys sitting beside an agent on the way to unknown dangers are unforgettable.'[25] It may have been at this point that she was given a copy of the cookery book.

Terwindt was despatched into the field that night by Room 900 in Operation Chicory, the objectives of which remain obscure and the full files still classified.[26] The only declassified file on Operation Chicory is slim and reveals nothing of the purpose of her mission, and the same is true of Terwindt's equally thin personal file at the National Archives.

Nothing alerted Trix or Room 900 that the reception committee were not members of the Dutch resistance. They were, in fact, Abwehr agents, who captured her upon landing and prevented her from taking a cyanide pill. Escorted to Dreibergen and brought before Giskes, she was interrogated for at least three days and subjected to sleep deprivation. Her interrogators believed she was working for SOE, which was in fact not true. She revealed nothing about SOE or Room 900.

She was held at Haaren concentration camp with the other SOE agents who had been captured in see p. 348 re Englandspiel the Englandspiel. An MI6 agent, Van der Reijden, who was sent by boat in 1941 and captured, was also held there. The Gestapo decided to save them for reasons which have never become clear. News of her incarceration in Haaren reached Neave and Langley four months later via two SOE agents who had successfully escaped from the camp. At some point, Trix was transferred to Ravensbrück concentration camp.

Leo Marks, author of the memoir *Between Silk and Cyanide*, believed it suspicious that SOE files on Englandspiel, including his own lengthy reports, were destroyed in a fire in early 1946. This meant that the Dutch Parliamentary Commission inquiry in 1949 could not establish the truth behind the catastrophe of SOE's agents in Holland. Major Bingham, who was appointed head of SOE Dutch Section in March 1943, was blamed for it all. He always maintained his innocence and tried to clear his name. He could not have been responsible for the compromise of SOE agents in 1941 and 1942 because he did not take up his post until 1943. As head of the Dutch Section, he had argued strongly against the use of reception committees in Holland and instead favoured blind drops.[27]

Colonel Cordeaux of SIS maintained in a private meeting in 1943 that there was no connection between SIS and SOE over Holland. He said SIS did not know that SOE had been penetrated by the Germans and there had been no connection between their respective operations.[28] At that same meeting, Colonel Brook stated that SOE suffered from 'a grave lack of intelligence and this was aggravated by our failure to get people back from Holland to conduct an investigation. The German counterespionage system is better in Holland than anywhere else.'[29]

In January 1945 the Germans transferred Trix from Ravensbrück to Mauthausen. Before the final surrender of Germany in May 1945 she was moved by the Red Cross to Switzerland where she received medical treatment. Neave wrote: 'The first attempt to set up an organisation in Holland had been a tragic failure and I never sent a woman on a similar mission from England during the rest of the war.'[30]

IS9 Agents

According to Neave, Mary Lindell and Beatrice Terwindt were the only women to be sent behind enemy lines by Room 900.[31] Today, with the benefit of a small number of declassified IS9 personnel files, it is possible to see that this was not the case. Other women were despatched into enemy territory on top-secret missions for IS9/Room 900. Their missions are deemed top-secret even today, such that the files have not been declassified. There is reference to an operation codenamed 'Chicken I', but its primary files remain classified. What is known is that it was an attempted rescue of Jews by field officers of IS9(ME) in the Black Sea region.[32]

Hannah Szennes (Senesh) was parachuted into Yugoslavia with two other agents on 14 June 1944 as part of Operation Chicken I. She took the codename 'Minnie' and, with her fellow parachutists, was ultimately heading towards the Black Sea region. Jewish, and originally from Hungary, Szennes had escaped to Palestine, where she was recruited by Zionist leaders to join IS9.[33] She enlisted in the WAAF and was paid £30 a month as an aircraftwoman by special agreement between the RAF and the Jewish Agency, with part of her salary paid by IS9 in the Middle East. She and her comrades linked up with local partisans and awaited further instructions about when to cross into Hungary. Their mission for IS9 was first and foremost the rescue of Allied pilots trapped behind enemy lines in Eastern Europe. Only then were these agents permitted a secondary purpose and that was to link up with partisans to rescue the 1.25 million Jews believed to be in hiding in Hungary, Romania and Czechoslovakia.[34]

Szennes was arrested on the Hungarian border and taken to Conti Street prison in Budapest. She underwent thorough interrogation, then torture by the Gestapo. While in prison, she managed to pass information to a colleague who escaped and he passed the information by radio transmission to Cairo. Szennes was shot on 6 November 1944. Her official file records that she was 'killed by enemy action, whilst in the course of her duties'.[35] Notification of her death was sent to Teddy Kollek, head of the Jewish Agency for Palestine, a liaison officer for IS9 who had left Vienna in the mid-1930s. He went on to become the first Israeli mayor of Jerusalem after the foundation of the State of Israel in 1948. Years later, an eyewitness gave an account of the events surrounding Hannah Szennes' final days.[36] Szennes was tried by a Hungarian court and executed.

Martha Martinovic worked for IS9 in the Middle East. She was originally from Czechoslovakia and had enlisted in the WAAF on 4 April 1944. She was missing in action for a considerable period, believed killed. All attempts to trace her had failed and IS9(ME) issued a death certificate, giving the date of her death as 1 September 1945.[37] IS9 wrote to Teddy Kollek and paid £500 to the Jewish Agency in settlement for her death.

Antonia Maria Hamilton was dropped behind enemy lines on 9/10 August 1944 for IS9, but no further details are available. Miss Poumboura, another of IS9's female agents, was arrested in Athens while engaged on MI9/IS9 work.[38] She was imprisoned in Greece and Italy.

It is not known how many agents were dropped by IS9 into occupied Europe because the majority of the personal files remain classified. Around twenty personal files have been released: these are for Jewish émigré women and men who had fled Hitler who carried out clandestine missions and died in the service of IS9. It is possible that the IS9 missions overlapped with MI6 and this could account for why the files remain classified. It is hoped that the intelligence files may be released in the future.

Escape Lines

While Room 900 sent agents behind enemy lines in top-secret operations, there were thousands of women and men working for MI9 on the escape routes. Women were central to MI9's work in bringing Allied personnel back from enemy-occupied territories via a number of escape lines. They escorted airmen and soldiers to safety along the escape lines, and some of them smuggled intelligence over the border via the Pyrenees and into Spain to be passed on to MI9 in England.

Neave understood the importance of women's involvement in the escape lines and said that they made excellent guides on trains for the airmen. The women had to be discreet: to pose as the kind of glamorous spies beloved of espionage literature was counter-productive. They brought, he said, 'a human touch to the escape movement. It was this that helped to contrast Room 900 with the Secret Service of fact and fiction.'[39]

It is not known exactly how many women helped in the escape lines because their helper files have not been released into the public domain. British intelligence promised never to disclose the identities of agents, helpers and personnel to protect them and their families, in case of a future conflict which might place them at risk of reprisals. However, some personal memoirs and writings have given an insight into their achievements and legacy. The three main MI9 escape lines operating in Western Europe were the Pat Line, the Comet and the Shelburne.

The Comet Line ran from Brussels into France via Paris and down to the far side of the Pyrenees via San Sebastian and to Bilbao in Spain. The Shelburne Line was a sea evacuation route from the Brittany coast in northern France to the Helford River in Cornwall that took place at night and never by moonlight. The line dropped secret agents into France and evacuated evaders and escapers to Cornwall. The Pat Line operated from Marseille and ran to the Pyrenees via Perpignan and into Spain where MI9's man, Michael Creswell ('Monday'), waited to meet evaders and escapers. One of the women who worked for the Pat Line was Elisabeth Furse.

Elisabeth Furse

Elisabeth Furse was born Elisabeth Louise Ruth Wolpert in 1910 in Königsberg (today Kaliningrad) to a German mother and Russian father. In 1934 she married Peter Haden-Guest, an English communist, and they had one child, Anthony. In 1939, twenty-nine-year-old Elisabeth trained as an ambulance driver with SAAF (Section ambulance Alliée Française) at the Hertford British Hospital in a suburb of Paris. With German forces advancing in May 1940, she left for Brittany and helped with the evacuation of British soldiers at Saint-Malo. For a time, she was site manager for Château Les Essarts at Saint-Briac, on behalf of her friends, the owners, who had left the area. Always resourceful and quick thinking, she placed a notice at the entrance to the drive which read 'American property' to protect it from requisition by the Germans.

Following the German occupation of the Channel Islands, just 40 miles off the coast from Saint-Briac, German soldiers were billeted in the château on 1 July 1940. Elisabeth pretended to be an American, but the Germans discovered she was British and interned her in a camp at Dinan, where she witnessed the mass internment of British people in France, alongside her son and nanny. While being transferred to a detention centre in Paris in 1941, she escaped with her son by saying she needed to use the toilet at the Gare de Lyon. She knew the station well and escaped into the street. She was sent false identity papers by a friend, and a courier explained how she could get into Vichy France. She headed to Marseille with her young son.

In Marseille, Elisabeth met with British consuls Hugh Dodds and Arthur Dean who had been permitted to operate from a room in the US embassy. She initially received a frosty reception, but their attitude changed when they learnt she was the wife of Peter Haden-Guest, a British diplomat. They gave her money and asked Jimmy Langley – an escaper who worked for MI9 and Room 900 and was helping the Pat Line until he made it back to England – to lend her his flat. A few days later while in a café, Elisabeth was approached by Captain Ian Garrow, founder of the Pat Line.

Elisabeth began to help the Pat Line, which ran over the Pyrenees to Barcelona in Spain, from where soldiers made their way back to the UK via Gibraltar or Lisbon. Garrow said he needed a woman to look after the escapers before they left, to find safe houses and hide them. He explained that the work was dangerous and if caught she faced the death penalty. As protection for herself and her young son, she moved into a brothel at 5 Rue Belloi, knowing that it was a good hiding place for them. When she needed to work for the escape line, the women and young girls there took care of her child.

Elisabeth recruited trusted people for the escape line. The local doctor, Dr Rodocanachi, and his wife allowed the use of their home as a safe house for nearly 200 evaders from June 1941 to February 1943. By 1943 Garrow was in hiding. British POWs and evaders had been moved to Saint-Hippolyte-du-Fort, near Nîmes, some 160 km from Marseille. The Seaman's Mission in Marseille had been aiding the escape line. Elisabeth became the contact between the mission and Saint-Hippolyte-du-Fort. She spoke fluent French to the guards at the fort to liaise over the release of the POWs; the guards thought she was

American. When a batch of POWs were being released, she travelled by train from Marseille to Nîmes to escort them back to Marseille and the safe houses.

She commented, 'I was a professional, trained in undercover work, and knew what was safe and what was not.'[40] At times, she changed her disguise and deliberately dressed in a flamboyant manner, placing a big Mexican hat on her young son Anthony's head, so no one would suspect her of being engaged on partisan work. On other occasions, she dressed dowdily and kept a low profile, sliding into invisibility. She hid airmen in brothels until the time for their escape. Nadia de Pastre, the young daughter of Countess Lily de Pastre, hid men for Elisabeth in the Château de Montredon, near Marseille, and did not tell her mother.

Elisabeth smuggled messages and intelligence hidden in toothpaste, face cream and balloons to Donald Darling (aka 'Sunday'), MI9's man in Lisbon, who then operated out of Gibraltar. 'My work was often routine,' she commented, but this belied the personal danger that she risked every day to save lives and smuggle intelligence back to England. She continued to pass messages to members of the network and arranged couriers between Vichy France, Spain and Lisbon. They had to be incredibly security conscious and careful, but she suspected – and was proved right – that it already had a traitor in its midst: Harold Cole 247.[41] Elisabeth and her son survived the war.[42]

The Comet Line

The Comet Line was founded entirely by women. Their heroine was Edith Cavell, whose bravery during the First World War inspired a new generation of women to help the Allies on clandestine operations. In June 1941, Dédée De Jongh, a twenty-five-year-old Belgian girl, was staying with the de Greef family at Villa Voisin in Anglet, between Biarritz and Bayonne, on the French side of the Pyrenees. The de Greef family had fled there the previous year after the German occupation of Belgium. While there, De Jongh and the de Greef family planned to establish an escape line from Brussels into Spain. To do this they needed to make contact with the British, so, in early September 1941, De Jongh arrived at the British embassy in Bilbao and asked to see the consul general. With her were two Belgians who wanted to fight for the Allies and a Scottish soldier of the 1st Gordons, an evader.[43] Vice Consul Arthur Dean agreed to see her. She explained that she had escorted the three men across the enemy countries of Belgium and France on a journey that had taken approximately a week and her companions were waiting in a room downstairs. He remained cautious, concerned that she might be a Nazi agent who had been planted to infiltrate the area.

Dean's initial scepticism changed to surprise as he learnt that an escape line had already been established and that, a few months earlier, De Jongh had accompanied a party of ten Belgians wanted by the Gestapo and an Englishwoman out of Belgium with false identity papers on the dangerous journey across Nazi-occupied France to the Pyrenees. But Dean had to convince Claude Dansey in London, the MI6 deputy who had final authority over the MI9 and MI6 escape lines. Dansey believed it was folly to allow a woman to run a network, even though he had made one exception with the Noah's Ark network in France, headed by Marie-Madeleine Fourcade (p. 312).[44]

Dansey finally agreed to her working after hearing the testimony of three men she had brought out of occupied Europe who spoke of her 'incomparable courage'.[45] And he would be proved wrong in his assessment of women's capabilities too. Women showed themselves able to run a network as professionally and efficiently as men, with the advantage of not being readily suspected by the Germans. De Jongh remained operational until January 1943 precisely because the Nazis did not believe that such a young woman could be the head of a network.

Madame Elvire de Greef (known as 'Tante Go'), with her husband Fernand, seventeen-year-old son Freddie and fifteen-year-old daughter Janine, became central to the foundation and running of the Comet Line along the Pyrenees. They operated from autumn 1941 until the end of the war, working with De Jongh until her arrest in January 1943.[46] They hired Basque smugglers to smuggle the 'parcels' (airmen and others) over the Pyrenees. Tante Go built up her own network of smugglers and agents in Bayonne and Saint-Jean-de-Luz, used the black market and arranged for airmen and others to be hidden in safe houses. She and her network organised guides and smugglers to escort the escapers and evaders into Spain. Her daughter Janine escorted evaders from Paris to the railway station at Biarritz and to the safe houses. Tante Go and her husband, Fernand, smuggled intelligence to MI9 via the couriers. Examples of this included information sent about the airfield at Palme and a gunpowder factory at Blancpigeon, details about the port of Bayonne and the 12-kilometre stretch of the coastline of Anglet.[47] 'She was a match for the Gestapo over three years of continuous underground activity. She bribed, cajoled and threatened the Germans and deceived them to the end. Her contribution to victory was tremendous.'[48]

Monique Hanotte worked for the Comet Line on the French – Belgian border in 1943–44, from Rumes, where she lived. She operated as a guide to Paris and sometimes later to Bordeaux and Saint-Jean-de-Luz. She was asked by MI9 to guide some important people out of Belgium, including a member of the Dutch royal family and army personnel.

Elsie Maréchal was just sixteen years old and still at school when she began to work for the Comet Line, along with her entire family. She was sent north in Belgium to find an airman who was known to be hiding in the woods and awaiting rescue. The whole family were betrayed and arrested in what became known as the 'Maréchal Affair' in November 1942.[49]

Andrée Dumont (aka 'Nadine') was operational for the Comet Line until 15 August 1942, when she was arrested and taken to prison. She had escorted airmen from Brussels to the border, then later smuggled them to Paris. After Nadine's arrest, her elder sister, twenty-three-year-old Micheline Dumont (aka Michou or 'Lily'), continued to work for the Comet Line. She helped photographers in putting together false documents, organised safe houses and ferried food and clothing between them. She cycled around Brussels, delivering messages, giving out money to the owners of safe houses and checking on the progress of operations. She was not caught by the Gestapo because she looked only fifteen years old.

Michou was staying at a safe house in Bayonne with Tante Go when she learnt that there had been more arrests and killings of helpers of the Comet Line. 'I am going back to Paris,' she told de Greef. 'There is a traitor in the line and I am going to find out who it is.' She telephoned her friend Martine to say she would be arriving late at her house in

Paris, but a strange voice answered. She realised that Martine must have been arrested and would be held in Fresnes prison on the outskirts of Paris. Michou went straight to the prison and stood outside the women's wing, shouting, 'Martine! Martine!'

Eventually a shout came back. It was Martine's voice.

'Who betrayed you?' asked Michou.

'It was Pierre! Pierre Boulain!' Martine yelled back.

Pierre Boulain was a young Belgian guide for the escape line. Michou hurried back down to Bayonne and warned Tante Go that the line was compromised, thus saving it ahead of D-Day. But Michou herself had been compromised and MI9 exfiltrated her to England. She had personally escorted at least 150 airmen to safety in Spain and saved their lives.

When she arrived in London in 1944, she was debriefed by Neave and earmarked to join the 'Retrievers', a unit working to repatriate airmen and soldiers after the Allied forces had advanced into Normandy after D-Day. The idea was to send retrievers as agents into no-man's-land, putting themselves at high personal risk of losing their own lives. In the end, Michou's services as a retriever were not needed, but, as one of the few women asked to join the unit, it was a sign of how highly she was regarded that she was considered suitable for this dangerous work.[50]

For Freedom

During its four-year history of operations for MI9, the Comet Line – like other MI9 escape lines – suffered repeated infiltration by traitors. The line went down, but, time and again, courageous women and men resurrected it and continued to save the lives of Allied airmen and soldiers, as well as smuggling vital intelligence out to MI9. Hundreds of women worked for the Comet Line, risking – and losing – their lives for aiding the Allies. The fiercely independent figure of Dédée De Jongh, and the women who worked with her, became 'symbols of courage and defiance . . . and to the last she [Dédée] made her own decisions'.[51]

When asked why she risked her life, Elsie Maréchal replied, 'We had to do something against the Nazi occupation. That's why my family fought back and was involved with the escape line. For me, democracy is essential everywhere.'[52] In the words of her friend Peggy van Lier, also a helper on the Comet Line, 'The despair, the humiliation, the anger [at German occupation] was so deep that one felt ready to do anything to regain the priceless treasure of freedom. It is only when one has lost freedom that one realises that it is the most precious thing.'[53]

So many women risked and lost their freedom during the war at the hands of the Nazi regime. Like Elsie Maréchal and her mother, they spent years in horrific conditions in Gestapo prisons and Ravensbrück concentration camp. These women of the Comet Line remained defiant until their liberation by the Swiss Red Cross in April 1945. Little Elsie and her mother survived to be liberated. Although her mother was desperately ill with pneumonia, they were both able to live in freedom again in Brussels – the freedom for which they and others of the Comet Line had sacrificed so much.

19
WOMEN OF MI6

The women of MI6 remain among the most unknown in the history of women in intelligence. Their names remain classified, making it difficult to provide a full assessment of their contribution to this history. It has been possible to ascertain that, as 'secretaries', they undertook roles in the 1920s and 1930s that went beyond clerical duties: they were agent handlers, helped to run spy networks and were at the heart of developing the tradecraft of espionage. By the Second World War, many had had over thirty years of service with SIS and had become valuable experts who were given important postings abroad in wartime or jobs of high responsibility at MI6 headquarters in London. Regarding those women who can be known about, it is clear that they achieved a great deal, taking on high levels of responsibility, including as heads of stations abroad, even if the organisational structure was not in place for the same levels of promotion as their male colleagues – much like civilian jobs during this era.

Some of the most significant work during the Second World War (and beyond) was conducted by MI6's women abroad, especially those working under cover from passport control offices or embassies in neutral countries like Switzerland, Spain, Portugal, Sweden, Turkey and Morocco. The capital cities became important espionage hubs for spies of all countries moving in and out of the regions and therefore were excellent bases for MI6 operatives. From neutral countries, MI6's women ran agents, became handlers of defectors and 'turned' enemy personnel to work for the Allies. These women became intelligence-gatherers in their own right. They, too, were caught up in the two major catastrophes to befall MI6 in August 1938 and November 1939.

The first disaster was the arrest of MI6's most senior spymaster in Europe, Thomas Joseph Kendrick, who was betrayed to the Gestapo by a double agent in Vienna in August 1938. A large number of SIS officers across Europe were recalled to London. After Kendrick's release from Gestapo custody, the network returned to Europe, including the women. The second catastrophe was the Venlo incident in November 1939 when two MI6 officers were abducted at Venlo on the Dutch–German border in a sting operation by the Germans. The officers believed they were meeting anti-Nazi military officers who would overthrow Hitler, but it turned out not to be the case – a deception that saw them spend the rest of the war in concentration camps. After Venlo, MI6 struggled to return its officers to Europe, but they did return and that included MI6's female staff. It was often the case that these women continued to work in MI6 abroad during the Cold War. One of the women who did so was Marjorie 'Peggy' Weller.

Sweden

Marjorie 'Peggy' Weller had returned to London in August 1938 after the arrest of her boss Kendrick in Vienna (p. 95). When the risk was over, and already well versed in MI6 operations, she was transferred to Stockholm. Sweden was an important staging post from where British intelligence could mount clandestine operations into Germany and Nazi-occupied Norway. Weller arrived in the capital to run covert missions into Germany and Nazi-occupied Norway and remained there for the rest of the war. She aided her new boss, Major Malcolm Munthe, MC, who had been recruited by SOE as a spy and saboteur and who led the operations in Norway against the Vemork power station in Telemark. The Special Forces operation against Telemark was essential to destroy all German attempts to acquire heavy water for its atomic weapons programme. Weller's precise role in support of it for Munthe has never been made known, but she was a key player in the operation from an MI6 perspective.

Aged thirty-five at the end of the war, she was promoted to officer level, which seems to have been a rare occurrence for women in MI6 at that time. She travelled by land convoy to Tehran for her next and final posting, where her new boss was Robert Charles Zaehner, a distinguished Orientalist and Fellow of All Souls. Although the specific details of Weller's involvement in Tehran is unknown, it seems that she was engaged in activities against the Russians and communists. It was in Tehran that she met her husband, John Somers Cocks, of the Foreign Office, and they married in the Catholic church there. She worked with Norman Darbyshire, who became head of MI6's Persia station in Cyprus, and in 1953 aided the overthrow of Iranian Prime Minister Mohammad Mosaddegh.[1] After her marriage, she had to leave MI6 to raise a family.

The 'Firm' – MI6 – heard of her husband's death in 1964 and, because Weller had no pension from MI6, invited her to rejoin the service. On the surface she worked for the Diplomatic Service, but in reality she was an MI6 intelligence officer in the Information Department of MI6 in London. Her stint in MI6 lasted from 1965 until her retirement in 1975 and involved frequenting many embassy parties. Her daughter Anna commented, 'My mother was an adventurer; she had a fun career. She was a career spook.'[2]

Weller was not alone in her achievements. Another SIS colleague from 1930s Vienna went on to lead equally important operations for MI6.

MI6 Station Riga

Peggie Lambert had been undercover as a secretary in the Commercial Department of the British Legation in Vienna. In the autumn of 1938, Peggie was posted to Riga, Latvia, with her new husband, SIS officer Kenneth Benton. They had met at the Legation in Vienna, where she was compiling economic reports for MI6 and liaising with local intelligence agencies. They married in the British consulate in Vienna on 2 March 1938 and made a swift exit from Austria to Riga after the arrest of Kendrick.

Now, as Mrs Benton, Peggie became part of a successful husband-and-wife team for MI6 that lasted through the Second World War and beyond. Their first year in Riga was fairly relaxed and relatively stable compared to elsewhere in Europe, where there was growing political upheaval and instability from the threat of Nazi Germany. The couple had two sons and, importantly, Peggie was not required to give up her MI6 work to become a full-time mother and housewife. The boys' upbringing was divided between the various postings of their parents and a boarding school in England.

In Riga, Kenneth Benton was acting vice consul and managed the daily visa work. The real purpose for the couple's presence there was for both of them to run key agents and double agents.[3] For the remainder of 1938 and during 1939, they ran two Latvian sources for MI6, one an unnamed Latvian agent and the other a liaison officer with the head of the Latvian military intelligence service. The intelligence reports which emanated from these two agents were sent to 'C' in London. Peggie taught the agents how to transmit in Morse using a special device supplied by the technical team at Broadway Buildings.

The signing of the Molotov–Ribbentrop non-aggression pact between Germany and Russia in late 1939 brought changes: Germany was to have Poland (largely) as its sphere of influence, and the Russians were to have the Baltic states. The pact between the two countries was highly unexpected given that the Germans were vehemently anti-communist. Neither Britain nor the US had any prior knowledge of it. In June 1940 the Soviet Union invaded Latvia, resulting in increasing chaos in the British passport control office in Riga. Long queues of would-be émigrés wanted to flee the country, in scenes reminiscent – for the Bentons – of Vienna the previous year. Amidst this turmoil, the intelligence work had to continue and Peggie reported the changing events on the ground to London. The Latvian State Optical Works had produced the first miniature Minox camera – a 'spy camera' – that became an icon of espionage and tradecraft in the twentieth century. Peggie arranged for a number of the first Minox cameras to be smuggled out of Riga via the diplomatic bag for use in the West.[4]

By 1 August 1940 all foreign diplomats were required by the Russian authorities to leave the Baltic states. Food was becoming scarce and the Russians increased their military presence with reinforcements to integrate Latvia into the USSR. Not for the first time, the Bentons had to flee a country under occupation. They prepared to leave, burnt sensitive papers and their codes and wound up the British passport control office. Communication with head office was temporarily broken.

The story of their long dramatic escape from Riga via the Trans-Siberian Railway to Vladivostok is told in Peggie's own memoirs.[5] They returned to the UK in September 1940 and were despatched to Bletchley Park to explain the indecipherable messages being picked up by the codebreakers from their Latvian agent. Peggie had been the one to train him as a 'stay-behind' agent and wireless operator and taught him a special code which she and Kenneth had devised.[6] Messages from the Latvian agent ceased and it was concluded that he had been picked up by the Soviet police.

Having seen an advert for a passport control officer in Madrid, which in reality was a cover for MI6's counter-espionage work, Benton applied. Peggie would be a valuable asset because of her proficiency in agent-running, and no German would suspect her – a woman – of such activities. She would be perceived by the outside world as the housewife who supported her husband's diplomatic posting. The couple were interviewed by Colonel Felix Cowgill, deputy head of Section V, at Glenalmond House, an MI6 property in St Albans, Hertfordshire.[7]

Cowgill was keen to apprehend German spies before they made it into the UK and one of the best places to track them was in Madrid and Lisbon. He explained to the couple how ISOS decrypts from Bletchley Park gave access to messages from the Abwehr to its agents in many of the countries where they operated. Intercepts had confirmed that the Germans were training agents to infiltrate Britain and passing them via Spain and Portugal. ISOS material had been used successfully to identify German agents in Lisbon, so the same was believed to be possible for Madrid. The Bentons were despatched to Madrid in neutral Spain for what became one of the most important periods of Peggie's career with MI6.

Madrid Spynest

The Iberian Peninsula, incorporating Spain and Portugal, was the central point for many British intelligence operations with double agents. The Bentons were posted to Madrid to identify and track German spies moving in and out of the capital. They monitored passenger lists of flights and trains for the movement of German agents, sometimes having advance warning of their travel via ISOS from Bletchley Park. Their task was helped by the fact that the Abwehr accommodated their spies in good hotels and they often travelled first class on trains. The office from where the counter-espionage effort was orchestrated had a row of sixteen cabinets of card indexes with names of individuals, and these were cross-referenced and checked by five women against suspected German agents entering the country. It proved an effective method, even if labour intensive. Within three years, the index system had grown to 14 ft in length, which provides an insight into the volume of data being collected.

Peggie and her husband coded and decoded messages back and forth with London. During their posting to Madrid, they identified nineteen German agents, about a third of whom were 'walk-ins', and the majority of whom were already Abwehr officers.[8] As we have seen, one of the female 'walk-ins' in the summer of 1943 was Nathalie Lily Sergueiev, who went on to become double agent 'Treasure' in MI5's Double Cross System (p. 207). Another was the double agent 'Artist', aka Johnny Jebsen, who was initially debriefed by the Bentons in Madrid, before being run via the Lisbon office.[9] Informants were recruited at hotels, railways stations and airports. Axis agents who turned themselves in to the Bentons revealed that their instructions by the Abwehr were given in secret ink and by micro-dot, a process by which their instructions had been photographed and shrunk to the size of a postage stamp. The best way for intelligence officers to read these messages was via an ultra-violet lamp.

In 1943, after the Allied landings in Salerno, Peggie and her husband were transferred to Rome on MI6 work. Kenneth Benton commented on their careers, 'Our work was done in the utmost secrecy . . . The morale amongst the staff employed in what was often boring, repetitious work, was high, perhaps because they knew that whatever disasters might be occurring in North Africa and elsewhere, in their own special field they were winning.'[10] That was certainly true of MI6's operations in Lisbon that were linked to the double agents in Madrid.

Lisbon

By the early 1940s Lisbon had become the new European 'centre of espionage', a hotbed of enemy spies and Abwehr officers, and a major staging post for MI6's operations into North Africa and the Mediterranean. MI6's counter-espionage activities were extraordinarily successful in the Portuguese capital. MI6 controlled five 'secret sections' in Lisbon, all engaged in the clandestine collection of intelligence.[11] They comprised sixty-two intelligence staff – which was a large number to be operating in Lisbon, but it was dictated by the workload. Weekly intelligence meetings were held between the heads of each secret section. Menzies, aka 'C', wrote, 'It is true of course that I have had two separate offices in Lisbon, which has meant that in practice there have been two SIS organisations there.'[12] As soon as he was able, he planned to merge them under the control of one junior officer, rather than under the passport control office. That officer appears to have been Marguerita 'Rita' Winsor, who ran agents and defectors for MI6 in Lisbon. Aspects of her story have remained hidden until now, but, as we shall see, her career begins to shift our understanding of the position of some women – occupying responsible, more senior roles – within MI6 from the 1940s on. The full picture of the progress and achievements of MI6's women in the Second World War is still shrouded in mystery and secrecy.

Winsor was an expert on Germany, having in the 1930s worked in the British passport control office in Berlin – in what one account calls 'an important position'[13] – alongside her close SIS colleague Ena Molesworth. Indeed, for much of the 1930s, the careers of Winsor and Molesworth were interlinked as both had worked as agent handlers for SIS head of station Frank Foley in Berlin. With Britain and Germany at war in September 1939, the British passport control office in Berlin closed down. Winsor and Molesworth were posted by Claude Dansey to Switzerland for a year on unstated clandestine duties. Winsor was almost certainly working as an agent handler in Switzerland because this had been the nature of her job in the 1930s and it was usual to follow a woman's line of expertise when posting her to a new MI6 station.

By May 1940 Dansey believed that it was likely that Germany could invade Switzerland, having already occupied much of Western Europe. He therefore decided to move some of his team out of the country. That included Winsor and Molesworth, who fled across Nazi-occupied France on bicycles to Bordeaux. They arrived back in London, after which Dansey assigned Winsor to a post in Lisbon. This was a period when MI6 started to appoint women as officers in their own right.[14] Winsor was despatched to Lisbon in 1941 as a fully fledged MI6 officer and First Head of the Secretariat, working for the new SIS chief of station, Commander Philip Johns.[15] Johns described her as 'dark, quite tall with an attractive personality and an exceedingly genuine sense of the ridiculous . . . I could have imagined her in fancy dress as a sort of gypsy queen. She was particularly suited to the job, quick thinking and with just that devious approach to problems so important to operations.'[16]

Winsor organised safe passage for visiting intelligence officers to Lisbon, including Ian Fleming, Malcolm Muggeridge and Somerset Maugham. She worked alongside agent handler 'Klop' Ustinov and became a senior, very experienced officer, rising to become head of one of MI6's two stations there. She is designated as 'BD001' in reports emanating from the Lisbon station (itself codenamed 24000). This sheds new light on the status of female intelligence officers – that as early as the 1940s MI6 did appoint a woman (and possibly women) as head of station and not from a later date in the Cold War, as previously thought. This assessment seems to be confirmed by the fact that Carl Eitel (aka 'Ellerman'), an Abwehr officer run by OSS, was reported as being 'regularly interviewed by staff from the local SIS station led by Rita Winsor'.[17]

Eitel was a naval Abwehr officer who was posted from Bremen in Germany to Portugal. He passed intelligence to Winsor about submarine nets at the entrance of various ports and information on German aircraft and anti-aircraft defence, as well as the names of Abwehr chief agents and material from their intelligence reports. Winsor's handling of Eitel led to the creation of a notional agent, codenamed 'Winchester', allegedly a Portuguese man employed by Imperial Airways.[18] High-quality chickenfeed – some of it real information – was prepared for 'Winchester' (the fictitious agent) to be passed to Eitel by Winsor.[19] She led Eitel to believe that she was the intermediary between him and Winchester. Winchester – even though he was fake – was allocated an Abwehr handler by the Germans. That handler was Theodore Schmoele, who was collecting political intelligence in Madrid from a source called

Pelizaeus. At the end of May 1944 Carl Eitel was transferred by the Abwehr from Lisbon to Berlin and then posted back to Bremen, from where he was able to send four letters in secret ink to an OSS safe address.[20]

The whole world of double agents and spies centred around Lisbon and Madrid was incredibly complex. Some were genuinely working for who they said they were, others were 'turned' or wholly fictitious. Winsor navigated her way around this world and succeeded as head of station in Lisbon. Perhaps Dansey knew she would – after all, it was he who recognised her ability and posted her to Lisbon as a full MI6 officer in the first place. Perhaps there is more to emerge in the future about the role that Dansey himself played in developing the careers of women within MI6, even though such progress for women was slow. This was from a man who was originally reluctant to send female agents behind enemy lines as agents – yet now emerging as a potential figure of interest in progressing the careers of women in MI6.

Operation Valkyrie

New information in declassified files sheds further light on another complex MI6 operation from Lisbon that involved Rita Winsor. It related to the defector Otto John (an MI6 asset) and Operation Valkyrie – the plot to assassinate Hitler in July 1944.[21] John, a lawyer working for the German airline Lufthansa, used his position to fly to Lisbon and elsewhere in order to meet his British handlers Rita Winsor and Graham Maingot without arousing suspicion. Codenamed 'Whiskey', John had already met with them twelve times in the two years leading up to Operation Valkyrie. He is believed to have acted as an intermediary between the German resistance chief Colonel Georg Hansen and MI6.

One night in 1944, in a quiet back street of Lisbon, Winsor, as a handler of German defectors, collected John and drove him around the dark, dimly lit streets of the Portuguese capital. He explained to her about a plot being devised by a growing number of prominent anti-Nazis in Germany to assassinate the Führer that July.[22] Winsor heard how it was to be carried out while Hitler was at a meeting at Wolf's Lair, his headquarters on the Eastern Front near Görlitz (now in

Poland). The leader of the plotters was Count Claus von Stauffenberg, who would instigate a new government once Hitler was dead. With General Ludwig Beck as the new leader of Germany and Field Marshal Erwin Witzleben as head of the German armed forces, they would seek a peace settlement with the Allies. Winsor relayed this intelligence to Dansey at once.[23]

On 20 July 1944 Stauffenberg managed to detonate a bomb hidden in a briefcase that he had placed under the table where Hitler was speaking at his headquarters. Unfortunately the briefcase was innocently moved by another German officer before the bomb went off, thus saving the Fuhrer's life. The failed assassination attempt had ramifications for the plotters, most of whom were executed along with their families.

After the unsuccessful plot, Otto John attempted to flee Germany and defected to the West.[24] Winsor made the necessary, complex arrangements to smuggle him to Britain under protection as a defector.[25] Espionage historian Nigel West concluded: 'Based on this astonishing new evidence, it is completely inconceivable that the British did not know, have an opinion on, nor participate in such a momentous plot. We now know that Otto John was an MI6 asset, and has a large MI6 file . . . If this can be released, it will show the British involvement in Valkyrie and the role of Otto John as the missing link.'[26]

Lisbon continued to be a centre of global espionage during the war and a successful neutral capital from which MI6, in conjunction with MI5, could run the brilliant double agents in the Double Cross System.

Admiral Canaris

Over the decades there has been speculation as to whether Admiral Canaris, head of the German secret service, was working secretly for the Allies. Declassified material may answer this question to a fairly reliable degree.

It is now clear that MI6 had been tracking Canaris since at least 1936.[27] One of the main aims of British intelligence in the 1940s was to surreptitiously destroy the German intelligence service without the Nazi regime even realising. One way to do that would be to 'turn'

Canaris to work for the Allies. Towards the end of 1940, Guy Liddell, head of counter-espionage at MI5, suggested to Valentine Vivian of MI6 that 'we ought to try and get at Admiral Canaris'.[28] One line of communication came through a Polish woman called Halina Szymanska, who became an important source of intelligence for MI6.

Halina was the wife of the Polish military attaché in Berlin. She had been captured after Soviet forces invaded the east of Poland on 17 September 1939. Canaris smuggled her into neutral Switzerland, where he met with her on a couple of occasions, and she became his confidant and possibly his mistress. Dubbed by the British as 'Source Warlock', she passed full details to the British about German plans to invade Greece via Bulgaria and Yugoslavia.[29]

At the beginning of January 1941 Canaris deliberately leaked information to Halina about Germany's intention to invade Russia the following June.[30] They had an unspoken agreement that she would pass the information to MI6. Her report containing this information, dated 7 January 1941, was passed to MI6 officer Frank Foley via his network in Switzerland. Szymanska was interviewed after the war by Nigel West, who recalled, 'although she was then seventy-seven years old, she was able to recall many of her wartime experiences and meetings with Canaris'.[31]

With clear information that Hitler had designs to expand eastwards, Menzies ('C') decided it was time to make contact with German officers who did not agree with Hitler's plans. In his sights were senior figures like Canaris. Menzies believed that Canaris might be the catalyst for the anti-Nazi officers who, as loyal and patriotic Germans, did not support Hitler.[32] Consideration was given as to how Canaris could cooperate with the Allies. By early 7 January 1942, Liddell reported to Menzies that Canaris might lead an army revolt against Hitler.[33] A few months later, on 17 April, Canaris arrived in North Africa, then travelled to Madrid to meet 'the head of this Service' and his Lisbon representative.

Another conduit to Canaris came through one of MI6's secret networks in France and again involved women – this time a group of nuns in a French convent. The network was called Jade/Amicol and its headquarters were based in a convent of the Sisters of St Agonie, an order of nuns that had its roots in twelfth-century Jerusalem. Jade/Amicol was founded in 1943 by Claude Ollivier, a Jesuit priest of the French secret service, and Major Philippe Keun, a British soldier and resistance fighter. The network had approximately 1,500 sub-agents and was controlled from London by Claude Dansey.

Major Keun was instructed to find a channel to Canaris. This he did by mixing in high-level German military circles. He had connections to the Austrian Baron Posch-Pastor, private secretary to Karl Heinrich von Stülpnagel. Stülpnagel was head of a circle of anti-Nazis in the West who wished to overthrow Hitler, a group which included von Stauffenberg. Stülpnagel was close to Canaris and made contact with MI6 via Baron Posch-Pastor. On 30 May 1944 Keun flew to England by Lysander on a secret mission to be briefed on the role of Jade/Amicol in the D-Day invasions.[34] Menzies gave him a letter to deliver to Canaris and then Vera Atkins (F Section, SOE) despatched Keun on his final mission into France.

Just a few days before D-Day, and carrying the letter for Canaris, Keun stayed in the convent of the Sisters of St Agonie. The convent had nine resident sisters and Mother Superior Henriette Frede, all of whom worked as couriers for Jade/Amicol and MI6; they collected secret mail destined for 'C' in London, and the convent also served as one of the main secret radio posts in Paris for MI6. One of the network's major intelligence achievements was to obtain plans for the Atlantic Wall defences which the Germans had constructed from Norway to Spain.

Colonel Ollivier, co-founder of Jade/Amicol, met Canaris in Paris and told him that he had a letter for him from London that was too important to risk giving him in public. He persuaded Canaris to secretly visit the convent, where there would be total privacy. With the nuns confined to their cells, Ollivier handed over 'C's letter to Canaris in a private room. Ollivier was not privy to its contents, but Canaris read it and exclaimed, '*Finis Germaniae!*' ('Germany is finished!').[35] After a brief meal, Canaris left. While it is not clear precisely what 'C' had written to Canaris, it is thought that Canaris was asked to open the Atlantic Wall to Allied forces for an invasion and to allow airborne forces to land.

The convent became a location for a number of secret meetings between Canaris and MI6. And, while much remains in the shadows of secrecy, Jade/Amicol was one of the most secure and effective intelligence networks in France until 1944. It was one in which women played their part, but unlike the Alliance – Noah's Ark – it did not survive until the end of the war.

Female Heads of Station

We have but glimpses of that most secret of world of MI6, but it transpires that it was one in which Rita Winsor was not the only female head of an MI6 station. For the first time in the history of women in intelligence, an exciting new understanding is emerging of the high-level and responsible roles given to MI6 women in the field.

A source who wishes to remain unnamed has confirmed that Margaret 'Teddy' Dunlop was one of MI6's heads of station in Lisbon and described her as 'a legend in SIS'. Very few personal details can be traced about her, except she was born in Darjeeling in 1906, was married and died in Tangier in 1969. Only scant evidence is known for her career in MI6. However, by 1949 she was stationed in Tangier as MI6 head of station there. The port of Tangier on the Strait of Gibraltar was strategically significant as the gateway between Europe and Africa. Here she monitored skirmishes among the Arab population and had 'never required large funds for agents, and the way she ran her field was her own affair'.[36]

During her time in Tangier, she crossed paths with Guy Burgess after he and his mother visited there. Burgess attended social parties and moved in the circles of MI6 officers and agents. He drank heavily and was in need of money. Dunlop contacted Desmond Bristow, head of the Iberian Section of MI6 in Madrid, and told him that Burgess was rude, kept pestering her for money and was 'generally behaving in an appalling fashion'.[37] Bristow advised her not to give him any money. She then reported that Burgess was broadcasting the name of the Swiss diplomat who was allowing the British to use the Swiss diplomatic bag to bring rare pieces of equipment and information out of Switzerland. Burgess was clearly a security risk. Dunlop and her colleague Kenneth Mills (MI6 head of station in Gibraltar) drafted a letter to the Foreign Office stating that Burgess should not be in their employment. Not long afterwards, Burgess returned to London and, in 1951, defected to Russia with Donald Maclean.

Although nothing further has come to light on Dunlop's career, the above offers a rare view into a world where, contrary to traditional narratives, women did in fact become heads of MI6 stations. Their wider legacy is still obscured by official secrecy.

In 1946 Rozanne Medhurst met and married a young intelligence officer, Halsey Colchester. She had applied for a transfer to 'the Office' (MI6) from the secret world of codebreaking at Bletchley Park and was posted to the MI6 station in Cairo as an intelligence officer. As Mrs Colchester, she worked for Rodney Dennys (Graham Greene's brother-in-law) as head of station and had responsibility for preparing scores of MI6 agents for clandestine insertion into Yugoslavia. No one understood why these men, who had been trained down to the last detail, were caught on landing and executed. Gradually, the truth about the Cambridge spies emerged. In 1950 Rozanne moved with her husband to Istanbul, after his transfer there. In the Turkish capital she met Kim Philby at an office party. After the defection of Burgess and Maclean in 1951, she commented, 'it was a terrible time in MI6. There was a witch hunt. People were given the most awful grilling.'[38]

During her career with MI6, Rozanne met intelligence officer Graham Greene and also felt first-hand the effect of Philby's penetration of the organisation. She was closely involved with MI6 officer Nicholas Elliott in trying to obtain a confession from Philby. Although that was the limit of her 'acquaintance' with the Cambridge spies, she found the mood of post-war intelligence so different from her Bletchley Park days. She believed that the poisoned atmosphere in MI6 caused by Philby's betrayal contributed to her husband's decision to quit the service. He decided to ordain as a priest – a world familiar to both of them as their fathers were vicars. For several years Rozanne was content to be a vicar's wife in Oxfordshire, although after 'the Office', she found life boring.

Queen of Spies

Daphne Park had a long and exceptional career in MI6 with high-level promotion within the service.[39] Dubbed 'queen of spies', by 1975 she had risen to become Controller Western Hemisphere, the highest SIS/MI6 posting ever occupied by a woman at that time. When asked once about her drink of choice, she replied with typical wry humour, 'Earl Grey tea, stirred not shaken'.[40] Her MI6 career, which spanned forty years, began during the Second World War. Born in 1921 in Surrey, she had graduated with a BA in Modern Languages from Somerville College, Oxford in 1943 and turned down the opportunity to take a number of prestigious jobs at the Treasury and the Foreign Office because she wished to do something more active for the war effort. She enlisted in the FANY and served with SOE in its North Africa operations during 1944, almost certainly selected because of her early childhood experiences in East Africa (where her father was recovering from tuberculosis) and her knowledge of coding. SOE gave her charge of briefing and despatching the Jedburgh teams ('the Jeds'), who were to be deployed from Algiers to southern France as part of the 'second invasion' (the first being D-Day). The Jeds were inter-Allied teams of special forces (British, US and French) who were tasked with coordinating an armed uprising by resistance groups at the same time as the Allied forces landed in southern France.

At the end of the war Park transferred to the Allied Commission for Austria, hunting down German and Austrian scientists to ensure they worked for the West rather than the Russians. In 1947 she transferred to MI6 and worked under cover of various diplomatic positions in the Foreign Office, including a posting to Moscow in the 1950s. During the Cold War she was one of MI6's toughest top female intelligence officers; it was said that even the KGB (Russian intelligence) admired her tenacity and brilliance. She served in other global hotspots, including a posting to Lusaka, Zambia, then as consul general in Hanoi, Vietnam, in 1969, where her movements were severely restricted by the Vietnamese as they suspected her of being a spy. Her final posting before retirement was to Ulan Bator in Mongolia. She once commented, 'I must have been arrested and condemned to be shot several times. It was a hazard that I got used to.'[41]

Described after her death as 'the greatest woman intelligence officer in the world', Park was somewhat dismissive of her groundbreaking achievements as a female officer in MI6.[42] What she minded was not being named as a spy, she said, but the highlighting of her sex. 'Why,' she would ask, 'woman intelligence officer?'[43] Perhaps surprisingly for us today, Park appeared unconcerned about the lack of equality for women in the intelligence services, saying instead that the only time she ever experienced sexism was when an African chief gave her a special gift of a hoe instead of a spear. In fact, several African leaders so respected her that they often relied on her judgement and advice. Reflecting with a measure of realism on her unusual career, she once said, 'There are frightening moments and there are moments when you should have been frightened but weren't. I do not have courage, but I do have a mixture of curiosity and optimism.'[44] Park retired from MI6 in 1979.[45] She became a legend among her colleagues because she was one of a small number of women who, prior to the end of the Cold War, led the way for women in MI6 to take higher positions as intelligence officers and in command of some of MI6's most important postings abroad.

Daphne Park and her female colleagues blazed a trail for the women who came later. It has been a slow, hard-fought journey, but the talents of women are now commonly employed by the British Secret Service. Today, three out of the four heads of sections at MI6 who report to 'C' are women.[46]

'The Office'

The story of MI6 women is not just about the glamour and excitement of operations abroad. Back at MI6 headquarters in Broadway Buildings the hidden female workforce was vital to the service in support roles. Women like Kathleen Pettigrew have had little light shone on their careers. As personal assistant to Stewart Menzies, who became the chief of MI6 in 1939, she had one of the most trusted roles. Passing across her desk was pretty much everything that crossed Menzies's desk. She was intimately acquainted with the highest levels of classified operations and had a rare overview of all of the sensitive work. She had a fearsome reputation and protected Menzies from anyone trying to push into his office for an unscheduled meeting.

In 1956, Monica Washburn (née Paterson) was posted to MI6 in London and was working in the Registry or library. Her son Lorin commented, 'Mother had lots of male friends, not so many female friends. She met intelligence officer Graham Greene.'[47] She had had a career with SIS in Izmir, Turkey, in the 1930s. It was the country of her birth; her family originated from Scotland and made their wealth by purchasing land in Mesopotamia and mining chrome. Monica was educated in England and was fluent in English, French, Turkish and Greek. During the 1930s and 1940s, Turkey was neutral and the British consulate in Izmir had an extension from where spy networks operated. Here Monica handled documents and information and was the site librarian, responsible for overseeing books and cataloguing intelligence documents. Within the SIS circles in Turkey she knew senior SIS/SOE officer Eric Gedye. At the end of the war she transferred to Athens with British military intelligence, attached to the consulate, never in uniform and always as a civilian.

Monica never remarried after the death of her husband in 1938. She continued to work for MI6 even with a child to support. In 1947 she arrived in the UK with her twelve-year-old son and secured his private education at Blundell's School in Tiverton, Devon. While he remained in England, Monica was posted to Paris in an intelligence role for the Supreme HQ Allied Powers Europe (SHAPE), where she ran the library at its headquarters near Fontainebleau. Her son Lorin recalled, 'She must have been very senior in the organisation because she had access to the senior officers' dining room. I remember her taking me to the dining room for a meal.' Monica remained in Paris for four or five years, attending cocktail parties every night – a characteristic of her world of espionage. From there she was posted to MI6 headquarters in London.

At Broadway Buildings, women are known to have coordinated MI6 agents and operations, but the careers of these women are extremely difficult to reconstruct. At best, we have a sketchy picture. This is the case with Diana Neave (née Giffard), the wife of Airey Neave. Diana, who was the daughter of Thomas Giffard of Chillington Hall, Wolverhampton, and Angela Trollope (heir to the estate of Sir William Trollope), began her war work as a nurse, before being talent-spotted by 'a scout' and recruited to MI6. During the Second World War she had a liaison job with the Ministry of Information of the Polish government-in-exile. Though she was discreet about her wartime work, it is known that it involved contact with agents and work that involved agents' propaganda missions. Her family only glimpsed her secret past after the war when former unnamed agents greeted her with affection in the Polish Hearth Club in Kensington.

Diana's close friend and colleague in MI6 was Yvonne Maslinksa (née Medlicott), the daughter of Lieutenant-Colonel Henry Medlicott. She was fluent in German and French, with a working knowledge of Polish, and was responsible for receiving information coming into MI6 headquarters from overseas agents, translating them where necessary. She collated the information into a coherent form and passed the reports to senior personnel. While on night duty at the office, she occasionally interviewed returning agents; in one case an exhausted agent, on the point of collapse, became rather irritated because neither she nor her colleague were sufficiently proficient in shorthand to write down quickly enough all he urgently needed to report.

On the rare occasions that Yvonne mentioned the war, she was always vague. She described one incident to her family about how she was assembling a file of top-secret papers when some of them blew out of the open window. She managed to collect them in the street below and took them home to iron, before handing them to the chief. These snippets throw merely a chink of light onto that secret world. Yvonne may have been in intelligence in the 1930s as she travelled to Innsbruck in early April 1938 and observed the Nazi occupation in that region of Austria. Before the war, she learnt to fly and obtained her flying licence with the Air Transport Auxiliary, flying Tiger Moths and possibly Spitfires, before illness prevented her from continuing.[48] One of her sons commented, 'The problem is that, despite being very courageous and extraordinarily confident, my mother tended to understate everything about herself.'[49] His comment highlights again just how difficult it is to know very much about MI6's women.

Another hidden woman in the history of MI6 was Margaret Priestley. She was special assistant to Ian Fleming and helped to run 30 Assault Unit, a commando unit formed and trained by Fleming from 1943 in Amersham, Buckinghamshire. The unit went on to carry out special tasks, especially in 'smash and grab' raids, to acquire German technology, military equipment, German personnel and, from 1945, German scientists for the West.

Joan Bright Astley was assigned to the Joint Planning Committee and tasked with running a secret intelligence centre in an office in the Cabinet War Rooms under Whitehall. In this role, she had responsibility for secret papers and reports. Afterwards, she became personal assistant to General Sir Hastings Ismay. She had been born in Argentina to an English accountant and Scottish governess. She had experience as a secretary at the British Legation in Mexico, and then in the 1930s declined a job to teach English to the family of Hitler's deputy, Rudolf Hess. In the early part of the war she was recruited to D Section, MI(R), a secret SIS section of the War Office, by a mysterious colonel whom she met at an underground station. She was told to wear a pink carnation – an identifying feature used by Claude Dansey (a colonel and deputy head of MI6). It is likely that he recruited her. Her job was to find ways to disrupt the flow of Romanian oil to the Third Reich and thereby interrupt Germany's production for its war machine.

Sheila Trevaskis was a wireless operator, recruited by MI6 over tea in Harrods on 21 July 1943.[50] Having been given a password she met Major Beatrice Temple (ATS), the niece of the Archbishop of Canterbury, and accepted a post in special duties – the nature of which she did not know until her training by MI6 in Hans Place, behind Harrods. Sheila became part of a secret defence force of over 3,000 agents who were based in coastal locations to provide the first alerts of a German invasion of Britain.[51] They were trained in how to encode reports and transmit them to a local underground control station and to drop intelligence reports in dead letter boxes, such as hollowed out trees and gaps in walls. She and her auxiliary agents were stood down in December 1944 when a German invasion was no longer a possibility.

MI6's history is full of these hidden women.

20
CLOAK AND DAGGER

On 7 May 1945 the unconditional surrender of the German Third Reich was signed, bringing to an end six years of war in Europe. The Nazi regime was finally defeated, but the war in the Far East would continue for another three months. For the vast majority of women who had served in intelligence, their world was about to change again. Many of the female intelligencers were sent to post-war Germany and Austria to aid the reconstruction of Europe, often with intelligence units or attached to US intelligence operations. Gilian Gambier-Parry, daughter of Major-General Michael Gambier-Parry, was one of the women who served as an intelligence officer in General Eisenhower's headquarters (SHAEF). During the course of her work, she visited Hitler's bunker and acquired some items, now on display in the Military Intelligence Museum in Chicksands, Bedfordshire. Midge Holmes (of MI6 and SOE) was transferred to Vienna with some of her former male SOE agents to aid the restoration of laws in Austria. She was also engaged in the recovery of the art treasures which the Nazi leadership had looted from Jewish families across Europe and stored in the salt mines in Austria. Other women transferred to Klagenfurt in Austria to monitor subversive groups and other security threats to the restoration of peace.

As the Second World War drew to a close, Russia emerged as the new threat. A deep divide that was both physical and ideological descended on Europe, termed 'the Iron Curtain' by Winston Churchill. In the immediate aftermath of the defeat of Nazi Germany, it was imperative for the counter-espionage teams of the closest Allies – Britain, the United States and France – to find German scientists and technological experts and exfiltrate them to the West to avoid them and their technology falling into the hands of the Russians. A handful of women – no more than eight – from Bletchley Park and CSDIC joined their male colleagues at a secret interrogation centre at Bad Nenndorf in Germany, known as No. 74 CSDIC, and headed by Colonel Robin 'Tin Eye' Stephens. The unit became the centre of controversy, centred on Stephens, for the mistreatment of some of the inmates. It was here that German technologists and civilian scientists were bugged in their cells after interrogation. The women there seem to have been engaged primarily on typing and transcription duties, although the majority of the files remain classified.

Tracing the Missing SOE Agents

A major element of the restoration of democracy involved justice and the hunt for Nazi war criminals. Journalist Rebecca West, who worked for MI6 on undisclosed duties, covered the Nuremberg Trial.[1] Vera Atkins, who sent SOE agents into France for F Section, conducted her own personal mission in 1945–46.

Before hostilities were over, in autumn 1944 Atkins travelled to France, determined to discover the exact fate of her missing agents, bring the perpetrators to justice and thereby honour the memory of the dead.[2] She carried a list of their names and information about their last-known whereabouts and whether they were known to have been arrested. Initially, her intention to investigate and interrogate was not taken seriously in London. The world of interrogation was still largely a male domain, but Atkins was determined. However, there was the debacle over her nationality to overcome. Originating from Romania, Atkins had tried and failed to gain British nationality in 1942; but by 1945 her application had acquired a new urgency. Major Thomas Roche, head of General Security in SOE, wrote in the strongest terms to the Home Office: 'If she does not have British nationality, she will be unable to work in the British and American zones and will be treated as an alien. This will place on her special restrictions, and of course the essence of her work for the British would be to move freely and unobtrusively through areas of Europe.'[3] He went on to describe her as 'quite irreplaceable'. In the end, her application for naturalisation succeeded because of references from two long-serving MI6 officers who had known her since her childhood: Thomas Kendrick and his brother-in-law, Rex Pearson.[4] Her application succeeded with Kendrick vouching for her: 'I believe her to be completely pro-British and loyal to this country. I consider her to be a person in whom absolute reliance may be placed.'[5] In a report of her naturalisation interview she was described as 'a woman of intelligence and discretion, well able to keep her own counsel'.[6]

The type of investigative work that she was to about to undertake required an experienced officer who could identify the agents; it was she who had despatched them behind enemy lines and had known them for up to three years. Only two other officers could have conducted the investigations, but they were engaged on other intelligence work, and Atkins was regarded as the most efficient person for the job. Atkins did not rest until she had confirmed the fate of all her agents. This led to a period of extraordinary interrogation work by her that saw her travel extensively in France and Germany, piecing together evidence and interrogating Nazi war criminals. She was the only female interrogator known to have entered the secret interrogation centre in Kensington Palace Gardens in London. During the war the site was known as the London Cage; from 1945 until 1948 it became the War Crimes Investigation Unit.[7] Copies of statements signed by Nazi war criminals and witnesses survive in Atkins's personal file and declassified files in the National Archives. Atkins countersigned all the interrogations that she personally undertook, which makes it possible to know exactly who she interrogated.

Atkins is a rare example of a female intelligence officer in post-war Europe who worked with the War Crimes Section (Judge Advocate General, or JAG). She showed 'the greatest qualities of determination and single-mindedness of purpose in following up innumerable fragments of information and has covered a great deal of ground in interviewing personally anyone who might conceivably have information to give, and that included German prisoners and suspected Nazi War criminals'.[8] She learnt the horrifying truth that thirteen of her female agents were murdered by the Nazis, that others were captured and suffered ghastly and unspeakable torture but survived the concentration camps.[9] The investigations were slow and on many occasions distressing.

In the end, with sheer determination and hard work, she succeeded in tracing 117 of the 118 missing F Section agents, both women and men. Armed with this knowledge, she did so much to highlight *specifically* the women's contributions to SOE, ensuring they had a voice even in death. Furthermore, she ensured that the British government recognised their service, which included the awarding of the George Cross to Odette Sansom (who had survived Ravensbrück) in 1946 and a posthumous George Cross to Violette Szabo and Noor Inayat Khan in 1946 and 1949 respectively.

Atkins's own discharge papers summed her up as 'a capable administrator and organiser . . . [who] remains undaunted both by the difficulties or amount of work. She has courage and drive, but is somewhat disinclined to accept instructions without argument. She requires handling, but has proved a capable officer.'[10] It was precisely this strong personality which defined her success as an agent handler and intelligence officer during the war.

Decades later, questions are still being asked by historians about the catastrophe that befell SOE's agents in France. How were they betrayed? And why did SOE continue to send more agents behind enemy lines? But, interestingly, Atkins's personal SOE file has this citation: 'On countless occasions her foresight and intelligent appreciation have saved both French and British clandestine workers in enemy-occupied France from running into danger and her constant encouragement and the confidence which it inspired have been the greatest value.' This hints at a different picture of operations in France.

Atkins was successful in ascertaining the fate of every one of her agents, except one. Her single-minded and single-handed achievement in this respect is a credit to her determined and strong character. She was a woman of honour and compassion.

Intelligence under Fire

Molly Sasson, who enjoyed a career with SIS/MI6, is another good example of the hidden stories of women who worked in the field of intelligence at the end of the war.[11] Her mother was a professional pianist who had studied at the Royal Academy and who had, prior to and during the First World War, spent three years in France working secretly for the War Office in England and France. The nature of her intelligence work was never discussed.[12]

During Molly's childhood, the family travelled from their home in Putney, south London, for holidays in Germany, Austria, Holland, Belgium, Switzerland, Hungary and France. At the age of seventeen, Molly attended the International Ladies College, six miles from The Hague. There was a strong emphasis on language, the arts and etiquette as prerequisites for university education. She was on course to become a classical singer when war intervened. She enlisted in the WAAF and was sent to RAF Wilmslow in Cheshire for training. After this, she took several specialist courses because of her knowledge of languages, and these covered intelligence matters. Her first posting was to the Special Investigation Branch headquarters, then located in a large block of flats on Exhibition Road in Kensington. Her work initially involved censorship of thousands of German letters. If any raised security concerns, she had to annotate them. She translated documents from German and Dutch into English and interviewed German prisoners of war and civilians who were of interest to the security services. She was then transferred to the Air Intelligence Unit in Monck Street, which was processing thousands of documents captured by the Allies as they advanced through Europe. The documents needed to be translated and the intelligence extracted.

In November 1944, Molly became the sole German interpreter for a detachment of the Allied Military Government for Occupied Territories. Their final destination was Verden, a town in Lower Saxony in Germany. She commented, 'It was a hazardous, dangerous time even though we all knew that Germany had lost the war . . . Our task was to bring law and order, closely following our troops and the retreating German army . . . We were confronted with the true horror of war, death, destruction and misery.'[13]

Her memoirs provide a vivid account of the dangers of intelligence work under fire. As their convoy of eight vehicles travelled through Belgium, Holland and Germany, they came under attack from both Allied Spitfires and German Stukas (dive bombers). On the Dutch–German border there were seriously wounded German soldiers, many of them dying of gangrene. Molly's task was to interview the wounded men to gain useful information and most urgently gather intelligence on the location of SS troops. While she did so, the authorities were removing the corpses of their comrades behind her. She wrote, 'I cannot describe the agony and pain I witnessed while gaining much intelligence from these helpless, disillusioned, dying men . . . Many wanted to pray with me and needed reassurance in prayers and tears, as well as help and sympathy, in order not to die alone. These were enemy soldiers reaching out in the last hour of life. It was a sobering experience.'[14]

Molly's detachment was empowered to arrest any citizen, confiscate vehicles and requisition buildings. As the only interpreter for this detachment, she helped to conduct interviews, house searches and investigations. Ahead of them, advancing Allied forces were engaged in heavy fighting with SS troops as they liberated towns and villages. When the detachment moved into the newly liberated areas, Molly was tasked with long hours of interrogation of suspected Nazi war criminals.

When the detachment reached the town of Bocholt, the personnel rested overnight in a florist shop. Several hours later, while they were sleeping, they were bombed. Molly was pulled out of the rubble alive, but many of townsfolk were killed or wounded that night.

Once in Verden, Molly spent three days a week on war crimes work, interpreting and translating documents, and this was sent on to the British war crimes trials at Hamburg. The dangers were ever present as die-hard SS troops hid in the woods and buildings in town. One of the despatch riders was attacked on his way back from Hamburg and his body later pulled out of the river.

In early 1946 Molly was posted to Bueckeburg, a city in Lower Saxony, where the headquarters of the Special Investigation Branch was based in a 700-year-old castle. Again, she translated documents for the war crimes trials and interviewed arrested suspects. In June 1947 she returned to London for an interview at the Air Ministry in Kingsway and a whirlwind romance that led to marriage a few months later. Her life in intelligence continued as a married officer, while her husband was posted to Singapore. It is interesting that, contrary to popular belief, some women were able to continue their intelligence work after marriage.

For a short time, Molly was posted back to Bueckeburg in Germany, only to be suddenly recalled to England. She was greeted at Hendon aerodrome and driven to Kensington where she was interviewed by an air commodore and officers from MI5 and MI6. She agreed to work for the British Secret Service and was told she would become a civilian and be given a new name and identity.

Russian Defector

Molly was about to undertake a hugely responsible role within the cloak-and-dagger world of MI6. She was given a German passport and ration cards and briefed on her assignment: she was to assist the world's pre-eminent rocket scientist, his wife and nine-year-old daughter, who were about to be smuggled out of the Soviet occupation zone of Berlin and brought to the UK. Gregory Aleksandrovich Tokaev was a colonel in the Soviet air force and formerly head of the Zhukovsky Air Force Engineering Academy in Moscow. In 1946 he had been sent by Moscow to Berlin to head all Russian troops in the Soviet occupied zone, but he had become disillusioned with Stalin's brutal regime and its purges of enemies of the state. His exfiltration to the West became extremely urgent and he was flown out of Berlin to London under top-level secrecy. He was one of the most valuable Soviet defectors in the early Cold War.

At a safe house in the UK, Molly was the minder and companion for Tokaev and his family, tasked with preparing them for a new life in the West. She recalled, 'my all-absorbing task was as an escort, confidant, guard, guide and translator in the German language, spoken and understood by this family during the first eighteen months of debriefings, acclimatisation and adaptation to the British way of life'.[15] Molly lived with the Tokaevs for two years.

Afterwards, and following a period of further training, she worked in the Directorate of Foreign Liaison (DFL) in Whitehall. Her intelligence job covered Belgium, the Netherlands, Thailand, Burma and Indonesia. From there she was posted to RAF Nuneham Park in Oxfordshire on photographic interpretation – still required in the Cold War – and joined the newly created Joint Air Photographic Intelligence

Centre (JAPIC) to monitor Soviet troop movements in Eastern Europe and the Soviet nuclear capability.

Her service with the RAF ended in 1954 and she was transferred to The Hague with her husband. Tragically, while there she lost a baby during a caesarean operation and this took its toll on her. Keen to return to intelligence work, she was interviewed in 1955 by an Australian security intelligence organisation attached to the Australian embassy's Migration Office in The Hague, which screened migrants wishing to enter Australia; this was an extension of her expertise in interrogation and security. She processed thousands of applications by would-be migrants and cleared them for security purposes. In 1967 she was recruited by Sir Charles Spry, director general of ASIO (the Australian intelligence service), to track down suspected moles in the intelligence services. It was not only MI5, MI6 and the Foreign Office that had been penetrated by Russian intelligence via double agents like the Cambridge spies – the Australian intelligence services were also believed to have been similarly breached in the Cold War.

Molly's life offers a glimpse into a closed, still-classified clandestine world – a world shrouded in such total secrecy that it is almost impossible to assess and evaluate the role of women in it. However, her life demonstrated that women could be, and were, selected for interesting and diverse intelligence work – exciting, and sometimes dangerous, and with a huge responsibility placed on their shoulders.

MI5 after 1945

During the Cold War, the section of MI5 that employed the most women was the Registry. Astoundingly, it was not until 1976 that the first man joined it.[16] In the years immediately after the Second World War, MI5 continued to primarily recruit the daughters of former officers or debutantes. The new female recruits rarely served for long in MI5 because when they married they had to leave the service as, without the provision of childcare, there was no structure to support having a family and a career. This meant that the turnover of female staff was high and they rarely progressed up the ranks or gained sufficient expertise in the job. By the late 1960s the younger generation of women were professionals, drawn from universities and less content with the lifestyle and lack of career promotion in MI5. On one occasion in the late 1960s, a batch of new female recruits were told that women were happier in subordinate positions.[17]

It appears that in the post-war period, the Security Service generally failed to progress the careers of its women, with the exception of figures like Jane Archer and Milicent Bagot (pp. 103, 106). But their operational roles in MI5 were limited to surveillance; and, even then, their job was to act as camouflage or a decoy for the male officer.

A certain amount of sexism lingered on in the service. As one director wrote about women and counter-surveillance work, 'once we allow a woman to stay for over five years, you should find it very difficult in practice to get rid of her at all'.[18] In spite of this negative attitude, the Security Service had been recruiting a higher proportion of women at executive and officer level than any other branch of government. Even so, it still took until 1992 to appoint a woman to the top job.

Stella Rimington began as a junior assistant officer in MI5 in 1969.[19] She recalled her beginnings there, when men were recruited as officers and the women had their own career structure as assistant officers. It was, in effect, a second-class career. They carried out a wide range of support work, but not 'the sharp-end of intelligence gathering operations'.[20] When Rimington became the first female director general of MI5 in 1992, she was not invited to apply for the post. There was no interview or selection panel. She learnt about her promotion after Prime Minister John Major had approved her appointment, and she was not even asked if she wanted the job.

Rimington made history as the first female head of any of the world's leading intelligence or security agencies. Importantly, she was chosen on her ability, not her sex, and not because MI5 thought it politically correct to appoint a woman as its head. She was simply the best person for the job. She was also the first director general to be named publicly. This had unforeseen consequences, because it brought her unwanted attention from the media and paparazzi. Every detail of her private life was aired to the public in newspapers and articles. The *Evening Standard* published an unattractive photograph of her. The *Sun* ran a story about her separation from her husband under the headline 'MI5 Wife in

Secret Love Split'. Her life that had, thus far, been totally secret was played out in the full glare of the media spotlight.

Ten years later, in 2002, Eliza Manningham-Buller became the second woman to become director general of the Security Service. And in 2023 history was made again for women in intelligence when Anne Keast-Butler was appointed the first female director of GCHQ. She took up the post from her former position as Deputy Director General of MI5. At the time of her appointment, details emerged about her existing thirty-year career in intelligence, counter-terrorism and security. Such biographical information offers a rare and tangible glimpse of the progress women have been, and are, making in these highly secretive agencies.

To mark 100 years of women's suffrage in the UK, in 2018 MI5 commented openly on the legacy of its women, who had given 'ungrudging service to what they rightly considered to be war work of great importance . . . in many cases they were women of ability . . . It was the union of men and women in the work to which the department owed its success, each bringing into the common stock their own peculiar qualities and thus complementing the work of the other.'[21]

In spite of ongoing secrecy, it has finally been able to open a window onto that compelling world of female spies, intelligence and espionage and to begin to understand and acknowledge the hidden contribution of women to this work. A far-reaching assessment of women in intelligence across all eras, especially after the Cold War, currently remains challenging, however, because the vast majority of the women are anonymous and their experiences continue to be shrouded by the Official Secrets Act.

EPILOGUE
A LIFE IN SECRETS

Across the twentieth century's two world wars, women were a vast, hidden workforce of intelligencers, codebreakers, spies, secret agents, handlers and double agents. Ironically, their enormous contribution to the secret world of intelligence has not been eclipsed solely by men or a focus on male agents. Women in intelligence and their precise work within the services has been obscured primarily by official secrecy.

It is true to say that, even when the files have been declassified, there has been a tendency to glamorise the female spies and a reluctance to discover their true stories. That is now changing as historians begin to focus on the previously under-reported dimension of women in intelligence, in particular, and within conflict more broadly. There is a welcome movement away from an overemphasis on a handful of *femmes fatales*, like Mati Hari. These female spies have served to distract and detract from the true legacy of women in intelligence.

What emerges in this book is a complex picture and one that crosses all aspects of the British secret services. Today, the declassification of files and other archives are making it possible to begin to restore many of the often unnamed women of intelligence to their rightful place in history. Some have been named here for the first time, personalising what is so often an anonymous crowd of female intelligencers. It has been an exciting journey and a privilege for me to highlight the indispensable contributions to intelligence made by the women in this book across two world wars. These stories began to emerge unexpectedly during the research for my other books on military intelligence, including *The Walls Have Ears*, *MI9* and *Spymaster*.

An examination of the stories of individual women in this book has revealed that, beneath the surface of their seemingly routine intelligence roles, they carried out work previously unattributed to women. This is beginning to shift our understanding and enable an assessment of what women actually achieved in clandestine missions and networks and as intelligencers. Generally, in the intelligence field, women were not automatically restricted by their sex. Some services in wartime – especially within military, naval and air intelligence – appointed women to roles because they were either the best person for the job or had the right skills for it. But it is true, and has been acknowledged in the book, that women operated against a backdrop of gender inequality in respect of pay and the opportunities for promotion to the highest ranks. That has changed, and is changing, in the twenty-first century.

Between 1915 and 1945 some women in Sigint had more senior roles than at any time during the Cold War.[1] And there were discreet women who collected intelligence for the British during their travels, especially during the 1920s and 1930s. But before the Second World War Britain was, nevertheless, an overridingly patriarchal society, and opportunities for most women to work and live a life outside the confines of domesticity and motherhood were few. For the majority of middle- and working-class women in Britain, war was liberating in that it provided them with opportunities to take up roles hitherto performed by men that would not have been available to them in peacetime. Given the opportunities afforded by male conscription, women comprised a greater proportion of the available workforce and were selected on the basis of their particular skillsets. This meant that they were not incidental to intelligence in wartime, but central to it.

As we have seen, women were recruited for a host of different reasons which varied across the field of intelligence and the exigencies of the wartime picture. Women were agent handlers and runners – jobs no woman had been permitted to take on before – simply if they could do the job. The first female interrogators were used in CSDIC and Naval Intelligence, where it was discovered that women could make prisoners talk. We have seen brilliant women in technology, as in the case of Catherine Townshend, who headed the M Room tech, and those who went on to work in GCHQ. Academic and creative skills were drawn on, for example, with the archaeologists and artists at RAF Medmenham, such backgrounds making them experts in their particular fields of intelligence. The SIS secretaries of the inter-war period are another instance of women whose extensive knowledge of European countries from their intelligence work meant they were taken up by SOE to mount operations into those countries in the 1940s. This book has made it abundantly clear that the myth that women were 'just' secretaries or clerks should be debunked. Women were indispensable to uniformed and civilian intelligence organisations and at the heart of operational and strategic intelligence.

At the beginning of both world wars, women in occupied countries displayed extraordinary bravery and resilience in getting intelligence to the Allies, often at great risk to their own lives. They moved invisibly across occupied territories and lived and died for the cause of freedom. They were part of amateur spy networks behind enemy lines that developed into highly efficient and vitally important sources of intelligence for the Allies. These female agents used their intuition and common sense, and learnt from their experiences in setting up their networks and keeping them secure. None of the women, nor their male colleagues, were professional intelligencers. Nevertheless, they provided the Allies with eyewitness material from behind enemy lines that could not be gained any other way. Those women who survived the war enjoyed the knowledge that their efforts and sacrifice were not in vain. La Dame Blanche, Clarence and Noah's Ark networks are good examples of this.

An important thread in this history is that there were men of vision who used the skills of women, especially in wartime, even when the social limitations placed on women in the workplace diminished the salaries they received and their opportunities for advancement. Sir Edward Travis, who became head of Bletchley Park in February 1942, had such foresight, dramatically increasing the female personnel to number two-thirds of the total workforce ahead of D-Day. Ian Fleming, too, a Naval Intelligence officer and later bestselling author, initiated the practice of using women to interrogate enemy prisoners of war. Women like these carried out roles that made a real difference to the end game.

Decades of Silence

It is notable that many histories of intelligence, spies and espionage contain few women in their indexes. Women's intelligence careers so often took place in the shadows, their work then further shrouded by the cloak of official secrecy. But another factor in their invisibility has also been historians' unconscious bias – an assumption that if women's roles were not evidenced to the same degree as men's, then they must not have been of importance. Women have simply been left out of their writings. Just as damaging has been the enduring fascination with glamorous female spies, honey traps and seduction, which has obscured the real role of women in espionage. What is far more exciting – and to be celebrated – is what this book has revealed again and again: women in intelligence, across two world wars, emerged as specialists in their field.

The activities of women who served in intelligence roles in the First World War are only now materialising more fully in declassified files over a hundred years after their clandestine work. For the inter-war years, there remains a huge lack of declassified material which would enable operations to be assessed – especially SIS operations, carried out by both men and women. Even so, this book has highlighted a hidden history of women who quietly served their country. There have been surprises and examples of where they have been trailblazers, for example in being appointed SIS heads of station abroad, as in the case of Teddy Dunlop, Rita Winsor and Daphne Park. Also brought into sharp focus has been how some women enjoyed long careers spanning two or three decades, providing MI5 and MI6 with indispensable expertise in a range of roles. But ascertaining their numbers is exceedingly difficult, given the mystery and secrecy surrounding these organisations. There are aspects of the hush-hush world of intelligence that MI5 and MI6 have decided must remain classified for reasons that cannot be understood by members of the public.

While revealing the prevalence of women across the British intelligence services, this book has also charted the challenges they faced. Although remarkable individuals shattered glass ceilings, and male allies fought for recognition of their staff, women did not achieve equality with their male colleagues, especially with regard to pay – though this was of course true also for women in civilian jobs. Happily, there has been some progress in areas of military intelligence. It wasn't until 1975 that women were recruited directly into the Intelligence Corps and had a formal military intelligence role, but since 1992 women have been able to apply directly into its ranks. In 2022 the Princess Royal, HRH Princess Anne, became the first female patron of the Intelligence Corps, following her father's death the previous year. Yet challenges remain, with gaps in women achieving the highest positions.

The majority of women who had served in the two world wars returned to their old lives afterwards. Whether involved as civilians or as intelligencers in the army, navy or air force, they went back to their pre-war existences. Having signed the Official Secrets Act, they never revealed the reality of their wartime roles, even to their closest family. They got on with their lives – the majority of them married and raised children – but always carried with them the guarded memories of a past lived in secret.

It would be over six decades before their files were declassified and an insight gained into what they had achieved in the Second World War. Now that their work is in the open, the veterans of Bletchley Park can hold annual reunions. The same is true for the veterans of the clandestine eavesdropping programme whom I interviewed. When the files were released, decades after they signed the Official Secrets Act, they were able to connect with their wartime colleagues and finally speak about their work. Hundreds of their colleagues, though, had already gone to their graves without breaking their vow of silence.

At the end of the Second World War, Joan 'Panda' Carter, one of the ATS girls at RAF Medmenham, drew a sketch of her female colleague waving goodbye as their service came to an end. It was captioned: 'Although we have all gone our different ways and are scattered far apart, our life together during the Second World War left a bond between us for the rest of our lives.' That bond was not simply collegial: it was a deeper connection forged from a life lived in the utmost secrecy. In a sense, this has been the unspoken bond between women in intelligence across every generation.

Today, historians have the benefit of thousands of declassified files to begin to shine a light on these stories and to analyse the contribution of women to intelligence. The picture can probably never be complete, but we can now start to understand how their expertise became central to some of the most important intelligence networks and counter-espionage operations of the twentieth century. Women, as well as men, have shaped the ways in which intelligence has been carried out and methodologies developed. They have been catalysts for many high-level and successful operations in the history of British intelligence. Their stories have been hidden for far too long.

We can celebrate the heroism and legacy of the women in intelligence and espionage through those whose stories can now be told. We salute the women who cannot be known and whose legacy remains in the shadows. To them all, a grateful nation owes a profound sense of gratitude for their self-sacrifice and their diverse efforts in the fight for freedom and democracy.

NOTES

Prologue

1. Lesley Wyle, *Becoming Lesley*, p. 54.
2. Interview with the author.

Introduction

1. There are many other glimpses of women's role in informal espionage over the centuries. During the seventeenth century, for example, they passed confidential political and religious information, sometimes for money or power, and at other points operated as successful codebreakers and users of invisible ink: see Nadine Akkerman, *Invisible Agents*.
2. For an official history see Christopher Andrew, *The Defence of the Realm* and his book *Secret Service*.
3. MI1(c) later became later SIS, the Secret Intelligence Service/MI6.
4. Brian Parritt, *The Intelligencers*, p. 139.
5. A.F. Judge, 'The Intelligence Corps: 1914 to 1929', p. 9, Military Intelligence Museum.
6. Female spies can be traced back to over 2,500 years ago, invariably depicted in the bible as spy-harlots. We might think of Rahab and Delilah – one a prostitute who hid two Israelite spies scouting out the Promised Land, thereby enabling the Israelites to capture the land; the other the archetypal *femme fatale* bribed by her lover's enemies to discover and give away the source of his strength. The image of the female spy who seduces the enemy and steals secrets has continued to cast women in intelligence as seductresses and exotic spies – and not much more. The remnants of this image exist to an extent even in popular spy fiction and film today. See Tammy Proctor, *Female Intelligence*, p. 123.
7. Ibid., p. 126.
8. Mata Hari's MI5 file has been declassified, KV 2/1.
9. Brigadier Brian Parritt, correspondence with the author.

Chapter 1: Invisible Spies

1. Helen Fry, *Spymaster*, pp. 6–10.
2. For the formation of the Intelligence Corps, see Judge, 'The Intelligence Corps, 1914 to 1929', p. 14. For an overview of the history, see also Anthony Clayton, *Forearmed: A History of the Intelligence Corps*.
3. Proctor, *Female Intelligence*, p. 99.
4. See her personal MI5 file, KV 2/822.

5. Agents named as working for Cavell in the evacuation of soldiers included Evance Maillard, his wife and daughter, Miss Balligan and Madame Debrève. See interrogation report of Miss Jeanne Cleve, 19 August 1918, KV 2/844. Also working for her were Mrs Bodard (Bodaert), Mrs van Baer, Mrs Adam, Mr Maillard and Mr Capiau. Information from the National Archives, Brussels.
6. Proctor, *Female Intelligence*, p. 102.
7. Countess de Borchgrave was living at Broughton House, Crowthorne.
8. Report, 2 November 1915, KV 2/822.
9. Letter signed on behalf of Kell, the head of MI5, 10 August 1915, KV 2/822.
10. Details in her personal MI5 file, KV 2/822.
11. Reported in the *Daily Sketch*, 25 October 1915. Copy in KV 2/822.
12. Those who received the death penalty were Cavell, Baucq, Belleville, Thuliez and Louis Severin. The latter three later had their sentences commuted to hard labour. Proctor, *Female Intelligence*, p. 102.
13. For her work for the British she was awarded an OBE, ref: WO 372/23/10006.
14. Report in KV 2/844.
15. Cavell's death was officially reported on 27 October 1923 in the National Archives of Belgium, Brussels, dossier No. 111153.
16. German chaplain's report in KV 2/844.
17. The photographs survive in KV 2/822 and were sent to Vernon Kell in 1917.
18. Undated, handwritten letter from Mrs Cavell to Kell, KV 2/822.
19. Note dated 28 July 1918 to Stewart Menzies, GHQ I(b), KV 2/844. The interrogators of the Intelligence Corps were working out of offices of British military intelligence in Paris, Cambrai and Rouen.
20. Quien's arrest and interrogation, including his betrayal of Edith Cavell, are reported in his personal MI5 file, KV 2/844.
21. Interrogation report of Madame van Baer on 24 August 1918, KV 2/844.
22. The names of women who helped Cavell's organisation were given by Madame L'Hotelier, as reported by Major Bruce to MI5 from GHQ I(b), 28 November 1918, KV 2/844.
23. Report by J. Capiau, 7 July 1919, National Archives of Belgium.
24. Ibid.
25. Interrogation report of Miss Jeanne Cleve by Sigismund Payne Best (GHQ Hesdin, northern France), 19 August 1918, KV 2/844. Corroborated by a report from military intelligence office at Rouen, dated 19 July 1918 in the same KV file.
26. Interrogation of Aubertine Houet on 22 July 1918 by M. Gayot, interpreter at Intelligence Corps in Rouen, KV 2/844.
27. Affidavit of Octave Malice, 20 January 1921, National Archives of Belgium.
28. Malice wrote three separate affidavits describing his escape and evasion, as well as espionage work, for the British. These survive in the National Archives of Belgium and are dated 22 February 1920, 5 March 1920 and 20 January 1921.
29. Affidavit of Mrs Marie Charlet, 6 October 1919, National Archives of Belgium. The French intelligence officers were named by her as Count de Molincourt and Guy de St Ignon.
30. Louise de Bettignies spoke English, French, Flemish, German and Italian.
31. Elizabeth P. McIntosh, 'The Role of Women in Intelligence', p. 11.
32. Major Thomas Coulson, *The Queen of Spies*.
33. Kirke diaries, entry for 7 October 1915, IWM.
34. Memo, 29 November 1915, Kirke papers, ref: 82/28/1, IWM.

35. Marthe McKenna, *I Was à Spy!*, p. 148.
36. Ibid., p. 189.
37. Ibid., p. 191.
38. Ibid., p. 196.
39. Ibid., p. 220–2.

Chapter 2: Espionage behind Enemy Lines

1. Clayton, *Forearmed*, p. 35.
2. 'Service de passage: Vicomtesse Gabrielle de Monge de Franeau', in the archives of La Dame Blanche, IWM.
3. See www.1914-1918.be/civil_gabrielle_petit.php, and Kathryn Atwood, *Women Heroes of World War I*, p. 57.
4. Atwood, *Women Heroes of World War I*, p. 54.
5. The young women were Laure Butin, Adèle Collet and Hélène Petit.
6. Report entitled 'The journeys of Gabrielle Petit at Tournai', dated 2 July 1920, signed by Henri Philippart and witnessed by L. Tandel (one of the Tandel sisters who worked for La Dame Blanche network).
7. Atwood, *Women Heroes of World War I*, p. 59.
8. See www.1914-1918.be/civil_gabrielle_petit.php.
9. Atwood, *Women Heroes of World War I*, p. 60.
10. Proctor, *Female Intelligence*, p. 111.
11. Documentary series *David Jason's Secret Service*, episode 1.
12. Henry Landau, *The Spy Net*; Keith Jeffery, *MI6*; and Michael Smith, *Six*.
13. Landau, *Spy Net*, p. 245.
14. Proctor, *Female Intelligence*, p. 89.
15. Other women working for La Dame Blanche were Lieutenant Henriette Dupuich; sisters Sergeant Jeanne Henne and Lieutenant sécretaire Yvonne Henne, Julienne and three sisters Sergeant Jeanne Cambier, Corporal Valentine Cambier and Corporal Marguerite Cambier, Marcelle Dutilleux and Mrs Walther Dewé.
16. Proctor, *Female Intelligence*, p. 76.
17. Landau, *Spy Net*, pp. 110–11.
18. Copy of the citation in the archives of La Dame Blanche, IWM.
19. Report of espionage (rapport d'espionage) written by Hélène Levy survives in the archives of La Dame Blanche, IWM.
20. Other women working for the Paulin Jacquemin platoon were Mrs Tutiaux, Hélène Jacquemin, Marthe Baijot, Mrs Bottes (a guide), Mrs Leleuch, Mrs Remacle and Mrs Jacquemin.
21. BA_OBE_Props_Ldb_EM-12, National Archives of Belgium.
22. Working also in the Service of the Guard (Security) were Anna Barée, Rosa Collin, Eliza Renward, Joseph Bory, Christine Molitor, Angelina Timmermans, Marie Crahay, Desirée Crahay, Emilie Jammé, Dièudoneel Salmon and Henri Ville.
23. In Squad 1 were Juliette Durieu, Lucie Neujean and Camille Hemon. Squad 2: Marie Delcourt, Jenny Jacques and Jeanne Foettinger. Squad 3: Marie Thérèse Collard and Irene Bastin. Squad 4: Marguerite de Radiguès, Françoise de Villermont, Anne de Villermont, Clémie de L'Epine and Marie Antoinette de Radiguès. 'Conseil Supreme du Corps', in Commission des Archives des Services Patriotiques, Secrétariat de Liège.
24. OBE citation: BA_OBE_Props_Ldb_EM-7, National Archives of Belgium.
25. Proctor, *Female Intelligence*, p. 82.

26. Jeanne Menage and Josephine Detrooz helped Louise Tandel with administration.
27. Laure Tandel's citation: BA_OBE_Props_Ldb_EM-7 and Louise Tandel's citation: BA_OBE_Props_Ldb_EM-8, National Archives of Belgium.
28. BA_OBE_Props_Ldb_EM-19, National Archives of Belgium.
29. Henri Bernard, *Un géant de la résistance: Walthère Dewé*, p. 74.
30. Citations for Julienne and Anne Demarteau: BA_OBE_Props_Ldb_EM-10 and BA_OBE_Props_Ldb_EM-11, National Archives of Belgium. Marie Delcourt later became a renowned Hellenist scholar.
31. Citation for Thérèse de Radiguès: BA_OBE_Props_Ldb_EM-21. Women working for Platoon 49 included Countess Caroline d'Aspremont Lynden, Baroness de Moffarte and Mrs Dubois-Lefevre. Belgian female agents Marie Louise Donnay de Casteau and Emma Van Hamme de Corte were awarded the British Medal. See WO 372/23/1008 and Peter Verstraeten, 'The Secrecy of Awards to Belgian Secret Service Agents'.
32. Other agents working directly for Thérèse de Radiguès were Viscountess Marie-Antoinette du Parc, warrant officer Marie Joseph Poswick, Elisabeth Plissart and warrant officer Thérèse Marie Plissart.
33. Report dated 27 January 1919, archives of La Dame Blanche, IWM.
34. Citation, BA_OBE_Props_Ldb_EM-3, National Archives of Belgium.
35. Proctor, *Female Intelligence*, p. 92.
36. Ibid., p. 93.
37. Quoted in ibid., p. 94.
38. Bernard, *Un géant de la résistance: Walthère Dewé*, p. 6
39. La Dame Blanche, Box 2, folder 13, newspaper report from *Moniteur*, 31 January 1919.
40. Landau, *Spy Net*, p. 170.
41. Letter from Henry Landau to Captain Vigors of MI1(c), 24 February 1919, La Dame Blanche, Box 2, Folder 12a/b.
42. Landau, "*Spy Net*"?, p. 252.
43. Jeffery, *MI6*, p. 81.
44. Judge, article entitled 'Ladies of the Intelligence Corps', p. 1, November 2019, Military Intelligence Museum.
45. Information from the Military Intelligence Museum.
46. Charlotte and Sylvia Bosworth were the sisters of Lieutenant Arthur F. Bosworth (Intelligence Corps) and Major L.O. Bosworth.
47. Judge, 'The Intelligence Corps, 1914 to 1929', p. 41, Military Intelligence Museum.
48. The special passes of Charlotte and Sylvia Bosworth for the French War Office are held in the Military Intelligence Museum.
49. Clarke's 'History of Room 40', p. 149, HW 3/3.
50. Diary of Mavis Peel, pp. 9–10, Military Intelligence Museum.
51. Ibid., p. 7.
52. Ibid., p. 21.
53. Mavis Peel founded the Rouen branch of the British Legion. Her medals are in the Military Intelligence Museum.
54. The story is told in full by Janet Morgan in *The Secrets of Rue St Roch*.
55. The postcard was addressed c/o Madame Fresez-Settegast at Villa Allmer in Grindelwald.

56. *Herald*, Scotland, 30 July 2004, and *Guardian*, 7 August 2004.
57. Smith, *Six*, p. 83.

Chapter 3: Intelligence on the Home Front

1. Fred Judge, 'Ladies of the Intelligence Corps', p. 2, November 2019.
2. For the early wartime work of Room 40, see its logbook and diary, 1914–15, ADM 223/767.
3. Paul Gannon, *Inside Room 40*, p. 149.
4. A list of their names appears in William F. Clarke's history of Room 40, pp. 147–8, HW 3/3.
5. Gannon, *Inside Room 40*, p. 24.
6. HW 3/35.
7. The women who stayed on with Denniston were Misses Anderson, Watkins, Spurling and Haylar and Lunn (the latter two as translators).
8. In subsequent years, the headquarters would move to several different locations. From September 1912 to August 1916, it was at Watergate House, York buildings on the Strand; then from February 1915 to August 1916 at Adelphi Court as an extension to Watergate House and still on the Strand. From August 1916 to December 1919, still under the name of Watergate House, the HQ moved to 16 Charles Street (now Charles II Street in Haymarket, SW1).
9. Report on women's work in MI5, April 1920, KV 1/50.
10. Around 400 women were employed in the Registry, and over 200 as clerks across MI5 and other roles.
11. Report dated 17 October 1915, KV 2/822.
12. Report on women's work in MI5, April 1920, KV 1/50.
13. H1 covered office records, reports, specialists; H2 registration and indexing; H3 distribution of correspondence; H4 finance; H5 control, selection and discipline of female clerks; H6 War Office and interviews; H7 office routines; H8 Black lists; and H9 Military Intelligence index. See KV 1/50 and KV 1/63. For more detailed study of each section, see declassified files at the National Archives and Andrew, *Defence of the Realm*.
14. Andrew, *Defence of the Realm*, p. 60.
15. Report on women's work in MI5, April 1920, KV 1/50.
16. Report, p. 10, KV 1/54.
17. The full list of qualifications for female clerks is contained in the report of KV 1/54: a high sense of honour, discretion and reliability, sound common sense, accuracy, readiness to take responsibility, keenness, physical fitness, good temper and tact.
18. Andrew, *Defence of the Realm*, p. 60.
19. Report on women's work in MI5, p. 19, April 1920, KV 1/50.
20. Report, p. 11, KV 1/54.
21. Report on women's work in MI5, p. 49, April 1920, KV 1/50.
22. The women were Miss D. Bowie, Miss H.M. Cribb, Miss E.L. Harrison, Miss S. Holmes and Miss H.M. Newport. *London Gazette*, 2 September 1918.
23. Miss L.H. Andrew, Miss A.D. Bliss, Miss G. Buckler, Miss F. Dalton, Mrs M.D. George, Miss V. Herne, Miss Betty Hodgson and Miss H. Matheson. *London Gazette*, 18 August 1919.
24. KV 1/50.
25. Report on Special Branch, KV 4/443.

26. Report by Sir Trevor Bingham, 23 March 1929, MEPO 2/9844.
27. They were listed as Misses Bidwell, Eggett, Mayer, Symons, Tirrell, Stirling, Molesworth, Capleton, Bracey, Appleton, Dunning and Penley in MEPO 2/9844.
28. Letter dated 11 April 1928, MEPO 2/9844.
29. Sir Trevor Bingham, 23 March 1929, MEPO 2/9844.
30. Letter dated 7 May 1932, MEPO 2/9844.
31. 'History of Intelligence, British Expeditionary Force, France, from January 1917 to April 1919: The Secret Service', pp. 19–21, WO 106/45. See also Clayton, *Forearmed*, p. 56.

Chapter 4: Spies and Infiltrators

1. For MI5's surveillance of Edith Suschitzky, see KV 2/1012.
2. Henry Hemming, *M: Maxwell Knight, MI5's Greatest Spymaster*, p. 91.
3. Joan Miller, *One Girl's War*, p. 19.
4. 'Notes which might be useful for cross-examination at the Old Bailey trial', KV 2/1022.
5. Undated report, KV 2/1022.
6. Report dated 22 February 1934, KV 2/1020.
7. CX/ correspondence dated 28 February 1938, from MI6 to Miss Sissmore at MI5, KV 2/1022.
8. The photographs, which survive in Glading's MI5 file, were taken ahead of Glading's trial at the Old Bailey in March 1938.
9. Valentine Vivian to MI5, 24 February 1938, KV 2/1020.
10. Guy Liddell's diary, entry for 13 October 1939, in Nigel West (ed.), *The Guy Liddell Diaries*, vol. 1.
11. Report, 26 January 1942, KV 2/1023.
12. Anthony Masters, *The Man Who Was M*, p. 77.
13. Details of the case in KV 4/227.
14. See his MI5 file, KV 2/2257.
15. Wolkoff case is in MI5 files, KV 2/2257, KV 2/2258 and KV 2/2259.
16. Hemming, *M*, p. 252.
17. Bernard O'Connor, *Agent Fifi*, p. 133.
18. Hemming, *M*, p. 217.
19. Andrew, *Defence of the Realm*, p. 182. This information was found by Andrew in the Security Service Archives.
20. Robert Hutton, *Agent Jack*, pp. 132–6.
21. The KV file notes that she still had a brother in Austria who was described as violently pro-Nazi. Gartner's original address in Austria was 30 Heidel, Wels, Austria.
22. For a biography of Kendrick, see Fry, *Spymaster*.
23. Report from Stewart Menzies to Guy Liddell of MI5, 18 May 1938, KV 2/1280.
24. MI5 report, 30 May 1938, KV 2/1280.
25. MI5 to Stewart Menzies at MI6, 21 September 1938, KV 2/1280.
26. Report, 28 September 1938, KV 2/1280. Eight photographs of Friedl Gartner survive in her original MI5 files but these photographs have been retained under Section 3(4) of the Official Secrets Act.
27. In September 1938, Gärtner visited a married friend in the south of France. She brought back intelligence that the Germans had decided to make her hometown of Wels, upper Austria, an increasingly important centre for German military strategy.

Her friend told her that there had been an increase in German activity there, including the construction of military barracks and a new camouflaged aerodrome.
28. Details in her personal file KV 2/1280.
29. 'Anglo-German Fellowship dinner, Claridge's Hotel, October 19th', report dated 24 October 1938, KV 2/1280.
30. MI5 report, 15 November 1938, KV 2/1280.
31. Report on Weissblatt, 3 January 1939, KV 2/1280.
32. Report, 30 November 1938, KV 2/1280.
33. Report, 29 February 1939, KV 2/1280.
34. Gärtner's full report on Greene is dated April 1940, KV 2/1280.
35. Hemming, *M*, p. 337.
36. Ibid., *M*, p. 293.

Chapter 5: Secret Secretaries

1. Jeffery, *MI6*, p. 202.
2. Fry, *Spymaster*.
3. Michael Smith, *Foley*.
4. The first problem is establishing the names of the SIS secretaries before any research can be carried out to find out the nature of their work. Occasionally, their names appear in general lists of personnel in Foreign Office files. For example, the women who were recalled to MI6 headquarters from passport control offices across Europe after Kendrick's arrest by the Gestapo in mid-August 1938. Recalled from Vienna were Miss Steedman, Miss Birkett, Miss Mapleston, Miss Wood and Mrs Howe; from Berlin, Miss de Fossard, Miss Lloyd, Miss St Clair and Miss Molesworth (the latter worked for MI5 prior to the 1920s); and from Prague, Miss Williams.
5. Kenneth Benton, 'The ISOS Years: Madrid 1941–3', *Journal of Contemporary History*, vol. 30, no. 3 (July 1995), pp. 362–3.
6. Evelyn Stamper died in 1960.
7. Interviews with daughter Prudence Hopkinson.
8. Ibid.
9. Unpublished short memoir, held by the family.
10. Hanns Vischer transferred to Vienna for a short time, returning to Africa in the 1920s. In the Second World War he was stationed at Bletchley Park. Jeffery, *MI6*, pp. 201–2.
11. From 1936 until 1946, Carlile Aylmer Macartney was in charge of the Hungarian section of the Foreign Office Research Department.
12. For espionage in Vienna in 1933/34, see Fry, *Spymaster*.
13. Jeffery, *MI6*, p. 363.
14. Interview with the author, February 2022.
15. Letter 19 March 1938 from Phyllis Bottome to Frank and Esther Adams, Ms 88921/3/1. Phyllis Bottome archive at the British Library.
16. Frank Foley, SIS chief of station in Berlin, saved over 10,000 German Jews. See Smith, *Foley: The Spy who Saved 10,000 Jews*.
17. Marjorie 'Peggy' Weller was born in 1910.
18. Smith, *Foley*, p. 125.
19. Interview with Prudence Hopkinson.
20. Short unpublished memoir held by the family.
21. Letter dated 10 July 1939, copy given to the author by the family.

22. For a list of secret and confidential files destroyed, see FO 741/4.
23. During the war, Arthur Knight had been a liaison officer for the Ministry of Economic Warfare and SOE. Obituary in the *Daily Telegraph* and the *Guardian*, 10 April 2003.
24. For a full explanation, see the Afterword in Fry, *Spymaster*.
25. *Guardian*, 16 April 1985.
26. Peter Lane, *Princess Michael of Kent*, p. 36.
27. 'Marianne Szápáry – interview for *The Times* of London', 24 April 1985.
28. Barry Everingham, *MC*, p. 24; and 'Marianne Szapáry – interview for *The Times* of London', 24 April 1985. See also Fry, *Spymaster*.
29. The Germans had produced a basket which could be lowered from the Zeppelin and, using a variety of equipment, could collect intelligence on sites below.
30. Towards the end of the war in 1945 it meant that Countess Marianne endured the permanent presence of an SS officer at the family estate. See 'Marianne Szápáry – interview for *The Times* of London', 24 April 1985.
31. Fry, *Spymaster*.
32. Smith, *MI6*, p. 341.
33. Ibid., p. 354.
34. Ibid., p. 151. I am grateful to Michael Smith (Foley's biographer) for his help with research material.
35. Andrew, *Defence of the Realm*, p. 132.
36. Ibid., p. 132.
37. Ibid., p. 122.
38. 'Centenary of Women's Suffrage – 100 Years of Women in MI5', https://www.mi5.gov.uk/news/celebrating-vote-100.
39. Ibid.
40. Andrew, *Defence of the Realm*, p. 268.
41. Liddell's diary, entry for 18 November 1940, in West (ed.), *The Guy Liddell Diaries*, vol. 1.
42. Ibid., entry for 20 November 1940.
43. Andrew, *Defence of the Realm*, p. 131.
44. Obituary, *Guardian*, 17 June 2006.
45. Teresa 'Tess' Mayor (later Rothschild) was born in September 1915, died May 1996. Obituary, *Independent*, 30 May 1996.
46. Liddell's diary, entry for 21 March 1945, in West (ed.), *The Guy Liddell Diaries*, vol. 2.

Chapter 6: The Codebreakers

1. Tessa Dunlop, *The Bletchley Girls*, p. 33.
2. Obituary, *Guardian*,1 November 1995.
3. Obituary, *Independent*, 1 November 1995.
4. In India Margaret Godfrey was active as secretary of the Women's Voluntary Services, responsible for welfare work, for which she was awarded the Kaiser I Hind medal, awarded by the emperor for public service in India.
5. Michael Smith, *The Debs of Bletchley Park*, and Dunlop, *The Bletchley Girls*.
6. Obituary, *Herald*, 18 October 2017.
7. *The Intelligence Factory* exhibition, Bletchley Park.
8. 'General Report on Tunny: With Emphasis on Statistical Methods', 1945, HW 25/4 and HW 25/5.

9. Obituary by Michael Smith, *Daily Telegraph*, 28 August 2018.
10. Ibid.
11. Ibid.
12. Ibid.
13. Obituary, *Daily Telegraph*, 15 February 2013.
14. Ibid. See also her memoir: Sarah Baring, *The Road to Station X.*
15. Dunlop, *The Bletchley Girls*, p. 175.
16. Smith, *The Debs of Bletchley Park*, pp. 154–5.
17. John Ferris, *Behind the Enigma*, p. 437.
18. For a biography of Emily Anderson, see Jackie Uí Chionna, *Queen of Codes*.
19. Obituary by Michael Smith, *Guardian*, 12 May 2021.
20. For a history of Hut 8, see HW 25/2 and HW 50/65.
21. Joel Greenberg, *Gordon Welchman*, p. 37.
22. Obituary, *Daily Telegraph*, 25 May 2016, and *New York Times*, 28 May 2016.
23. Obituary, *Daily Telegraph*, 25 May 2016.
24. For a full profile of her career at Bletchley, see Smith, *The Debs of Bletchley Park*, pp. 34ff.
25. Ibid., p. 38.
26. After the war, Jane Hughes trained as a professional singer. She married Ted Fawcett, a former Royal Navy officer.
27. In the late 1970s, under her married name Joan Murray, she produced a document for the US National Security Agency about her personal memories of Turing's bombe development.
28. Robert McCrum, 'Women Spies in the Second World War', *Observer*, 7 November 2010.
29. Ibid.
30. Obituary, *Observer*, 7 November 2010.
31. Tessa Dunlop, 'An Unlikely Asset', 9 April 2016, DangerousWomenProject.org.
32. Obituary, *Guardian*, 13 November 2013.
33. Smith, *The Debs of Bletchley Park*, p. 176.
34. Ibid., pp. 180–1.
35. By 2 December 1940, Hut 6 had 93 staff, Hut 3 had 60, Hut 8 had 37 and Hut 4 had 40.
36. Denniston, a codebreaker in Room 40, was appointed deputy head of GC&CS in 1919, and Travis was a cryptographer on naval cyphers. Travis became the first head of GCHQ in 1946.
37. Letter from Welchman to Travis, from Room 11 in Hut 6, dated 4 July 1941, HW 14/17.
38. Letter dated 10 July 1941, HW 14/17.
39. Report of 31 July 1941, HW 14/17.
40. Ralph Curtis of MI6(e), Hut 3 to Denniston, 23 October 41, HW 14/21.
41. Greenberg, *Gordon Welchman*, p. 46.
42. Curtis to Saunders, 23 October 1941, HW 14/21.
43. Undated and unsigned report, HW 14/21.
44. Correspondence about Travis's increase in personnel is contained in HW 14/48 and HW 14/50.
45. Obituary, *Daily Telegraph*, 22 March 2018.
46. Ibid.
47. Obituary, *Herald*, 5 February 2018.

48. At the height of the Cold War, Caroline Chojecki and her husband set up a card index of the extensive intelligence uncovered by the Soviet Studies Research Centre (SSRC), established in 1972 to gather intelligence from open-source material on Soviet military capabilities. Caroline's achievements were recognised by the mid-1980s and she was invited to the US Army Combined Arms Center, Fort Leavenworth, to provide advice on establishing a similar system there.
49. Correspondence with Richard Aldwinckle.
50. Obituary, *Guardian*, 13 July 2020.
51. For a history of the UK–US special relationship, see Michael Smith, *The Real Special Relationship*.
52. Obituary, *Guardian*, 13 July 2020.
53. Richard Aldwinckle, 'Helene Aldwinckle – Dulwich's Secret Codebreaker', https://www.dulwichsociety.com/the-journal/winter-2022/helene-aldwincke.
54. Qwatch worked in Room 64, which adjoined Watch A, and Room 78, with thirteen personnel across the two rooms.
55. John Jackson, *Solving Enigma's Secrets*, p. 152.
56. Or P was possibly Puma, a key also managed by the Qwatch and used by the German air force to deal with Axis army–air cooperation in Sicily and afterwards during Allied operations in northern Italy.
57. Helene and John married in February 1945, and he worked in RAF intelligence and with MI6. Helene worked as a broadcaster for the British Forces Network.
58. The official history is now declassified in HW 43/72.
59. 'Women in Diplomacy: The FCO, 1782–1999', pp. 11–12.
60. Obituary, *The Times*, 27 September 2021.
61. 'I Wanted to Do Something More for the War Effort Than Bake Sausage Rolls', *National Geographic*, 6 May 2020.
62. Dunlop, *The Bletchley Girls*, p. 153.
63. Permanent exhibition entitled *The Intelligence Factory*, Block A, Bletchley Park.
64. Ferris, *Behind the Enigma*, p. 213. The official numbers were Wrens, 2,594; ATS 408; WAAF 1,096; and civilians 2,660. See *The Intelligence Factory* exhibition.
65. I am grateful for the support of Melissa Davis of the George C. Marshall Foundation in Lexington (USA), which holds the archive of Elizebeth Smith Friedman.
66. For a history of Beaumanor, see Joan Nicholls, *England Needs You*.
67. For a history of the Radio Security Service, see David Abrutat, *Radio War: The Secret Espionage War of the Radio Security Service 1938–1946*.
68. Telephone interviews with the author on 22 May and 4 June 2004.
69. According to the archivist of the Vienna Symphony Orchestra, there were no women in the orchestra in the 1930s. A similar enquiry to the Vienna Philharmonic Orchestra was inconclusive.
70. Helen Fry, *Jews in North Devon during the Second World War*, pp. 157–60.
71. Edmund David Fry, *The Life and Times of a Knowle Boy*, p. 12.
72. *Short Wave Magazine*, vol. 11, no. 2, April 1938, p. 21.
73. It has not been possible to find the citation for which she was awarded the BEM, however – it possibly remains within the unreleased MI6 files.
74. Information provided by the late Ted Verney of Barnstaple and Vic Thompson, who received information regarding Myler's work on detecting submarines.
75. Myler died on 23 August 1948 and is buried in the disused cemetery in Ilfracombe.
76. Fry, *Jews in North Devon*, p. 159.

Chapter 7: When the Walls Had Ears

1. For a biography of Thomas Kendrick, see Fry, *Spymaster*.
2. Ibid.
3. For a detailed history of the life of the generals at Trent Park, see Fry, *The Walls Have Ears*.
4. Pauline Rubin, unpublished reminiscences, 12 December 1992.
5. Catherine Jestin, *A War Bride's Story*, p. 225.
6. Correspondence in WO 208/3437.
7. See WO 208/3248, Appendix C. There were women intelligence personnel at the CSDIC sites abroad in Cairo, Algiers, Italy, the Middle East and the Far East. For CSDIC Algiers, see WO 208/3461.
8. WO 208/3248, Appendix C.
9. Family correspondence with the author.
10. Interview with the author, 2013.
11. Jestin, *A War Bride's Story*, p. 204. Catherine Townshend became Jestinsky/Jestin after her marriage in 1945.
12. Diary entry, copy sent to the author.
13. Jestin, *A War Bride's Story*, p. 229.
14. Ibid., p. 211.
15. 'The history of CSDIC', WO 208/4970. See also WO 165/41, July 1943.
16. Jestin, *A War Bride's Story*, p. 215.
17. Ibid.
18. Details of MI19(e) in WO 208/3554.
19. The bulk of the files of Camp 020 have been declassified at the National Archives in series KV. See also Oliver Hoare, *Camp 020: MI5 and Nazi Spies*.
20. Jestin, *A War Bride's Story*, pp. 230–1.
21. Doust to Jestinsky, 11 May 1945, WO 208/3554.
22. Doust to Jestinsky, 9 June 1945, WO 208/3554.
23. Equipment supplied to 5th Army CI Section for use in Austria, dated 13 July 1945, WO 208/3554.
24. Jestin, *A War Bride's Story*, p. 234.
25. Ibid., p. 223.
26. Interrogation section in paper entitled 'No. 9 intelligence school', in WO 208/3242.
27. Evelyn Barron, interview with the author; see also Fry, *The Walls Have Ears*, p. 50. Information confirmed in ADM 223/257 and ADM 223/472.
28. Personnel lists in ADM 223/257.
29. Interview with the author.
30. S/O Hughes drafted a summary report on this on behalf of Major I/O, dated 23 January 1944 for IS9(W), WO 208/3248.
31. Paper entitled 'No. 9 intelligence school', in WO 208/3242.
32. Colin McFadyean's report, ADM 223/84.
33. 'Intelligence from Prisoners of War', section 289, AIR 40/2636.
34. Interviews with Susan Lustig by the author across a decade of research.
35. Ibid.
36. Fritz Lustig, *My Lucky Life*.
37. Interview with the author.
38. Jestin, *A War Bride's Story*, p. 211.
39. Rubin, unpublished reminiscences.

Chapter 8: Women of Naval Intelligence

1. Donald McLachlan, *Room 39* and C.I. Hamilton, 'The Character and Organization of the Admiralty Operational Intelligence Centre during the Second World War', *War in History* (July 2000), pp. 295–324.
2. Godfrey, quoted in footnote on p. 418 of McLachlan, *Room 39*.
3. Details of the work of each section is covered by ADM 223/472.
4. Another NID section producing geographical handbooks was based at Cambridge and consisted primarily of a male workforce.
5. Personnel list for 1944, naval censorship abroad, ADM 223/257.
6. From August 1943, the chief officer in charge of censorship was First Officer Mrs Dent, WRNS. Second Officer Mrs Baker was deputy officer in charge. Mrs Cooper and Miss Guthrie were in charge of other mobile sections.
7. Second Officer (S/O) J. Stewart was in charge of the first unit of the mobile naval section of Censorship, Postal and Daily Telegraph. S/O N.A. Ford headed the second unit; S/O D. Sinclair Scott the third unit, and S/O I.R. Kerr was in charge of trainees.
8. The Suez section was run by Second Officer Miss E. Webb, and Haifa, Palestine, by Second Officer Miss M. Fletcher. The post at Port Said was operated by Second Officer Miss J. Sykes and Third Officer Miss F. Cousins.
9. Kristie Macrakis, *Prisoners, Lovers and Spies*, p. 228.
10. Author's correspondence with Michael Smith.
11. 'History of Room 29 from March 1943 to 1945', written by Miss Kiddy, in ADM 223/286.
12. Ibid., p. 2.
13. 'History of Room 29 . . .', in ADM 223/286, and Patrick Beesly, *Very Special Intelligence*.
14. For life in the OIC, see 'Reminiscences of the O.I.C', by Margaret Stewart, ADM 223/286.
15. The four new women were Mrs C. Church, Mrs B. Llewellyn, Mrs P. Tweedie and Miss J. Lewis-Smith.
16. 'Reminiscences of the O.I.C', by Margaret Stewart, ADM 223/286.
17. Ibid., p. 4.
18. Ben Macintyre, *Operation Mincemeat*, pp. 27–8.
19. 'Organisation and history of Naval Intelligence Section 12', ADM 223/792.
20. Macintyre, *Operation Mincemeat*, p. 73.
21. Copy of her personal service record given to the author.
22. Barbara Bond, *Great Escapes*, p. 15. Photograph attributed to Getty Images.
23. 'Reminiscences of the O.I.C', by Margaret Stewart, p. 9, ADM 223/286.

Chapter 9: Eyes in the Sky

1. Christine Halsall, *Women of Intelligence*, p. 20.
2. Taylor Downing, *Spies in the Sky*, p. 39.
3. Halsall, *Women of Intelligence*, p. 29.
4. Ibid., p. 23.
5. Downing, *Spies in the Sky*, p. 73–6. For the WAAF in intelligence roles, see Sarah-Louise Miller, *The Women Behind the Few*.
6. Halsall, *Women of Intelligence*, p. 24.
7. For an overview of the work of each section, see 'The Chalk House with the Tudor Chimneys', published by the Medmenham Collection. Photographic interpretation

was carried out at other sites, as well as other RAF bases, including Morecambe and Bomber Command at High Wycombe, RAF Benson, near Wallingford (Oxfordshire); RAF St Eval, near Wadebridge (Cornwall); RAF Wick (Aberdeenshire); and RAF Leuchars on the coast of Fyfe, Scotland.

8. Halsall, *Women of Intelligence*, p. 109.
9. The Chalk House, p. 55.
10. Ibid., p. 156.
11. Ibid., p. 24.
12. She had read history at Newnham College, Cambridge, but, because women could not formally be awarded degrees, she was given only a certificate. She was formally awarded her degree by Cambridge University in 1948.
13. Constance Babington Smith, *Evidence in Camera*, p. 154.
14. Downing, *Spies in the Sky*, p. 288.
15. Ibid., p. 295.
16. Halsall, *Women of Intelligence*, p. 189.
17. Ibid., p. 225.
18. Downing, *Spies in the Sky*, p. 342.
19. Halsall, *Women of Intelligence*, p. 220.

Chapter 10: Double Cross Agents

1. Masterman's history of Double Cross, p. 27f, KV 4/5.
2. Benton, 'The ISOS Years', p. 359.
3. The Twenty Committee was a sub-committee of the 'W Board'. The 'W Board' was made up of the directors of Intelligence. The Twenty Committee had representatives from MI5, MI6, Naval Intelligence Division, the London Controlling Section (LCS), MI11 and later the Supreme Headquarters Allied Expeditionary Force (SHAEF).
4. Smith, *Foley*.
5. Mrs A.M. Pitt appears to have been head of a section within B.1.g and wrote up counter-espionage reports. Report by Pitt to Harmer of B.1.A (MI5), 11 December 1942, KV 2/2098.
6. For the Venlo incident, see FO 1093/200 and FO 1093/201, and Jeffery, *MI6*, p. 382–6.
7. Ben Macintyre, *Double Cross*, p. 152.
8. Gleam was a notional member of Garbo's organisation named Theresa Jardine.
9. Liddell's diary entry for 6 August 1943 notes that Robertson came to see him about running 'Josephine' for deception. She was a female agent run by Richmond Stopford. Two entries exist for 'Redhead' in the minutes of the Twenty Committee, August 1942, KV 4/65.
10. 'Machinery of deception outside NID', p. 14, ADM 223/794.
11. Letter from Stewart Menzies to John Masterman, 11 June 1942, KV 4/65.
12. Appendix to Masterman's report mentions around 120 double cross agents in MI5 records.
13. Report by Frank Foley (MI6), 26 May 1942, KV 2/1275.
14. MI5 memo, 13 September 1939, KV 2/1275.
15. Letter to New Scotland Yard, 27 September 1939, KV 2/1275.
16. Anthony Cave Brown, *C: The Secret Life of Sir Stewart Graham Menzies, Spymaster to Winston Churchill*, p. 306.
17. Dusko Popov, *Spy, Counter-Spy*, pp. 73–4.
18. Ibid., p. 72.

19. Ibid., p. 83.
20. Extensive details are contained in Tricycle's personal MI5 files: KV 2/845–KV 2/866.
21. MI5 report, 27 February 1941, KV 2/1275.
22. Report by Bill Luke, 18 May 1941, KV 2/1275.
23. Tricycle's report, 1 May 1941, KV 2/1275.
24. MI5 report, 7 April 1942, KV 2/1275.
25. Memo, 5 March 1942, KV 2/1275. Examples of her writing in secret ink survive in her personal MI5 file.
26. Liddell's diary, entries for 7 June 1943 and 22 October 1943, in West (ed.), *The Guy Liddell Diaries*, vol. 2.
27. 'Paper for Discussion', p. 3, ADM 223/794.
28. Report by Bill Luke, 18 May 1941, KV 2/1275. Hess had his own intelligence organisation called the Verbindungstab. See Popov, *Spy, Counter-Spy*, p. 55.
28. As is clear in the Hess files in the FO 1093 series.
30. Report by Bill Luke, 18 May 1941, KV 2/1275.
31. Balloon's personal files: KV 2/1070 to KV 2/1083.
32. See also report dated 26 May 1942 from Foley to MI5 about Balloon in KV 2/1275.
33. He received £358.4.2 from the Germans in July 1942 and £325 in October 1942.
34. The address was 164 Rue da Rosa, Lisbon.
35. Report, 10 May 1942, KV 2/1275.
36. MI5 report, 7 April 1942, KV 2/1275.
37. Report 10 April 1942, KV 2/1275.
38. Report 22 April 1942, KV 2/1275. Wilson made similar accusations again in a report of 9 May 1942.
39. Frank Foley directed Gelatine's operations to the XX Committee and acted as liaison on behalf of MI6. Correspondence between Frank Foley and Robertson, June 1942, KV 2/1275.
40. John Masterman, *The Double-Cross System*, p. 87.
41. Ibid., p. 136–47.
42. Urgent message from Cowgill (SIS) to Marriott (MI5), KV 2/1275.
43. Present at the meeting were Cowgill and Foley (SIS) and Marriott (MI5), Masterman and Wilson.
44. Masterman, *The Double-Cross System*, pp. 220ff.
45. It used double agents Gelatine, Father, Mutt, Jeff, Tate, Garbo, Careless, Balloon and Dragonfly.
46. 'Extract from SIS file on Cyril', 9 January 1942, KV 2/2098.
47. In the early part of the war the interrogators were based at a camp at Cockfosters, in North London.
48. Elvira Chaudoir's personal file, KV 2/2098.
49. Jimmy Langley, *Fight Another Day*, p. 132. See also Anthony Read and David Fisher, *Colonel Z*, pp. 268–9.
50. 'Paper for discussion', p. 3, ADM 223/794.
51. For Beau Baschwitz's background see Morgan, *The Secrets of Rue St Roch*.
52. 'Extract from SIS file on Cyril', 9 January 1942, KV 2/2098. This is a rare extract because her SIS file has not been released.
53. Letter from NID to Guy Liddell (MI5), 12 April 1942, KV 2/2098.

54. CX/22666/A, 4 June 1942, KV 2/2098.
55. MI5 to Kim Philby (SIS), 1 May 1942, KV 2/2098.
56. Report by J.C. Masterman, 21 October 1942, KV2/2098.
57. Interrogation report titled 'Cyril', dated 16 November 1942, KV 2/2098.
58. Report by J.C. Masterman, 21 October 1942, KV2/2098.
59. Summary report for the XX Committee, 4 November 1942, KV 2/2098.
60. 'Paper for discussion', p. 3, ADM 223/794.
61. T.A. Robertson to Frank Foley, 11 July 1943, KV 2/2098.
62. CX/12678/DK, H.A.R. Philby to Christopher H. Harmer at MI5, 11 December 1942, KV 2/2098.
63. SIS to MI5, 30 September 1942, KV 2/2098.
64. Between March 1943 and December 1943, Bronx received over £1,400 from the Germans.
65. Report dated 15 March 1944, KV 2/2098.
66. Report by Harmer, 2 September 1943, KV 2/2098.
67. Ibid.
68. Summary report to Major Robertson by C.H. Harmer, 25 February 1943, KV 2/2098.
69. On 23 July 1943 Bronx received another £88 for her monthly salary and a further £360 on 16 August 1943 that year.
70. Masterman's history of Double Cross, p. 66, KV 4/5.
71. Scant details have appeared in KV 4/10.
72. Entry for 13 August 1942, Minutes of the Twenty Committee, KV 4/65.
73. Entry for 20 August 1942, KV 4/65. Other agents who appear fleetingly in the files include Jeannot, an I-Heer female agent. Her identity is not given and it is not clear for whom she was working. Minutes of the 212 Committee, 30 October 1944, KV 4/101.
74. The Snark's files have been released: KV 2/669 to KV 2/673.
75. 'Life story of The Snark', report 29 July 1941, KV 2/669.
76. Liddell's diary, entry for 26 July 1941, in West (ed.), *The Guy Liddell Diaries*, vol. 1.
77. Marriot to Cowgill, 29 July 1941, KV 2/669.
78. An interrogation report, 29 July 1941, KV 2/699.
79. Cyril Mills' report, July 1941, KV 2/699.
80. Letter from Masterman to Cowgill 27 July 1941, KV 2/669.
81. Details in KV 2/670.
82. Sherer's report, 27 August 1941, KV 2/670.
83. Letter 19 September 1941, KV 2/670.
84. Letter dated 6 August 1941, KV 2/670.
85. 'Paper for discussion', p. 3, ADM 223/794.
86. Minutes for 13 July 1944, KV 4/68.
87. Sergueiev's MI5 personal files are in KV 2/464 to KV 2/466.
88. Interrogation of Treasure by Captain R.H. Osborne, 14 November 1943.
89. Memo by Mary Sherer, 14 November 1943, KV 2/464.
90. Liddell's diary, entry for 18 November 1943, in West (ed.), *The Guy Liddell Diaries*, vol. 2.
91. December 1943, KV 2/465.
92. Masterman's history of Double Cross, p. 78, KV 4/5.
93. Nigel West, *Hitler's Nest of Vipers*, p. xxxii.

94. Jeffery, *MI6*, p. 570.
95. Peter Day, *The Bedbug*, pp. 175–6.
96. Nigel West and Oleg Tsarev, *Triplex*.
97. KV 4/192, p. 104. The word 'Triplex' has been blanked out in the original diary entry when it was declassified. The real identity of this agent is obscure and might be fictitious.
98. J.G. Dickson to Anthony Blunt, 19 April 1945, in Nigel West and Oleg Tsarev, *Triplex*, p. 24.
99. For Plan Hegira, instigated in March 1941, see KV 4/211.
100. Order issued on 3 April 1941, KV 4/211.
101. Letter from Captain Finney (in Wales) to Robertson, 9 April 1941, KV 4/211.
102. SIS instructions issued on 3 December 1941.
103. 'Victoire' (an SIS/SOE agent) and 'Mrs Weasel' were to be placed on a suspect list for arrest in an emergency. Reasons for this were not given.
104. Instructions issued on 24 July 1942, KV 4/211.

Chapter 11: Double Cross Deception

1. Masterman, *The Double-Cross System*, p. 182.
2. Diary entry for 29 April 1943, KV 4/66.
3. ADM 223/794.
4. Minutes, 10 May 1945, KV 4/70.
5. For a history, see 'Organisation and history of Naval Intelligence Section 12', ADM 223/792. Montagu was appointed head of the section towards the end of November 1940,
6. The women listed as working in Sections 17M and 17P of NID 12 were Mrs Helen Mary Brown, Mrs Joan Saunders, Mrs J.P. Fenley, Miss Patricia Trehearne, and Miss Marjorie Boxall. Typists and clerical were Miss K. Tattersall, Mrs Robbins, Miss Barnes, Miss S. McCarthy, Mrs Onslow, Miss Vera Sylvester, Miss Juliette Ponsonby and Miss P. Hall. Section 17P dealt with non-operational Special Intelligence. See personnel listed in 'Organisation and history of NID Section 12', ADM 223/792. The section also used female agents to gather gossip at cocktail parties. See 'Deception on naval matters', ADM 223/794.
7. For Montagu's report on Operation Mincemeat, see entry for 6 May 1943, KV 4/66.
8. Report, 22 October 1945, WO 208/3163.
9. Report on Operation Mincemeat, 23 April 1943, p. 14, ADM 223/794.
10. Ibid.
11. Appendix: Proof of success of Mincemeat, ADM 223/794.
12. Masterman's history of Double Cross, p. 79, KV 4/5.
13. 'Machinery of deception outside NID', pp. 4–5, ADM 223/794.
14. Liddell's diary, entry for 20 February 1944, in West (ed.), *The Guy Liddell Diaries*, vol. 2. Details also in KV 4/67.
15. Minutes for 9 March 1944, KV 4/67.
16. Minutes for 15 June 1944, KV 4/68.
17. Minutes for 28 May 1944, KV 4/67.
18. MI5 history – footnote 80.
19. Minutes 19 May 1944, KV 4/67.
20. Liddell's diary, entry for 28 May 1944, in West (ed.), *The Guy Liddell Diaries*, vol. 2.

21. 'Machinery of deception outside NID', p. 12, ADM 223/794.
22. For the male double agents, see their individual MI5 files and Ben Macintyre, *Double Cross*.
23. Masterman, *The Double-Cross System*, p. 153.
24. Minutes, 8 June 1944, KV 4/68.
25. Bronx's plain language code is in KV 2/2098.
26. Masterman's history of Double Cross, KV 4/5. Report entitled 'Bronx and Plan Ironside', 25 May 1944, KV 2/2098.
27. Liddell diary, entry 20 September 1944.
28. Report dated 27 May 1944, KV 2/2098.
29. Report on Bronx's activities, 13 July 1944, KV 2/2098.
30. Masterman, *The Double-Cross System*, p. 186.
31. T.A. Robertson to Frank Foley, 15 February 1944, KV 2/2098.
32. Minutes, 10 May 1945, KV 4/70.
33. Liddell's diary, entry for 1 January 1945, in West (ed.), *The Guy Liddell Diaries*, vol. 2.
34. Kliemann was the Abwehr handler for MI5's double agents Brutus, Dragonfly, Weasel, Basket and Job.
35. Minutes for 28 September 1944, KV 4/68 and Liddell's diary, entry 24 September 1944, in West (ed.), *The Guy Liddell Diaries*, vol. 2. For a history of the bugging operation, see Fry, *The Walls Have Ears*.
36. Memo from D.I. Wilson, 23 October 1944, KV 4/68, which reported from Captain Davis (interrogator of CSDIC) that Kliemann had suggested British intelligence should use Treasure and Dragonfly as agents.
37. Liddell's diary, 22 October 1944, in West (ed.), *The Guy Liddell Diaries*, vol. 2.
38. Minutes for 20 July 1944, KV 4/68.
39. Liddell's diary, entry for 13 November 1944, in West (ed.), *The Guy Liddell Diaries*, vol. 2.
40. Masterman, *The Double-Cross System*, p. 174.
41. Ibid., footnote on pp. 174–5.
42. Minutes, 23 November 1944, KV 4/69.
43. Minutes, 9 November 1944, KV 4/69.
44. Minutes, 30 November 1944, KV 4/69.
45. Minutes 14 December 1944, KV 4/67.
46. Minutes for 17 March 1945, KV 4/68.
47. Known agents working for Double Cross were Gleam, Bullseye, Sunrise, Purple Whale, Hiccups, Angel I, Father, Pawnbroker, Doubtful, Audrey, Silver, Mary Oliver, Mary Tom, and Mary Rhino. Minutes for 18 January 1945, KV 4/68.
48. Gleam's traffic had some bearing on the work of Sunrise. See 19 October 1944, KV 4/69.
49. Minutes for 25 January 1945, KV 4/68.
50. Minutes for 8 February 1945, KV 4/69.
51. Minutes for 26 October 1944, KV 4/69.
52. Minutes for 11 January and 25 January 1945, KV 4/68.
53. Friedrich Blaum, KV 2/1976.
54. Peter Day, *The Bedbug*, p. 176.
55. Liddell's diary, entry for 23 February 1945, in West (ed.), *The Guy Liddell Diaries*, vol. 2.
56. Ibid., 22 February 1945.

57. Copy of text of Bronx's letter in correspondence from Hugh Astor to Marriott, 7 August 1944, KV 2/2098.
58. Bronx died in the south of France in 1996, aged eighty-five.
59. Masterman's history of Double Cross, KV 4/5.
60. Ibid.
61. Minutes of W Board, KV 4/70.
62. Masterman, *The Double-Cross System*, p. 188.
63. 'Memorandum on the double agent system', 27 December 1940, KV 4/70.
64. Masterman's history of Double Cross, p. 9, KV 4/5.

Chapter 12: Baker Street Irregulars

1. For an overview see Giles Milton, *Churchill's Ministry of Ungentlemanly Warfare*; and M.R.D. Foot, *An Outline History of the Special Operations Executive.*
2. For a history, see Hugh Popham, *The FANY in War and Peace.*
3. Leo Marks, *Between Silk and Cyanide*, pp. 60–5.
4. For a detailed history, see Kate Vigurs, *Mission France*, and Foot, *An Outline History of the SOE.* For the life of Vera Atkins, see Sarah Helm, *A Life in Secrets.*
5. Note from AQ/C to P/SO.1, 11 December 1943, HS 9/1065/4.
6. C/D Reg. to AQ/CR, 27 January 1944, HS 9/1065/4.
7. Note, 22 August 1944, HS 9/1065/4.
8. For Operation Periwig, see FO 898/354, FO 898/356, HS 6/224 (Belgium) and HS 6/178.
9. In July 1975 Margot Morse took over temporarily as the CEO of the Special Forces Club and navigated it through its most difficult financial period, including an overhaul of its records. Her exceptional organisational skills, used so adeptly for SOE in the war, came to the fore in her post-war activities.
10. Letter from Squadron Leader H.E. Park to Guy Liddell at MI5, 10 August 1945, HS 9/1141/8.
11. Letter dated 1 August 1945 from MI5, HS 9/1141/8.
12. Barbara Keeley, personal SOE file HS 9/824/7.
13. Report of 26 June 1943, HS 9/824/7.
14. Ibid.
15. Fry, *Spymaster*, pp. 6–7.
16. Vera Atkins's naturalisation papers: HO 505/45567.
17. Report, 24 May 1945, HS 9/59/2.
18. Note dated 21 October 1942, HS 9/59/2.
19. Popham, *The FANY in War and Peace*, p. 98.
20. For a detailed account, see Vigurs, *Mission France.*
21. Personal HS 9/307/3; see also O'Connor, *Agent Fifi* and FO 1004/591.
22. They were Eliane Sophie Plewman, Yolande Beekman and Madeleine Damerment.
23. Odette Sansom was also known as Odette Churchill / Odette Hallowes.
24. Report, 23 September 1944, HS 9/356.
25. Report by unnamed officer in her personal SOE file, HS 9/849/7.
26. Report dated 14 December 1945, HS 9/849/7. An eleven-page report by her of her mission is contained in her personal file.
27. Personal SOE file, HS 9/1274/4.
28. Citation in her personal SOE file HS 9/1274/4.
29. For her full biography see Clare Mulley, *The Spy Who Loved.*
30. Granville's statement, 23 February 1941, HS 9/1274/4.

31. Letter signed by 'F', 15 December 1939, from 46 Lexham Gardens, W8, an SOE safehouse.
32. Eric Sanders, SOE's Austrian section, interview with author.
33. Letter from Frederick Voigt to Holmes at Electra House, Victoria Embankment, 17 May 1940.
34. SOE report, 7 December 1939, HS 9/1274/4.
35. Fredrick Voigt was a British journalist with German roots. Based in Germany from 1920 to 1933, he transferred to Paris in 1933. He spent time in Vienna in 1933–4. See Fry, *Spymaster*, p. 48.
36. Report, no date, HS 9/1274/4.
37. Report, 25 March 1944, HS 9/1274/4. She was designated X/A/513 in SOE reports.
38. Letter in her personal SOE file, HS 9/647/4.
39. Virginia Hall was born on 6 April 1906 in Baltimore, Maryland.
40. Report dated 1 April 1941 to F Section, HS 9/647/4.
41. Personal file HS 9/647/4.
42. Citation for the Croix de Guerre, HS 9/647/4.
43. Memo dated 2 April 1942, HS 9/647/4.
44. Report by Virginia Hall, 18 January 1943, HS 9/647/4.
45. For Harold Cole's MI5 files, see KV 2/415, KV 2/416 and KV 2/417.
46. Statement to the War Office by Lilias, 12 March 1943, HS 9/647/4.
47. Ibid.
48. Report by Virginia Hall, 15 January 1943, HS 9/647/4.
49. Citation for the Croix de Guerre, HS 9/647/4.
50. Correspondence with Kate Vigurs, March 2022.
51. Quoted in the permanent exhibition at the Soldiers of Oxfordshire Museum, Woodstock.

Chapter 13: Section X

1. Copy of the citation given to the author by the family.
2. Ibid.
3. Report dated 18 November 1940, HS 8/304.
4. For a history of the German and Austrian section of SOE, see HS 7/145 and HS 7/146.
5. Ronald Thornley was known by the cover name 'Major Thurston' to other government departments that did not know of SOE's existence.
6. Fritz Molden, *Fires in the Night*, p. 69.
7. Appendix A: 'Short note on the organisation and activities of X Section', HS 7/145.
8. History of X Section, p. 2, HS 9/145.
9. Ibid., p. 16.
10. For Operation Champagne, see 'History of the German and Austrian section of SOE', HS 7/145.
11. Ibid.
12. Letter from MI6, 20 September 1946, FO 371/60516.
13. Letter from R. Brook of the Ministry of Economic Warfare, to J.M. Addis at the Foreign Office, 28 July 1941, FO 369/2715.
14. 'History of the German and Austrian section of SOE', HS 7/145.
15. Letter from MI6, 20 September 1946, FO 371/60516.

16. For information on Hodgson's case, see FO 371/60516.
17. For reports of the missions into Austria from Italy, see 'Activities of X Section in Italy', HS 7/146.
18. Activities of X Section, HS 7/146.
19. For a fuller history, see Helen Fry, *Churchill's German Army*.
20. Information provided to the author by the family.
21. Personal unpublished memoir.
22. Interview with the author.
23. A detailed history of these missions is contained in HS 7/146.
24. See Walter Freud, 'Before the Anticlimax', and Helen Fry, *Freuds' War*.
25. Fry, *Spymaster*, pp. 29 and 47–50.'
26. Evelyn Stamper, Squadron Leader Matthey and R. Jellinek, 'SOE history: Austria, links with PWE; operations from Turkey and Switzerland', HS 7/146.
27. Report from X Section to D/HT, 6 January 1944, HS 9/915/2.
28. Personal SOE file, HS 9/915/2.
29. Memo: 'Salary and status of D/H.98. Sec. [Secretary]', 2 August 1944, HS 9/915/2.
30. Memo, 2 May 1944, HS 9/915/2.
31. Stamper, Matthey and Jellinek, 'SOE history: Austria, links with PWE; operations from Turkey and Switzerland', HS 7/146.
32. No personal SOE file exists for Mary Vischer. Scant details of her life are to be found in her obituary (1995), a copy of which survives in Vera Atkins's papers, ref: file 12/1/3–12/1/7, IWM 08/1/8.
33. Ibid.
34. 'Work into the Sudetenland from Turkey', HS 7/146.
35. Eric Gedye died in 1971, Alice in 2005.
36. Interview with Robin Gedye.
37. R. Jellinek, report entitled 'Work into Austria', p. 2, HS 7/146.
38. Cipher from Hungary to the War Office, 17 August 1945, HS 4/129.
39. Copy of citation given to the author.
40. Captain E.M. Hodgson, 'Activities of X Section in Italy', HS 7/146.

Chapter 14: Spy Swap

1. Letter from New Scotland Yard to MI5, 29 May 1943, KV 2/3324.
2. Details of the spy exchange are contained in KV 2/3324.
3. Mary Walters was born 11 February 1894. Other documents in KV 2/3324 suggest her date of birth could be 17 February 1892.
4. Baron Miske had been brought up in Vienna at the Theresianum and the Court of the old Emperor Franz Joseph. See 'Autobiographical details', report dated 17 February 1965, FO 950/2522.
5. Memo, 20 September 1942, HS 9/1041; confirmed by a letter dated 29 November 1943 from MI5 to SIME general headquarters, Middle East, KV 2/3324. Commander V. Wolfson was also the MI9 /IS9 representative; see ADM 1/26884.
6. For background to SOE in these countries, see Alan Ogden, *Through Hitler's Back Door*.
7. Pants personal SOE files, HS 5/826–829.
8. Personal Record Sheet, HS 9/1041. This record states that Baroness Miske worked for the SOE office in Istanbul.

9. Cipher from the clandestine SOE station in Istanbul, 11 August 1943, HS 9/1041.
10. Jeffery, *MI6*, pp. 424–5. SIS reports for the Abyssinian crisis and agents of the Italian secret service are in KV 3/316.
11. Laszlo Bekeffy's personal SOE file, HS 9/117/1.
12. Report dated 10 February 1942 sent from DH18 in Istanbul to SOE Cairo, HS 9/1041.
13. Report from DH18 (Captain J. Craig) to SOE Cairo, 10 February 1942, HS 9/1041.
14. Report from DH18 to SOE Cairo, 3 April 1942, HS 9/1041.
15. Report dated April 17, 1942, HS 9/1041.
16. Report to SOE Cairo, 23 April 1942 from Istanbul, HS 9/1041.
17. Report from Istanbul, 10 February 1942, HS 4/129.
18. Report on the debriefing of Baroness Miske, 21 April 1942, HS 9/1041. See also HS 5/826-829.
19. For Pants, see HS 5/826–829.
20. Report on Fruit by B/H6, HS 9/1041.
21. Report on the arrest of Fruit, from DH18 to SOE Cairo, 17 June 1942, HS 9/1041.
22. Untitled report, 6 July 1942, HS 9/1041.
23. Letter from the Foreign Office, 31 January 1955 to the Aliens Department, Home Office, HO 382/108.
24. Mary Walters (Baroness Mary Miske), 'Details of persecution', FO 950/2522.
25. Wieser's case is covered in KV 2/3400, KV 2/3401 and KV 2/3402. He was repatriated in August 1943: letter dated 1 September 1943 from New Scotland Yard to MI5, KV 2/3402.
26. Memo, 11 May 1943, KV 2/3324.
27. Profile of Eugene Wieser by MI5, 12 March 1941, KV 2/3401.
28. Application B, signed by Major Sefton-Watson, HS 9/1041.
29. Extract from a Foreign Office file dated 30 December 1954 to British Representative in Moscow, KV 2/3324. She resided with Miss Stephens, 26 Moss Hall Grove, North Finchley.
30. Autobiographical details, dated 17 February 1965, FO 950/2522
31. Extract from SIS to the attaché at the US embassy, 9 September 1947, KV 2/3324.
32. Memo to Director of Military Intelligence, London from Intelligence Organisation, Allied Commission for Austria, 23 September 1946, KV 2/3324.
33. Letter from Mr R.T. Reed to Kim Philby, 11 October 1946, KV 2/3324.
34. Letter from Philby at SIS to Reed at MI5, 30 October 1946, KV 2/3324.
35. Cipher telegram from the War Office to MI5, 11 June 1947, KV 2/3324.
36. Article in *The People*, 2 November 1958.
37. Top-secret extract from US Army, 20 November 1947, KV 2/3324.
38. Extract of correspondence from the attaché at the US embassy to MI6, 2 September 1947, copy sent to MI5, KV 2/3324.
39. Copy of a letter from SIS to the attaché of the US embassy, 9 September 1947, KV 2/3324.
40. Extract from Foreign Office file, 30 December 1954 to British Representative in Moscow (C.C. Parrott, CMG, OBE), KV 2/2334.
41. Ibid.

42. 'Women Slaves of the Russians', interview with Mary Miske in *The People*, 5 October 1958.
43. Article in *The People*, 2 November 1958.
44. Ibid.
45. Background note, 21 December 1970, FO 950/2522. See also letter from MI6 to MI5, 29 November 1956, FO 950/2522.
46. Letter from MI6 to MI5, 29 November 1956, FO 950/2522.
47. Letter to the Foreign Office from unknown department, 3 May 1956, FO 950/2522.

Chapter 15: SOE and Intelligence

1. 'SOE's relationship with SIS', section in the report on intelligence, FO 1093/155.
2. Major S.A. Truelsen, 'Report on the Danish Military Naval Intelligence Services in Denmark during the period following 29 August 1943', June 1944, HS 7/110.
3. 'Evaluation of SOE activities in Denmark', HS 7/110.
4. Ibid., p. 4.
5. Ibid., p. 12.
6. Letter from SOE to Colonel Baxter at MI5, 6 November 1944, HS 9/605/3.
7. Memo, 2 November 1944 from SOE officer known only as 7404, HS 9/605/3.
8. Citation for her MBE, signed by Gubbins on 11 January 1946, HS 9/605/3.
9. Report, 23 December 1944, HS 9/605/3.
10. Memo, 13 March 1945, HS 9/605/3.
11. Letter with prefix CX: 22666/A, no date, HS 9/605/3.
12. Personal file HS 9/605/3.
13. Report, 4 November 1944, HS 9/605/3.
14. Memo, on 24 December 1944, HS 9/605/3.
15. Citation for her MBE in HS 9/1081/2.
16. Training report from STS 51, HS 9/1081/2.
17. Report from STS 32c, HS 9/1081/2.
18. For a history of this section and a list of personnel, see HS 2/248.
19. See David Howarth, *The Shetland Bus*, and Stephen Wynn, *The Shetland Bus*.
20. Operation Grouse, HS 2/172.
21. Operation Gunnerside, HS 2/184–190.
22. Operation Claymore, HS 2/224.
23. Operation Wallah, HS 2/244, and see also HS 2/198 and HS 2/199.
24. Operation Archery, HS 2/225. The dawn raid succeeded in its objectives and prisoners were captured.
25. Citation for her MBE, on 23 May 1945, HS 9/52/6.
26. Information provided by Lee Richards.
27. Memo, 18 February 1942, HS 9/860/7.
28. Ibid.
29. Ibid.
30. Details in HS 6/112.
31. Report on Operation Amelia (aka Mission Imogen with 'Alice'), 22 November 1944, HS 6/11. Elaine Marie Madden's personal file HS 9/973/7.
32. Sue Elliott, *I Heard My Country Calling*, p. 60.
33. Ibid., pp. 171–2.
34. Mission details in HS 6/77.

35. Report on Operation Amelia (aka Mission Imogen with 'Alice'), 22 November 1944, HS 6/11.
36. For the SOE mission to exfiltrate Prince Charles to the UK, see HS 6/216.
37. Elliott, *I Heard My Country Calling*, p. 197.
38. Citation, 1 October 1945, HS 9/973/7.
39. The missions were codenamed Violet, Daisy, Bluebell and Poppy.
40. Report, p. 2, FO 898/94.
41. I am grateful to Lee Richards, leading expert on the Political Warfare Executive and propaganda, for sharing his research.
42. Training report, 9 May 1944, HS 9/784/1.
43. Report from STS 19, dated 24 May 1944, HS 9/784/1. STS 19 was Gardener's End, Ardeley, Stevenage in Hertfordshire.
44. Report 'Emilia Babette (Mrs Olga Jackson)', CAB 102/610.
45. 'Belgium – missions. Emelia: independent propaganda mission', p. 2, HS 6/84.
46. The towns and cities were Brussels, Liège, Antwerp, Ghent and Charleroi.
47. Lee Richards, *The Black Art*, p. 36.
48. Ibid.
49. Citation in her personal file, HS 9/784/1.
50. Report by Lieutenant Colonel H. Aimes to Captain G.J. Kidd, HS 9/973/7.
51. Elliott, *I Heard My Country Calling*, p. 212.
52. See HS 9/289. Many of their profiles can be found on https://soeinburma.com/females-in-the-far-east/
53. See memos dated 21 November 1944 and 29 November 1944 in her personal file, HS 9/416/5.

Chapter 16: Noah's Ark

1. Marie-Madeleine Fourcade, *Noah's Ark*, p. 60.
2. Ibid., p. 80; and obituary in *The Times*, 22 July 1989.
3. Edward Wake-Walker, *A House for Spies*, p. 137.
4. Fourcade, *Noah's Ark*, p. 126.
5. Ibid., pp. 152–3.
6. There is some suggestion that Bla was sent by Marie-Madeleine to London to be dealt with there.
7. Fourcade, *Noah's Ark*, p. 232.
8. Ibid., p. 211.
9. Wake-Walker, *A House for Spies*.
10. Fourcade, *Noah's Ark*, p. 255.
11. Ibid., p. 272.
12. Ibid., pp. 317–18.
13. Ibid., p. 309.
14. Ibid., pp. 328–9.
15. Obituary in *The Times*, 22 July 1989 and the *Daily Telegraph*, 22 July 1989.
16. Lynne Olson, *Madame Fourcade's Secret War*, p. 130.
17. Among them were Christiana Battu (Cricri), Marguerite Brouillet (Bee), Henriette Amable (Tomboy) and Marguerite Grimprel (Scarab), a society woman.
18. The Wachtel Report is reproduced in R.V. Jones, *Most Secret War*, p. 447–8.
19. Quoted in Fourcade, *Noah's Ark*, p. 253.
20. Jones, *Most Secret War*, p. 476.
21. Fourcade, *Noah's Ark*, p,208.

22. Ibid., p. 143.
23. Ibid., p. 57.
24. In 1987, Marie-Madeleine was one of the moral witnesses called at the trial of Klaus Barbie in Lyon. She died in Paris on 20 July 1989 and became the first woman to have her funeral in the church of Saint-Louis des Invalides in Paris, where Napoleon and other senior French military figures are buried.
25. The six women are Berty Albrecht (co-founder of the 'Combat' movement) who died in Fresnes prison in 1943; Simone Michel-Levy of the resistance; agent Marie Hackin, who was lost at sea in February 1941; Laure Diebold, a liaison officer for the Mithridate network; and Emilienne Moreau-Evrard of the Brutus resistance network.
26. Olson, *Madame Fourcade's Secret War*, p. 378.

Chapter 17: The Clarence Service

1. Dewé called up the following figures from La Dame Blanche network of the First World War; their ages in 1940 are in brackets: Thérèse de Radiguès (75), Alexandre Neujean (71), Arsène Scheurette (66), Herman Chauvin (64), Jeanne Goeseels (64), Jeanne Delwaide (59), Franz Creusen (47), Robert Boseret (55), two sisters Laure Tandel (warrant officer, aged 65) and Louise Tandel (warrant officer, aged 61), two sisters Emma Weimerskirsch (warrant officer, aged 61) and Alice Weimerskirsch (warrant officer, aged 57), three sisters Jeanne, Valentine and Marguerite Cambier (aged 53, 49, 46) and Henriette Dupuich (59).
2. Thérèse de Radiguès was born in Liège on 27 June 1865 and died in Brussels on 16 June 1963. She had medals from the First World War, including Officer of the Order of Leopold, with palm.
3. Bernard, *Un géant de la résistance: Walthère Dewé*, p. 133.
4. Citation for Chevalier, WO 373/107/179.
5. Interview with the author.
6. Citation signed by chief of the Clarence Service, Brussels, 7 February 1946, in their personal files at CegeSoma (part of the Belgian State Archives), Brussels.
7. Citation in her personal file, CegeSoma.
8. Correspondence with the author.
9. Clarence to London, report for 25 to 31 August 1944.
10. Ibid.
11. Jeffery, *MI6*, pp. 521–2.
12. The female members who lost their lives are listed in Appendix 5 in Bernard, *Un géant de la résistance*. They were Madame Dewé (née Dieudonnée Salmon), who died in service on 14 January 1943, and the following women, who died in Ravensbrück concentration camp: Madeleine Dewé (17 January 1945); Lieutenant Elisabeth Plissart (January 1945); Nelly Durieu (29 January 1945), Juliet Durieu (March 1945); and Madame Bertha Morimont (née Bertha Lambrecht, died March 1945).
13. Jeffery, *MI6*, p. 521.

Chapter 18: MI9 Secret Agents

1. For a history of MI9, including Room 900, see Helen Fry, *MI9*, and also Airey Neave, *Saturday at MI9*, and Foot and Langley, *MI9*.
2. Neave, *Saturday at MI9*, p. 68.
3. Airey Neave, 'We Brought Them Home Alive', *Observer*, 27 October 1974. See also 'Historical record of MI9, IS9 and RAF Intelligence Course B', WO 208/3243.

4. Fry, *MI9*, pp. 77 and 285.
5. Information provided to the author by the Neave family. Obituary in the *Independent*, 1 December 1992.
6. The letter is dated January 1944 and written by Airey Neave from Room 900. Copy sent to the author.
7. Neave, *Saturday at MI9*, p. 190.
8. Ibid., p. 194.
9. Foot and Langley, *MI9*, pp. 87–8.
10. Hasler's escape report No. 1140, WO 208/3312. Spark's escape report No.1162, WO 208/3313. Both were interrogated by a female interrogator, Commander Jackson (ATS).
11. Mary Lindell's personal file, FO 950/1898.
12. Ibid.
13. Neave, *Saturday at MI9*, p. 204.
14. Report, July 1964, FO 950/1646.
15. The friend was Madame Chatenay of La Romanerie (an English woman, married to Frenchman) who lived in St Barthélemy d'Anjou in the Loire valley.
16. Christiaan Lindemans' MI5 files are KV 2/31– KV 2/37.
17. M.R.D. Foot, *SOE in the Low Countries*, and Leo Marks, *Between Silk and Cyanide*.
18. She became an agent and liaison officer under a number of aliases: Trix, Felix, Beatrice Thompson and Joanna Maria ven der Velden.
19. Neave, *Saturday at MI9*, p. 206.
20. Ibid., pp. 207–8.
21. HS 9/1452/8.
22. Personal file, HS 6/762.
23. HS 9/1452/8.
24. Neave, *Saturday at MI9*, p. 205.
25. Ibid., p. 208.
26. Operation Chicory in HS 6/762.
27. Inquiry commission, report dated 23 December 1948, FO 371/79558.
28. Report of the conversation between Sir Colin Gubbins, Brigadier Mockler-Terryman, Colonel Brook, Colonel Cordeaux and Dr Donker (Chair of the Netherlands Parliamentary Commission of Enquiry), 4 October 1943, FO 371/79558.
29. Ibid.
30. Neave, *Saturday at MI9*, p. 213.
31. Ibid., p. 205.
32. Operation Chicken I is mentioned in Phil Froom, *Evasion and Escape Devices*, p. 363, but no further details given.
33. Personal file WO 208/3401. She was born on 17 June 1921 in Budapest.
34. Eitan Senesh, preface to *Hannah Senesh: Her Life and Diary*, p. xiv.
35. Letter to the Jewish Agency from IS9(ME), dated 5 July 1945, in personal file WO 208/3401.
36. *Hannah Senesh: Her Life and Diary*, p. 245.
37. Personal file, WO 208/3415.
38. AIR 40/1533 contains limited details of her mission. Appendix A describes the torture she suffered from the Gestapo. Other details are in her personal file WO 208/3505.

39. Neave, 'We Brought Them Home Alive', *Observer*, 27 October 1974.
40. Elisabeth Furse, *Dream Weaver*, p. 116.
41. For Cole's treachery, see his MI5 files KV 2/415 to KV 2/417.
42. Obituary in *Guardian*, 16 October 2002.
43. Andrée De Jongh, citation for George Medal, no date, WO 208/5452.
44. Fourcade, *Noah's Ark*.
45. Ian Dear, *Escape and Evasion*, p. 138.
46. Fernand de Greef, unpublished notes entitled 'Details of the activity of M. Fernand De Greef from 26 June 1940 to the end of the war', report by Tante Go about the Comet Line. Copy given to the author by the family.
47. Ibid.
48. Foot and Langley, *MI9*, p. 138.
49. Elsie Maréchal's full story is told in Fry, *MI9*.
50. Michou married a paratrooper and after the war raised funds for the families of Comet Line agents who had died in action. She was awarded the George Medal by Britain and the Golden Medal of Freedom by the US.
51. Foot and Langley, *MI9*, p. 132.
52. Interview with the author, October 2019.
53. Fry, *MI9*, p. 287.

Chapter 19: Women of MI6

1. 'British Spy's Account Sheds Light on Role in 1953 Iranian Coup', *Guardian*, 17 August 2020.
2. Interview with Anna Somers Cocks, March 2022.
3. See Benton, 'The ISOS Years', pp. 359–410.
4. Peggie Benton, *Baltic Countdown*, p. 110.
5. Ibid., pp. 148–90.
6. The code is explained on pp. 368–9 of Benton's paper.
7. Glenalmond House was in King Harry Lane, St Albans.
8. Benton, 'The ISOS Years', p. 394.
9. For the operations by Artist (Johnny Jebsen), see KV 2/845–866.
10. Benton, 'The ISOS Years', p. 359.
11. The five secret sections are listed in Appendix 2 of correspondence between 'C' and the Foreign Office, FO 1093/268. With the number of their personnel in brackets, they were: the financial attaché's section (19), the passport control office (17), the naval control section of the shipping office (16), the Danegeld section, which operated on instructions from the Ministry of Economic Warfare (2), and the honorary attaché's section (SOE) (8).
12. C/3862, from 'C' to Sir A. Cadogan at the Foreign Office, 14 July 1943, FO 1093/268.
13. Read and Fisher, *Colonel Z*, p. 239.
14. In peacetime Rita Winsor and her MI6 colleague Ena Molesworth set up a high-end travel agency that specialised in exotic, remote destinations abroad. They even scheduled trips to the moon to start from 2040.
15. For his career in Lisbon and mention of Rita Winsor, see Philip Johns, *Within Two Cloaks*.
16. Read and Fisher, *Colonel Z*, p. 239.
17. West, *Hitler's Nest of Vipers*, p. 140.

18. The codename was taken from a real employee of US Lines and Pan American whose name was Tarleton Winchester, but who was not a spy.
19. Ibid., p. 141.
20. In August 1944, Eitel was captured by the Free French and handed over to the US Third Army. He was transferred to England in October 1944 and interrogated at MI5's Camp 020, Latchmere House. There may be a further SIS connection here via the Bentons in Madrid, although the files do not confirm this for certain.
21. Article in the *Sun* newspaper, 21 November 2021, about Nigel West's book *Hitler's Nest of Vipers*.
22. Day, *The Bedbug*, p. 166.
23. Read and Fisher, *Colonel Z*, p. 239.
24. Otto John later re-defected to the East and then re-defected to the West. Personal MI5 file, KV 2/2465.
25. Day, *The Bedbug*, p. 284.
26. 'The Wolf's Lair', about Nigel West's book *Hitler's Nest of Vipers*, *Sun*, 21 November 2021.
27. CX/4282, KV 3/8.
28. Liddell's diary, entry for 12 November 1940, in West (ed.), *The Guy Liddell Diaries*, vol. 1.
29. Michael Smith, *The Spying Game*, p. 172.
30. Nigel West, *A Thread of Deceit*, pp. 37–8.
31. Ibid., p. 37.
32. Brown, *C*, p. 310.
33. Liddell's diary, entry for 7 January 1942, in West (ed.), *The Guy Liddell Diaries*, vol. 2.
34. Brown, *C*, p. 583.
35. Ibid., pp. 586–7.
36. Desmond Bristow, *A Game of Moles*, p. 206.
37. Ibid., pp. 211–12.
38. 'Women Spies in the Second World War', *Observer*, 7 November 2010.
39. For a full biography, see Paddy Hayes, *Queen of Spies*.
40. Obituary, *Daily Telegraph*, 25 March 2010.
41. Obituary, *Guardian*, 28 March 2010.
42. Obituary, *Wall Street Journal*, 1 April 2010.
43. Ibid.
44. Ibid.
45. Daphne Park was elected Principal of Somerville College, Oxford and served until 1989. In 1990, she was granted a peerage as Baroness Park of Monmouth.
46. Helen Warrell, 'The Secret Lives of MI6's Top Female Spies', *Financial Times*, 8 December 2022.
47. Interview with the author.
48. Sara Taylor, 'Yvonne Maslinksa, War Intelligence Worker', https://www.hertsmemories.org.uk/content/herts-history/people/yvonne-maslinksa-war-intelligence-worker..
49. Correspondence with the author.
50. Obituary, *Daily Telegraph*, 2 January 2020.
51. Andrew Chatterton, *Britain's Secret Defences*.

Chapter 20: Cloak and Dagger

1. Day, *The Bedbug*, p. 247.
2. For a full account, see Helm, *A Life in Secrets*.
3. Report written in support of her application for naturalisation by Major Roche, 31 January 1944, HO 505/45567.
4. The references survive in Vera Atkins's archive at the IWM.
5. Kendrick's attestation of 28 February 1944, HO 505/45567.
6. Report in HO 505/45567.
7. For the London Cage and war crimes investigations, see Helen Fry, *The London Cage*.
8. Atkins's personal SOE file, HS 9/59/2.
9. For a detailed history, see Vigurs, *Mission France*.
10. Discharge papers, dated 12 October 1945, HS 9/59/2.
11. Molly J. Sasson, *More Cloak Than Dagger*.
12. It is possible that Sasson's mother was a Hush-WAAC, but the author has not been able to establish this.
13. Sasson, *More Cloak Than Dagger*, p. 26.
14. Ibid., p. 28.
15. Ibid., p. 46.
16. Andrew, *Defence of the Realm*, p. 338.
17. Ibid., p. 339.
18. Ibid., p. 774.
19. For her autobiography see Stella Rimington, *Open Secret*.
20. 'Tinker, Tailor, Soldier, Mum', *Guardian*, 10 September 2001.
21. 'Centenary of Women's Suffrage – 100 Years of Women in MI5', https://www.mi5.gov.uk/news/celebrating-vote-100.

Epilogue

1. Ferris, *Behind the Enigma*, p. 437.

BIBLIOGRAPHY

Interviews

This book draws on interviews with former female intelligence staff: Susan Lustig (née Cohn), Elizabeth Bruegger, Evelyn Barron and Cynthia Turner, and Lesley Wyle; and Fritz Lustig, Eric Mark and Eric Sanders.

Papers and Archives

Imperial War Museum

Diaries and papers of General Sir Walter Kirke, IWM 82/28/1.
Papers of La Dame Blanche, uncatalogued.
Papers of the Clarence Service, uncatalogued.
Private papers of Squadron Officer Vera M. Atkins CBE, IWM, ref.: 12636.
Papers and unpublished memoirs of Anton Walter Freud, including 'Before the Anticlimax'.

Military Intelligence Museum

Diary of Mavis Peel, 'The Story of the Hush-WAACs'.
Judge, A.F., 'The Intelligence Corps 1914 to 1929', unpublished.
Judge, A.F., 'Ladies of the Intelligence Corps', November 2019, unpublished.

Other Archives and Collections

Bletchley Park Trust
The Medmenham Collection
Archives Générale du Royaume de Bélgique, Brussels
Cegesoma Studies & Documentation Institute, Brussels
Commission des Archives des Services Patriotiques, Secretariat de Liège
Walter L. Pforzheimer papers, Yale University
Townshend/Jestin private family papers

The National Archives, London

ADM 223/84, ADM 223/257, ADM 223/286, ADM 223/464, ADM 223/472, ADM 223/478, ADM 223/521, ADM 223/792, ADM 223/794, AIR 40/1533, AIR 40/2636, CAB 102/610, FO 369/2715, FO 371/60516, FO 371/79558, FO 741/4, FO 898/94, FO 898/354, FO 898/356, FO 950/1646, FO 950/1898, FO 950/2522, FO 1004/591, FO 1093/155, FO 1093/268, FO 1093/200, FO 1093/201, HO

382/108, HO 505/45567, HS 2/172, HS 2/184–190, HS 2/198, HS 2/199, HS 2/224, HS 2/225, HS 2/244, HS 2/248, HS 4/129, HS 5/826–829, HS 6/11, HS 6/77, HS 6/84, HS 6/112, HS 6/178, HS 6/216, HS 6/224, HS 6/762, HS 7/110, HS 7/145, HS 7/146, HS 8/304, HS 9/24/6, HS 9/59/2, HS 9/52/6, HS 9/92/1, HS 9/106/1, HS 9/112/2, HS 9/117/1, HS 9/307/3, HS 9/355/2, HS 9/356, HS 9/416/5, HS 9/417/1, HS 9/488/3, HS 9/498/6, HS 9/605/3, HS 9/644/6, HS 9/647/4, HS 9/733/4, HS 9/783/4, HS 9/784/1, HS 9/824/7, HS 9/849/7, HS 9/860/7, HS 9/915/2, HS 9/973/7, HS 9/1041, HS 9/1065/4, HS 9/1081/2, HS 9/1141/8, HS 9/1274/4, HS 9/1299/3, HS 9/1299/7, HS 9/1309/4, HS 9/1320/1, HS 9/1327/1, HS 9/1350/3, HS 9/1432/3, HS 9/1432/7, HS 9/145, HS 9/1452/8, HS 9/289, HW 3/3, HW 3/35, HW 14/17, HW 14/21, HW 14/48, HW 14/50, HW 25/2, HW 25/4, HW/25/5, HW 43/72, HW 50/65, KV 1/50, KV 1/54, KV 1/63, KV 2/1, KV 2/2, KV 2/31–37, KV 2/415, KV 2/416, KV 2/417, KV 2/464, KV 2/465, KV 2/466, KV 2/669, KV 2/670, KV 2/673, KV 2/822, KV 2/844, KV 2/845–866, KV 2/1012, KV 2/1020, KV 2/1022, KV 2/1023, KV 2/1067, KV 2/1083, KV 2/1275, KV 2/1280, KV 2/1696, KV 2/1976, KV 2/2098, KV 2/2257, KV 2/2258, KV 2/2259, KV 2/3324, KV 2/3400, KV 2/3401, KV 2/3402, KV 2/2465, KV 2/4531 – KV 2/4534, KV 3/8, KV 3/291, KV 3/316, KV 4/5, KV 4/65, KV 4/66, KV 4/67, KV 4/68, KV 4/70, KV 4/10, KV 4/69, KV 4/101, KV 4/192, KV 4/211, KV 4/227, KV 4/443, MEPO 2/9844, WO 106/45, WO 165/41, WO 208/3163, WO 208/3242, WO 208/3243, WO 208/3248, WO 208/3312, WO 208/3313, WO 208/3401, WO 208/3415, WO 208/3437, WO 208/3461, WO 208/3505, WO 208/3554, WO 208/4970, WO 208/5452, WO 372/5/143615, WO 372/23/100006, WO 372/23/100008, WO 372/23/100009, WO 373/107/179

Published Works

Abrutat, David. *Radio War: The Secret Espionage War of the Radio Security Service 1938–1946*, Fonthill, 2019.

Akkerman, Nadine. *Invisible Agents: Women and Espionage in Seventeenth-century Britain*, Oxford University Press, 2020.

Andrew, Christopher. *The Defence of the Realm: The Authorized History of MI5*, Allen Lane, 2009.

Andrew, Christopher. *Secret Service: The Making of the British Intelligence Community*, Book Club Associates, 1985.

Ashcroft, Michael. *In the Shadows: The Extraordinary Men and Women of the Intelligence Corps*, Biteback Publishing, 2022.

Atwood, Kathryn. *Women Heroes of World War I*, Chicago Review Press, 2014.

Babington Smith, Constance. *Evidence in Camera: The Story of Photographic Intelligence in World War II*, David & Charles, 1974.

Baring, Sarah. *The Road to Station X*, privately published, 2021.

Basu, Shrabani. *Spy Princess: The Life of Noor Inayat Khan*, The History Press, 2010.

Beesly, Patrick. *Very Special Intelligence: The Story of the Admiralty's Operational Intelligence Centre, 1939–1945*, Seaforth Publishing, 2015.

Benton, Kenneth. 'The ISOS Years: Madrid 1941–3', *Journal of Contemporary History*, vol. 30, no. 3 (July 1995), pp. 359–410.

Benton, Peggie. *Baltic Countdown*, Centaur Press, 1984.

Bernard, Henri. *Un géant de la résistance: Walthère Dewé*, La Renaissance du Livre, 1971.

Bijl, Nick van der. *Sharing the Secret: The History of the Intelligence Corps, 1940–2010*, Pen and Sword, 2020.
Blake, George. *No Other Choice*, Jonathan Cape, 1990.
Bond, Barbara. *Great Escapes: The Story of MI9's Second World War Escape and Evasion Maps*, Times Books, 2015.
Bristow, Desmond. *A Game of Moles: The Deceptions of an MI6 Officer*, Little, Brown, 1993.
Brown, Anthony Cave. *C: The Secret Life of Sir Stewart Graham Menzies, Spymaster to Winston Churchill*, Macmillan, 1987.
Burgh, Lucy de. *My Italian Adventures: An English Girl at War 1943–47*, The History Press, 2013.
'The Chalk House with the Tudor Chimneys: A Photographic Record of the Allied Central Interpretation Unit', published by the Medmenham Collection.
Chatterton, Andrew. *Britain's Secret Defences: Civilian Saboteurs, Spies and Assassins during the Second World War*, Casemate, 2022.
Chionna, Jackie Uí. *Queen of Codes: The Secret Life of Emily Anderson, Britain's Greatest Female Codebreaker*, Headline, 2023.
Clayton, Anthony. *Forearmed: A History of the Intelligence Corps*, Brassey's, 1993.
Coulson, Major Thomas. *The Queen of Spies: Louise de Bettignies*, Constable, 1935.
Day, Peter. *The Bedbug – Klop Ustinov: Britain's Most Ingenious Spy*, Biteback, 2015.
Dear, Ian. *Escape and Evasion: POW Breakouts in World War Two*, Cassell, 1997.
Dixon, Peter. *Return to Vienna: The Special Operations Executive and the Rebirth of Austria*, Cloudshill Press, 2023.
Dorril, Stephen. *MI6: Fifty Years of Special Operations*, Fourth Estate, 2001.
Downing, Taylor. *Spies in the Sky*, Little, Brown, 2011.
Dunlop, Tessa. *The Bletchley Girls*, Hodder, 2015.
Elliott, Sue. *I Heard My Country Calling: Elaine Madden, SOE Agent*, The History Press, 2021.
Everingham, Barry. *MC: The Adventures of a Maverick Princess*, Bantam Press, 1985.
Ferris, John. *Behind the Enigma: The Authorised History of GCHQ, Britain's Secret Cyber-Intelligence Agency*, Bloomsbury, 2020.
Foot, M.R.D. *An Outline History of the Special Operations Executive*, Bodley Head, 2014.
Foot, M.R.D. *SOE in the Low Countries*, St Ermin's Press, 2001,
Foot, M.R.D. and Jimmy Langley. *MI9: Escape and Evasion 1939–1945*, BCA, 1979.
Fourcade, Marie-Madeleine, *Noah's Ark: The Story of Alliance Intelligence Service in Occupied France*, Allen & Unwin, 1973.
Froom, Phil. *Evasion and Escape Devices Produced by MI9, MIS-X & SOE in World War II*, Schiffer Publishing Ltd, 2015.
Fry, Edmund David. *The Life and Times of a Knowle Boy*, Braunton Museum, 2003.
Fry, Helen. *Spymaster: The Man Who Saved MI6*, Yale University Press, 2021.
Fry, Helen. *MI9: A History of the Secret Service for Escape and Evasion in World War Two*, Yale University Press, 2020.
Fry, Helen. *The Walls Have Ears: The Greatest Intelligence Operation of World War II*, Yale University Press, 2019.
Fry, Helen. *The London Cage: The Secret History of Britain's World War II Interrogation Centre*, Yale University Press, 2017.
Fry, Helen. *Churchill's German Army*, The History Press, 2009.

Fry, Helen. *Freuds' War*, The History Press, 2009.
Fry, Helen. *Jews in North Devon during the Second World War*, Halsgrove, 2005.
Furse, Elisabeth. *Dream Weaver: From the Russian Revolution to the Fall of the Berlin Wall, One Woman's Witness*, Chapmans, 1993.
Gannon, Paul. *Inside Room 40: The Codebreakers of World War I*, Ian Allan Publishing, 2010.
Greenberg, Joel. *Gordon Welchman: Bletchley Park's Architect of Ultra Intelligence*, Frontline, 2014.
Halsall, Christine. *Women of Intelligence*, Spellmount, 2012.
Hamilton, C.I. 'The Character and Organization of the Admiralty Operational Intelligence Centre during the Second World War', *War in History*, July 2000, pp. 295–324.
Hastings, Max. *The Secret War: Spies, Codes and Guerrillas 1939–1945*, William Collins, 2017.
Hayes, Paddy. *Queen of Spies: Daphne Park, Britain's Cold War Spy Master*, Gerald Duckworth & Co., 2015.
Helm, Sarah. *A Life in Secrets: The Story of Vera Atkins and the Lost Agents of SOE*, Little, Brown, 2005.
Hemming, Henry. *M: Maxwell Knight, MI5's Greatest Spymaster*, Preface Publishing, 2017.
Hoare, Oliver. *Camp 020: MI5 and Nazi Spies – The Official History of MI5's Wartime Interrogation Centre*, Public Record Office, 2000.
Howarth, David. *The Shetland Bus: A WWII Epic of Courage, Endurance and Survival*, Lyons Press, 2017.
Hutton, Robert. *Agent Jack: The True Story of MI5's Secret Nazi Hunter*, Weidenfeld & Nicolson, 2018.
Jackson, John (ed.). *Solving Enigma's Secrets: The Official History of Bletchley Park's Hut 6*, BookTower Publishing, 2014.
Jeffery, Keith. *MI6: The History of the SIS, 1909–1949*, Bloomsbury, 2010.
Jestin, Catherine. *A War Bride's Story*, privately published.
Johns, Philip. *Within Two Cloaks: Missions with SIS and SOE*, William Kimber, 1979.
Jones, R.V. *Most Secret War*, Coronet, 1978.
Kenyon, David. *Bletchley Park and D-Day: The Untold Story of How the Battle of Normandy Was Won*, Yale University Press, 2019.
Knightley, Phillip. *The Second Oldest Profession: Spies and Spying in the Twentieth Century*, Pan Books, 1987.
Landau, Henry. *The Spy Net: The Greatest Intelligence Operations of the First World War*, Biteback, 2015 (originally published as *Secrets of the White Lady*, G.P. Putnam's Sons, 1935).
Lane, Peter. *Princess Michael of Kent*, Fontana, 1986.
Langley, Jimmy. *Fight Another Day*, Pen & Sword, 2013.
Lustig, Fritz. *My Lucky Life*, privately published.
McIntosh, Elizabeth P. 'The Role of Women in Intelligence', Association of Former Intelligence Officers, 1989.
Macintyre, Ben. *Double Cross: The True Story of the D-Day Spies*, Crown Publishers, 2012.
Macintyre, Ben. *Operation Mincemeat*, Crown, 2010.
McKenna, Marthe. *I Was a Spy!* Pool of London Press, 2015 (first published 1934).

McLachlan, Donald. *Room 39: Naval Intelligence in Action 1939–45*, Weidenfeld & Nicolson, 1968.

Macrakis, Kristie. *Prisoners, Lovers and Spies: The Story of Invisible Ink from Herodotus to Al-Qaeda*, Yale University Press, 2014.

Marks, Leo. *Between Silk and Cyanide*, Sutton, 2007.

Masterman, John. *The Double-Cross System*, Yale University Press, 1950.

Masters, Anthony. *The Man Who Was M: The Life of Maxwell Knight*, Blackwell, 1984.

Miller, Joan. *One Girl's War: Personal Exploits in MI5's Most Secret Station*, Brandon, 1986.

Miller, Sarah-Louise, *The Women Behind the Few, The Women's Auxiliary Air Force and British Intelligence in the Second World War*, Biteback Publishing, 2023.

Milton, Giles. *Churchill's Ministry of Ungentlemanly Warfare*, John Murray, 2017.

Molden, Fritz. *Fires in the Night*, Westview Press, 1989.

Morgan, Janet. *The Secrets of Rue St Roch: Intelligence Operations behind Enemy Lines in the First World War*, Allen Lane, 2004.

Morris, Wright. *Solo: An American Dreamer in Europe: 1933–1934*, Penguin, 1983.

Mulley, Clare. *The Spy who Loved*, Macmillan, 2012.

Neave, Airey. *Saturday at MI9: The Classic Account of the WWII Allied Escape Organisation*, Pen & Sword, 2010.

Nicholls, Joan. *England Needs You: The Story of Beaumanor*, privately published, 2000.

Nudd, Derek. *Castaways in Question: A Story of British Naval Interrogators from WW1 to Denazification,* Cottage Grove Editions, 2020.

Nudd, Derek. *Castaways of the Kriegsmarine: How Shipwrecked German Seamen Helped the Allies Win the Second World War*, Createspace, 2017.

O'Connor, Bernard. *Agent Fifi and the Wartime Honeytrap Spies*, Amberley Publishing, 2015.

Ogden, Alan. *Through Hitler's Back Door: SOE Operations in Hungary, Slovakia, Romania and Bulgaria 1939–1945*, Pen & Sword, 2010.

Oliver, Mary and Mary Benedetta. *Marriage Bureau*, B7 Enterprises Ltd, 2021 (first published 1942).

Olson, Lynne. *Madame Fourcade's Secret War*, Scribe, 2019.

Parritt, Brian. *The Intelligencers: British Military Intelligence from the Middle Ages to 1929*, Pen & Sword, 2011.

Philipps, Roland. *Victoire: A Wartime Story of Resistance, Collaboration and Betrayal*, Bodley Head, 2021.

Popham, Hugh *The FANY in War and Peace: The Story of the First Aid Nursing Yeomanry 1907–2003*, Pen & Sword, 2019.

Popov, Dusko. *Spy, Counter-spy*, HarperCollins, 1976.

Proctor, Tammy. *Female Intelligence: Women and Espionage in the First World War*, New York University Press, 2003.

Purnell, Sonia. *A Woman of No Importance: The Untold Story of Virginia Hall, WW2's Most Dangerous Spy*, Virago, 2019.

Purvis, Stewart and Jeff Hulbert. *Guy Burgess: The Spy who Knew Everyone*, Biteback Publishing, 2016.

Read, Anthony and David Fisher. *Colonel Z: The Life and Times of a Master of Spies*, Hodder & Stoughton, 1984.

Richards, Lee. *The Black Art: British Clandestine Psychological Warfare Against the Third Reich*, 2010: www.psywar.org.

Rimington, Stella. *Open Secret: The Autobiography of the Former Director-General of MI5*, Hutchinson, 2001.
Ruis, Edwin. *Spynest: British and German Espionage from Neutral Holland 1914–1918*, The History Press, 2012.
Sanders, Eric. *From Music to Morse*, privately published.
Sasson, Molly J. *More Cloak than Dagger: One Woman's Career in Secret Intelligence*, Connor Court Publishing, 2015.
Senesh, Eitan, Preface, in *Hannah Senesh: Her Life and Diary*, Jewish Lights Publishing, 2004.
Smith, Michael. *The Real Special Relationship: The True Story of How the British and US Secret Services Work Together*, Simon & Schuster, 2022.
Smith, Michael. *The Debs of Bletchley Park and Other Stories*, Aurum Press, 2015.
Smith, Michael. *The Secrets of Station X: How Bletchley Park Helped Win the War*, Biteback Publishing, 2011.
Smith, Michael. *Six: A History of Britain's Secret Intelligence Service*, Dialogue, 2010.
Smith, Michael. *Foley: The Spy who Saved 10,000 Jews*, Politico's, 2004.
Smith, Michael. *The Spying Game: The Secret History of British Espionage*, Politico's, 1996.
Sullivan, Matthew Barry. *Thresholds of Peace: German Prisoners and the People of Britain*, Hamish Hamilton, 1979.
Szabo, Tania. *Young, Brave and Beautiful: The Missions of Special Operations Executive Agent Lieutenant Violette Szabo*, The History Press, 2015
Verstraeten, Peter. 'The Secrecy of Awards to Belgian Secret Service Agents', *Journal of the Orders and Medals Society of America*, vol. 70, no. 2 (2019), pp. 3–14.
Vigurs, Kate. *Mission France: The True History of the Women of SOE*, Yale University Press, 2021.
Wake-Walker, Edward. *A House for Spies: SIS Operations into Occupied France from a Sussex Farmhouse*, independently published, 2021.
West, Nigel. *Churchill's Spy Files: MI5's Top-Secret Wartime Reports*, The History Press, 2018.
West, Nigel (ed.). *The Guy Liddell Diaries, vol. 1, 1939–1942*, Routledge, 2009.
West, Nigel (ed.). *The Guy Liddell Diaries, vol. 2, 1942–1945*, Routledge, 2009.
West, Nigel. *Hitler's Nest of Vipers: The Rise of the Abwehr*, Frontline, 2022.
West, Nigel. *A Thread of Deceit*, Westintel, 1985.
West, Nigel and Oleg Tsarev. *Triplex: More Secrets from the Cambridge Spies*, Yale University Press, 2009.
'Women in Diplomacy: The FCO, 1782–1999', Records and Historical Services, Foreign and Commonwealth Office, 1999.
Wyle, Lesley. *Becoming Lesley: A Memoir in Letters and Other Writings*, independently published, 2021.
Wynn, Stephen. *The Shetland Bus*, Pen & Sword, 2021.

Unpublished Manuscripts

Rubin, Pauline. *Family History*, 12 December 1992.

Media Interviews and Programmes

Secrets and Spies: The Untold story of Edith Cavell, BBC, 16 September 2015.
David Jason's Secret Service, three-part documentary series, Channel 4, 2018.

INDEX